Understanding Child Abuse and Neglect

Panel on Research on Child Abuse and Neglect

Commission on Behavioral and Social Sciences and Education

National Research Council

NATIONAL ACADEMY PRESS
Washington, D.C. 1993

NATIONAL ACADEMY PRESS • 2101 Constitution Avenue, N.W. • Washington, D.C. 20418

NOTICE: The project that is the subject of this report was approved by the Governing Board of the National Research Council, whose members are drawn from the councils of the National Academy of Sciences, the National Academy of Engineering, and the Institute of Medicine. The members of the committee responsible for the report were chosen for their special competences and with regard for appropriate balance.

This report has been reviewed by a group other than the authors according to procedures approved by a Report Review Committee consisting of members of the National Academy of Sciences, the National Academy of Engineering, and the Institute of Medicine.

This report was undertaken with the sponsorship of the Administration for Children, Youth, and Families of the U.S. Department of Health and Human Services.

Library of Congress Cataloging-in-Publication Data

National Research Council (U.S.). Panel on Research on Child Abuse and Neglect.
    Understanding child abuse and neglect / Panel on Research on Child Abuse and Neglect, Commission on Behavioral and Social Sciences and Education, National Research Council.
      p. cm.
    Includes bibliographical references and index.
    ISBN 0-309-04889-3
    1. Child abuse—United States—Prevention. 2. Abused children—United States—Psychology. I. Title.
    HV6626.52.N38   1993
    362.76'0973—dc20   93-29640
                                                                CIP

Cover: Photograph by Eric Futran, copyright 1993.

Printed in the United States of America

First Printing, October 1993
Second Printing, November 1994

PANEL ON RESEARCH ON CHILD ABUSE AND NEGLECT

ANNE C. PETERSEN (Chair), Vice President for Research and Dean of the Graduate School, Professor of Adolescent Development and Pediatrics, University of Minnesota

J. LAWRENCE ABER, Associate Professor of Clinical and Developmental Psychology, Barnard College, Columbia University

ANDREW BILLINGSLEY, Professor and Chair, Department of Family and Community Development, University of Maryland-College Park

JEANNE BROOKS-GUNN, Virginia and Leonard Marx Professor of Child Development, Teachers College, Columbia University

DONALD J. COHEN, Director, Child Study Center, Yale University

MICHAEL I. COHEN, Chairman, Department of Pediatrics, Albert Einstein College of Medicine

JON ROBERT CONTE, Associate Professor, School of Social Work, University of Washington

BYRON EGELAND, Irving B. Harris Professor of Child Psychology, Institute of Child Development, University of Minnesota

E. MAVIS HETHERINGTON, James Page Professor of Psychology, University of Virginia

SARAH McCUE HORWITZ, Associate Professor of Public Health, Department of Epidemiology and Public Health, Yale University

JILL E. KORBIN, Associate Professor, Department of Anthropology, Case Western Reserve University

DOROTHY OTNOW LEWIS, Professor, Department of Psychiatry, New York University

RODERICK J. A. LITTLE, Professor, Department of Biomathematics, University of California-Los Angeles

MURRAY A. STRAUS, Professor of Sociology, Founder and Co-Director of the Family Research Laboratory, University of New Hampshire

CATHY SPATZ WIDOM, Professor in the School of Criminal Justice and Director of the Hindelang Criminal Justice Research Center, State University of New York-Albany

GAIL WYATT, Clinical Psychologist and Professor in the Department of Psychiatry and Biobehavioral Science, University of California-Los Angeles

ROSEMARY CHALK, Study Director

JESSICA BACKER, Research Assistant

DEBBIE MacGUFFIE, Senior Project Assistant

The National Academy of Sciences is a private, nonprofit, self-perpetuating society of distinguished scholars engaged in scientific and engineering research, dedicated to the furtherance of science and technology and to their use for the general welfare. Upon the authority of the charter granted to it by the Congress in 1863, the Academy has a mandate that requires it to advise the federal government on scientific and technical matters. Dr. Bruce M. Alberts is president of the National Academy of Sciences.

The National Academy of Engineering was established in 1964, under the charter of the National Academy of Sciences, as a parallel organization of outstanding engineers. It is autonomous in its administration and in the selection of its members, sharing with the National Academy of Sciences the responsibility for advising the federal government. The National Academy of Engineering also sponsors engineering programs aimed at meeting national needs, encourages education and research, and recognizes the superior achievements of engineers. Dr. Robert M. White is president of the National Academy of Engineering.

The Institute of Medicine was established in 1970 by the National Academy of Sciences to secure the services of eminent members of appropriate professions in the examination of policy matters pertaining to the health of the public. The Institute acts under the responsibility given to the National Academy of Sciences by its congressional charter to be an adviser to the federal government and, upon its own initiative, to identify issues of medical care, research, and education. Dr. Kenneth I. Shine is president of the Institute of Medicine.

The National Research Council was organized by the National Academy of Sciences in 1916 to associate the broad community of science and technology with the Academy's purposes of furthering knowledge and advising the federal government. Functioning in accordance with general policies determined by the Academy, the Council has become the principal operating agency of both the National Academy of Sciences and the National Academy of Engineering in providing services to the government, the public, and the scientific and engineering communities. The Council is administered jointly by both Academies and the Institute of Medicine. Dr. Bruce M. Alberts and Dr. Robert M. White are chairman and vice chairman, respectively, of the National Research Council.

Preface

The abuse or neglect of a child is a human tragedy. The print and broadcast media have been flooded in recent years with stories of babies abandoned by their mothers; toddlers who are beaten by their parents or who are deprived of essential forms of nutrition, compassion, emotional and physical comfort; school-age children who are sexually abused; and adolescents who run away from homes after they have been subjected to years of neglect or abuse.

Although these stories attract tremendous interest and empathy for the victims of abuse and neglect, media accounts fail to reveal the complex interplay of factors that influences the origins and consequences of child maltreatment. Simple answers are often proposed for cruel behaviors against children, and easy-to-identify factors such as psychopathology, poverty, alcohol, drugs, and society itself are often blamed for destructive behaviors. Yet, after decades of research, we now recognize that no single risk factor provides the overriding catalyst for child abuse and neglect. Indeed, we have only recently discovered that a complex interplay of multiple risk factors paves the path to abuse and neglect, a discovery that challenges our search for the origins of maltreatment, but one that encourages us to recognize multiple opportunities for intervention.

As scientists, we have too long neglected the study of child maltreatment. For decades, social workers, clinicians, lawyers, and others have documented the pain of child victimization. But daunting obstacles inhibit the scientific study of this topic: the nature of the subject itself is emotionally overwhelming, the field lacks consistent definitions and valid instrumentation, data collection efforts are cumbersome and often unreliable, and the presence of multiple cofactors in the study populations—including poverty, violence, and other forms of victimization—makes it exceedingly difficult to isolate key factors.

In three decades of research with abusive and neglectful families, remarkable progress has been achieved. Theoretical assumptions have been revised and expanded to incorporate research findings about characteristics of individuals, families, neighborhoods, and social and cultural values that affect child maltreatment. The importance of the developmental cycle of the child has been recognized in studying the consequences of child maltreatment and in designing interventions and prevention programs. And the relationship between experiences with child abuse and neglect and a broad range of health and behavioral disorders has been explored through longitudinal studies with increasingly larger samples.

Despite this progress, we still lack a solid base of research information that can guide and enhance society's efforts to intervene and prevent child abuse and neglect. The existing scientific literature on child maltreatment, though extensive, is not definitive. It lacks cohesion and organization. The literature base is highly specialized and reflects the fragmentation of the field. Some scholars have focused exclusively on physical abuse of children within their family environments. Others have concentrated on the phenomenon of sexual abuse. Still others have studied the often hidden dimensions of child neglect or the more recently recognized forms of emotional abuse and neglect. The interdisciplinary nature of the field also fosters fragmentation and uncertainties. Health professionals tend to emphasize the physical manifestations of abuse or neglect: psychologists stress the internal dynamics that may foster maltreatment or protect an abused child from the more destructive consequences of abuse. Social workers concentrate on the factors and services that foster family strengths or risks to the child, while lawyers examine the effects of laws on outcomes, among other issues.

The fragmentation of the research literature, and the absence of research priorities in a field that is gaining increased attention, are the catalysts that stimulated our study. In 1991, the Commissioner for Children, Youth, and Families in the U.S. Department of Health and Human Services asked the National Academy of Sciences to convene an expert panel to develop a research agenda for future studies of child maltreatment. The charge to the panel was to examine the quality of the existing research, determine areas of strength and weakness, and offer guidance regarding ways in which current and future research resources might be directed to improve the development of this field.

The panel was set up by the Commission on Behavioral and Social

Sciences and Education (CBASSE) of the National Research Council in response to this request. This is the first study on child abuse and neglect undertaken by the National Research Council, but it was developed at a time of expanding activities in areas of violence and youth. For example, in early 1993 the Academy published the results of a major study on research on the causes, prevention, and control of violent behavior (*Understanding and Preventing Violence*, National Academy Press, 1993). The National Research Council was also engaged in developing a report on high-risk youth (*Losing Generations: Adolescents in High-Risk Settings*, National Academy Press, 1993), although the results of that effort were not available at the time that our study was in progress.

In carrying out its task, the panel undertook a number of activities. The panel formed three subpanels to help organize the research literature and to identify primary themes and initial recommendations. Review materials prepared by panel members and staff, as well as a set of background papers prepared by others, guided the initial discussions and, in some cases, were incorporated into draft chapters of the report. The panel is grateful to the many presenters, consultants, authors, readers, workshop participants, and federal agency officials who provided materials on specialized topics; they are listed individually in Appendix A. A few who deserve special recognition are Diana Baumrind, Jay Belsky, Jeanne Bertolli, Rosemary Bolig, Deborah Daro, Howard Dubowitz, Richard Gelles, Jeanne Giovannoni, David Kolko, John Leventhal, Howard Morgenstern, Joan Sieber, Susan Sorenson, Penelope Trickett, and Michael Wald. In addition, the panel developed outreach activities to a broad group of scholars and organizations through two working group sessions and a national survey of more than 170 professional, educational, and advocacy groups concerned with child abuse and neglect (listed in Appendix A).

With such a diversity of effort, disagreements were common, but the panel was able to achieve a consensus of views through discussions and analysis of research findings. This volume also includes two brief supplementary statements prepared and endorsed by three panel members (Appendix B). Although these members support the interactive approach taken in the panel's report, they wish to emphasize two of the risk factors identified as potential contributors to child maltreatment.

To ensure that this study could both build on what is currently known about child maltreatment and develop informed insights into related fields that may contribute theroetical and methodological research, the panel was composed of experts in child maltreatment as well as others who are notable for their work in other areas of epidemiology, biostatistics, child development, and pediatric medicine. Biographical sketches of panel members and staff appear in Appendix C.

Rosemary Chalk served as the study director for this project. Her extensive experience with earlier Academy reports as well as her wisdom about the process were essential to our steady progress and timely completion of this demanding task. Although the panel bears responsibility for any errors of inference, Rosemary deserves credit for much of the writing and for upholding high standards of evidence. Jessica Backer was the research assistant for the study, and she diligently identified and obtained hundreds of reference materials in addition to preparing background papers for the panel. Debbie MacGuffie, the project assistant, provided the panel with excellent support and guidance in organizing the panel meetings, preparing agenda materials, and guiding the report from the first drafts to the published volume.

Finally, the panel wishes to acknowledge the support and assistance of officials from the U.S. Department of Health and Human Services who were instrumental in the initiation and development of this study. Wade Horn, former Administrator of Children, Youth, and Families, was the key individual who sponsored this study. David Lloyd, director of the National Center for Child Abuse and Neglect, provided financial support, guidance, and information for the panel throughout the study. Marsha Liss, special assistant to the director of the National Center on Child Abuse and Neglect, served as the project monitor for this study and helped to negotiate administrative and information requests to keep the project moving smoothly through all phases of its operation.

In recognizing the contributions of these individuals, we want to affirm that the recommendations of this report are those of the panel members themselves. We have had a privileged opportunity to review, in an independent manner, the fruits of decades of research investments by governmental and private agencies. We hope that our report will stimulate those responsible for the development of this research to be encouraged by the progress that has been achieved, and to renew their sense of commitment to the tasks that must still be completed. Much remains to be done.

Anne C. Petersen, *Chair*
Panel on Research on
Child Abuse and Neglect

Contents

Tribute to Ray E. Helfer, M.D.

This report is dedicated to Ray E. Helfer, M.D., pediatrician and professor in the Department of Pediatrics and Human Development at Michigan State University in East Lansing. Dr. Helfer had agreed to serve as a member of the study panel, but he suffered a fatal stroke and died in December 1991, prior to the first panel meeting. His death is a significant loss for the community of professionals dedicated to research on child maltreatment.

Ray Helfer was a pioneer scientist and practitioner in the field of child maltreatment. As a pediatrician, he treated many children who were victims of abuse or neglect, and he worked closely with their families in striving to improve the quality of parent-child interactions. As a researcher, he was committed to a multidisciplinary effort to respond to, and prevent, child victimization. He collaborated with Henry Kempe in the publication of *The Battered Child*, a collection of research articles on child maltreatment first published in 1974, now in its fifth edition. And he was a strong advocate for national legislation that resulted in the passage of the Child Abuse Prevention and Treatment Act in 1974.

The panel's deliberations have been guided by the findings and insights of Dr. Helfer. This report is dedicated to his memory.

Summary

Child maltreatment is a devastating social problem in American society. In 1990, case reports involving over 2 million children were made to social service agencies. In the period 1979 through 1988, about 2,000 child deaths (ages 0-17) were recorded annually as a result of abuse and neglect (McClain et al., 1993), and an additional 160,000 cases resulted in serious injuries in 1990 alone (Daro and McCurdy, 1991). However tragic and sensational, the counts of deaths and serious injuries provide limited insight into the pervasive dimensions of child abuse and neglect. Reports of child maltreatment reveal little about the interactions among individuals, families, communities, and society that lead to such incidents. The services required for children who have been abused or neglected, including medical care, family counseling, foster care, and specialized education, cost more than $500 million annually, according to estimates by the General Accounting Office (1991).

No specific theories about the causes of child abuse and neglect have been substantially replicated across studies, yet significant progress has been gained in the past few decades in identifying the dimensions of complex phenomena that contribute to the origins of child maltreatment. Furthermore, research in the field of child maltreatment studies is relatively undeveloped when compared with related fields such as child development, social welfare, and criminal violence.

In part, this underdevelopment is influenced by a lack of funds as well as the methodological difficulties of research on topics with a complex etiology. But in part it is underinvestment due to bias, prejudice, and the lack of a clear political constituency for children in general, and disadvantaged children in particular, in the competition for scarce research funds. Substantial efforts are now required to reach beyond the limitations of current knowledge and to gain new insights that can lead to the prevention of maltreatment and also improve the quality of social services and public policy decisions affecting the health and welfare of abused and neglected children and their families. Long-term research and collaborative ventures are necessary to develop knowledge that can improve understanding of, and response to, child maltreatment.

The panel has identified five key reasons why child maltreatment research should be viewed as a central focus of more comprehensive research activity.

1. Research on child maltreatment can provide scientific information that will help with the solution of a broad range of individual and social disorders. Research in this field is demonstrating that experiences with child abuse and neglect are a major component of many child and adult mental and behavioral disorders, including delayed development, poor academic performance, delinquency, depression, alcoholism, substance abuse, deviant sexual behaviors, and domestic and criminal violence.

2. Research on child maltreatment can provide insights and knowledge that can directly benefit victims of child abuse and neglect and their families. Individuals who have been victimized as a result of child maltreatment deserve to have research efforts dedicated to their experience, in the same manner as our society invests in scientific research for burn victims, victims of genetic or infectious diseases, or those who are subjected to other forms of trauma.

3. Research on child maltreatment can reduce long-term economic costs associated with treating the consequences of child maltreatment, in areas such as mental health services, foster care, juvenile delinquency, and family violence. Economic issues must also be considered in evaluating long-term treatment costs and loss of earnings associated with the consequences of child victimization.   One analysis cited by the General Accounting Office that used prevalence and treatment rates generated from multiple studies (Daro, 1988) calculated that the future lost productivity of severely abused children is $658-1300 million annually, if their impairments limit their potential earnings by only 5-10 percent.

4. Research on child maltreatment can provide empirical evidence to improve the quality of many legal and organizational decisions that have broad-based social implications. Government officials, judges, legislators, social service personnel, child welfare advocates, and others make hundreds of crucial decisions each day about the lives and futures of child victims and their offenders. These decisions will benefit from informed guidance on the effectiveness and consequences of various social interventions that address child maltreatment. Such guidance can evolve from research on the outcomes of alternative responses to reports of child abuse and neglect, results of therapeutic and social service interventions, and cost-effectiveness studies.

5. **Research on the etiology of child maltreatment can provide a scientific basis for primary prevention of child abuse—that is, through programs that will counteract etiological factors before they have a chance to produce child abuse in the next generation.**

CHARGE TO THE PANEL

The commissioner of the Administration for Children, Youth, and Families (ACYF) in the U.S. Department of Health and Human Services requested that the National Academy of Sciences convene a study panel to undertake a comprehensive examination of the theoretical and pragmatic research needs in the area of child maltreatment. The Panel on Research on Child Abuse and Neglect was asked specifically to:

• Review and assess research on child abuse and neglect, encompassing work funded by ACYF and other known sources under public and private auspices;
• Identify research that provides knowledge relevant to the field, and
• Recommend research priorities for the next decade, including building blocks for knowledge development, new areas of research that should be funded by public and private agencies, and suggestions regarding fields that are no longer a priority for funding.

The report resulting from this study provides recommendations for allocating existing research funds and also suggests funding mechanisms and topic areas to which new resources could be allocated or enhanced resources could be redirected.

A DEVELOPMENTAL AND ECOLOGICAL PERSPECTIVE

Over the past several decades, a growing number of state and federal funding programs, government reports, specialized journals, and research centers, as well as national and international societies and conferences, have examined various dimensions of the problem of child maltreatment. The results of these efforts have been inconsistent and uneven. In addressing aspects of each new revelation of abuse or each promising new intervention, research efforts often have become diffuse, fragmented, specific, and narrow. What is lacking is a coordinated approach and a general conceptual framework that can add new depth to our understanding of child maltreatment. A coordinated approach can accommodate diverse perspectives while providing direction and guidance in establishing research priorities and synthesizing research knowledge. Collaborative efforts are also needed to facilitate the integration and application of research on child maltreatment with related areas such as child development, spousal violence, substance abuse, and juvenile delinquency.

In contrast to conceptualizing this report in terms of categories of maltreatment or responses of the social system to child maltreatment, the panel presents a **child-oriented** research agenda that emphasizes the importance of knowing more about the backgrounds and experiences of developing children and their families, within a broader social context that includes their friends, neighborhoods, and communities. This framework stresses the importance of knowing more about the qualitative differences between children who suffer episodic experiences of abuse or neglect and those for whom maltreatment is a chronic part of their lives. And this approach highlights the need to know more about circumstances that affect the consequences, and therefore the treatment, of child maltreatment, especially circumstances that may be affected by family, cultural, or ethnic factors that often remain hidden in small, isolated studies.

The panel has adopted an *ecological developmental perspective* to examine factors in the child, family, and society that can exacerbate or mitigate the incidence and destructive consequences of child maltreatment. In the panel's view, this perspective reflects the understanding that development is a process involving *transactions* between the growing child and the social environment or ecology in which development takes place. Positive *and* negative factors in the cycle of child development merit attention in shaping a research agenda on child maltreatment. The panel's ecological perspective recognizes that dysfunctional families are often part of a dysfunctional environment. This report extends beyond what is—to what could be, if children and families were supported to attain healthy development. We cannot simply build a research agenda for the existing social system; we need to develop one that independently challenges the system to adapt to new perspectives, new insights, and new discoveries.

IDENTIFICATION AND DEFINITIONS

Four categories of child maltreatment are now generally distinguished: (1) physical abuse, (2) sexual abuse, (3) neglect, and (4) emotional maltreatment. These four categories have become the focus of separate studies of incidence and prevalence, etiology, prevention, consequences, and treatment, with uneven development of research within each area and poor integration of knowledge across areas. Each category has developed its own typology and framework of reference terms. As a result, we know very little about the extent to which different types of child abuse and neglect share common risk factors or the ways in which they respond to different types of interventions.

The co-occurrence of different forms of child maltreatment has been examined only to a limited extent and the specific causes, consequences, prevention, and treatment of selected types of child abuse and neglect is relatively unknown. Inconsistencies in definitions often preclude comparative analyses of clinical studies.

The complexity of studies on child maltreatment also reflects the fragmentation of services and responses by which our society addresses specific cases. Furthermore, the duration, source, intensity, timing, and situational context of incidents of child victimization are important. Yet information about these factors is rarely requested or recorded by social agencies or health professionals in the process of identifying or documenting reports of child maltreatment.

Despite vigorous debate over the last two decades, little progress has been made in constructing clear, reliable, valid, and useful definitions of child abuse and neglect. The difficulties in constructing definitions include such factors as lack of social consensus over what forms of parenting are dangerous or unacceptable; uncertainty about whether to define maltreatment based on adult characteristics, adult behavior, child outcome, environmental context, or some combination; conflict over whether standards of endangerment or harm should be used in constructing definitions; and confusion as to whether similar definitions should be used for scientific, legal, and clinical purposes.

Standardization of definitions is difficult and carries with it dangers of oversimplification. However, consistent definitions are necessary for better measurement and instrumentation in the field. Attempts to reach consensus on clear operational measures must be made to overcome existing limitations and to develop more refined measures. The formulation of research definitions of child maltreatment should be guided by four key principles: consideration of the specific objectives the definition must serve; division into homogeneous subtypes; conceptual clarity; and feasibility in practice.

SCOPE OF THE PROBLEM

From 1976, when the first national figures for child maltreatment were generated, to 1990, the most recent year covered by the National Child Abuse and Neglect Data System, reports of maltreatment have grown from 416,033 per year (affecting 669,000 children) to 1,700,000 per year (affecting 2,712,917 children). This alarming rise in the number of reported cases of child maltreatment has promoted the view that there is an epidemic of child maltreatment in the United States.⌐

The panel's review of national prevalence and incidence child maltreatment studies has revealed important methodological problems that greatly affect the usefulness of these data for drawing conclusions about both the scope and origins of the problem. These methodological problems include definitional issues, confusion of prevalence and incidence, the source of maltreatment data, sampling and design considerations, a paucity of reliable and valid measurement instruments, the problem of retrospective bias, the impact of mandatory reporting requirements on the reliability of survey respondents' reports, and scarce funding for methodological work (specifically instrument development). The paucity of rigorous epidemiological investigations has retarded progress in this field. However, the available evidence suggests that child abuse and neglect is an important, prevalent problem in the United States, with conservative estimates placing the annual number of children affected by this problem at more than 1 million, following an analysis of substantiated rates of reported cases. Child abuse and neglect are particularly important compared with other critical childhood problems because they are often directly associated with adverse physical and mental health consequences in children and families. Furthermore, given the prevalence of childhood maltreatment, the level of federal funds expended in this research area is extremely small when compared with the resources allocated for less prevalent childhood mental disorders, such as autism and childhood schizophrenia.

Specifically, the panel concludes:

•   Much of the tremendous increase in maltreatment is probably the result of increased reporting, although significant increases in the occurrence rate itself may have occurred as well.

•   Neglect is more common than any individual type of child maltreatment and has consistently accounted for approximately half of the cases of maltreatment. The chronic nature of child neglect cases needs to be considered in discussions of incidence and prevalence.

•   Total reports of physical abuse increased significantly between 1980 and 1986, although severe forms of physical abuse may actually have decreased.

•   Sexual abuse reported to child protective services has shown the largest reported increase of any form of abuse or neglect.

•   Emotional abuse is the least studied of all the types of abuse.

OVERVIEW OF ETIOLOGICAL MODELS

Most forms of maltreatment are part of a pattern of maladaptive behavior that emerges over time, but research evidence regarding the origins and maintenance of this pattern is not clear. Investigators disagree about whether child maltreatment is a continuum of behaviors (ranging from mild physical discipline to severe forms of physical or sexual abuse) or a set of unique behavioral problems with distinctive etiologies.

Since no single risk factor has been identified that provides a necessary or sufficient cause of child maltreatment, etiological models of child maltreatment have evolved from isolated cause-and-effect models to approaches that consider the combination of individual, familial, environmental, and social or cultural risk factors that may contribute to child maltreatment. The phenomenon of child abuse and neglect has thus been moved away from a theoretical framework of an individual disorder or psychological disturbance, toward a focus on extreme disturbances of childrearing, often part of a context of other serious family problems, such as substance abuse or mental illness.

Interactive models suggest that child maltreatment occurs when multiple risk factors outweigh protective, compensatory, and buffering factors. The role of particular risk or protective factors may increase or decrease during different developmental and historical periods, as individuals, their life circumstances, and the society in which they live change. These models show promise and suggest issues that need to be addressed in research on the etiology of child maltreatment.

Individual Ontogenic Factors

A parent's personality influences child development primarily through the interactive process of parenting. Disrupted parenting can occur in a variety of ways, especially when a parent's personality attributes (such as anger or anxiety) are compounded by additional stresses such as marital conflict, absence of the spouse, poverty, unemployment, and having a difficult child. Individual factors that have sometimes been associated with child maltreatment include adult attitudes, attributions, and cognitive factors; the intergenerational transmission of abusive parenting; the use of alcohol and drugs; characteristics of the child (such as temperament); and demographic factors such as maternal age, marital status, and household density. Research on the role of these individual factors in stimulating or maintaining neglectful or abusive behaviors has been contradictory and inconclusive, suggesting that no single factor, in isolation, can explain with satisfaction the origins of child maltreatment. For example, although alcohol often is cited as a principal risk factor in the etiology of child maltreatment, its relationship to child abuse and neglect remains uncertain. More needs to be known about the unique and immediate effects of alcohol, its co-occurrence with other problem behaviors such as antisocial personality disorder and substance abuse, the circumstances under which different types of drinking situations lead to or sustain violence against children, and cultural factors that mitigate or exacerbate connections between substance use or abuse and aggression.

Family Factors

Dysfunctions in all aspects of family relations, not just parent-child interactions, are often present in the families of maltreated children, and research is needed to examine whether such dysfunctions contribute to or are consequences of child maltreatment. Anger, conflict, and social isolation are pervasive features of maltreating families. In many cases of maltreatment, there often is not a single maltreated child, but multiple victims. Thus, maltreated children may be exposed to considerable violence involving other family members as well as violence directed toward themselves.

A distinctive feature associated with chronically neglecting families is the chaotic and unpredictable character of the family system. The effect on children of repeated acts of violence or constant fluctuations in the makeup of their household, in addition to child neglect, has not been examined in the research literature, although such factors may contribute to unrelatedness and detachment.

An important gap in the literature on child maltreatment is the lack of comparative analysis of the effects of parenting styles and dysfunctional parenting patterns (including abuse and neglect) on children in different social, ethnic, and cultural groups. The relationships among physical discipline, stress, and parental and family dysfunctions that give rise to the emergence of child maltreatment also need to be clarified.

Although a parent's own history of victimization during childhood is thought to predict child maltreatment, this association is based on retrospective studies that are sometimes methodologically suspect. The relationship between physical discipline and child maltreatment is also largely unknown, particularly in the context of cultural differences and practices. Finally, stressful life events are thought to play an important role on parental abilities, but relations between stress and poor parenting are complex and poorly understood at this time.

Environmental and Community Factors

Family functioning occurs within the context of various social institutions and external forces that influence family and parent-child behaviors. Research on environmental factors has concentrated on neighborhood and community environments, but other factors may affect individual and family functioning as well, including the workplace, the media, the school, church, and peer groups.

Discussion of the relationship of poverty to child maltreatment has persisted since publications of the early professional papers on child abuse in the 1960s. Although child maltreatment is reported across the socioeconomic spectrum, it is disproportionately reported among poor families. Furthermore, child maltreatment—especially child neglect—is not simply concentrated among the poor, but among the poorest of the poor. Whether this association results from greater stress due to poverty-related conditions that precipitate abuse, or from greater scrutiny by public agencies that results in overreporting, or whether maltreatment is but one characteristic of the pattern of disruption among the poorest of the poor continues to be debated. The link between unemployment and maltreatment is significant in understanding the relationship between poverty and maltreatment. Families reported for abuse often have multiple problems, and the abuse may simply be a part—or a consequence—of a broader continuum of social dysfunctions.

Although it occurs in all social levels, violent behavior toward children, particularly severe violence, is more likely in poor families. Despite the fact that the evidence on maternal age as a risk factor for child maltreatment is mixed, mothers with young children living below the poverty line have the greatest risk of behaving violently toward children.

Although neighborhoods are recognized as important in the ecology of child maltreatment, more insight is needed into the processes by which neighborhood conditions and factors affect maltreatment. Poor neighborhoods differ in their social and physical conditions and in their ability to influence specific risks posed to children by poverty, unemployment, and community violence. Socioeconomic conditions have predictive value for explaining child maltreatment rates, yet some neighborhoods have higher or lower child abuse rates than would be expected based on socioeconomic conditions alone.

Social isolation has been identified as an important etiological risk factor in child maltreatment, but its role as a consequence or cause of maltreatment is uncertain. The influence of family ties and organizational affiliations (including employment and education) are poorly understood but increasingly recognized as powerful forces in shaping parenting styles and family functioning. Financial stability, employment, and neighborhoods can create a context that either supports a family during periods of stress or enhances the potential for abuse.

Social and Cultural Factors

Family practices and policies that reflect social and cultural values can foster or mitigate stress in family life. Although the relationship of cultural factors is not well understood, some American societal values may contribute to child maltreatment and they have achieved new importance in emerging theoretical models of child maltreatment. Racism, for example, can lead to an inequitable distribution of resources, education, and employment that undermine many ethnic minority families' abilities to support their children (financially and emotionally) and to provide parental care. The term *societal neglect* has been suggested to characterize American tolerance for a situation in which one-fifth of all preschool children live below the poverty line, with a substantially higher rate among ethnic minorities. Societal fascination with violence, including violence toward children, has been suggested as a risk factor for child maltreatment, as has the lack of coherent family leave and family support policies, particularly the absence of preventive health care for infants, children, and adolescents at risk for maltreatment.

Conclusions

Many factors have been identified as contributing to the occurrence of child maltreatment, but single-factor theories of child maltreatment have not been able to identify specific mechanisms that influence the etiology of child maltreatment. Such environmental factors as poverty and unemployment and such individual characteristics as a prior history of abuse, social isolation, and low self-esteem have been significantly associated with child maltreatment offenders, but the relationships among such factors are not well understood in determining the origins of child maltreatment. The panel believes that the etiology of maltreatment involves complex clusters of variables that interact along various dimensions of a child's ecological/transactional system. Factors that increase risk for maltreatment and factors that decrease the likelihood for maltreatment are found at all ecological levels and interact to produce child maltreatment. Although theoretical models that describe the etiological complexity of maltreatment have been developed, they have not been subjected to testing and adequate research. Our recommendations seek to address these limitations.

PREVENTION

In the past, the risk factor literature for child maltreatment has been dominated by an orientation that emphasizes correction of perceived weaknesses or problem behaviors and ignores protective factors that may influence outcomes. In recent years, some researchers have begun to examine variables that foster healthy relationships and reduce risk for child maltreatment. The reduction of multiple vulnerabilities as well as the development of compensatory behaviors should be a goal for future prevention research.

Risk Factors and Pathways to Prevention

Until recently, the primary focus in designing preventive interventions was the identification and modification of problematic or damaging parental practices associated with child maltreatment, such as physical discipline, failure to provide children with basic necessities and care, and mismatches between a parent's expectations and a child's ability.

This singular focus on parental roles was altered with the recognition of the prevalence of sexual abuse in the late 1970s. Research on victims of child sexual abuse suggested that risk factors with respect to perpetrator characteristics, victim characteristics, and sociodemographic variables are far more heterogeneous than they are for physical abuse or neglect victims. As a result, prevention advocates focused on ways to strengthen potential victims of sexual abuse through classroom-based instruction for children of all ages.

In recent years, schools have placed a new emphasis on violence prevention programs, designed to equip students to develop nonviolent methods of conflict resolution. Although the generalizability of these programs to the field of child maltreatment has not been systematically assessed, such programs represent a promising direction for future research.

Parental Enhancement Programs

Parental practices in families with young children are a major focus of research on prevention strategies for child maltreatment. Prevention strategies have built on individual, familial, and community-level risk and protective factors that contribute directly to both parental practices and to child well-being. This research foundation has provided the basis for identifying vulnerable families that are at high risk for maladaptive parental practices. Increasingly, at-risk communities are becoming the target of early intervention programs.

Four major types of prevention strategies have been developed for families with young children (defined as the prenatal period through age 8): (1) comprehensive programs, often including home visitor services that vary widely in both scope and content, (2) center-based programs that include a family support component, parent information services, and early childhood education services, (3) community-based interventions that offer a range of family support services, and (4) hospital-based interventions.

Although some well-designed, randomized control, clinical trials exist (such as the Olds study [1986a,b] in upstate New York), many early intervention services lack a theoretical framework and their mission is not always well defined. Some interventions demonstrate that knowledge about child development can be transferred to parents in a relatively brief period of time (i.e., 6-12 weeks), but a time commitment of six months or more is needed to change attitudes and strengthen parenting and interpersonal skills. Prevention programs need to focus directly on families at most risk for maltreatment, to accommodate families with differing needs and experiences, and to adapt to changing family situations.

Community-Based Prevention Programs

The large majority of existing community-based programs focus on prevention of physical and sexual abuse. Child maltreatment prevention programs that are found in the schools are primarily child sexual abuse prevention programs designed for children in elementary and high schools. In addition to major efforts in child sexual abuse prevention, the panel reviewed two other efforts that may have implications for the prevention of child abuse and neglect. These are community-based antipoverty programs, some of which involve vocational or educational assistance, and the violence prevention programs in the schools designed to educate children, primarily adolescents, about conflict resolution skills. Such programs may be important in helping improve the welfare of many families and peer relations, but they have not been systematically evaluated in terms of their outcomes for child abuse and neglect.

Although sexual abuse prevention education programs have generally achieved the goals of teaching prevention knowledge and skill acquisition, it is not clear that these gains are retained over time or are useful to a child under assault, especially if the offender is a relative or trusted adult. Less is known about the efficacy of child sexual abuse prevention programs compared with prevention efforts directed primarily at the physical abuse and neglect of children. There is disagreement in the child safety field about the theories that should guide child sexual abuse prevention programs. At this juncture, it seems critical for child sexual assault prevention programs to evaluate the contributions of extensive parent and teacher training components. Research efforts should be expanded to include extended afterschool programs and in-depth discussion programs for certain high-risk groups (e.g., former victims, teen-age parents).

Since poverty has consistently been associated with child maltreatment, particularly child neglect, programs designed to improve the income of poor families could become a major source of prevention of child neglect. At a time when education has become an important requirement for better-paying jobs, programs designed to increase the career options of young parents through educational and vocational training efforts are commonly viewed as part of the preventive spectrum for child maltreatment.

Day care providers, teachers, principals, and others who have ongoing and long-term contact with children are in a position to identify suspected victims of maltreatment and report them to child protective services. Such interventions can be a source of reduced incidence for the recurrence or the prevention of child maltreatment. However, the low percentage of suspected cases identified by educators and other personnel in the school system that are eventually reported to child protection agencies may be a cause for concern. Day care providers, educators, and other youth service personnel require training in the identification of child abuse and neglect, guidance in reporting suspected cases, and methods for supporting maltreatment victims and their families, including referrals to relevant treatment services and peer support groups for victims.

Since many families who are reported for child maltreatment are characterized by other forms of violence (including spouse abuse and involvement in criminal assaults), interrupting the cycle of violence in one area of life may have spillover effects on others, but this assumption needs to be tested empirically. School-based interventions have several advantages, including accessibility to a broad youth population, mandated attendance, ease in scheduling, and cost effectiveness. Although school-based violence prevention programs are a promising development, no firm conclusions can be drawn at this time regarding their effectiveness or generalizability for the prevention of child abuse, and it is not known if participants will be less likely to be perpetrators of family violence.

Media representatives can become important participants in public education about prevention in child abuse and neglect. Media efforts to prevent child maltreatment may benefit from lessons derived from the role of the media in addressing public health issues. Similarly, media programs could be developed to promote community support for appropriate parental practices, especially in the use of physical discipline, and to improve the response of bystanders who witness acts of child maltreatment in public places.

Community-based prevention efforts show promise, especially in the design of multisystem approaches that can build on family-school-media-community approaches. Many avenues can be considered in designing prevention programs, but well-designed program evaluations are critical for developing a knowledge base to guide future efforts. The community mental health approach and community-based interventions designed to reduce smoking and heart disease represent much promise, but such efforts have not yet been developed or tested in the area of child maltreatment.

The Role of Cultural and Social Values in Prevention

Prevention programs increasingly focus on ways to foster cultural changes that could lead to regulatory and voluntary approaches to reinforce health messages at other system levels. Several areas that have relevance for prevention research on child maltreatment include attitudes toward the use of corporal punishment, the effects of criminal sanctions on the maltreatment of children, and the use of violence as a means of resolving conflict. Reliance on corporal punishment by parents has been identified by some researchers as an important risk factor for physical abuse, but corporal punishment is usually not dealt with in programs to prevent physical abuse. Research is needed on whether the inclusion of alternatives to spanking in such programs reduces physical abuse.

In considering the effectiveness of criminal sanctions in the area of child maltreatment, associated problems of abusive and neglectful families need to be recognized. Many of these families are already involved with the legal system because of other behaviors, including substance abuse, juvenile delinquency, and other crimes. Assessment of the impact of criminal sanctions solely in the area of child maltreatment is challenging, since the perpetrators may be removed from the home in a variety of other ways involving the court system.

Conclusions

Evaluations of home visitation programs, school-based programs for the prevention of sexual abuse and violence, and other community-based child maltreatment prevention programs are quite limited. Many evaluations are compromised by serious methodological problems, and many promising preventive interventions do not systematically include child maltreatment as a program outcome. Children and families who are most at risk for child maltreatment may not participate in the interventions, and those that do may not be sufficiently motivated to change or will have difficulty in implementing skills in their social context, especially if they live in violent neighborhoods.

The panel's primary conclusion is that comprehensive and intensive prevention programs that incorporate a theoretical framework, identifying critical pathways to child maltreatment, offer the greatest potential for future programmatic efforts. New theoretical models that incorporate ecological and developmental perspectives have complicated the development of prevention research, but these models hold much promise, for they suggest multiple opportunities for prevention. Prevention research needs to be guided by rigorous evaluation that can provide knowledge about the importance of different combinations of risk and protective factors, the developmental course of various forms of maltreatment, and the importance of replacing or supplementing risk behaviors with compensatory skills. In the face of uncertainty as to whether etiologies of the various forms of child maltreatment are similar or different, a diverse range of approaches to prevention research should be encouraged.

CONSEQUENCES

For over 30 years, clinicians have described the effects of child abuse and neglect on the physical, psychological, cognitive, and behavioral development of children. Physical consequences range from minor injuries to severe brain damage and even death. Psychological consequences range from chronic low self-esteem to severe dissociative states. The cognitive effects of abuse range from attention problems and learning disorders to severe organic brain syndromes. Behaviorally, the consequences of abuse range from poor peer relations to extraordinarily violent behaviors. Thus, the victims of abusive treatment and the society in which they live pay an enormous price for the results of child maltreatment.

Yet empirical studies of child maltreatment have identified important complexities that challenge our understanding of factors and relationships that exacerbate or modify the consequences of abusive experiences. The majority of children who are abused do not show signs of extreme disturbance. Research has suggested a relationship between child maltreatment and a variety of short- and long-term consequences, but considerable uncertainty and debate remain about the effects of child victimization on children, adolescents, and adults.

The scientific study of child maltreatment and its consequences is in its infancy. Until recently, research on the consequences of physical and sexual child abuse and neglect has been limited by delays between the child's experience and official identification of maltreatment. Maltreatment often occurs in the presence of multiple problems within a family or social environment, including poverty, violence, substance abuse, and unemployment. Distinguishing consequences that are associated directly with the experience of child maltreatment itself rather than other social problems is a daunting task for the research investigator.

As a result, we do not yet understand the consequences on children of particular types or multiple forms of abuse. Nor do we yet know the importance of the particular timing, intensity, and context of abuse on the outcome. Factors such as age, gender, developmental status, family relationships, and placement experiences of the child may influence the outcomes of maltreatment experiences. Disordered patterns of adaptation may lie dormant, only to appear during times of stress or in conjunction with particular circumstances. Furthermore, certain intrinsic strengths and vulnerabilities within a child and the child's environment may affect the extent to which abuse will have adverse consequences.

Victims of child abuse and neglect are at increased risk for delinquency and running away, but the majority of childhood victims do not manifest these problem behaviors. Significantly less is known about connections between childhood victimization and other problem behaviors, such as teenage pregnancy, use of alcohol and illicit drugs, and self-destructive behavior. Alcohol and illicit drug use are both illegal for teenagers, creating a natural confounding of alcohol and substance use with delinquency. Diagnoses of alcoholism are complicated by the presence of antisocial personality disorder, which in turn may include components of criminal behavior and sexual promiscuity. Engaging in any one of these behaviors, then, might increase the likelihood of involvement in other high-risk behaviors.

Issues of Stigma, Bias, and Discrimination

Problem behaviors may result from the chain of events occurring subsequent to the victimization rather then the victimization experience per se. For example, being separated from one's biological parents, subsequent to the abuse and neglect incident(s), and placed in foster care can be associated with deleterious effects. Furthermore, children can encounter discrimination against their race, color, language, life and family styles, and religious and cultural beliefs that affect their self-esteem and magnify the initial and lasting effects of both types of victimization. The observed relationship between early childhood victimization and later problem behaviors may also be affected by practices of the juvenile justice system that disproportionately label and treat maltreatment victims as juvenile offenders.

Protective Factors

Not all abused and neglected children grow up to become dysfunctional adults. A broad range of protective factors, such as temperamental attributes, environmental conditions, and positive events, can mitigate the effects of early negative experiences. The consequences of childhood maltreatment vary by demographic, background, and clinical variables—such as the child's gender, the family's socioeconomic status, and the level of marital and family violence.

Individual characteristics, such as high intelligence, certain kinds of temperament, the cognitive appraisal of victimization experiences, a relationship with a significant person, and out-of-home placement experiences protect some childhood victims. But conflicting or indirect evidence about most of these characteristics and experiences results in a major gap in knowledge about what factors make a difference in the lives of abused and neglected children. Research is needed to determine the role of protective factors and mediating individual characteristics, particularly how they operate to increase or decrease vulnerability for problem behaviors.

Placement outside the home may act to protect abused and neglected children from serious long-term consequences, but such an action is controversial. Foster care placements may pose additional risks for the abused or neglected child, and the trauma of separation from one's biological family can also be damaging. Although some out-of-home placements may exacerbate stress in children from abusive and neglectful households, such placements may not always be deterimental. However, abused and neglected children in foster care and other out-of-home placement experiences, who typically come from multi-problem families, are a particularly vulnerable group because they have experienced both a disturbed family situation and separation from their natural parents.

Conclusions

Knowledge of the long-term consequences of childhood maltreatment into adulthood is extremely limited, with sparse information on intellectual and academic outcomes and medical and physiological consequences. Some research has addressed parenting behaviors (particularly the intergenerational effects of abuse), but the vast majority of existing research has focused on psychosocial outcomes and, in particular, psychopathology.

Childhood victimization often occurs in the context of multiproblem homes. Other family variables, such as poverty, unemployment, parental alcoholism or drug problems, and other factors that affect social and family functioning, need to be disentangled from the specific effects of childhood abuse and neglect. Few studies have assessed the long-term consequences on the development of abused and neglected children, beyond adolescence and into adulthood. Control groups matched on socioeconomic status and other relevant variables become necessary and vital components of this research, in order to determine the effect of childhood victimization on later behavior, in the context of family and demographic characteristics.

INTERVENTIONS AND TREATMENT

Research on interventions in child maltreatment is complicated by ethical, legal, and logistical problems, as well as difficulties in isolating factors specifically associated with child abuse and neglect in programs that often include families with multiple problems. Interventions include the assessment and investigation of child abuse reports by state child protection agencies, clinical treatment of physical injuries, legal action against the perpetrator, family and individual counseling, self-help services, and informal provision of goods and services (e.g., homemaker and respite care). Multiple agencies determine policies that guide interventions in child abuse and neglect and coordinate human and financial resources to fulfill these objectives. Researchers in this area have limited resources to collect compatible data, the results of project evaluations are rarely published in the professional literature, and issues of service delivery and accessibility are difficult to document.

The fragmentary nature of research in this area inhibited the panel's ability to evaluate the strengths and limitations of the intervention process. Furthermore, we did not have sufficient time to evaluate the full spectrum of administrative and legal procedures associated with reports of child maltreatment. The panel has thus focused its attention on those areas in which significant theory and empirical evidence exist.

Treatment of Child Victims

Despite the large literature on the detrimental effects of child maltreatment, the majority of treatment programs do not provide services directed at the psychosocial problems of the abused child. Children's involvement in treatment programs has generally occurred in the context of family-based services in which some children have received direct programmatic attention but others have not. Treatment interventions for child victims of abuse and neglect draw extensively from approaches for treating other childhood and adolescent problems with similar symptom profiles, but the psychological effects of abuse have not been well formulated in terms of theoretical constructs that can provide a basis for intervention.

Treatment of Adult Survivors

The treatment of adult survivors of childhood sexual victimization is a newly emerging field; the first programs appeared in the late 1970s. Many adult survivors of child abuse do not identify themselves as such, and most treatment programs or studies for adult survivors focus on child sexual abuse rather than other forms of child maltreatment. Research on the treatment of adult survivors is submerged in the literature on adult psychological disorders such as addiction, eating disorders, borderline personality disorders, and sexual dysfunction.

Treatment for Adult and Adolescent Sex Offenders

The treatment of child molesters is a controversial issue. Treatment programs are frequently offered to adult and adolescent offenders as part of plea bargaining negotiations in criminal prosecutions. The traditional assumption has been that children and society are better protected by offender treatment than by traditional prosecution and incarceration if the treatment service is effective. However, there is currently considerable debate about whether child molesters can be effectively treated. Until recently, adolescent sexual offenders have been neglected in clinical and research literature.

Empirically tested models to explain why adolescents commit sexual crimes or develop deviant sexual interest patterns are lacking.

The most common approaches to treating child molesters are comprehensive treatment programs aimed at simultaneously treating multiple aspects of deviant sexual behavior. Although many different approaches to the treatment of sexual offenders have been tried (including group therapy, family systems treatment, chemical interventions, and relapse prevention), scientific data indicating sustained reductions in recidivism are not available. Most studies follow offenders for only one year after treatment, and the effectiveness of the treatments in eliminating molestation behavior beyond that period is not known. Preliminary outcome data on the treatment of juvenile sex offenders show positive outcomes, although there is a lack of substantive research in the field and a lack of consensus regarding basic principles of treatment.

Family-Oriented Interventions

Most treatment interventions for physical abuse, child neglect, and emotional abuse seek to change parenting practices or the home environment. Only recently have treatment services incorporated empirical findings that examine the interactions of family members, abusive parents' perceptions of their children, behavioral characteristics that may restrict parenting abilities, and emotional reactions to stressful childrearing situations.

A lack of consensus exists regarding the effectiveness of a wide range of treatment services for maltreating families, including parental enhancement programs, family systems treatment, home-based services, and family support programs. Outcome studies have indicated positive behavioral and attitudinal changes as a result of family or parent treatment, but few studies have examined the effects of such interventions on subsequent reports of child abuse and neglect beyond one year. Definitive conclusions about the generalizability of the findings from studies of family-oriented programs in reducing subsequent child maltreatment are difficult to develop because the participants in these programs often present varied types of parental dysfunction.

Family Income and Supplemental Benefits

Government programs designed to alleviate or mitigate the effects of poverty on children are often part of a comprehensive set of services for low-income, maltreating families. Such programs include Social Security supplemental income programs, Aid to Families with Dependent Children, Women with Infants and Children food supplement program, Head Start, rent-subsidy programs, and school lunch programs, among others. While national and local child welfare programs designed to improve the well-being of all poor families may provide food, shelter, and other necessary resources for children in households characterized by neglect or abuse, the relationship between income support, material assistance, and the subsequent reduction of maltreatment has not been systematically addressed.

Community-Based Interventions

Family-oriented interventions often exist within a context of a broad range of diverse services provided by community agencies. Understanding these responses to child maltreatment is important in understanding the experiences of children and families following reports of maltreatment. Yet little is known about the efficacy of these community-based interventions.

A few treatment programs have been developed at the community level to provide services to families, such as counseling and educational services for the parents, supervised day care, and specialized referrals for community services, including mental health care, housing, and substance addiction treatment. Although such neighborhood-focused programs may assist children who are victims of abuse or neglect, program evaluations usually do not consider outcomes in terms of maltreatment subpopulations.

Medical Treatment of Child Abuse

Health professionals in private practice, community health clinics, and hospitals are often the first point of contact for abused children and their families when physical injuries are sustained. Little is known about treatments recommended for abused children in medical settings, and even less is known about specific treatment outcomes. Studies suggest, however, that many health professionals may not be sufficiently trained to detect or validate signs of abuse or to deal with the emotional, technical, and legal aspects of evaluating maltreated children, particularly sexually abused children.

Child Protective Services

Child protection agencies receive and screen initial reports of child abuse and neglect from educators, health personnel, police, members of the public (e.g., neighbors, family friends), relatives (including siblings and parents), and others to determine whether investigation is required. The processes that determine their responses to children and families have not attracted much research attention, although a few studies have attempted to document and characterize various stages of the process and their effects on children and families. Evaluations of operations of child protective services are complicated by the emergency situation in which most investigations occur, the confidential nature of the process, limited budgets, staff turnover, variations in definitions of child maltreatment and the absence of clear objectives, procedures, and standards of evaluation. The lack of systematic record-keeping and compatible data, and political sensitivity also inhibit the observation and analysis of decisions made by child protective services workers.

Research on the nature and effectiveness of risk assessment and referral decisions involving maltreating families is difficult, and we know little about factors that influence the assessment, investigation, and substantiation of specific cases; the operation of the referral system and follow-up services; the character of cases that are likely to receive services; the nature, intensity, and length of the services provided; and outcomes resulting from intervention services for different types of child maltreatment. Many factors can affect referral decisions, including availability of services, costs to clients and sponsors, ease of access, client attitudes, perceived need, and organizational relations. Recent clinical reports of child abuse cases suggest that many cases are closed immediately after services have been initiated and, in some instances, even prior to actual service delivery.

Child Welfare Services

The decision to allow a maltreated child to remain with family members or relatives during treatment is a critical and controversial aspect of the case management process. In some cases, temporary or permanent foster care is provided to children on the premise that protection of the child from physical harm is paramount.

Research on services provided to children in foster or kinship care is difficult. Information about children in foster care is often dispersed among biological parents, foster parents, relatives, and caseworkers, and cooperation among agencies providing services is frequently hampered by issues of confidentiality, funding and eligibility requirements, budgetary restrictions, and the specialized nature of professional services, that tend to focus on isolated problems.

Legal Intervention in Child Maltreatment

A small proportion of child maltreatment cases that are reported to child protection agencies become involved with juvenile courts, family courts, and criminal courts. Areas of convergence and conflict between the goals of service providers and the legal system in the treatment of child abuse and neglect have been documented, but much uncertainty remains in this area. Legal interventions in child maltreatment are complicated by many factors, such as the absence of physical evidence, difficulties in obtaining consistent and reliable testimony from children, emotional trauma that might be incurred in forcing a child victim to testify against a parent or other adult who may have harmed him or her, and inconclusive scientific evidence regarding the effectiveness of treatment in halting abusive and neglectful behavior. Even though relatively low numbers of sexually abused children are involved in court proceedings, the legal treatment of child sexual abuse cases has attracted significant research attention. Almost nothing is known about the quality of court experiences for children or adults who are affected by physical abuse, neglect, and emotional maltreatment.

Social and Cultural Interventions

National policies, professional services, and institutional programs sometimes reveal inconsistent policies and fundamental value conflicts. Values that strongly influence the current American social context for responding to reported or suspected child maltreatment include respect for child safety and family preservation. The rights of individual privacy, confidentiality, and other liberties that are often constitutionally guaranteed also influence both the provision of social and professional interventions as well as evaluations of their effectiveness.

The conditions under which child, parental, or community rights should supersede all other rights and obligations, and the criteria that should be considered in balancing long-term dangers against immediate threats, are unclear. Research defining the "best interests of the child" is becoming a significant issue in determining the outcomes of assignment of visitation and custodial rights in court decisions.

Conclusions

Medical, psychological, social, and legal interventions in child maltreatment cases seek to reduce the negative physical, behavioral, and emotional consequences of child abuse and neglect, foster attitudes and behaviors that improve the quality of parent-child interactions, and limit or eradicate recurrences of maltreatment. Interventions have been developed in response to public, professional, legal, and budgetary pressures that often have competing and sometimes contradictory policies and objectives. Some interventions focus on protecting the child or protecting the community; others focus on providing individual treatment for the child or the offender; others emphasize developing family coping strategies and improving skills in parent-child interactions. Assumptions about the severity of selected risk factors, the adequacy of caretaking behaviors, the impact of abuse, and the steps necessary to prevent abuse or neglect from recurring may vary.

Little is known about the quality of existing interventions in treating different forms of child maltreatment. No comprehensive inventory of treatment interventions currently exists, and we lack basic descriptive and evaluative information regarding key factors that influence the delivery and results of treatment for victims and offenders at different developmental stages and in different environmental contexts. A coherent base of research information on the nature and the effectiveness of treatment is not available at this time to guide the decisions of case workers, probation officers, health professionals, family counselors, and judges.

Investigations of child maltreatment reports often influence the development and availability of other professional services, including medical examinations, counseling, evaluation of risk factors, and substantiation of complaints. Research on various federal, state, and private agency involvement and interactions in treatment interventions has not been systematically organized. Although the panel acknowledges the challenges of performing research in this area, future study designs require adequate sample sizes, well-characterized and well-designed samples, and validated and comparable measures.

HUMAN RESOURCES, INSTRUMENTATION, AND RESEARCH INFRASTRUCTURE

Child maltreatment research in the 1990s will require a diverse mix of professional skills and collaborative efforts. The development of human resources, measurement tools, and research infrastructure in this field is complicated by the absence of support for problem-oriented research efforts in academic centers; the legal and ethical complexities associated with this kind of research; the lack of a shared research paradigm that can integrate interdisciplinary efforts across types of maltreatment; problems in gaining access to relevant data and study populations; the absence of data and report archives; and funding inconsistencies associated with shifting research priorities.

The Research Community

A variety of disciplines and subject areas contributes to studies of child maltreatment, including medicine (especially pediatrics and psychiatry), psychology, social work, criminal justice, law, sociology, public health, nursing, anthropology, demography, statistics, and education. Few systematic efforts have been made to integrate research on child maltreatment with the knowledge that has evolved from recent studies of normal child development, family systems, adult and child sexual behavior, family violence, community violence, substance abuse, poverty, and injuries.

Academic training for professionals who must work in the area of child maltreatment has not kept pace with the demands for expertise. About a dozen child maltreatment research programs exist at various universities, medical centers, and child advocacy organizations, but the depth and quality of these centers as well as the skills and affiliations of their research staff are generally unknown. Consequently, considerable effort is needed to deepen and broaden the human resources, instrumentation, and research infrastructure available for addressing the key research questions.

The number of doctorates and other advanced degrees that involve dissertations on child maltreatment studies has been increasing over the past decade, reflecting a growing interest in research in this field. Although many universities offer graduate courses in child abuse and neglect, less than half a dozen universities now sponsor graduate or postgraduate training programs in this field. Graduate training programs have achieved consensus regarding the general body of information necessary in the field of child maltreatment, but considerable variability exists in the length of the programs, student eligibility requirements, time requirements for classroom instruction and practical experience, and the availability of financial support.

Methodological Issues

The absence of support for methodological research has impeded scientific progress in child maltreatment studies. The development of adequate research tools is essential to move a research field beyond theoretical or design problems toward the collection and analysis of empirical data.

Methodology and instrumentation issues present one of the most significant barriers to the development of child maltreatment research. A number of issues deserve particular attention:

• Uncertainties about the nature and significance of the phenomena to be measured.

• Absence of empirical data and inconsistencies in the type of data collected.

• Absence of documentation of the reliability and validity of measures used in child maltreatment research.

In many cases research instruments may simply be unavailable. Measures have been developed to assess "normal" child behavior or other problems in samples of unabused children, but they may not be adequate to assess child maltreatment issues and they may not be standardized on diverse cultural or ethnic populations. Furthermore, available research instruments adapted from other fields may not provide significant information for the practitioner. Difficulties in the use of instruments may result from training—researchers have often come from disciplines that give inadequate attention to the importance of valid and reliable measures and empirical results. Overall, the use of standard measures of family characteristics and social environmental characteristics seems to be less frequent in child maltreatment research than in child development and family research in general.

The development and use of standardized measures in child maltreatment research is complicated by an additional set of pragmatic and professional factors, including the lack of budgetary support for instrumentation research projects, publication policies that discourage discussions of psychometric work in reporting research results, and research sponsors' preference for substantive rather than methodological topics.

Although some useful resources can be identified, the field of child maltreatment studies has not successfully developed a comprehensive information service designed to integrate research publications from diverse professional and private sources in an easily accessible format. In contrast to effective dissemination programs focused on criminal justice research, limited efforts exist to summarize and disseminate maltreatment research findings from the fields of psychology, social work, medicine, and other relevant disciplines.

Federal Funding for Research

Federal support for child maltreatment research is currently divided among 28 separate offices in 5 federal departments—the departments of Health and Human Services, Justice, Education, Defense, and Transportation. The forms of federal research support are diverse, including large research center program awards, individual research awards, data collection efforts, individual training grants, and evaluations of demonstration projects. With the exception of the National Center for Child Abuse and Neglect, which has a research program focused explicitly on studies of child maltreatment, most federal agencies support child maltreatment research in the context of other scientific objectives and program responsibilities, such as research on violence, maternal and child health care, family support, mental health, and criminal justice. As a result, federally supported research activities that may advance scientific knowledge of the identification, causes, consequences, treatment, and prevention of child abuse and neglect are often embedded within other research studies that have multiple objectives. No central repository exists to maintain an ongoing index of federally supported research on child maltreatment.

A 1992 forum sponsored by the Federal Interagency Task Force on Child Abuse and Neglect indicated that the total federal research budget for studies directly related to child maltreatment research is in the $15-20 million range. It is important to note that these figures reflect only research that is "primarily relevant" to child abuse and neglect studies. Additional research efforts related to child maltreatment are also sponsored by federal agencies, although the level of investment in these secondary research efforts depends on the perceived significance of studies about parent-child interactions, substance abuse, family violence, and juvenile delinquency to child maltreatment.

The relevance of child maltreatment research to the central mission of each federal department appears to be idiosyncratic and uneven. Adopting a comprehensive view of research on child maltreatment presents certain difficulties of identification, organization, and taxonomy. Efforts to prevent child abuse and neglect and improve child welfare are dispersed among a wide range of federal programs within the U.S. Department of Health and Human Services alone. However, most of these efforts are not "child abuse" in name, and no systematic effort has been made to evaluate the lessons for child maltreatment learned from them. Various direct services for abused children and their families, demonstration projects, and educational and information dissemination activities are scattered throughout other federal program efforts as well.

Clearly, not all research on children, families, poverty, and violence is relevant to studies of child maltreatment. However, the fragmented and specialized character of the current federal research portfolio in these issues can hamper systematic efforts to organize and build on advances in research. The specialized roles of federal programs that have relevance for studies of child maltreatment continue to inhibit the development of this field. Research investigators and program officers in separate agencies are often unaware of previous studies or active projects related to their research interests. Researchers funded by separate agencies to conduct studies on aspects of child maltreatment often work with separate theoretical paradigms, use different sample populations, develop project-specific methodologies, draw on separate research databases, and present their results in a wide variety of journals and professional meetings. The absence of a central tracking and documentation resource center and the diffuse organization of the federal research portfolio, as well as the fragmented bureaucratic and legislative requirements that are associated with child maltreatment, inhibit the development of a dynamic and interdisciplinary research field.

State Roles in Research on Child Maltreatment

No comprehensive inventory of state research programs exists for studies on child maltreatment issues, but it is unlikely that the total amount of research funds available from individual state agencies is significant (i.e., greater than $1 million per year). However, individual scientists reported to the panel that they have received occasional research support from various state agencies, including the maternal and child health departments and family services offices in the states of Hawaii, Illinois, and Minnesota, the children's trust funds administered by the states, and other offices. The decentralized and sporadic nature of state-funded research efforts discourages efforts to build collaborative interdisciplinary research teams or long-term studies focused on complex research topics.

States are a potential source of future support for specific training and data collection programs in areas such as the criminal justice, education, and public health systems that need to be integrated into comprehensive studies of outcomes and consequences of child abuse and neglect. It is useful to think of the state agencies as important partners in building an expanded research base for studies of child maltreatment.

State science programs are expected to assume a larger role in sponsoring and using research related to domestic health, social, and environmental issues in the decades ahead. The 1992 report of the Carnegie Commission on Science, Technology and Government, for example, concluded that new scientific and technological advisory organizations will be needed to foster better communication between and within the states. These organizations will need to improve the gathering of scientific knowledge, of identifying best practices, and of suggesting research priorities in national science and technology forums. Studies on child maltreatment should be viewed as an important opportunity for building collaborative state and federal research organizations directed toward long-term improvements in social service programs in areas such as child protection, child welfare, family counseling, and foster care.

Private Foundations

In addition to research funding from governmental agencies, at least eight private foundations have selected child abuse and neglect as a priority funding area. Despite this interest, the amount of funds provided by private foundations for studies on child maltreatment is quite limited.

The nongovernmental sector may be an important source of potential funding for dissertation and graduate student support in funding studies on the relationships among child maltreatment, child development, family welfare, poverty, and others. It is most important, therefore, to see the private sector as a collaborator in strengthening the research foundation for studies on child maltreatment.

Conclusions

Support for child maltreatment research has developed in a haphazard, piecemeal fashion, reflecting the absence of a national plan for providing research, educational, and professional support for studies of child abuse and neglect. Governmental roles in this area have been complicated by poor leadership, the absence of sufficient funds to support a robust research program, uncertainties about the most promising research directions to pursue, tensions between the role of the federal and state governments in sponsoring projects in such areas as child maltreatment and child and family welfare, and conflicting social values about the proper interventions to develop in response to child maltreatment incidents. Tensions also exist in the allocation of funds between professional and social services for maltreated children and their families and research projects that seem to provide no immediate benefits for these groups.

Given the current status and evolution of child maltreatment studies, a broad diversity of parallel efforts should be maintained. Top-down or centralized approaches should be avoided that may discourage or fail to recognize the significance of emerging theoretical paradigms, instrumentation research, and other approaches that seek to extend the boundaries of current knowledge about the origins, scope, and consequences of child abuse and neglect. In particular, attention to cultural and ethnic issues that affect our understanding of childhood needs, child development, and family life require a breadth of effort that currently does not exist in the research community.

While diversity of effort is important to maintain, the panel concludes that better national leadership is needed to organize the research base. Such leadership requires more informed documentation of research efforts so that scientific findings, instrumentation, theory, and data can be better recorded, integrated, and disseminated to researchers and practitioners. There is also a pressing need to connect education, research, and practice so that individuals who become caseworkers, family counselors, administrators, legal officials, and future scientists have a richer understanding of the complexities of child maltreatment. Finally, the development of both young and mature scientists needs attention to build a foundation for future explorations of the intricate scientific questions that lie ahead.

ETHICAL AND LEGAL ISSUES

Ethical and legal issues for studies of child maltreatment will gain increasing prominence with the growth of research activities on child maltreatment, especially as researchers acquire the ability and resources to conduct long-term prospective studies of nonclinical samples involving large numbers of children and families.

Human Subjects Research Issues

Many ethical issues arise in the course of human subjects research, some of which have special relevance for studies of child maltreatment.

Five issues that deserve special attention are: (1) the recruitment of research subjects; (2) informed consent and deception; (3) assignment of subjects to experimental or control programs; (4) issues of privacy, confidentiality, and autonomy; and (5) debriefing or desensitizing of research subjects following research on matters that may involve deception or significant stress.

Issues Derived from Research on Children and Families

The validity of scientific research takes on special relevance in studies of children and other vulnerable populations, when research results are likely to influence social policy and public perceptions of the problem under study. Information that scientists disseminate about child victimization is often socially and politically sensitive and can affect both parental and professional behavior as well as public policy. Scientific information, communicated through the popular media, can influence the manner in which abusive parents view abuse, and the ways in which victims view themselves. High-quality research is needed to provide information that has a factual, scientific basis, rather than information based on conjecture or opinion.

Because validity is so important but hard to achieve in research on children and families, factors that affect validity are receiving increased attention. These factors include the definitions of child maltreatment, instrumentation and research methods, selection of subject samples, collection of data, interpretation of findings, and safeguards for ensuring privacy, confidentiality, and reliability in the research study.

Research on Socially Sensitive Topics

Scientific studies of child maltreatment require extraordinary care and confidentiality in eliciting, safeguarding, and disclosing information from respondents because of the socially sensitive nature of the research subject. Family disciplinary practices, the use of violence between family members, and expressions of anger or rage are difficult to detect, observe, and record. Research on children's sexual development is one of the most unexamined areas in all of social science, impeded by a variety of social taboos, political sensitivities, and ethical ambiguities in general and discussions of sexual behavior with children in particular.

Conclusions

Researchers who seek to foster valid and creative research projects must address fundamental ethical issues in the recruitment of research subjects; the process of obtaining informed consent; the assignment of subjects; debriefing, dehoaxing, and desensitizing subjects when deception or stressful research is involved; and in providing referrals for children and family members in distress.

RESEARCH PRIORITIES

Despite the clear significance of child maltreatment, the panel concludes that research in this area is in an early stage of development. Although much insight has been gained over the past three decades, the field has not yet developed an integrated and organized base of knowledge or ongoing data collection efforts that can inform practice, guide the development of programs and policies relevant to child maltreatment, and shape the formation and testing of major hypotheses in this field. As a result, research is needed in diverse areas to explore promising directions. At the same time, research on child maltreatment requires guidance, coordination, and leadership to organize the research base and cultivate future generations of researchers who are well trained and informed about the complex research questions in this field.

The panel concludes that a research agenda for child maltreatment studies should address four separate objectives. We need knowledge that can:

(1) Clarify the nature and scope of child maltreatment, guided by well-developed research definitions and instrumentation.

(2) Provide an understanding of the origins and consequences of child maltreatment in order to better inform theories regarding its etiology and to establish a foundation for improving the quality of future policy and program efforts to address this problem.

(3) Determine the strengths and limitations of existing approaches and interventions in preventing and treating child maltreatment to guide the development of new and more effective interventions; and

(4) Develop a science policy for child maltreatment research that recognizes the importance of developing national leadership, human resources, instrumentation, financial resources, and appropriate institutional arrangements for child maltreatment research.

Each chapter in this report includes key research recommendations within the topic under review. In the final chapter of the report (Chapter 10) the panel uses the four headings listed above as a framework for organizing the research priorities that it selected as the most important to address in the decade ahead. Details regarding each priority area appear in the individual chapters of the report.

Under each general heading below, the panel has organized the research priorities in order of their importance, with the most important recommendation listed first within each section.

The Nature and Scope of Child Maltreatment

Research definitions of child maltreatment are inconsistent, and the breadth and quality of instrumentation for child maltreatment studies are seriously incomplete. The variation in existing definitions and inadequate instrumentation impedes high-quality research, inhibits the comparison of studies of related phenomena, and restrains the development of good evaluations of intervention efforts. Improved definitions and instrumentation will facilitate the development of small- and large-scale epidemiologic investigations. These investigations would provide solid information on the occurrence of these important problems as well as on key etiologic agents.

Research Priority 1. A consensus on research definitions needs to be established for each form of child abuse and neglect. The development of consensus requires a major federal and professional commitment to a dynamic, evolutionary process, guided by a series of expert multidisciplinary panels and developed in conjunction with existing agencies, that could review existing work on research definitions.

Research Priority 2: Reliable and valid clinical-diagnostic and research instruments for the measurement of child maltreatment are needed to operationalize the definitions discussed under Research Priority 1. The absence of appropriate instrumentation and methodology is a second serious barrier to the development of good child maltreatment research. The reliability and validity of these instruments must be established by sound methodology, including testing their relevance and usefulness for economically and culturally diverse populations.

Research Priority 3: Epidemiologic studies on the incidence and prevalence of child abuse and neglect should be encouraged, as well as the inclusion of research questions about child maltreatment in other national surveys. After considerable work on instrumentation, including investigations into effective questioning strategies, the panel recommends funding several epidemiologic studies of different size and scope (including different age groups and ethnic groups) to address several different questions relating to child maltreatment (for example, the extent of the hidden nature of abuse).

Understanding the Origins and Consequences of Child Maltreatment

Research Priority 4: Research that examines the processes by which individual, family, community, and social factors interact will improve understanding of the causes of child maltreatment and should be supported. Theoretical models that integrate a variety of risk and protective factors are a promising development in research on the origins of child maltreatment and deserve further research attention. Rather than endorsing a single approach, the panel recommends that diverse models be tested using a variety of research strategies so that researchers can test theory and generate hypotheses about mechanisms that activate or protect against individual child maltreatment.

Research Priority 5: Research that clarifies the common and divergent pathways in the etiologies of different forms of child maltreatment for diverse populations is essential to improve the quality of future prevention and intervention efforts. Studies that compare the etiologies of different types of maltreatment, and the patterns of risk and protective factors among populations that vary by ethnicity, cultural, and economic status, should be supported. It is particularly important at this time to uncover key pathways for child victimization that may be amenable to prevention or other forms of intervention.

Research Priority 6: Research that assesses the outcomes of specific and combined types of maltreatment should be supported. Research is needed that assesses direct and indirect consequences of child maltreatment across different domains of life, such as health, cognitive and intellectual skills, and social behavior in a variety of cultural contexts.

Research Priority 7: Research is needed to clarify the effects of multiple forms of child victimization that often occur in the social context of child maltreatment. The consequences of child maltreatment may be significantly influenced by a combination of risk factors that have not been well described or understood. The presence or absence of certain characteristics and other adverse events may influence a child's response to childhood victimization, and in some cases the combined effects of two stresses (such as family environment and poor caretaking) may be greater than the sum of the two considered separately. The social context is particularly important, since the effects of abuse or neglect often cannot be separated from other problems confronting families experiencing a variety of problems. It is not yet known whether a syndrome of problem behaviors or combined risks have common origins or whether discrete behaviors have different etiologies. These contrasting pathways have different implications for intervention strategies.

Research Priority 8: Studies of similarities and differences in the etiologies and consequences of various forms of maltreatment across various cultural and ethnic groups are necessary. The effects of risk potentiating and protective factors on child maltreatment in diverse cultural and ethnic groups have not been adequately explored.

Improving Treatment and Preventive Interventions

At present, we have limited knowledge about the range or nature of treatment and preventive services for child maltreatment or the context in which these services are available to children and their families. Research evaluations in this area therefore must seek to broaden understanding of what currently exists as well as documenting what services appear to work for which individuals or groups, under what circumstances. Research on service interventions must also seek to identify factors and mechanisms that facilitate, or impede, the transfer of knowledge between researchers who study the origins, nature, scope, and outcomes of child maltreatment and those who develop and implement policies and programs for child and family services in the public sector.

Research Priority 9: High-quality evaluation studies of existing program and service interventions are needed to develop criteria and instrumentation that can help identify promising developments in the delivery of treatment and prevention services. Independent scientific evaluations are needed to clarify the outcomes to be assessed for service delivery programs in the area of child maltreatment. Such evaluations should identify the outcomes to be assessed, clarify the instrumentation and measures that can provide effective indicators of child and family well-being or dysfunction, and develop the criteria that should be considered in evaluating the effectiveness of a specific program or service. Evaluation studies currently rely heavily on reported incidents of child maltreatment as a measure of program effectiveness. Given the uncertainties associated with official detection of child maltreatment, such outcomes may have limited value in measuring the achievements or limitations of a selected program intervention.

Rigorous evaluation studies should be an essential part of all major demonstration projects in the area of child maltreatment, and funds should also be available for investigator-initiated evaluation studies of smaller program efforts. Smaller programs should be encouraged to use similar assessment instruments, so that results can be compared across studies. Scientific program evaluations, published in the professional literature, are an important means of transferring the knowledge and experience gained in the service sector into the research community. Such information exchange can improve the quality of studies on the origins, consequences, and other aspects of child maltreatment, ultimately leading to improved services and programs.

Evaluation research is particularly important in the following areas:

• Evaluation studies of specific program interventions, such as foster care, family preservation services, and self-help programs that examine the conditions and circumstances under which selected programs are beneficial or detrimental to the child are needed.

• Empirical research is also needed to determine the degrees to which criminal sanctions deter child abuse and the degree to which removal of offenders or children from the home protects the child from abuse.

• Rigorous scientific evaluations of home visiting programs, focused on the prenatal, postnatal, and toddler periods, are necessary prior to the development of nationwide home visiting programs.

• Evaluations of treatments for specific forms of child maltreatment are needed to identify criteria that promote recovery and to identify treatments that are appropriate for children and offenders depending on their sex, age, social class, spoken language or culture, and type of abuse.

• Research evaluations of sexual abuse prevention programs are necessary, particularly to determine the outcomes of personal reports of sexual abuse that are often disclosed as a result of such programs.

• Research is needed on the extent to which community-based prevention and intervention programs (such as school-based and domestic violence prevention programs, Head Start) focused on families at risk of multiple problems may affect the likelihood of child maltreatment.

Research Priority 10:   Research on the operation of the existing child protection and child welfare systems is urgently needed. Factors that influence different aspects of case handling decisions and the delivery and use of individual and family services require attention. The strengths and limitations of alternatives to existing institutional arrangements need to be described and evaluated. We have very poor information about the methods and mechanisms used to identify and confirm cases of child maltreatment, to evaluate the severity of child and family dysfunction, to assess personal and social resources, family strengths, and extrafamilial influences, and to match clients to appropriate treatments based on these formulations. An analysis is needed of interactions among different agencies involved in intervention and treatment and the degree to which decisions made by one agency affect outcomes in others. A research framework that provides standardized classifications and descriptions of child maltreatment investigations, adjudications, and treatment services should be developed. Comparative studies are needed to describe the agencies involved in the system, the types of interventions available for selected forms of maltreatment, the costs of investigating and responding to reports of child maltreatment, and the outcomes of case reports. Such studies should also consider the development of alternatives to existing institutional arrangements to improve the quality of service delivery systems.

Research Priority 11: Service system research on existing state data systems should be conducted to improve the quality of child maltreatment research information as well as to foster improved service interventions. Variations in state definitions of child abuse and neglect as well as differences in verification procedures result in significant unevenness in the quality of research data on child maltreatment reports.

Research Priority 12: The role of the media in reinforcing or questioning social norms relevant to child maltreatment needs further study. Important lessons can be learned from the role of the media in fostering healthy or unhealthy behaviors in areas such as the use of alcohol, smoking, drug use, and condom use. Research is needed that can identify the significant pathways by which key factors and behaviors affect child maltreatment, such as parenting styles, the use of corporal punishment, the use of violence and time-out periods in stress management and conflict resolution, and young children's relationships with strangers and abusive caretakers.

A Science Policy for Research on Child Maltreatment

The complexity of the problem of child maltreatment requires a sustained commitment to high-quality research, national leadership, human resources, and adequate funds. Scientific knowledge can contribute to our understanding of the nature, scope, origins, and consequences of child maltreatment, but such knowledge cannot be developed in a haphazard manner. Thus the panel has formulated priorities for science policy and the research infrastructure that supports child maltreatment studies in order to highlight key strengths and existing deficiencies in the research system.

Research Priority 13: Federal agencies concerned with child maltreatment research need to formulate a national research plan and provide leadership for child maltreatment research. Existing fragmentation in the federal research effort focused on child maltreatment requires immediate attention. National leadership is necessary to develop a long-term plan that would implement the child maltreatment research priorities identified by the panel, help coordinate the field, and focus it on key research questions. The panel believes that Congress, federal agency directors, and the research community should weigh the strengths and limitations of alternative federal research management approaches presented in this report in considering how to implement a national research plan for child maltreatment. Once a course of action has been formulated, current and proposed agency research activities need to be examined so that areas of strength, duplication of effort, and gaps in current efforts can be identified.

Research Priority 14: Governmental leadership is needed to sustain and improve the capabilities of the available pool of researchers who can contribute to studies of child maltreatment. National leadership is also required to foster the integration of research from related fields that offer significant insights into the causes, consequences, treatment, and prevention of child maltreatment.

Research Priority 15: Recognizing that fiscal pressures and budgetary deficits diminish prospects for significant increases in research budgets generally, special efforts are required to find new funds for

research on child abuse and neglect and to encourage research collaboration and data collection in related fields. The federal government spent about $15 million in fiscal year 1992 on research directly related to child maltreatment. As a first step in strengthening the research portfolio, the panel recommends that the research budgets of the National Center on Child Abuse and Neglect, the National Institute of Mental Health, the National Institute of Child Health and Human Development, the Centers for Disease Control and Prevention, and the Department of Justice that are relevant to child maltreatment studies be doubled over the next three years. Second, the panel recommends that the National Center on Child Abuse and Neglect convene a consortium of government agencies, private foundations, and research scientists to develop a task force to identify ways in which research on programs relevant to child maltreatment (such as substance abuse, spousal violence and child abuse, child homicides, juvenile delinquency, and so forth) can be more systematically integrated into the research infrastructure for child abuse and neglect.

Research Priority 16: Research is needed to identify organizational innovations that can improve the process by which child maltreatment findings are disseminated to practitioners and policy makers. The role of state agencies in supporting, disseminating, and utilizing empirical research deserves particular attention. Research on the information dissemination process can strengthen the ways in which science is used to inform and advise legislative and judicial decision makers. Such research can also contribute to the effective partnerships among scientists, practitioners, clinicians, and governmental officials to encourage the use of sound research results in formulating policies, programs, and services that affect the lives of thousands of children and their families.

State agencies have an important role in developing and disseminating knowledge about factors that affect the identification, treatment, and prevention of child maltreatment. The National Center on Child Abuse and Neglect should encourage the development of a state consortium that can serve as a documentation and research support center, allowing the states to collaborate in sponsoring child maltreatment studies and facilitating the dissemination of significant research findings to state officials.

Research Priority 17: Researchers should design methods, procedures, and resources that can resolve ethical problems associated with recruitment of research subjects; informed consent; privacy, confidentiality, and autonomy; assignment of experimental and control research participants; and debriefings. Research is needed to clarify the nature of individual and group interests in the course of research, to develop clinical advice and experience that can resolve such conflicts among such interests, and to identify methods by which such guidance could be communicated to researchers, institutional review boards, research administrators, research subjects, and others.

REFERENCES

Daro, D.
1988   *Confronting Child Abuse: Research for Effective Program Design.* New York: The Free Press, Macmillan.

Daro, D., and K. McCurdy
1991   *Current Trends in Child Abuse Reporting and Fatalities: The Results of the 1990 Annual Fifty State Survey.* Chicago: National Committee for Prevention of Child Abuse.

General Accounting Office
1991   *Child Abuse Prevention: Status of the Challenge Grant Program.* May. GAO:HRD91-95. Washington, DC.

McClain, P.W., J.J. Sacks, R.G. Froehlke, and B.G. Ewigman
1993   Estimates of fatal child abuse and neglect, United States, 1979 through 1988. *Pediatrics* 91(2):338-343.

Olds, D.L., C.R. Henderson, R. Chamberlin, and R. Tatelbaum
1986a   Preventing child abuse and neglect: A randomized trial of nurse home visitation. *Pediatrics* 78:65-78.

Olds, D.L., C.R. Henderson, R. Tatelbaum, and R. Chamberlin
1986b   Improving the delivery of prenatal care and outcomes of pregnancy: A randomized trial of nurse home visitation. *Pediatrics* 77:16-28.

1

Introduction

Child maltreatment is a devastating social problem in American society. In 1990, over 2 million cases of child abuse and neglect were reported to social service agencies. In the period 1979 through 1988, about 2,000 child deaths (ages 0-17) were recorded annually as a result of abuse and neglect (McClain et al., 1993), and an additional 160,000 cases resulted in serious injuries in 1990 alone (Daro and McCurdy, 1991). However tragic and sensational, the counts of deaths and serious injuries provide limited insight into the pervasive long-term social, behavioral, and cognitive consequences of child abuse and neglect. Reports of child maltreatment alone also reveal little about the interactions among individuals, families, communities, and society that lead to such incidents.

American society has not yet recognized the complex origins or the profound consequences of child victimization. The services required for children who have been abused or neglected, including medical care, family counseling, foster care, and specialized education, are expensive and are often subsidized by governmental funds. The General Accounting Office (1991) has estimated that these services cost more than $500 million annually. Equally disturbing, research suggests that child maltreatment cases are highly related to social problems such as juvenile delinquency, substance abuse, and violence, which require additional services and severely affect the quality of life for many American families.

THE IMPORTANCE OF CHILD MALTREATMENT RESEARCH

The challenges of conducting research in the field of child maltreatment are enormous. Although we understand comparatively little about the causes, definitions, treatment, and prevention of child abuse and neglect, we do know enough to recognize that the origins and consequences of child victimization are not confined to the months or years in which reported incidents actually occurred. For those who survive, the long-term consequences of child maltreatment appear to be more damaging to victims and their families, and more costly for society, than the immediate or acute injuries themselves. Yet little is invested in understanding the factors that predispose, mitigate, or prevent the behavioral and social consequences of child maltreatment.

The panel has identified five key reasons why child maltreatment research should be viewed as a central nexus of more comprehensive research activity.

1. Research on child maltreatment can provide scientific information that will help with the solution of a broad range of individual and social disorders. Research in this field is demonstrating that experiences with child abuse and neglect are a major component of many child and adult mental and behavioral disorders, including delayed development, poor academic performance, delinquency, depression, alcoholism, substance abuse, deviant sexual behaviors, and domestic and criminal violence.

Many forms of child abuse and neglect are treatable and avoidable, and many severe consequences of child maltreatment can be diminished with proper attention and assistance. Research on child abuse and neglect provides an opportunity for society to address, and ultimately prevent, a range of individual and social disorders that impair the health and quality of life of millions of America's children as well as their families and communities.

2. Research on child maltreatment can provide insights and knowledge that can directly benefit victims of child abuse and neglect and their families. Individuals who have been victimized as a result of child maltreatment deserve to have research efforts dedicated to their experience, in the same manner as our society invests in scientific research for burn victims, victims of genetic or infectious diseases, or those who are subjected to other forms of trauma. Yet the families of child abuse and neglect victims are often not active in social and political organizations. Unable to speak for themselves or employ paid representatives to promote their interests, they have been discounted and overlooked in the process of determining what social problems deserve public resources and attention from the American research community.

3. Research on child maltreatment can reduce long-term economic costs associated with treating the consequences of child maltreatment,

in areas such as mental health services, foster care, juvenile delinquency, and family violence.

Economic issues must also be considered in evaluating long-term treatment costs and loss of earnings associated with the consequences of child victimization. One analysis cited by the General Accounting Office that used prevalence and treatment rates generated from multiple studies (Daro, 1988) calculated potential fiscal costs resulting from child abuse estimates as follows: (1) Assuming a 20 percent delinquency rate among adolescent abuse victims, requiring an average of 2 years in a correctional institution, the public cost of their incarceration would be more than $14.8 million. (2) If 1 percent of severely abused children suffer permanent disabilities, the annual cost of community services (estimated at $13 per day) for treating developmentally disabled children would increase by $1.1 million. (3) The future lost productivity of severely abused children is $658-1300 million annually, if their impairments limit their potential earnings by only 5-10 percent.

4. **Research on child maltreatment can provide empirical evidence to improve the quality of many legal and organizational decisions that have broad-based social implications.** Government officials, judges, legislators, social service personnel, child welfare advocates, and others make hundreds of crucial decisions each day about the lives and futures of child victims and their offenders. These decisions include the selection of cases of suspected child abuse and neglect for investigation and determinations about which children should remain with families in which abuse has occurred. Individuals making such decisions will benefit from informed guidance on the effectiveness and consequences of various social interventions that address child maltreatment. Such guidance can evolve from research on the outcomes of alternative responses to reports of child abuse and neglect, results of therapeutic and social service interventions, and cost-effectiveness studies. For example, research that describes the conditions under which family counseling and family preservation efforts are effective has tremendous implications for the importance of attachment relationships for children and the disruption of these relationships brought on by foster care.

5. **Research on the etiology of child maltreatment can provide a scientific basis for primary prevention of child abuse—that is, through programs that will counteract etiological factors before they have a chance to produce child abuse in the next generation.**

RESEARCH ON CHILD MALTREATMENT IS CURRENTLY UNDERVALUED AND UNDEVELOPED

Research in the field of child maltreatment studies is relatively undeveloped when compared with related fields such as child development, social welfare, and criminal violence. Although no specific theory about the causes of child abuse and neglect has been substantially replicated across studies, significant progress has been gained in the past few decades in identifying the dimensions of complex phenomena that contribute to the origins of child maltreatment.

Efforts to improve the quality of research on any group of children are dependent on the value that society assigns to the potential inherent in young lives. Although more adults are available in American society today as service providers to care for children than was the case in 1960, a disturbing number of recent reports have concluded that American children are in trouble (Fuchs and Reklis, 1992; National Commission on Children, 1991; Children's Defense Fund, 1991).

Efforts to encourage greater investments in research on children will be futile unless broader structural and social issues can be addressed within our society. Research on general problems of violence, substance addiction, social inequality, unemployment, poor education, and the treatment of children in the social services system is incomplete without attention to child maltreatment issues. Research on child maltreatment can play a key role in informing major social policy decisions concerning the services that should be made available to children, especially children in families or neighborhoods that experience significant stress and violence.

As a nation, we already have developed laws and regulatory approaches to reduce and prevent childhood injuries and deaths through actions such as restricting hot water temperatures and requiring mandatory child restraints in automobiles. These important precedents suggest how research on risk factors can provide informed guidance for social efforts to protect all of America's children in both familial and other settings.

Not only has our society invested relatively little in research on children, but we also have invested even less in research on children whose families are characterized by multiple problems, such as poverty, substance abuse, violence, welfare dependency, and child maltreatment. In part, this slower development is influenced by the complexities of research on major social problems. But the state of research on this topic could be advanced more rapidly with increased investment of funds. In the competition for scarce research funds, the underinvestment in child maltreatment research needs to be understood in the context of bias, prejudice, and the lack of a clear political constituency for children in general and disadvantaged children in particular (Children's Defense Fund, 1991; National Commission on Children, 1991). Factors such as racism, ethnic discrimination, sexism, class bias, institutional and professional jealousies, and social inequities influence the development of our national research agenda (Bell, 1992, Huston, 1991).

The evolving research agenda has also struggled with limitations imposed by attempting to transfer the results of sample-specific studies to diverse groups of individuals. The roles of culture, ethnic values, and economic factors pervade the development of parenting practices and family dynamics. In setting a research agenda for this field, ethnic diversity and multiple cultural perspectives are essential to improve the quality of the research program and to overcome systematic biases that have restricted its development.

Researchers must address ethical and legal issues that present unique obligations and dilemmas regarding selection of subjects, provision of services, and disclosure of data. For example, researchers who discover an undetected incident of child abuse in the course of an interview are required by state laws to disclose the identities of the victim and offender(s), if known, to appropriate child welfare officials. These mandatory reporting requirements, adopted in the interests of protecting children, may actually cause long-term damage to children by restricting the scope of research studies and discouraging scientists from developing the knowledge base necessary to guide social interventions.

Substantial efforts are now required to reach beyond the limitations of current knowledge and to gain new insights that can improve the quality of social service efforts and public policy decisions affecting the health and welfare of abused and neglected children and their families. Most important, collaborative long-term research ventures are necessary to diminish social, professional, and institutional prejudices that have restricted the development of a comprehensive knowledge base that can improve understanding of, and response to, child maltreatment.

DIMENSIONS OF CHILD ABUSE AND NEGLECT

The human dimensions of child maltreatment are enormous and tragic. The U.S. Advisory Board on Child Abuse and Neglect has called the problem of child maltreatment "an epidemic" in American society, one that requires a critical national emergency response.

The scale and severity of child abuse and neglect has caused various public and private organizations to mobilize efforts to raise public awareness of individual cases and societal trends, to improve the reporting and tracking of child maltreatment cases, to strengthen the responses of social service systems, and to develop an effective and fair system for protecting and offering services to victims while also punishing adults who deliberately harm children or place them in danger. Over the past several decades, a growing number of state and federal funding programs, governmental reports, specialized journals, and research centers, as well as national and international societies and conferences, have examined various dimensions of the problem of child maltreatment.

The results of these efforts have been inconsistent and uneven. In addressing aspects of each new revelation of abuse or each promising new intervention, research efforts often have become diffuse, fragmented, specific, and narrow. What is lacking is a coordinated approach and a general conceptual framework that can add new depth to our understanding of child maltreatment. A coordinated approach can accommodate diverse perspectives while providing direction and guidance in establishing research priorities and synthesizing research knowledge. Organizational mechanisms are also needed to facilitate the application and integration of research on child maltreatment in related areas such as child development, family violence, substance abuse, and juvenile delinquency.

Child maltreatment is not a new problem, yet concerted service, research, and policy attention toward it is just beginning. Although isolated studies of child maltreatment appeared in the medical and sociological literature in the first half of the twentieth century, the publication of "The Battered Child Syndrome" by C. Henry Kempe and associates (1962) is generally considered the first definitive paper in the field in the United States. The efforts of Kempe and others to publicize disturbing medical experience with child abuse and neglect led to the passage of the first Child Abuse Prevention and Treatment Act in 1974 (P.L. 93-247). The act, which has been amended several times (most recently in 1992), established a governmental program designed to guide and consolidate national and state data collection efforts regarding reports of child abuse and neglect, conduct national surveys of household violence, and sponsor research and demonstration programs to prevent, identify, and treat child abuse and neglect.

However, the federal government's leadership role in building a research base in this area has been complicated by changes and inconsistencies in research plans and priorities, limited funding, politicized peer review, fragmentation of effort among various federal agencies, poorly scheduled proposal review deadlines, and bias introduced by competing institutional objectives.[1] The lack of comprehensive, long-term planning for a research base has resulted in a field characterized by contradictions, conflict, and fragmentation. The role of the National Center for Child Abuse and Neglect as the lead federal agency in supporting research in this field has been sharply criticized (U.S. Advisory Board, 1991). Many observers believe that the federal government lacks leadership, funding, and an effective research program for studies on child maltreatment.

THE COMPLEXITY OF CHILD MALTREATMENT

Child maltreatment was originally seen in the form of "the battered child," often portrayed in terms of physical abuse. Today, four general categories of child maltreatment are generally recognized: (1) physical abuse, (2) sexual abuse, (3) neglect, and (4) emotional maltreatment. Each category covers a range of behaviors, as discussed in Chapter 2.

These four categories have become the focus of separate studies of incidence and prevalence, etiology, prevention, consequences, and treatment, with uneven development of research within each area and poor integration of knowledge across areas. Each category has developed its own typology and framework of reference terms, revealing certain similarities (such as the importance of developmental perspectives in considering the consequences of maltreatment) but also important differences (such as the predatory behavior associated with some forms of sexual abuse that do not appear in the etiology of other forms of child maltreatment).

In addition to the category of child maltreatment, the duration, source, intensity, timing, and situational context of incidents of child victimization are now recognized as important factors in studying the origin and consequences of child maltreatment. Yet information about these factors is rarely requested or recorded by social agencies or health professionals in the process of identifying or documenting reports of child maltreatment. Furthermore, research is often weakened by variation in research definitions of child maltreatment, bias in the recruitment of research subjects, the absence of information regarding circumstances surrounding maltreatment reports, the absence of measures to assess selected variables under study, and the absence of a developmental perspective in many research studies.

The co-occurrence of different forms of child maltreatment has been examined only to a limited extent. Relatively little is known about areas of similarity and differences in terms of causes, consequences, prevention, and treatment of selected types of child abuse and neglect. Inconsistencies in definitions often preclude comparative analyses of clinical studies. For example, studies of sexual abuse have indicated wide variations in its prevalence, often as a result of differences in the types of behavior that might be included in the definition adopted by each research investigator. Emotional abuse is also a matter of controversy in some quarters, primarily because of broad variations in its definition.

Research on child maltreatment is also complicated by the fragmentation of services and responses by which our society addresses specific reports of child maltreatment. Cases may involve children who are victims or witnesses to single or repeated incidents of child abuse and neglect. Sadly, child maltreatment often involves various family members, relatives, or other individuals who reside in the homes or neighborhoods of the affected children. Adult figures may be perpetrators of offensive incidents or mediators in intervention or prevention efforts.

The importance of the social ecological framework of the child has only recently been recognized in studies of maltreatment. Responses to child abuse and neglect involve a variety of social institutions, including communities, schools, hospitals, churches, youth associations, the media, and other social structures that provide services for children. Such groups and organizations present special intervention opportunities to reduce the scale and scope of the problem of child maltreatment, but their activities are often poorly documented and uncoordinated. Finally, governmental offices at the local, state, and federal levels have legal and social obligations to develop programs and resources to address child maltreatment, and their role is critical in developing a research agenda for this field.

In the past, the research agenda has been determined predominantly by pragmatic needs in the development and delivery of treatment and prevention services rather than by theoretical paradigms, a process that facilitates short-term studies of specialized research priorities but impedes the development of a well-organized, coherent body of scientific knowledge that can contribute over time to understanding fundamental principles and issues. As a result, the research in this field has been generally viewed by the scientific community as fragmented, diffuse, decentralized, and of poor quality.

Selection of Research Studies

The research literature in the field of child maltreatment is immense—over 2000 items are included in the panel's research bibliography, a portion of which is referenced in this report. Despite this quantity of literature, researchers generally agree that the quality of research on child maltreatment is relatively weak in comparison to health and social science research studies in areas such as family systems and child development. Only a few prospective studies of child maltreatment have been undertaken, and most studies rely on the use of clinical samples (which may exclude important segments of the research population) or adult memories. Both types of samples are problematic and can produce biased results. Clinical samples may not be representative of all cases of child maltreatment. For example, we know from epidemiologic studies of disease of cases that were derived from hospital records that, unless the phenomenon of interest always comes to a service provider for treatment, there exist undetected and untreated cases in the general population that are often quite different from those who have sought treatment. Similarly, when studies rely on adult memories of childhood experiences, recall bias is always an issue. Longitudinal studies are quite rare, and some studies that are described as longitudinal actually consist of hybrid designs followed over time.

To ensure some measure of quality, the panel relied largely on studies that had been published in the peer-reviewed scientific literature. More rigorous scientific criteria (such as the use of appropriate theory and methodology in the conduct of the study) were considered by the panel, but were not adopted because little of the existing work would meet such selection criteria. Given the early stage of development of this field of research, the panel believes that even weak studies contain some useful information, especially when they suggest clinical insights, a new perspective, or a point of departure from commonly held assumptions. Thus, the report draws out issues based on clinical studies or studies that lack sufficient control samples, but the panel refrains from drawing inferences based on this literature.

The panel believes that future research reviews of the child maltreatment literature would benefit from the identification of explicit criteria that could guide the selection of exemplary research studies, such as the following:

• The extent to which the study is guided by theory regarding the origins and pathways of child abuse and neglect;

• The use of appropriate and replicable instrumentation (including outcome measures) in the conduct of the study; and

• The selection of appropriate study samples, including the use of experimental and control groups in etiological studies or in the analysis of outcomes of child maltreatment or intervention efforts.

For the most part, only a few studies will score well in each of the above categories. It becomes problematic, therefore, to rate the value of studies which may score high in one category but not in others.

The panel has relied primarily on studies conducted in the past decade, since earlier research work may not meet contemporary standards of methodological rigor. However, citations to earlier studies are included in this report where they are thought to be particularly useful and when research investigators provided careful assessments and analysis of issues such as definition, interrelationships of various types of abuse, and the social context of child maltreatment.

A Comparison With Other Fields of Family and Child Research

A comparison with the field of studies on family functioning may illustrate another point about the status of the studies on child maltreatment. The literature on normal family functioning or socialization effects differs in many respects from the literature on child abuse and neglect. Family sociology research has a coherent body of literature and reasonable consensus about what constitutes high-quality parenting in middle-class, predominantly White populations. Family functioning studies have focused predominantly on large, nonclinical populations, exploring styles of parenting and parenting practices that generate different kinds and levels of competence, mental health, and character in children. Studies of family functioning have tended to follow cohorts of subjects over long periods to identify the effects of variations in childrearing practices and patterns on children's competence and adjustment that are not a function of social class and circumstances.

By contrast, the vast and burgeoning literature on child abuse and neglect is applied research concerned largely with the adverse effects of personal and social pathology on children. The research is often derived from very small samples selected by clinicians and case workers. Research is generally cross-sectional, and almost without exception the samples use impoverished families characterized by multiple problems, including substance abuse, unemployment, transient housing, and so forth. Until recently, researchers demonstrated little regard for incorporating appropriate ethnic and cultural variables in comparison and control groups. In the past decade, significant improvements have occurred in the development of child maltreatment research, but key problems remain in the area of definitions, study designs, and the use of instrumentation.

As the nature of research on child abuse and neglect has evolved over time, scientists and practitioners have likewise changed. The psychopathologic model of child maltreatment has been expanded to include models that stress the interactions of individual, family, neighborhood, and larger social systems. The role of ethnic and cultural issues are acquiring an emerging importance in formulating parent-child and family-community relationships. Earlier simplistic conceptionalizations of perpetrator-victim relationships are evolving into multiple-focus research projects that examine antecedents in family histories, current situational relationships, ecological and neighborhood issues, and interactional qualities of relationships between parent-child and offender-victim. In addition, emphases in treatment, social service, and legal programs combine aspects of both law enforcement and therapy, reflecting an international trend away from punishment, toward assistance, for families in trouble.

CHARGE TO THE PANEL

The commissioner of the Administration for Children, Youth, and Families in the U.S. Department of Health and Human Services requested that the National Academy of Sciences convene a study panel to undertake a comprehensive examination of the theoretical and pragmatic research needs in the area of child maltreatment. The Panel on Research on Child Abuse and Neglect was asked specifically to:

• Review and assess research on child abuse and neglect, encompassing work funded by the Administration for Children, Youth, and Families and other known sources under public and private auspices;
• Identify research that provides knowledge relevant to the field; and
• Recommend research priorities for the next decade, including new

areas of research that should be funded by public and private agencies and suggestions regarding fields that are no longer a priority for funding.

The report resulting from this study provides recommendations for allocating existing research funds and also suggests funding mechanisms and topic areas to which new resources could be allocated or enhanced resources could be redirected. By focusing this report on research priorities and the needs of the research community, the panel's efforts were distinguished from related activities, such as the reports of the U.S. Advisory Board on Child Abuse and Neglect, which concentrate on the policy issues in the field of child maltreatment.

The request for recommendations for research priorities recognizes that existing studies on child maltreatment require careful evaluation to improve the evolution of the field and to build appropriate levels of human and financial resources for these complex research problems. Through this review, the panel has examined the strengths and weaknesses of past research and identified areas of knowledge that represent the greatest promise for advancing understanding of, and dealing more effectively with, the problem of child maltreatment.

In conducting this review, the panel has recognized the special status of studies of child maltreatment. The experience of child abuse or neglect from any perspective, including victim, perpetrator, professional, or witness, elicits strong emotions that may distort the design, interpretation, or support of empirical studies. The role of the media in dramatizing selected cases of child maltreatment has increased public awareness, but it has also produced a climate in which scientific objectivity may be sacrificed in the name of urgency or humane service. Many concerned citizens, legislators, child advocates, and others think we already know enough to address the root causes of child maltreatment. Critical evaluations of treatment and prevention services are not supported due to both a lack of funding and a lack of appreciation for the role that scientific analysis can play in improving the quality of existing services and identifying new opportunities for interventions. The existing research base is small in volume and spread over a wide variety of topics. The contrast between the importance of the problem and the difficulty of approaching it has encouraged the panel to proceed carefully, thoroughly distinguishing suppositions from facts when they appear.

Research on child maltreatment is at a crossroads—we are now in a position to merge this research field with others to incorporate multiple perspectives, broaden research samples, and focus on fundamental issues that have the potential to strengthen, reform, or replace existing public policy and social programs. We have arrived at a point where we can recognize the complex interplay of forces in the origins and consequences of child abuse and neglect. We also recognize the limitations of our knowledge about the effects of different forms of social interventions (e.g., home visitations, foster care, family treatment programs) for changing the developmental pathways of abuse victims and their families.

THE IMPORTANCE OF A CHILD-ORIENTED FRAMEWORK

The field of child maltreatment studies has often divided research into the types of child maltreatment under consideration (such as physical and sexual abuse, child neglect, and emotional maltreatment). Within each category, researchers and practitioners have examined underlying causes or etiology, consequences, forms of treatment or other interventions, and prevention programs. Each category has developed its own typology and framework of reference terms, and researchers within each category often publish in separate journals and attend separate professional meetings.

Over a decade ago, the National Research Council Committee on Child Development Research and Public Policy published a report titled *Services for Children: An Agenda for Research* (1981). Commenting on the development of various government services for children, the report noted that observations of children's needs were increasingly distorted by the "unmanageably complex, expensive, and confusing" categorical service structure that had produced fragmented and sometimes contradictory programs to address child health and nutrition requirements (p. 15-16). The committee concluded that the actual experiences of children and their families in different segments of society and the conditions of their homes, neighborhoods, and communities needed more systematic study. The report further noted that we need to learn more about who are the important people in children's lives, including parents, siblings, extended family, friends, and caretakers outside the family, and what these people do for children, when, and where.

These same conclusions can be applied to studies of child maltreatment. Our panel considered, but did not endorse, a framework that would emphasize differences in the categories of child abuse or neglect. We also considered a framework that would highlight differences in the current system of detecting, investigating, or responding to child maltreatment. In contrast to conceptualizing this report in terms of categories of maltreatment or responses of the social system to child maltreatment, the panel presents a **child-oriented** research agenda that emphasizes the importance of knowing more about the backgrounds and experiences of developing children and their families, within a broader social context that includes their friends, neighborhoods, and communities. This framework stresses the importance of knowing more about the qualitative differences between children who suffer episodic experiences of abuse or neglect and those for whom maltreatment is a chronic part of their lives. And this approach highlights the need to know more about circumstances that affect the consequences, and therefore the treatment, of child maltreatment, especially circumstances that may be affected by family, cultural, or ethnic factors that often remain hidden in small, isolated studies.

AN ECOLOGICAL DEVELOPMENTAL PERSPECTIVE

The panel has adopted an *ecological developmental perspective* to examine factors in the child, family, or society that can exacerbate or mitigate the incidence and destructive consequences of child maltreatment. In the panel's view, this perspective reflects the understanding that development is a process involving *transactions* between the growing child and the social environment or ecology in which development takes place. Positive *and* negative factors merit attention in shaping a research agenda on child maltreatment. We have adopted a perspective that recognizes that dysfunctional families are often part of a dysfunctional environment.

The relevance of child maltreatment research to child development studies and other research fields is only now being examined. New methodologies and new theories of child maltreatment that incorporate a developmental perspective can provide opportunities for researchers to consider the *interaction* of multiple factors, rather than focusing on single causes or short-term effects. What is required is the mobilization of new structures of support and resources to concentrate research efforts on significant areas that offer the greatest promise of improving our understanding of, and our responses to, child abuse and neglect.

Our report extends beyond what is, to what could be, in a society that fosters healthy development in children and families. We cannot simply build a research agenda for the existing social system; we need to develop one that independently challenges the system to adapt to new perspectives, new insights, and new discoveries.

The fundamental theme of the report is the recognition that research efforts to address child maltreatment should be enhanced and incorporated into a long-term plan to improve the quality of children's lives and the lives of their families. By placing maltreatment within the framework of healthy development, for example, we can identify unique sources of intervention for infants, preschool children, school-age children, and adolescents.

Each stage of development presents challenges that must be resolved in order for a child to achieve productive forms of thinking, perceiving, and behaving as an adult. The special needs of a newborn infant significantly differ from those of a toddler or preschool child. Children in the early years of elementary school have different skills and distinct experiential levels from those of preadolescent years. Adolescent boys and girls demonstrate a range of awkward and exploratory behaviors as they acquire basic social skills necessary to move forward into adult life. Most important, developmental research has identified the significant influences of family, schools, peers, neighborhoods, and the broader society in supporting or constricting child development.

Understanding the phenomenon of child abuse and neglect within a developmental perspective poses special challenges. As noted earlier, research literature on child abuse and neglect is generally organized by the *category* or *type* of maltreatment; integrated efforts have not yet been achieved. For example, research has not yet compared and contrasted the causes of physical and sexual abuse of a preschool child or the differences between emotional maltreatment of toddlers and adolescents, although all these examples fall within the domain of child maltreatment. A broader conceptual framework for research will elicit data that can facilitate such comparative analyses.

By placing research in the framework of factors that foster healthy development, the ecological developmental perspective can enhance understanding of the research agenda for child abuse and neglect. The developmental perspective can improve the quality of treatment and prevention programs, which often focus on particular groups, such as young mothers who demonstrate risk factors for abuse of newborns, or sexual offenders who molest children. There has been little effort to cut across the categorical lines established within these studies to understand points of convergence or divergence in studies on child abuse and neglect.

The ecological developmental perspective can also improve our understanding of the consequences of child abuse and neglect, which may occur with increased or diminished intensity over a developmental cycle, or in different settings such as the family or the school. Initial effects may be easily identified and addressed if the abuse is detected early in the child's development, and medical and psychological services are available for the victim and the family. Undetected incidents, or childhood experiences discovered later in adult life, require different forms of treatment and intervention. In many cases, incidents of abuse and neglect may go undetected and unreported, yet the child victim may display aggression, delinquency, substance addiction, or other problem behaviors that stimulate responses within the social system.

Finally, an ecological developmental perspective can enhance intervention and prevention programs by identifying different requirements and potential effects for different age groups. Children at separate stages of their developmental cycle have special coping mechanisms that present barriers to—and opportunities for—the treatment and prevention of child abuse and neglect. Intervention programs need to consider the extent to which children may have already experienced some form of maltreatment in order to evaluate successful outcomes. In addition, the perspective facilitates evaluation of which settings are the most promising locus for interventions.

PREVIOUS REPORTS

A series of national reports associated with the health and welfare of children have been published in the past decade, many of which have identified the issue of child abuse and neglect as one that deserves sustained attention and creative programmatic solutions. In their 1991 report, *Beyond Rhetoric*, the National Commission on Children noted that the fragmentation of social services has resulted in the nation's children being served on the basis of their most obvious condition or problem rather than being served on the basis of multiple needs. Although the needs of these children are often the same and are often broader than the mission of any single agency emotionally disturbed children are often served by the mental health system, delinquent children by the juvenile justice system, and abused or neglected children by the protective services system (National Commission on Children, 1991). In their report, the commission called for the protection of abused and neglected children through more comprehensive child protective services, with a strong emphasis on efforts to keep children with their families or to provide permanent placement for those removed from their homes.

In setting health goals for the year 2000, the Public Health Service recognized the problem of child maltreatment and recommended improvements in reporting and diagnostic services, and prevention and educational interventions (U.S. Public Health Service, 1990). For example, the report, *Healthy People 2000*, described the four types of child maltreatment and recommended that the rising incidence (identified as 25.2 per 1,000 in 1986) should be reversed to less than 25.2 in the year 2000. These public health targets are stated as reversing increasing trends rather than achieving specific reductions because of difficulties in obtaining valid and reliable measures of child maltreatment. The report also included recommendations to expand the implementation of state level review systems for unexplained child deaths, and to increase the number of states in which at least 50 percent of children who are victims of physical or sexual abuse receive appropriate treatment and follow-up evaluations as a means of breaking the intergenerational cycle of abuse.

The U.S. Advisory Board on Child Abuse and Neglect issued reports in 1990 and 1991 which include national policy and research recommendations. The 1991 report presented a range of research options for action, highlighting the following priorities (U.S. Advisory Board on Child Abuse and Neglect, 1991:110-113):

- To increase general knowledge about the causes, precipitants, consequences, prevention, and treatment of child abuse and neglect;
- To increase knowledge about the child protection system;
- To increase specific knowledge about the social and cultural factors related to child maltreatment;
- To increase human resources in the field of research on child abuse and neglect;
- To ensure that procedures for stimulation and analysis of research on child abuse and neglect are scientifically credible;
- To facilitate the planning of research; and
- To reduce obstacles to the generation of knowledge about child abuse and neglect.

This report differs from those described above because its primary focus is on establishing a research agenda for the field of studies on child abuse and neglect. In contrast to the mandate of the U.S. Advisory Board on Child Abuse and Neglect, the panel was not asked to prepare policy recommendations for federal and state governments in developing child maltreatment legislation and programs. The panel is clearly aware of the need for services for abused and neglected children and of the difficult policy issues that must be considered by the Congress, the federal government, the states, and municipal governments in responding to the distress of children and families in crisis. The charge to this panel was to design a research agenda that would foster the development of scientific knowledge that would provide fundamental insights into the causes, identification, incidence, consequences, treatment, and prevention of child maltreatment. This knowledge can enable public and private officials to execute their responsibilities more effectively, more equitably, and more compassionately and empower families and communities to resolve their problems and conflicts in a manner that strengthens their internal resources and reduces the need for external interventions.

REPORT OVERVIEW

Early studies on child abuse and neglect evolved from a medical or pathogenic model, and research focused on specific contributing factors or causal sources within the individual offender to be discovered, addressed, and prevented. With the development of research on child maltreatment over the past several decades, however, the complexity of the phenomena encompassed by the terms child abuse and neglect or child maltreatment has become apparent. Clinical studies that began with small sample sizes and weak methodological designs have gradually evolved into larger and longer-term projects with hundreds of research subjects and sound instrumentation.

Although the pathogenic model remains popular among the general public in explaining the sources of child maltreatment, it is limited by its primary focus on risk and protective factors within the individual. Research investigators now recognize that individual behaviors are often influenced by factors in the family, community, and society as a whole. Elements from these systems are now being integrated into more complex theories that analyze the roles of interacting risk and protective factors to explain and understand the phenomena associated with child maltreatment.

In the past, research on child abuse and neglect has developed within a categorical framework that classifies the research by the type of maltreatment typically as reported in administrative records. Although the quality of research within different categories of child abuse and neglect is uneven and problems of definitions, data collection, and study design continue to characterize much research in this field, the panel concluded that enough progress has been achieved to integrate the four categories of maltreatment into a child-oriented framework that could analyze the similarities and differences of research findings. Rather than encouraging the continuation of a categorical approach that would separate research on physical or sexual abuse, for example, the panel sought to develop for research sponsors and the research community a set of priorities that would foster the integration of scientific findings, encourage the development of comparative analyses, and also distinguish key research themes in such areas as identification, incidence, etiology, prevention, consequences, and treatment. This approach recognizes the need for the construction of collaborative, long-term efforts between public and private research sponsors and research investigators to strengthen the knowledge base, to integrate studies that have evolved for different types of child maltreatment, and eventually to reduce the problem of child maltreatment. This approach also highlights the connections that need to be made between research on the causes and the prevention of child maltreatment, for the more we learn about the origins of child abuse and neglect, the more effective we can be in seeking to prevent it. In the same manner, the report emphasises the connections that need to be made between research on the consequences and treatment of child maltreatment, for knowledge about the effects of child abuse and neglect can guide the development of interventions to address these effects.

> In constructing this report, the panel has considered eight broad areas:
> Identification and definitions of child abuse and neglect (Chapter 2)
> Incidence: The scope of the problem (Chapter 3)
> Etiology of child maltreatment (Chapter 4)
> Prevention of child maltreatment (Chapter 5)
> Consequences of child maltreatment (Chapter 6)
> Treatment of child maltreatment (Chapter 7)

Human resources, instrumentation, and research infrastructure (Chapter 8)
Ethical and legal issues in child maltreatment research (Chapter 9)

Each chapter includes key research recommendations within the topic under review. The final chapter of the report (Chapter 10) establishes a framework of research priorities derived by the panel from these recommendations. The four main categories identified within this framework—research on the nature and scope of child maltreatment; research on the origins and consequences of child maltreatment; research on the strengths and limitations of existing interventions; and the need for a science policy for child maltreatment research—provide the priorities that the panel has selected as the most important to address in the decade ahead.

NOTE

1.   The panel received an anecdotal report, for example, that one federal research agency systematically changed titles of its research awards over a decade ago, replacing phrases such as child abuse with references to maternal and child health care, after political sensitivities developed regarding the appropriateness of its research program in this area.

REFERENCES

Bell, D.A.
    1992   *Faces at the Bottom of the Well: The Permanence of Racism.* New York: Basic
            Books.
Children's Defense Fund
    1991   *The State of America's Children.* Washington, DC: The Children's Defense Fund.
Daro, D.
    1988   *Confronting Child Abuse: Research for Effective Program Design.* New York:
            The Free Press, Macmillan. Cited in the General Accounting Office, 1992. Child
            Abuse: Prevention Programs Need Greater Emphasis. GAO/HRD-92-99.
Daro, D., and K. McCurdy
    1991   *Current Trends in Child Abuse Reporting and Fatalities: The Results of the 1990
            Annual Fifty State Survey.* Chicago: National Committee for Prevention of Child
            Abuse.
Fuchs, V.R., and D.M. Reklis
    1992   America's children: Economic perspectives and policy options. *Science* 255:41-
            46.
General Accounting Office
    1991   *Child Abuse Prevention: Status of the Challenge Grant Program.* May. GAO:HRD91-
            95. Washington, DC.
Huston, A.C., ed.
    1991   *Children in Poverty: Child Development and Public Policy.* New York: Cam-
            bridge University Press.
Kempe, C.H., F.N. Silverman, B. Steele, W. Droegemueller, and H.R. Silver
    1962   The battered child syndrome. *Journal of the American Medical Association* 181(1):
            17-24.

McClain, P.W., J.J. Sacks, R.G. Froehlke, and B.G. Ewigman
  1993   Estimates of fatal child abuse and neglect, United States, 1979 through 1988. *Pediatrics* 91(2):338-343.

National Commission on Children
  1991   *Beyond Rhetoric: A New American Agenda for Children and Families.* Washington, DC: U.S. Government Printing Office.

National Research Council
  1981   *Services for Children: An Agenda for Research.* Commission on Behavioral and Social Sciences and Education. Washington, DC: National Academy Press.

U.S. Advisory Board on Child Abuse and Neglect
  1990   *Child Abuse and Neglect: Critical First Steps in Response to a National Emergency.* August. Washington, DC: U.S. Department of Health and Human Services. August.

  1991   *Creating Caring Communities.* September. Washington, DC: U.S. Department of Health and Human Services.

U.S. Public Health Service
  1990   Violent and abusive behavior. Pp. 226-247 (Chapter 7) in *Healthy People 2000 Report.* Washington, DC: U.S. Department of Health and Human Services.

2

Identification and Definitions

Despite vigorous debate over the last two decades, little progress has been made in constructing clear, reliable, valid, and useful definitions of child abuse and neglect. A 1977 report commissioned by the National Center on Child Abuse and Neglect summed up the situation as follows (Martin, 1978:1):

> The issue of defining abuse and neglect is one of central importance and logically precedes a discussion of incidence, etiology and treatment. The vagueness and ambiguities that surround the definition of this particular social problem touch every aspect of the field—reporting system, treatment program, research and policy planning.

The difficulties facing the field in constructing definitions are described elsewhere (Aber and Zigler, 1981; Cicchetti and Carlson, 1989; Giovannoni, 1989, 1992; Giovannoni and Becerra, 1979; McGee and Wolfe, 1991; Straus and Gelles, 1986; Zuravin, 1991). They include such factors as:

• lack of social consensus over what constitutes dangerous or unacceptable forms of parenting.

• uncertainty about whether to define maltreatment based on adult characteristics, adult behavior, child outcome, environmental context, or some combination.

• conflict over whether standards of endangerment or harm should be used in constructing definitions.

• confusion over the multiple purposes to which definitions are to be put: scientific, legal, and clinical.

• the fact that the meaning of an act toward a child may vary greatly with the child's age, gender, relation to the actor, ethnicity, and contextual factors.

• variations in age definitions of a "child" (which may range from 0 to 16 or 0 to 18 depending on state definitions) and the existence of a special subpopulation (commonly termed teens, youth, adolescents, teenagers) whose physical, developmental, and social characteristics are significantly different from those of children (Office of Technology Assessment, 1987).

• uncertainty as to whether definitions should reflect discrete categories of maltreating behaviors or draw on dimensions of maltreatment within a broader spectrum of "normal" behaviors.

• difficulties in developing definitions that are both meaningful and capable of being operationalized. An ideal theoretical construct that cannot be applied to real populations is of limited usefulness.

Given these difficulties, the development of standardized definitions is a challenging task. However, consistent definitions are necessary for better measurement and instrumentation in the field. Attempts to reach consensus on clear operational measures need to be made, and limitations recognized and researched. From these attempts, more refined measures can be developed. To take an analogy from the field of mental health, the system of classification of mental disorders contained in the *Diagnostic and Statistical Manual of Mental Disorders*, published by the American Psychiatric Association, currently undergoing its fourth revision (DSM-III-R, APA, 1987), has played a major role in modern advances in psychiatric research, despite its limitations. Research on child maltreatment could benefit greatly from the development of an analogous diagnostic system for child abuse and neglect. Cicchetti and Barnett (1991) wrote:

Perhaps investigators in the field of child maltreatment can learn a valuable lesson from research in the area of psychopathology (Askikal and Webb, 1978; Eaton and Kessler, 1985; Goodwin and Guze, 1984; Meehl, 1959/1973). Research in the diagnosis of mental disorders for research purposes has been greatly enhanced by two improvements: (1) the establishment of more operational, explicit, hence reliable criteria for each "type" of mental disorder; and (2) the development of standardized, structured diagnostic interviews. The first advance reduces the criterion or nosological variance in diagnosis, while the second significantly lowers the diagnostician variation—variance owing to different diagnosticians who may employ different clinical interviewing styles, disparate assumptions about signs and symptoms of disorders, and so on.

A basic requirement for scientific progress on research on child maltreatment is the availability of authoritative, valid and operational measures of child abuse and neglect. Definitions are essential to the development of such measures in order to conduct and interpret studies of prevalence and incidence of child maltreatment. In particular, issues of definition obscure comparisons of incidence rates from two governmental national incidence studies that rely heavily on administrative reports of child abuse and neglect (commonly referred to as NIS-1 and NIS-2) (National Center for Abuse and Neglect, 1981; 1988b). Technical issues such as the procedures used to generalize the findings of the NIS studies to the total U.S. population are complex and troublesome. The *Healthy People 2000* (NCCAN, 1990) report avoids specific targets for reducing the level of child maltreatment "because of difficulties in obtaining valid and reliable measurement of child maltreatment" (Institute of Medicine, 1990). Administrative data on child maltreatment from child protective service agencies are very difficult to interpret given the wide differences in the way definitions are operationalized in different localities.

Definitions are also essential in order to develop measures to compare and generalize results of different studies on the effects of maltreatment and on the primary, secondary or tertiary prevention of maltreatment. In the absence of consensus about child maltreatment measures, existing studies employ an array of different measures that can yield results that conflict or are hard to interpret.

REVIEW OF DEFINITIONS

A 1989 conference convened by the National Institute of Child Health and Human Development recommended that **maltreatment** be defined as "behavior towards another person, which (a) is outside the norms of conduct, and (b) entails a substantial risk of causing physical or emotional harm. Behaviors included will consist of actions and omissions, ones that are intentional and ones that are unintentional" (Christoffel et al., 1992). The term **child maltreatment** refers to a broad range of behaviors that involve risk for the child.

Four general categories of child maltreatment are now generally recognized: (1) physical abuse, (2) sexual abuse, (3) neglect, and (4) emotional maltreatment. Each category, in turn, covers a range of behaviors. *Physical abuse* includes scalding, beatings with an object, severe physical punishment, and a rare form of abuse called Munchausen by proxy, wherein an adult will feign or induce illness in a child in order to attract medical attention and support. *Sexual abuse* includes incest, sexual assault by a relative or stranger, fondling of genital areas, exposure to indecent acts, sexual rituals, or involvement in child pornography. *Child neglect* is the presence of certain deficiencies in caretaker obligations (usually the parent, although neglect can be found in residential centers or foster care homes) that harm the child's psychological and/or physical health. Child neglect covers a range of behaviors including educational, supervisory, medical, physical, and emotional neglect, and abandonment, often complicated by cultural and contextual factors. Several authors (Mrazek and Mrazek, 1985; Zuravin, 1991) have noted the relative lack of attention to definitional issues of child neglect, particularly given its greater reported prevalence (NCCAN, 1981, 1988b; Wolock and Horowitz, 1984). *Emotional maltreatment*, a recently recognized form of child victimization, includes such acts as verbal abuse and belittlement, symbolic acts designed to terrorize a child, and lack of nurturance or emotional availability by caregivers.[1]

Aber and Zigler (1981) distinguished medical-diagnostic, legal, sociological, and research approaches to the definition of child maltreatment. The medical-diagnostic approach "aims to identify a pathological process or condition underlying a symptom pattern in a way that enables a therapeutic intervention" (Aber and Zigler, 1981). It dates from published accounts of bone fractures to children of unspecified cause (Caffey, 1946). The seminal paper by Kempe and colleagues (1962) coined the term *battered child syndrome* to "characterize a clinical condition in young children who have received serious physical abuse, generally from a parent or foster parent."

The Kempe et al. (1962) article initiated a decade of supremacy of the medical diagnostic approach to the definition of child abuse that focused attention on identifying and treating the abusive parent. However, the approach has important limitations. The diagnosis through manifest physical symptoms in the child emphasizes the more extreme forms of physical abuse over other forms of maltreatment (such as child sexual abuse) and leads to a narrow definition of the problem. Also, the attempt to tie physical injury to the child, a descriptive characteristic with presumably high reliability, to an abusive act by the parent or caretaker is fraught with assumptions and difficulties. From a scientific perspective, the above definition lacks precision, and its reliability and validity are open to question.

Legislative activity in the 1970s, particularly the Child Abuse Prevention and Treatment Act of 1974, placed emphasis on the precise nature of abusive acts themselves and their consequences for the child. It formulated broader legal definitions of child abuse that encompass emotional injury, neglect, parental deprivation of medical services, and factors deleterious to children's moral development (Cicchetti and Barnett, 1991). Legal definitions in the Juvenile Justice Standards Project (Wald, 1977) encompass more than physical abuse, but stringent standards within each category are focused on the issue of legal intervention, and may not be commonly used in other settings:

- *Physical harm* is defined as "disfigurement, impairment of bodily functions or other serious physical injury."
- *Emotional damage* is evidenced by "severe anxiety, depression or withdrawal, or untoward aggressive behavior towards self or others, and the child's parents are unwilling to provide treatment for him/her."
- *Sexual abuse* is limited to those cases in which the child is "seriously harmed physically or emotionally thereby." Such a definition excludes many cases in which consequences are not immediately apparent but emerge at later points in the developmental cycle.

In these legal definitions, coercive state intervention on behalf of the child is weighed against the potential harm of separation from the caregiver and the problems of state intrusion into family autonomy. These standards, although influential in legal circles, were not adopted by the American Bar Association, largely due to opposition that they would tie the hands of judges. Indeed, the desire for judicial discretion conflicts with the precision and clarity needed for scientific definitions of child maltreatment.

The focus in the sociological approach is on the act of maltreatment; the goal is to label and control social deviance (Cicchetti and Barnett, 1991). The sociological view of the problem is broad and encompasses the study of milder forms of maltreatment that may not result in physical trauma requiring medical treatment or form legal grounds for state intervention (Gelles and Straus, 1988). Whereas a fair degree of consensus might be attainable about extreme forms of maltreatment, such as abuse or neglect leading to death of the child, definitional and measurement issues become more thorny when less severe manifestations are considered. Sociologists such as Gil (1975) and Pelton (1978) viewed child maltreatment from a sociocultural perspective and emphasized the need to take into account societal contexts such as overcrowding, poverty, inadequate services, and large family sizes.

Research definitions of child maltreatment aim at developing measures that allow reliable and valid empirical studies of incidence and prevalence rates, longitudinal studies of etiology and sequelae, and comparisons of treatments. Aber and Zigler (1981) recommended the formulation of broad research definitions, in which the main classification principle is the nature of acts, or "descriptive compartmentalization of behaviors" (Zigler and Phillips, 1981), as opposed to child outcomes.

In the absence of explicit definitions, the difficulty of operationalizing concepts of maltreatment in early studies (e.g., Giovannoni and Billingsley, 1970; Green et al., 1974) was usually resolved by simply using the label assigned to the act by responsible agencies, including hospitals, child protection agencies, police, and courts (Giovannoni and Becerra, 1979). This approach continues to be adopted in the use of empirical data based on child protective services records (NCCAN, 1988a,b). Defining child maltreatment by labels assigned by professionals in the field can provide useful descriptive information with minimal data collection efforts, but the absence of precise, objective criteria complicates comparability among measures of maltreatment in subpopulations defined by locality. For example, differences in incidence of case reports over time reported by social service agencies may reflect changes in definition imposed by legislation or resource changes, rather than changes in the incidence of maltreatment itself. Careful studies of the processes leading to case definitions are necessary to quantify and adjust for variations in the manner in which child maltreatment is operationalized.

Some recent studies have developed operational definitions that attempt to define acts of maltreatment more precisely, rather than relying on professional opinion. Zuravin (1991) noted this as a step in the right direction, but argued that comparability between studies is compromised by wide variations in the definitions adopted. Specifically, she analyzed and found differences in definitions of physical abuse, physical neglect, and child neglect from a number of empirical studies. Wyatt and Peters (1986) demonstrated empirically the impact of variations in definitions of sexual abuse on the estimated prevalence rates reported in a number of studies.

PRINCIPLES UNDERLYING RESEARCH DEFINITIONS

Zuravin (1991) suggested four general principles for formulating research definitions of child abuse:

1. *Formulation of the specific objectives the definition must serve.* Ross and Zigler (1980:294) noted that the current lack of agreement about definitions can be explained, at least in part, by failure to recognize that no single definition is capable of "fulfilling all the functions that social scientists and social service professionals would like." Aber and Zigler (1981) proposed the development of distinct sets of definitions for legal settings, case management settings, and research. Cicchetti and Barnett (1991:352) found this conceptualization useful but observed that "as the quality of data on the sequelae of maltreatment evolves sufficiently to allow stronger causal statements (e.g., about the role of emotional neglect in the development of emotional damage), then the legal thinker, the clinician and the researcher can begin to speak the same language, and the three sets of definitions will begin to converge."

2. *Division into homogeneous subtypes.* Cicchetti and Barnett (1991) delineated five major child maltreatment categories: physical abuse, physical neglect, sexual abuse, emotional maltreatment, and moral/legal/educational maltreatment. Emotional maltreatment was considered the least developed of the major subtypes. They recognized, however, that each of

these major categories displays considerable heterogeneity in character, severity, and potential consequences. Further subtyping into more homogeneous categories is an important consideration in developing a classification system.

An example of detailed subtyping was presented by Zuravin (1991), who proposed the 14 subtypes of physical neglect (which she defined as encompassing the category of moral/legal/educational maltreatment in Cicchetti and Barnett's [1991] schema): (1) refusal to provide physical health care; (2) delay in providing physical health care; (3) refusal to provide mental health care; (4) delay in providing mental health care; (5) supervisory neglect; (6) custody refusal; (7) custody-related neglect; (8) abandonment/desertion; (9) failure to provide a permanent home; (10) personal hygiene neglect; (11) housing standards; (12) housing sanitation; (13) nutritional neglect; (14) educational neglect. This scheme is presented as an illustration and is not necessarily endorsed by the panel.

3. *Conceptual clarity.* For a classification system to be reliable and valid, it is important to specify clearly every criterion that a behavior must meet in order to be classified in a category, and that categories are distinctly defined.

4. *Measurability of operational translations.* A classification scheme of great conceptual elegance is of limited utility in empirical research unless it can be operationalized. That is, the conceptual definition has to be converted into specific behaviors that can be measured by observation, interview, or some other practical means. The panel believes strongly that progress on child maltreatment research requires not only the development of intelligent classification schemes, but also the development of standardized field instruments, such as clinical checklists or structured survey questionnaires, with documented psychometric properties. In other words, instruments need to be developed, together with associated documentation such as training manuals; interrater reliability studies need to be conducted to document consistency together with studies of construct validity and (in the longer term) predictive validity; culturally sensitive versions of these instruments need to be developed for ethnic subpopulations;[2] and consideration for literacy or English as a foreign language needs attention. As noted above, work in psychiatric classification provides a useful paradigm for this work, although the approach needs to move beyond the diagnosis of a syndrome toward an effort to describe dimensions of maltreatment that may be embedded within a wide spectrum of behaviors.

SPECIFIC DEFINITIONAL ISSUES

In addition to these general principles, the following specific issues in the operationalization of child maltreatment definitions need to be considered. Our discussion borrows heavily from the useful discussions of Cicchetti and Barnett (1991) and Zuravin (1991).

Endangerment Versus Demonstrable Harm

Zuravin (1991) observed that there is general conceptual agreement that abuse represents acts of commission and neglect represents acts of omission (Giovannoni, 1971) by parents and/or caretakers that are "judged by a mixture of community values and professional expertise to be inappropriate and damaging" (Garbarino and Gilliam, 1988:7). An important distinction among existing operational definitions of child maltreatment is whether they require endangerment of the child or demonstrable harm to the child. Zuravin illustrates the difference in the context of definitions of physical abuse.

Altemeier et al. (1984) provide an example of a demonstrable harm definition as one in which an abused child is one who has incurred injuries (bruises, abrasions, cuts, burns, fractures, bites, and loss of hair) as a result of parental actions. The Second National Incidence Study (NIS-2) of 1986 provides an example of an endangerment definition: "Child abuse is physical assault with or without a weapon by a parent or temporary caretaker. It includes hitting with a stick, strap, or other hard object, as well as scalding, burning, poisoning, suffocating, and drowning. It also includes slapping, spanking with hand, hitting with fist, biting, kicking, shoving, shaking, throwing, nonaccidental dropping, stabbing, and choking" (NCCAN, 1988b). This definition clearly includes acts that may not result in physical injury. Demonstrable harm may be a useful standard in legal settings, but for research purposes we agree with Zuravin (1991) that endangerment is the more appropriate criterion, since it places emphasis on the act itself rather than the uncertain consequence of the act.

Severity of Acts

Acts of maltreatment can differ markedly and vary with respect to severity and the relative likelihood of injury. For example, acts of similar severity—a blow to the head—can result in significantly different injuries, such as a broken skull for a 6-month-old infant and a bruise for a 4-year-old. These developmental differences need to be considered in considering the severity of specific acts. The endangerment definition of Straus and Gelles (1986) is restricted to physical assaults. Although their definition of abuse and their cutoff level for abuse excludes less severe actions such as pushing and spanking that are included in the NIS-2 definition quoted above, their instrument (the Conflict Tactics Scales or CTS) records both mild and severe forms of physical attacks on a child and provides the capability of generating a variety of definitions at the analysis stage, depending on context. Other indices of physical abuse, along the lines of the Conflict Tactics Scales (Straus, 1979, 1990a,b) might be developed from the answers to a sequence of questions concerning the occurrence of abusive acts, giving higher weight to more severe acts. Similar indices could be developed for other forms of maltreatment and used in various ways according to context. By analogy, the National Institute of Mental Health developed a widely used index of depression, the Center for Epidemiologic Studies Depression Scale (CES-D). A particular cut off value of CES-D is often used to operationalize the concept of clinical depression, but other transformations of the scale may be of interest if subclinical depression is under study. Existing scales need to be calibrated so that they yield comparable conclusions on false positives and negatives.

Frequency of Acts

In addition to severity, measures of child maltreatment need to take into account the frequency of acts. Definitions need to distinguish between "chronic behavioral patterns" and "infrequent explosive episodes" (Widom, 1988:263). Wolock and Horowitz (1977) required a recurrent pattern of minor injury to establish abuse, but a single episode if the injury is severe. Zuravin and Taylor (1987) employed similar approaches. Many definitions do not take account of frequency, and definitions that do so often differ with respect to the number of times an act must occur before a recurrent or chronic pattern is established (Zuravin, 1991). Since frequency is often dependent on self-reports, a single reported incident may in fact represent repeated assaults, including the first assault that caused recognized harm. A consensus strategy for defining chronicity would enhance the comparability of results across studies.

Class of Potential Perpetrators

Abuse and neglect definitions vary with respect to whether they are applied to acts committed by a wide or narrow range of perpetrators. In definitions of neglect, the perpetrator should generally be restricted to the child's parent or legal caretaker, although there are exceptions to this rule— for example, when a parent believes she or he is leaving a child with a responsible temporary caretaker, but the child turns out to be at risk or is actually harmed by that caretaker. With child abuse, no consensus appears to exist as to how broadly the set of potential perpetrators should be defined.

Intent to Harm and Culpability of the Perpetrator

Zuravin (1991) concludes that intention to harm, a criterion that has been used mainly for physical abuse, is not included in most recent research definitions of abuse or neglect. However, culpability is used as a qualifier for definitions of physical neglect in NIS-2 (NCCAN, 1988b). For example, hazardous housing conditions are not considered neglect when they are attributed to a lack of financial resources.

Developmental Level

Several researchers have raised the link between a child's age or developmental stage when maltreated and long-term sequelae (Aber and Zigler, 1981; Cicchetti and Manly, 1990; McGee and Wolfe, 1991; Polansky et al., 1972). Age of child is clearly a key consideration in the development of valid operational criteria for child maltreatment. For example, leaving a 3-year old alone for 5 hours is clearly inappropriate, whereas leaving a 12-year old alone for the same period of time is not (Polansky et al., 1972). Aber and Zigler (1981) noted that "severe emotional damage due to separation and loss may be particularly easy to inflict during the child's earliest years." Clearly, successful measurement of maltreatment needs to be based on a developmental perspective of child rearing. Operationally, instruments developed to measure child maltreatment need to be carefully tuned to the age group and literacy level of the child. Documentation needs to be supplied to ensure that instruments are not administered to inappropriate age groups.

Culturally Informed Definitions

Although definitions of child abuse and neglect vary across time and across cultures, consensus exists around definitions of severe forms of child maltreatment—for example, all members of society would probably agree that battering a child to death is morally repugnant. Less obviously substandard behaviors seem more subject to genuine cultural differences. The challenge of formulating culturally informed definitions of child maltreatment is to accommodate cultural variability in child care beliefs and practices while taking care not to promote different standards of care for children on the basis of race, ethnicity, or economic class.

We lack information on the cultural parameters of child maltreatment. Research must differentiate cultural norms from individual deviations from those norms in defining and identifying maltreatment. Child maltreatment is a highly charged issue—a "diagnosis" of abusing or neglecting one's child constitutes a serious moral and value judgment not present in a strictly medical diagnosis. Hence definitions need to take into account sociological and ethnographic aspects of the problem and balance the scientific desire for comparability and uniformity of definition with the need to be sensitive to differences in cultural viewpoints.

Consistent with the need to identify incidents of abuse that are related to culturally condoned practices, we need to encourage research that identifies the long- and short-term consequences of these incidents and their prevalence. The prevalence and effects of practices such as "coining" (a curing practice that involves the forceful pressing of coins on a child's body that results in bruises) among the Vietnamese cultures or punishment with tree switches, cords, or ropes among African Americans also need to be assessed. Although such practices may meet some criteria for abuse in the United States, it is critical for researchers who identify them to understand the context of those practices, at least in the perceptions of the parents, in order to influence behavioral changes in parenting.

Finally, vignette studies have indicated that various cultures judge the seriousness of child maltreatment incidents differently (Giovannoni and Becerra, 1979; Hong and Hong, 1991). These differences are not always in the expected directions. Although ethnic minorities are often overrepresented in official reports of maltreatment, blacks and Hispanics judged maltreatment vignettes as more serious than did whites (Giovannoni and Becerra, 1979).

IDENTIFICATION OF CHILD MALTREATMENT

Detection in Medical Settings

Spurred by pediatric advocacy, reporting laws adopted in the mid-1960s were narrowly focused on encouraging physicians to recognize and initiate protective action for children who were victims of physical abuse inflicted by their caretakers. Medical professionals primarily identified multiple bruises and fractures at different stages of healing resulting from abuse (Krugman, 1984). Over the years, the laws have broadened in scope to include child neglect, emotional injury, parental deprivation of medical care, and factors injurious to a child's mental development (Dubowitz and Newberger, 1989). Current reporting laws require health professionals to identify a wide array of physical conditions resulting from child maltreatment. The diagnosis of maltreatment by physicians is complicated by the absence of a universal medical definition.[3]

Research and technological developments have enabled health professionals to become increasingly sophisticated in their ability to detect and diagnose abuse. Several diagnostic indicators of child maltreatment have emerged through clinical experiences in medical settings, including: discrepant, partial, or vague history; delay in seeking care; a family crisis; trigger behavior by the child; unrealistic expectations of the child by the parents; isolation of the family; and/or a history of the parent being abused as a child (Krugman, 1984).

Medical reports have described how to recognize specific patterns of immersion burns that result from intentional injuries (Purdue et al., 1988), and studies have determined the effects of the duration of heat exposure, water temperature, and thickness of skin (Moritz and Henriques, 1947). Medical research determining both the necessary force and resulting injury patterns of specific types of falls has aided medical professionals in assessing whether histories given by caretakers are consistent with a child's injury (Chadwick et al., 1991, Helfer et al., 1977; Nimityongskul and Anderson, 1987). Medical understanding of the "shaken baby syndrome" has benefited from technological developments, including computerized topography and magnetic resonance imaging. Numerous medical consequences, particularly damage to the central nervous system, brain hemorrhages, skull fractures, and respiratory problems have been identified (Ludwig, 1983; Levitt, 1992). Research developments have also strengthened diagnosis of abuse in skin injuries (Wilson, 1977) and fractures (King et al., 1988). Likely locations for nonaccidental injuries have been identified, as well as injuries that would require children to have certain developmental motor skills in order to be self-inflicted (Ludwig, 1983; Johnson, 1990).

The medical literature describing physical findings associated with sexual abuse has also grown rapidly. Although physical findings alone are rarely conclusive in the absence of a history of sexual abuse or specific lab findings (American Academy of Pediatrics, 1991),[4] recent studies have indicated that chafing, abrasions, or bruising of the inner thighs and genitalia, scarring in specific genital areas, and specific abnormalities of the hymen are "consistent with but not diagnostic of sexual abuse" (American Academy of Pediatrics, 1991:256). Documenting physical evidence of sexual abuse is complicated by variations in observations and descriptions of normal and abnormal genital appearance (Paradise, 1990).[5] Accurate diagnosis of sexual abuse in children is hindered by frequent delays between alleged molestations, disclosure, and medical examinations. Currently, physicians retrospectively interpret changes in anogenital anatomy without the benefit of clinical research describing the healing chronology of acute genital and anal trauma (Finkel, 1989).

Medical research in the area of sexual abuse is constantly changing, and many early studies have not been validated (Finkel and DeJong, in press). For example, specific physical findings, previously thought to result from sexual abuse, are now questioned because recent studies have revealed similar findings in "nonabused" children (Krugman, 1990). The presence of certain sexually transmitted diseases as indicators of sexual abuse is also questioned since some sexually transmitted diseases, such as condylomata, chlamydia, and genital herpes, can be transmitted nonsexually (Ludwig, 1983; American Academy of Pediatrics, 1991). Without precise understanding of the mode of transmission of each sexually transmitted disease, physicians cannot rely simply on the presence of these diseases as definitive evidence of sexual abuse.

Diagnosing emotional abuse and physical and emotional neglect is also problematic for medical professionals. Diagnosis of these conditions is complicated by social factors such as poverty and differing cultural definitions of adequate care. In the absence of specific definitive physical manifestations, diagnoses often depend on the value judgments of individual physicians (Ludwig, 1983; Bross, 1982).[6]

Although the medical diagnosis of child abuse has improved (particularly in the area of physical abuse), most medical research in child maltreatment has been retrospective and clinical, consisting primarily of observations of patients at one institution. Additional empirical research on physical indicators of child maltreatment could improve diagnostic assessments of child maltreatment victims by physicians (Johnson, 1990). Applying research from other public health concerns, such as automotive safety technology, to child maltreatment may be helpful.

Reports to Child Protection Agencies

Aside from the question of how child maltreatment is defined, the interpretation of results must take into account aspects of the research design, and in particular the method by which subjects in the study are sampled. Ideally, incidence and prevalence would be determined by a population-based survey, in which a random sample of the general population is studied to determine patterns of maltreatment.[7]

Such population-based studies are expensive and difficult to implement. In contrast, studies may instead be based on the system of reports of child maltreatment to legal and social service agencies.[8] Reports to child protective services or other agencies and their disposition are subject to biases from uncontrolled methods of detection, yielding problems analogous to those of clinic-based samples in medical studies. Comparatively mild forms of child maltreatment may not appear in such samples since they are never reported. Particular socioeconomic groups, such as the poor, are likely to be relatively overrepresented, since they often have more extensive contact with social service or other agencies liable to report maltreatment. Abusers who are capable of covering up their acts may go undetected, and certain ethnic groups may be overrepresented because of prejudice on the part of the reporters. Regional differences in maltreatment rates may reflect different patterns of reporting rather than true differences in underlying rates—

for example, a region with good child protection agencies may paradoxically appear to have higher rates of abuse, since there is an incentive to report cases when services are available to address the problem. For all these reasons and more, data based on reports and their disposition need careful analysis of the effects of known or potential detection biases.

Despite their limitations, data on reports of child maltreatment and their disposition provide important descriptive information. The scientific quality of the information may be enhanced by more detailed studies of the detection and selection processes involved, perhaps using stratified random samples of case reports, as well as the addition of data on types, severity, and frequency of maltreatment from multiple sources both within child protective services and the family (Cicchetti and Barnett, 1991).

Improvements on a research-based classification of child maltreatment can greatly enhance the scientist's ability to correctly identify child maltreatment cases. Research efforts in a variety of disciplines are currently severely restrained by a lack of good diagnostic instruments. The development of standardized instruments will lead to more consistency in the identification of cases and strengthen the scientific quality of data obtained.

RESEARCH RECOMMENDATIONS

2-1. Research Recommendation: Recognizing that the absence of consistent research definitions seriously impedes the development of an integrated research base in child abuse and neglect, a series of expert multidisciplinary panels should be convened to review existing work and to develop a consensus on research definitions of each form of abuse and neglect.

If definitions of abuse and neglect continue to be influenced by fluctuations in community norms and shifting administrative and legislative requirements, the incidence of "occurrence" will remain ambiguous and variations will continue over time and between individuals, agencies, and communities. Research definitions derived from scientific criteria rather than legal classification systems can reduce subjective variations and can improve the quality of objective standards of measurement. Research definitions should be coordinated with case-report and legal definitions, be developmentally appropriate and culturally sensitive, provide clear inclusion and exclusion criteria, adopt unified subtyping schemes, and provide clear guidelines on issues of severity, duration, and frequency of acts of maltreatment. Definitions must be developed in consultation with existing agencies.

2-2. Research Recommendation: Sound clinical-diagnostic and research instruments for the measurement of child maltreatment are needed to operationalize the definitions discussed under Recommendation 1.

The clinically based instruments need to classify children into categories of maltreatment based on the clinical picture they present. The reliability and validity of these instruments must be established by sound testing with economically and culturally diverse populations. The generalizability of these instruments then needs to be tested on nonclinical populations to strengthen the instruments' abilities to classify children demonstrating similar behaviors who have not been reported in abusive incidents.

2-3. Research Recommendation: Research should be conducted on the detection processes that lead to the definition of cases identified in child protective services records and other social agencies that handle child maltreatment.

Better understanding of the case assessment, investigation, and substantiation processes will lead to more consensus, and the development of useful standardized instrumentation for case assessment. In addition, programs must be developed to train clinicians in appropriate techniques for obtaining abuse histories. Pilot studies of clinically based instruments to determine the nature, incidence, and prevalence of abuse experiences in children and adolescents could be conducted in medical and educational settings commonly frequented by children. Survey instruments that incorporate clinical findings must also be developed. Recognizing that improved instruments may lead to detection of previously unreported cases of abuse, ways must be devised to enable clinicians and other service providers to refer potentially abusive parents for direct assistance without requiring clear evidence of maltreatment prior to the delivery of services.

A word of caution must be added. Because of the hazards of erroneous identification, pilot screening studies must incorporate measures to protect families from the possible consequences of misdiagnosis and labeling.

2-4. Research Recommendation: Empirical research that builds on existing medical knowledge of the physical indicators of child sexual and physical abuse would assist physicians in the identification of child maltreatment. Such identification would also be facilitated by the development of training programs that integrate research findings from child maltreatment studies into the education of health professionals.

Research should focus specifically on children because, although research on burns, bruises, and trauma conducted with adults may be revealing, the results may not directly apply to children. Studies of indicators of physical abuse should specifically include studies with large populations and attention to physical presentation and healing (such as bruises) in different ethnic groups. Studies should also evaluate the relationship of bone density to fracturability in children. Research on diseases and conditions that mimic abusive head trauma or malnutrition, such as metabolic diseases and genetic diseases, may also be revealing. Longitudinal studies of the genital anatomy of nonabused children as they progress through puberty as well as studies that document changes in the appearance of preexisting trauma (including the effect of hormonal influences during puberty) would be helpful to physicians in identifying victims of sexual abuse.

Such studies, however, may raise important ethical dilemmas, as discussed in Chapter 9. For example, what consideration should be given to the psychological impacts associated with studies of the physical characteristics of sexuality (such as hymenal anatomy) in young children? Is it appropriate to remind a child who has been sexually abused at a young age, or the child's parents, of this event annually?

NOTES

1. There are many reasons why emotional maltreatment has not received more attention, including lack of agreement as to its many forms and the difficulty of operationalizing the definition once the form of emotional maltreatment has been agreed upon. Most forms of emotional maltreatment are very subtle and are usually overlooked, especially in the presence of physical abuse and neglect. Hart and Brassard (1987, 1990) and others argue that all children who are physically abused and neglected are also emotionally maltreated at least to some extent. However, the converse is not always true. Egeland and Erickson (1987) found in their high-risk sample a number of children who were emotionally maltreated but not physically abused or neglected. They were well fed, clothed, and received proper health care, but their caregivers did not respond to their emotional needs at an early age, and as a consequence they displayed severe forms of developmental maladaptation. Another reason it has not received proper attention is that emotional maltreatment leaves no physical marks, whereas physical abuse often leaves obvious physical signs. One definitional controversy centers on whether it is necessary for the parental action (or inaction) to have an apparent impact on the child. Some argue that any definition must include substantial observable impairment in the child's ability to perform and behave within a normal range. Others would argue that actions can be considered maltreatment regardless of their immediate observable impact on the child's functioning (see Schakel, 1987). Other definitional issues include intentionality and cultural context (Korbin, 1980). (See McGee and Wolfe [1991] for a proposed model for a definition and criteria for emotional maltreatment.)

2. In a commentary on research with diverse populations, Brown et al. (1992) note that the selection of questions to be asked and instruments of assessment can all be subject to cultural influences. For example, parents and children may be asked to plan a family vacation or the child is presented with a story which involves the child breaking a mother's valued vase. How universal are these situations?

3. State laws mandating physician reporting define abuse and neglect with ambiguous terms such as "substantial, unjustified, and allowable" (Johnson, 1990). The American Medical Association's Diagnostic and Treatment Guidelines Concerning Child Abuse and Neglect (1985) have vague definitions of what physicians should report and suggest peer consultation in questionable cases.

4. Sexual abuse, particularly when there is no penetration, rarely results in physical trauma, and the elasticity of the internal genital anatomy also inhibits the detection of evidence of sexual or physical penetration (DeJong, 1992).

According to the American Academy of Pediatrics (1991), the presence of semen/sperm/ acid phosphatase, a positive culture for gonorrhea, or a positive serologic test for syphilis are the only physical findings that make the diagnosis of sexual abuse a "medical certainty" (p. 257).

5. Even in clinical texts and dictionaries, definitions of "normal" genital anatomy in children differ. Physicians are also often unfamiliar with the genital anatomy of children. In one study, 77 percent of a surveyed group of physicians routinely examined genitalia 50 percent of the time; 17 percent of these physicians routinely examined genitalia less than 10 percent of the time (Finkel and DeJong, in press).

6. Neglect is classified by medical practitioners as either nonorganic failure to thrive, medical neglect, or abandonment (Ludwig, 1983). Failure to thrive is indicated by decelerating growth rates, poor hygiene, excessive oral stimulation, and developmental delays but medical distinctions between organic and nonorganic causes of failure to thrive are not clear (Drotar, 1992). Medical neglect results when parents deny manifestations of serious illnesses and refuse appropriate medicine or surgical treatment, or when caretakers fail to provide minimal well-child care (Mrazek and Mrazek, 1985). Diagnosing abandonment, which may include symptoms such as excessive dirty diapers, poor hygiene, excessive hunger, and dehydration as well as burns, ingestions, and repeated accidents, also presents difficulty for the health professional.

7. Rates from such a survey may be distorted by nonresponse and response errors such as arise when respondents do not accurately report their experiences, but they are not subject to systematic bias from the method of ascertainment.

8. Over the years, reporting laws have expanded in scope and in the categories of professionals and lay persons who are mandated to report maltreatment. Although the original proponents of these policies had as one of their purposes the creation of a repository of reports for statistical purposes, this purpose has receded into the background given the wide variation in the states' laws and the mechanisms to implement them (Giovannoni, 1992).

REFERENCES

Aber, J.L., and E.F. Zigler
1981   Developmental considerations in the definition of child maltreatment. In D. Cicchetti and R. Rizley, eds., *New Directions for Child Development*. San Francisco: Jossey-Bass.

Altemeier, W., S. O'Connor, P. Vietze, H. Sandler, and K. Sherrod
1984   Prediction of child abuse: A prospective study of feasibility. *Child Abuse and Neglect* 8:393-400.

American Academy of Pediatrics
1991   Committee on Child Abuse and Neglect. Guidelines for the Evaluation of Sexual Abuse of Children. *Pediatrics* 87(2)(February):254-259.

American Medical Association
1985   Council report: AMA diagnostic and treatment guidelines concerning child abuse and neglect. Council on Scientific Affairs. *Journal of the American Medical Association* 254(6)(August 9):796-800.

Askikal H., and W. Webb, eds.
1978   *Psychiatric Diagnosis*. New York: Spectrum.

Bross, D.C.
1982   Medical care neglect. *Child Abuse and Neglect* 6:375-381.

Brown, E., P. Martinez, and M. Radke-Yarrow
1992   Diversity: Research with diverse populations. *Society for Research on Child Development Newsletter* (Fall).

Caffey, J.
1946   Multiple fractures in the long bones of infants suffering from chronic subdural hematoma. *American Journal of Roentgenology* 56(August):163-173.

Chadwick, D., S. Chin, C. Slarno, J. Landsverk, and L. Kitchen
1991   Deaths from falls in children: How far is fatal? *Journal of Trauma* 31(10):1353-1355.

Christoffel, K.K., P.C. Scheidt, P.F. Agran, J.F. Kraus, E. McLoughlin, and J.A. Paulson
1992   Standard definitions for childhood injury research: Excerpts of a conference report. *Pediatrics* 89:1027-1034.

Cicchetti, D., and D. Barnett
1991   Toward the development of a scientific nosology of child maltreatment. Pp. 346-377 in D. Cicchetti and W. Grove, eds., *Thinking Clearly About Psychology: Essays in Honor of Paul E. Meehl.* Minneapolis: University of Minnesota Press.

Cicchetti, D., and V. Carlson, eds.
1989   *Child Maltreatment: Theory and Research on the Causes and Consequences of Child Abuse and Neglect.* New York: Cambridge University Press.

Cicchetti, D., and J.T. Manly
1990   Problems and solutions to conducting research in maltreating families: An autobiographical perspective. In I.E. Sigel and G.H. Brody, eds. *Methods of Family Research: Biographies of Research Projects, Vol. 2.* Hillsdale, NJ: Erlbaum Press.

DeJong, A.R.
1992   Medical detection and effects of the sexual abuse of children. Pp. 71-99 in W. O'Donohue and J.H. Geer, eds., *The Sexual Abuse of Children: Clinical Issues Volume 2.* Hillsdale, NJ: Lawrence Erlbaum Press.

Drotar, D.
1992   Prevention of neglect and nonorganic failure to thrive. Pp. 115-149 in D.J. Willis, E.W. Holden, and M. Rosenberg, eds., *Prevention of Child Maltreatment: Developmental and Ecological Perspectives.* New York: Wiley.

DSM-III-R.
1987   *Diagnostic and Statistical Manual of Mental Disorders.* 3rd edition revised. Washington, D.C.: American Psychiatric Association.

Dubowitz, H., and E. Newberger
1989   Pediatrics and child abuse. Pp. 76-94 in D. Cicchetti and V. Carlson, eds., *Child Maltreatment: Theory and Research on the Causes and Consequences of Child Abuse and Neglect.* New York: Cambridge University Press.

Eaton, W., and L. Kessler, eds.
1985   *Epidemiologic Field Methods in Psychiatry.* Orlando, FL: Academic Press.

Egeland, B., and M.F. Erickson
1987   Psychologically unavailable caregiving. Pp. 110-120 in M.R. Brassard, R. Germain, and S.N. Hart, eds., *Psychological Maltreatment of Children and Youth.* New York: Pergamon Press.

Finkel, M.A.
1989   Anogenital trauma in sexually abused children. *Pediatrics* 84(2)(August):317-322.

Finkel, M.A., and A.R. DeJong
in press Draft chapter. Medical Findings in Sexual Abuse: Genital Findings, Anal Findings, and Sexually Transmitted Diseases. In R.M. Reece, ed., *Child Abuse Diagnosis and Treatment.* Philadelphia: Lee and Febiger.

Garbarino, J., and G. Gilliam
1988   *Understanding Abusive Families.* Lexington, MA: Lexington Books.

Gelles, R.J., and M.A. Straus
1988   *Intimate Violence.* New York: Simon and Schuster.
Gil, D.G.
1975   Unraveling child abuse. *American Journal of Orthopsychiatry* 45(3):346-356.
Giovannoni, J.M.
1971   Parental mistreatment: Perpetrators and victims. *Journal of Marriage and the Family* 33(November): 637-638.
1989   Definitional issues in child maltreatment. In D. Cicchetti and V. Carlson, eds, *Child Maltreatment: Theory and Research on the Causes and Consequences of Child Abuse and Neglect.* Cambridge: Cambridge University Press.
1992   Issues in the Definition of Child Maltreatment. Background paper prepared for the National Research Council's Panel on Research on Child Abuse and Neglect.
Giovannoni, J.M., and R.M. Becerra
1979   *Defining Child Abuse.* New York: Free Press.
Giovannoni, J.M., and A. Billingsley
1970   Child neglect among the poor: A study of parental adequacy in families of three ethnic groups. *Child Welfare* 49(April):196-204.
Goodwin, D., and S. Guze
1984   *Psychiatric Diagnosis.* Third edition. New York: Oxford University Press.
Green, A.H., R.W. Gaines, and A. Sandgrund
1974   Child abuse: Pathological syndrome of family interaction. *American Journal of Psychiatry* 131 (8): 882-886.
Hart, S.N., and M.R. Brassard
1987   A major threat to children's mental health: Psychological maltreatment. *American Psychologist* 43(2):160-165.
1990   Psychological maltreatment of children. Pp. 77-112 in R.T. Ammerman and M. Hersen, eds., *Treatment of Family Violence: A Sourcebook.* New York: John Wiley.
Helfer, R., T.L. Slovis, and M. Black
1977   Injuries resulting when small children fall out of bed. *Pediatrics* 60:533-35.
Hong, G.K., and L.K. Hong
1991   Comparative perspectives on child abuse and neglect: Chinese versus Hispanics and whites. *Child Welfare* 70(4):463-475.
Institute of Medicine
1990   *Healthy People 2000: Citizens Chart the Course.* Committee on Health Objectives for the Year 2000. Washington, DC: National Academy Press.
Johnson, C.F.
1990   Inflicted injury versus accidental injury. *Pediatric Clinics of North America* 37(4)(August):791-814.
Kempe, C.H., F.N. Silverman, B. Steele, W. Droegemueller, and H.R. Silver
1962   The battered child syndrome. *Journal of the American Medical Association* 181(1):17-24.
King, J., D. Diefendorf, J. Apthorp, V.F. Negrete, and M. Carlson
1988   Analysis of 429 fractures in 189 battered children. *Journal of Pediatric Orthopedics* 8(5):585-589.
Korbin, J.E.
1980   The cultural context of child abuse and neglect. *Child Abuse and Neglect* 4:3-13.
Krugman, R.D.
1984   Child abuse and neglect: The role of the primary care physician in recognition, treatment, and prevention. *Primary Care* 11(3)(September):527-534.

1990   Future role of the pediatrician in child abuse and neglect. *Pediatric Clinics of North America* 37(4):1003-1011.

Levitt, C.J.
1992   Shaken Baby Syndrome (Inflicted Cerebral Trauma). Draft statement in American Academy of Pediatrics, Committee on Child Abuse and Neglect.

Ludwig, S.
1983   Child abuse. Pp. 1127-1163 in G. Fleisher and S. Ludwig, eds., *Textbook of Pediatric Emergency Medicine*. Baltimore: Williams and Wilkins.

Martin, M.D.
1978   1977 Analysis of Child Abuse and Neglect Research. National Center on Child Abuse and Neglect, U.S, Children's Bureau, Administration for Children, Youth and Families, U.S. Department of Health, Education and Welfare.

McGee, R.A., and D.A. Wolfe
1991   Psychological maltreatment: Toward an operational definition. *Development and Psychopathology* 3:3-18.

Meehl, P.E.
1959/   Some ruminations on the validation of clinical procedures. Reprinted in P. Meehl,
1973   *Psychodiagnosis*. Minneapolis: University of Minnesota Press.

Moritz A.R., and F.C. Henriques
1947   Studies on thermal injuries: Pathology and pathogenesis of cutaneous burns experimental study. *American Journal of Pathology* 23:915-941.

Mrazek, D.A., and P.J. Mrazek
1985   Child maltreatment. Pp. 679-697 in M. Rutter and L. Hersor, eds., *Child and Adolescent Psychiatry: Modern Approaches* 2nd Edition. London: Blackwell Scientific Publications.

National Center for Child Abuse and Neglect
1981   *National Study of the Incidence and Severity of Child Abuse and Neglect*. 81-30325. Washington, DC: U.S. Department of Health and Human Services. [NIS 1]

1988a   *Report on Data Collection: Study of National Incidence and Prevalence of Child Abuse and Neglect*. Washington, DC: U.S. Department of Health and Human Services.

1988b   *Study Findings: Study of National Incidence and Prevalence of Child Abuse and Neglect*. Washington, D.C.: U.S. Department of Health and Human Services. [NIS 2]

Nimityongskul A., and A. Anderson
1987   Likelihood of injuries when children fall out of bed. *Journal of Pediatric Orthopedics* 7(2):184-186.

Office of Technology Assessment
1987   *Healthy Children: Investing in the Future*. Washington, DC: U.S. Congress, Office of Technology Assessment.

Paradise, J.
1990   The medical evaluation of the sexually abused child. *Pediatric Clinics of North America* 37(4):839-862.

Pelton, L.H.
1978   Child abuse and neglect: The myth of classlessness. *American Journal of Orthopsychiatry* 48(4)(October):608-617.

Polansky, N., R. Borgman, and C. DeSaix.
1972   *Roots of Futility*. San Francisco: Jossey Bass.

Purdue, G., J. Hunt, and P. Prescott.
1988   Child abuse by burning: An index of suspicion. *The Journal of Trauma* 28(2):221-224.

Ross, C.J., and E. Zigler
1980   An agenda for action. Pp. 293-305 in G. Gerbner, C.J. Ross, and E. Zigler, eds., *Child Abuse: An Agenda for Action*. New York: Oxford University Press.
Schakel, J.A.
1987   Emotional neglect and stimulus deprivation. Pp. 100-109 in M.R. Brassard, R. Germain, and S.N. Hart, eds., *Psychological Maltreatment of Children and Youth*. New York: Pergamon Press.
Straus, M.
1979   Measuring intrafamily conflict and violence: The Conflict Tactics Scales. *Journal of Marriage and the Family* 48:75-88.
1990a   The Conflict Tactics Scales and its critics: An evaluation and new data on validity and reliability. In M.A. Straus and R.J. Gelles, eds., *Physical Violence in American Families: Risk Factors and Adaptations to Violence in 8145 Families*. New Brunswick, NJ: Transaction Publications.
1990b   Measuring physical and psychological maltreatment of children with the Conflict Tactics Scales. Family Research Labratory, University of New Hampshire.
Straus, M.A., and R.J. Gelles
1986   Societal change in family violence from 1975 to 1985 as revealed by two national surveys. *Journal of Marriage and the Family* 48(August):465-480.
Wald, M.
1977   Juvenile Justice Standards Project. In M. Wald, *Standards Relating to Abuse and Neglect*. Cambridge, MA: Ballinger.
Widom, C.S.
1988   Sampling biases and implications for child abuse research. *American Orthopsychiatric Association* 58(2):260-270.
Wilson, E.F.
1977   Estimation of age of cutaneous contusions in child abuse. *Pediatrics* 60:750-752.
Wolock I., and B. Horowitz
1977   *Factors Relating to Levels of Child Care Among Families Receiving Public Assistance in New Jersey. Final Report to the National Center on Child Abuse and Neglect*. (DHEW Grant 90-C-418.) Washington, DC: Clearinghouse on Child Abuse and Neglect Information.
1984   Child maltreatment as a social problem: The neglect of neglect. *American Journal of Orthopsychiatry* 54(4)(October):530-543.
Wyatt, G.E., and S.D. Peters
1986   Issues in the definition of child sexual abuse in prevalence research. *Child Abuse and Neglect* 10:231-240.
Zigler, E.F., and L. Phillips
1981   Psychiatric diagnosis. *Journal of Abnormal and Social Psychology* 63:607-18.
Zuravin, S.J.
1991   Research definitions of child physical abuse and neglect: Current problems. In R. Starr and D. Wolfe, eds., *The Effects of Child Abuse and Neglect: Issues and Research*. New York: Guilford Press.
Zuravin, S., and R. Taylor
1987   Family Planning Behaviors and Child Care Adequacy. Final report submitted to the U.S. Department of Health and Human Services, Office of Population Affairs (Grant FPR 000028-01-1).

3

Scope of the Problem

From 1976, when the first national figures for child maltreatment were generated, to 1990, the most recent year covered by the National Child Abuse and Neglect Data System, reports of maltreatment have grown from 416,033 per year (affecting 669,000 children) to 1,700,000 per year (affecting 2,712,917 children) (NCCAN, 1981, 1988, 1992). Prominent groups, such as the U.S. Advisory Board on Child Abuse and Neglect, have labeled the increase in reported cases an "epidemic" of child maltreatment in the United States, calling the problems of child abuse and neglect a national emergency (U.S. Advisory Board on Child Abuse and Neglect, 1990).

The alarming rise in the number of reported cases of child maltreatment is a significant development, but the full dimensions of its meaning are not yet clear. A significant number of cases reported to child protective services (CPS) agencies are not substantiated. The results of the second National Incidence Study, for example, indicate that in 1986 the alleged maltreatment was unfounded for 47 percent of those children reported in CPS cases (NCCAN, 1988). However, the process of substantiating a reported case may be affected by a wide range of social and economic factors within the case investigation system (such as the number of case workers) as well as the characteristics of the case itself. Whether the rise in reported cases of maltreatment genuinely represents an epidemic, or whether, like apparent increases in other social problems, the epidemic is due to increased recognition rather than a true increase in the phenomenon, remains controversial due to methodological problems with the data collection efforts (Daro et al.,

1990; Eckenrode and Doris, 1987; Peters et al., 1986; Straus and Gelles, 1986). For example, recent research on child death rates suggest that child abuse and neglect (CAN) death rates have not changed during the period 1979 through 1988, but 85 percent of CAN deaths have been systematically misclassified as due to other causes (McClain et al., 1993; Ewigman et al., 1993).

The purpose of this chapter is to review the evidence on prevalence of maltreatment from a number of sources: congressionally mandated maltreatment reports, population-based surveys of specific types of maltreatment, surveys of maltreatment in special population subgroups (e.g., disabled children), and cross-national data. Following a review of the information available on the scope of these problems, the panel discusses methodological problems common to these data, including issues of sampling, research design, and measurement. Finally, the panel provides recommendations to improve the quality of research on the prevalence of child maltreatment.

CURRENT ESTIMATES

Governmental Case Report Surveys

National Studies

In 1974, the Child Abuse and Prevention Treatment Act (P.L. 93-247) stipulated that the newly created National Center on Child Abuse and Neglect (NCCAN) investigate the national incidence of child abuse and neglect (NCCAN, 1981). The act authorized reporting of suspected abuse or neglect and required reporting by a range of professionals (including educators, health professionals, and others) who come into contact with children. The American Humane Association (AHA) was asked to determine the feasibility of a national study of child maltreatment reports and, until 1987, AHA collected reports on various types of maltreatment from child protective services personnel in cooperating states. Data were collected in summary form (e.g., the number of cases of physical abuse in a calendar year) and by individual case.

The data collected in these congressionally mandated national studies of official reports show a dramatic rise over this period in the number of reported cases of maltreatment. Comparative analysis of the data across time indicates that between 1983 and 1986 the percentage of neglect cases decreased (45.7 percent to 36.1 percent) and the number of abuse reports increased (27.9 percent to 35.0 percent). Over the decade 1976 to 1986, estimates of the rates of sexual maltreatment rose drastically from 0.86 per 10,000 children in 1976 to 20.89 per 10,000 children in 1986.

The American Humane Association reports are difficult to interpret for a number of reasons. First, they were never intended to be studies of the true occurrence of child maltreatment but, rather, to reflect reports of maltreatment coming to the attention of child protective services and other designated personnel. Second, they set no admission criteria for cases, relying instead on varying agency definitions of maltreatment and individual caseworker applications of those definitions. Consequently, the precise nature of the incidents included in the reports is difficult to judge and is subject to multiple sources of bias. Third, the studies include all reported cases, including those that are duplicated or unsubstantiated. Fourth, there are historical inconsistencies in the data. For example, a report that is labeled unsubstantiated was either investigated and the evidence for maltreatment was not present, or the report was still under investigation and had not, at the time of the report, been confirmed. Finally, the data base was not generated from the same participants each year. States and territories voluntarily participated in the project and, over the years, the participants changed (American Humane Association, 1979, 1981; American Association for Protecting Children, 1986, 1987; NCCAN, 1981, 1988, 1992).

National Incidence Studies

Recognizing the need to estimate the true occurrence of child maltreatment rather than simply relying on reported cases, in 1976 NCCAN contracted with Westat to design and implement a study of the incidence and severity of child abuse and neglect. The first National Incidence Study (NIS-1) was conducted in 1979-1980, guided by the concept that the cases reported to state authorities represented only "the top of the iceberg" (NCCAN, 1981). To expand knowledge about incidence of maltreatment, reports were gathered from investigatory agencies (e.g., courts, police) and professionals from other community institutions (such as physicians and educators). In a probability sample of 26 counties, data regarding reported and unreported cases of maltreatment were gathered from child protective services agencies, investigatory agencies, and professionals in other community agencies. In addition to employing an operational definition of each type of maltreatment, NIS-1 collected information on a number of child and parent-related characteristics as well as two other important characteristics, the nature of maltreatment (omission or comission) and the effect of maltreatment. The injury or impairment resulting from the maltreatment must have been rated as moderate or severe for the act or omission to be classified as maltreatment. These data do not represent true occurrence of maltreatment but, once again, reports of maltreatment known to service providers. NIS-1 estimated the number of maltreated children in a 12-month period (5/1/79-4/30/80) and the incidence was expressed as a rate with the denominator being the number of children in the United States in an age range.

Data from child protective services agencies indicated that the reported incidence was 17.8 per 1,000 children with 42.7 percent of these reports substantiated, for a substantiated incidence rate of 7.6 per 1,000 children per year. Fifty-three percent of these substantiated cases did not meet the NIS-1 maltreatment definition that required moderate or severe harm, for a corrected incidence of 3.4 per 1,000 children per year. When data from other community agencies are added to the data from child protective services, the incidence increased to 10.5 per 1,000 children per year.

The second National Incidence Study (NIS-2) was compiled in 1986. Using the same design as NIS-1, NIS-2 estimated the current incidence of maltreatment and documented changes in the frequency, character, or severity of maltreatment since the completion of NIS-1 (NCCAN, 1988; Cicchetti and Barnett, 1991). NIS-2 employed two sets of operational standards. The first conformed to NIS-1 standards and required identifiable harm to establish maltreatment. The second set of standards was broader and included "endangered" children at risk for harm. When the more restrictive definitions were used, the reported incidence of substantiated maltreatment was estimated at 14.8 per 1,000 children.[1] If the broader "endangered" definition was employed, the reported incidence was 22.6 per 1,000 children.[2] The more conservative definition represents a 66 percent increase over the NIS-1 figure (NCCAN, 1988). Most of this increase was due to abuse, with physical abuse up 58 percent and sexual abuse up 300 percent (NCCAN, 1988). No increases in emotional abuse or any form of neglect were observed.

Looking at specific categories of maltreatment in corrected estimates of the NIS-2 survey employing the endangerment standard, the overall rates per 1,000 children per year for any type of abuse was 9.4, with a rate of 4.9 for physical abuse, 2.1 for sexual abuse, and 3.0 for emotional abuse[3] (Sedlak, 1990). There were 14.6 neglected children per 1,000 children, with physical neglect being most common (8.1 per 1,000). Factors associated with increased rates of maltreatment included older age of the child and lower family income.

National Child Abuse and Neglect Data System

In response to the 1988 Child Abuse Prevention, Adoption and Family Services Act (P.L. 100-294), NCCAN redesigned the national child maltreatment data collection and analysis system. Based on two years of work with national experts and state representatives, the National Child Abuse and Neglect Data System (NCANDS), like the National Incidence Studies, included two parts. The summary data component compiled information from state agencies on reports, investigations, victims, and perpetrators.

The detailed case component compiled case data to investigate trends and issues in the field.

The 1990 NCANDS information was gathered on reports from 49 states, the District of Columbia, 1 territory, and all branches of the armed services. In all, there were 1.7 million reports of maltreatment involving 2.7 million children. Forty-five percent of the reports were of neglect, 47 percent of the reports were of abuse: 25 percent of physical abuse, 16 percent of sexual abuse, 6 percent of emotional abuse. The rates of substantiation for reported cases remained reasonably constant at 40 percent (NCCAN, 1992).

Private Sector Studies Using Case Reports

In addition to the governmental data collection activities that rely on state reports, the National Committee for Prevention of Child Abuse (NCPCA) conducts an annual 50-state survey by contacting child welfare administrators in all 50 states and the District of Columbia to track trends in child abuse reporting, child abuse fatalities, and child welfare policy (Daro et al., 1990). Beginning in 1972, the committee conducted a telephone interview with each state's federal government liaison officer for child abuse and neglect. Trends indicate that reports increased from 1980 to 1985, stabilized between 1985 and 1987, and began to rise substantially in 1988. In 1989, reports involving approximately 2.4 million children were filed, up 10 percent from 1988. This increase in reports of maltreatment has been accompanied by a growing number of child abuse fatalities. Fatalities attributed to reports of abuse have grown from 899 in 1986 to 1,237 in 1989.[4] These data, like other data collection efforts based largely on official or unofficial reports, are problematic to interpret because of the noncomparability of case definitions across states and the inclusion of duplicated cases.

The National Committee for the Prevention of Child Abuse also estimated the scope of child neglect. On the basis of its 1990 50-state survey, the committee estimated that 46 percent of reported children (or 2 percent of all children) are reported for child neglect each year (Crittenden, 1992; Daro and McCurdy, 1991).

It is important to note that definitions of child neglect vary over time and circumstances as standards governing the acceptable level of adequate care of children have expanded from covering nutrition, shelter, and other material necessities to include medical, educational, and emotional care. Helfer (1987) has stated that "the true incidence of child neglect is unknown, since no consensus on the definition exists." Although extreme forms of maltreatment may be easy to recognize, gradations between satisfactory care and borderline neglect are difficult to measure, and variations within and between social service and child welfare agencies in handling reports of child neglect are common.

Population Surveys

A number of investigators have attempted to estimate the prevalence of child maltreatment through standard survey techniques rather than relying on official reports or reports of cases known to certain professionals (Gil, 1970).

Physical Abuse

After reviewing the incidence data available in the 1970s, Straus and Gelles (1986) concluded that little was known about patterns of violence against children. In 1975 they surveyed a national probability sample of 2,143 families consisting of a married couple or a man and woman who identified themselves as living together as a conjugal unit (Gelles, 1978). Violence was operationalized using the Conflict Tactics Scales, an instrument with 18 items in 3 categories: use of rational discussion and argument, use of verbal and nonverbal expression of hostility, and use of physical force or violence as a tactic in a conflict (Straus, 1979). Using a physical abuse index that included hitting a child with an object (such as a hairbrush or belt), the survey found a prevalence rate of 140 per 1,000 children ages 3-17 per year. If hitting with an object is omitted so that the index includes acts that are almost universally accepted as physical abuse (such as kicking and punching a child), the rate was 36 per 1,000 children.

Straus and Gelles (1986) repeated their survey in 1985 (with the same instrument) with 3,520 families using telephone interviews. The 1985 sample included children under three and single parents; after removing them for purposes of comparison with the rates generated by the 1975 survey, Straus and Gelles (1986) found a statistically significant decrease in the index of severe violence against children (from 140 to 107 per 1,000 children), a significant decrease in the very severe violence index (from 30 to 19 per 1,000 children), but no significant difference in the rate of minor violence, i.e., corporal punishment.

Straus and Gelles must be commended on two counts. First, they used a nationally representative sample and, second, they used an instrument with known reliability in determining whether abuse occured. The work is limited by its attention only to physical abuse and verbal forms of emotional maltreatment.

Sexual Abuse

Studies of the incidence and prevalence of sexual abuse, while initiated early in this century (Hamilton, 1929), became more common in the 1980s. Prior to 1976, surveys inquiring about sexual abuse were largely undertaken with volunteers or with college students (Peters et al., 1986). These studies mainly collected data on lifetime prevalence of noncontact (exhibitionism, solicitation) and contact sexual abuse. Depending on both the population used and the definition employed, lifetime rates of sexual abuse have ranged from 6 percent to 62 percent for females and 3 percent to 31 percent for males (Peters et al., 1986), with most investigators concluding that there has been a rise in the reported rates of being a victim of sexual abuse (Leventhal, 1988; Peters et al., 1986; Wyatt and Peters, 1986a,b).

Sexual abuse by adolescents has received increased attention. One study indicated that 56 percent of child molestations are committed by someone under age 18 (Fehrenbach et al., 1986), and the majority of adult sex offenders indicate that the onset of their deviant sexual behavior occurred before age 18 (Abel et al., 1988). Until recently, however, adolescent sexual offenders have been neglected in clinical and research literature. There are no empirically derived and tested models to explain why adolescents commit sexual crimes or develop deviant sexual interest patterns (Becker, 1991).

Prevalence of Abuse and Neglect in Disabled Children

Although early work in child maltreatment research pointed to a link between disabilities and maltreatment, studies in this area are limited. The chief problem, in addition to identifying the number of disabled children, is the temporal ordering of the two phenomena, determining whether disabled children are more likely to be abused or whether abused children are more likely to become disabled through abuse (Groce, 1988). Furthermore, most studies examining the relationship between disabilities and maltreatment have been inadequate due to small sample size, lack of appropriate comparison groups, and selection bias (Bertolli et al., 1992). In general, studies in this area find a higher rate of maltreatment of disabled children than of children without disabilities but the causal sequence is unknown (Groce, 1988). The possibility of disaggregating cause and effect by a comparative study of maltreatment in children whose disabilities are largely genetically determined, children whose disabilities could be caused by maltreatment, and children without disabilities has not been explored, even though it could provide significant insights in this area (Garbarino, 1987).

International Comparisons

Cross-national comparisons of the prevalence of child abuse and neglect are difficult because of anthropologists' focus on normative cultural behavior, the low base rate of the phenomenon, and the lack of a universal standard for what constitutes abuse and neglect (Korbin, 1987). Although abuse and neglect statistics are not collected across countries, the World Health Organization collects data on causes of death by age (Bertolli et al., 1992). Analyses of these data indicate that child homicide is more common in the United States than in comparison countries for every age group (Williams and Kotch, 1990; Division of Injury Control, 1990).

METHODOLOGICAL ISSUES

This review of the research on the scope of child maltreatment reveals important methodological problems that limit the usefulness of these data for drawing conclusions about both the dimensions of the problem and the factors that cause it. Such problems include definitional issues, confusion of prevalence and incidence, the source of maltreatment data, sampling and design considerations, the paucity of psychometrically sound instruments, and the impact of mandatory reporting requirements on the reliability of survey respondents' reports. Although some of these issues have been documented by investigators in the field, the panel believes their importance merits emphasis in this report because they must be remedied through research to improve the quality of data (Bertolli et al., 1992; Cicchetti and Barnett, 1991; Fromuth and Burkhart, 1987; Haugaard and Emery, 1989; Leventhal, 1982; Mash and Wolfe, 1991; Peters et al., 1986; Widom, 1988; Wyatt and Peters, 1986a,b).

Definitional Issues

As pointed out in the previous chapter, child maltreatment is not a uniform entity. Failure to recognize this stifles work on etiology, treatment, and prevention. While nominal definitions of maltreatment (e.g., physical, sexual, and emotional abuse) are common across studies, operational criteria, when available, differ greatly (Aber and Zigler, 1981; Bertolli et al., 1992; Cicchetti and Barnett, 1991; Peters et al., 1986; Wyatt and Peters, 1986a). Operational definitions can be based on the act itself (e.g., its form, intensity, duration, frequency), its consequences (e.g., bruising, developmental delay), the perpetrator's intent, the child's age, age differences and relationships between victims and perpetrators, and social norms on appropriate behavior (e.g., physical punishment as appropriate parental behavior) (Bertolli et al., 1992). Inconsistencies among definitions in these aspects, as pointed out in a rigorous comparison and adjustment of the operational criteria of sexual abuse by Wyatt and Peters (1986a), appear to account for much of the difference in prevalence estimates across studies.

Unreported Abuse

Given that only the most serious episodes of abuse are reported, such as those observed by outsiders such as physicians, neighbors, and teachers, child maltreatment is most likely underreported and underestimated in official records (Nagi, 1975; Widom, 1988; Wilbur, 1985). The 1975 National Family Violence Survey, for example, found a prevalence rate for physical abuse of 140 per 1,000 children per year, which is 21 times greater than the 6.8 per 1,000 for cases reported to child protective services in the United States, and also many times greater than the rates from the National Incidence Studies of cases known to all human service professionals (Straus and Gelles, 1986). Many severely abused children are brought to emergency rooms by parents or relatives who blame injuries on accidents that, in reality, never occurred. Children are reluctant to reveal abuse for fear of removal from their homes, feelings of shame, protection of their parents, selective inattention, or loss of memory of the event (Berger et al., 1988; Della Femina et al., 1990; Frischolz, 1985; Herzberger and Tennen, 1983; Lewis et al., 1991; Sullivan, 1956; Wilbur, 1985).

Few pediatricians and child psychiatrists are trained to elicit abuse histories, although the American Medical Association has recently recommended that these kinds of questions should be part of routine adolescent, pediatric, and psychiatric evaluations. Such procedures as looking at a child's or adolescent's back, inquiring about the origin of visible scars, and asking, "Are there any scars I can't see?" are rarely included in evaluations (Stein and Lewis, 1992).

Confusion of Prevalence and Incidence

Measuring the occurrence of child abuse and neglect has been difficult not only because of a lack of definitions but also because of confusion of what measure of occurrence is under investigation. To count an outcome under study, epidemiologists commonly use two measures: incidence and prevalence. Incidence, the number of new cases detected in a defined time period divided by the number of children who are eligible to become new cases, is the ideal measure for identifying etiologic factors. By using new cases, investigators can determine which features are related to occurrence of maltreatment rather than trying to disentangle features related to occurrence from those related to the continuation of maltreatment. In contrast, child protection services often rely on *total* occurrences, a different measure of incidence: the numerator is total occurrences of abuse and neglect during the defined period and the denominator is all children, whether or not they had previously been maltreated. Previously maltreated children are included in the denominator because they are at risk for new occurrences (Bertolli et al., 1992).

Prevalence consists of the number of existing cases of child abuse and neglect at any point in time divided by the total population from which the cases are identified. Use of prevalence data causes confusion between risk factors that are associated with new cases of abuse and neglect and those that influence continuation of the problem (Bertolli et al., 1992).

Research in this area does not always distinguish between incident and prevalent cases. It is sometimes difficult to distinguish between new and existing cases because the exact time of the occurrence must be arbitrarily determined. One approach for dealing with the confusion between incident and prevalent cases is to use a measure called period prevalence. In it the numerator is individuals in the population who, at any time in a defined period, experienced abuse or neglect divided by the total population. This strategy is commonly used by researchers in this field when they estimate the proportion of adults in a particular age group who have been maltreated at any time during childhood (Bertolli et al., 1992).

Use of Administrative Data

With the exception of a relatively small number of primary data collection efforts, the vast amount of information on the occurrence of child abuse and neglect is based on state child protective services records. The accuracy with which these data reflect the true incidence or prevalence of maltreatment is questionable for a number of reasons. First, although all states have mandatory reporting laws, the definitions of abuse and neglect vary across and within states chiefly as a result of the absence of structured assessment tools, the casework burdens of social services personnel, inaccurate or missing information, and the limited availability of services for families who are identified (Hoaglin et al., 1982; Leventhal, 1990). Second, the segments of the population at risk are subject to unequal surveillance. Specifically, families who, because of their demographic characteristics (e.g., poverty, unemployment, single parent), have more frequent contact with public sector services (e.g., welfare, housing) are more often exposed to mandated reporters and receive closer scrutiny. Consequently, the overrepresentation of families who are poor and members of minority groups in child protective services caseloads may be less likely to be due to poverty being a risk factor for maltreatment and more likely to be due to undetected abuse and neglect in more affluent families (Gelles, 1982; Newberger et al., 1977).

Conflicting evidence exists as to whether differences occur in rates of maltreatment by culture or ethnicity. The two National Incidence Studies did not find a significant relationship between race[5] and the incidence, type, or severity of child maltreatment (NCCAN, 1981, 1988). Some studies have reported that ethnic minorities are disproportionately reported for child abuse and neglect (e.g., Jason et al., 1982; Lauderdale et al., 1980). Others indicate that such overrepresentation is equivalent to the representation of ethnic minorities among the poor, thus supporting the confounding nature of ethnicity and poverty in child abuse and neglect reports (Horowitz and Wolock, 1981). Cultural and ethnic groups that are at the greatest risk of poverty, then, appear to have disproportionate incidence and prevalence rates of child maltreatment. Convincing evidence that disaggregates socio-economic status and cultural or ethnic identity in rates of reported child abuse and neglect has not been developed, although socioeconomic status may be strongly associated with some forms of child maltreatment. For example, child neglect occurs among the poorest of the poor (Giovannoni and Billingsley, 1970), and physical abuse is more severe among the poorest families (Straus, 1980).

Surveillance bias further complicates the issue. Poor and ethnic minority children are more likely to be identified as maltreated than more affluent white families (e.g., Newberger et al., 1977). A reanalysis of the first National Incidence Study (1981) found that class and race were the best predictors of whether an incident was reported by hospitals, with impoverished black families more likely to be reported than affluent white families, regardless of the severity of the incident (Hampton and Newberger, 1985). Furthermore, service availability and severity of worker caseloads may affect reporting by ethnicity (Light, 1973; Wolock and Horowitz, 1979).

Finally, use of substantiated administrative data is problematic because all cases of abuse and neglect are not pursued with equal rigor (Eckenrode et al., 1988a,b; Giovannoni, 1989). The availability of resources within individual state child protective service agencies clearly affects which cases are investigated and confirmed.

Rate of Occurrence Versus Rate of Reporting

Much of the tremendous increase in maltreatment rates is probably due to increased reporting (Straus and Gelles, 1986). Recent work by Leventhal and colleagues (1993) suggests that for two cohorts of adolescent mothers, one whose children were born from 1967-1970 and the other whose children were born 1979-1981, no differences in rates of maltreatment were detected when injury events were rated using predefined criteria by physicians who were blind to the social characteristics of the mothers. However, over the 14 year time span, reports of maltreatment to the Connecticut Department of Children and Youth Services tripled indicating little real difference in rates of maltreatment but considerable differences in *reported* rates of maltreatment. A recent study of the classification of child death rates also suggests that although the number of deaths from child abuse and neglect has been consistently underestimated because they are often misclassified as due to other causes[6], even expanded interpretations of child death reports suggest that the rate of child abuse and neglect deaths among children ages 0 to 17 has remained relatively stable (around 2,000 deaths per year) from 1979 through 1988 (McClain et al., 1993).

Changes in the proportion of child maltreatment reports that are substantiated may provide evidence as to whether the increased reported incidence involves changes in the rate of occurrence as well. One study conducted by Eckenrode and colleagues (1988a,b) observed that the percentage of substantiated reports declined from 1974 to 1984, although the number of reports filed increased significantly during the same period. The authors concluded that the reporting and investigation process was "cutting further into the tip of the iceberg of child maltreatment, but proportionally more social resources are being used to uncover new cases" (Eckenrode et al., 1988b; p. 9). Their findings are consistent with the summary findings of the NIS-2 study, which reported that although little change was reported between 1980 and 1986 in the severe categories of maltreatment (such as fatalities and serious injuries), dramatic increases occurred at the level of mild to moderate injury and impairment, where there was greater potential for improved recognition of cases (NCCAN, 1988).

In summary, the increase in reported incidence of child maltreatment is probably the result of a combination of factors: expanded definitions, increased recognition and reporting, and increases in the rate of occurrence. Increases in rate of occurrence cannot be ruled out since the number of children living in poverty has increased significantly since the 1970s and poverty is thought to be significantly associated with child maltreatment (see discussion in Chapter 4) (National Commission on Children, 1991). Changes over time in the proportion of reports for each type and severity of abuse, the source of the complaints, and the characteristics of perpetrators and victims can provide insight into whether significant increases in reported rates of maltreatment reflect increases in the actual occurrence of maltreatment (Knudsen, 1992). However, data for each of these factors are so limited that it currently provides no insight into the relative contributions of increased rates of reporting and increased rates of occurrence of child maltreatment.

Sampling and Design Issues

The design of a study is the blueprint through which the investigator achieves specific research objectives. These objectives determine what groups are to be compared, how subjects are selected, what factors should be measured, and what conclusions can be drawn (Bertolli et al., 1992; Leventhal, 1990).

A number of investigators have pointed out the inadequacy of the sampling strategies and study designs commonly used in child abuse research (Leventhal, 1982, 1990; Peters et al., 1986; Widom, 1988). The use of volunteers and college students in cross-sectional studies has produced disparate estimates of the problem, an inconsistent picture of the etiologic factors associated with these problems, and an inability to generalize findings to other population groups.

An ideal design for investigating etiology and sequelae of maltreatment would be a large, prospective cohort study in which random samples of children from different types of communities, and ethnic and sociodemographic groups would be followed from birth to adulthood. The study would measure all known and hypothesized risk factors for abuse and neglect at birth and at prespecified follow-up interviews, and all new cases of abuse and neglect would be identified as they occur with no loss to follow-up (Bertolli et al., 1992).

Although cohort studies are being conducted in this area, key factors of the ideal design, such as ascertainment of representative samples of cases of abuse and neglect, are missing due to reliance on administrative data for cases. Incidents of child maltreatment may also remain undetected and unreported if subgroups of the population at risk for abuse and neglect are not recruited into longitudinal studies.

In the area of abuse and neglect, cross-sectional designs are more common than cohort studies. These studies interview respondents about past experiences of abuse and neglect and risk factors of interest. While quicker, less costly, and easier than cohort studies, cross-sectional designs are not usually used to estimate incidence and, furthermore, because exposure variables are measured after the abuse or neglect occurred, the temporal ordering of cause and effect is problematic. Finally, retrospectively collected data are often subject to recall errors (Briere, 1992; Widom, 1989; Wolfe and Mosk, 1983).

Two other study designs are used less frequently in this area of research but should be mentioned because they are useful for studying phenomena with low base rates. The case-control study is a design in which two groups of individuals are selected separately (one with the outcome, the other without it) and then compared to determine the effects of hypothesized risk factors. To draw accurate conclusions about the effects of the risk factors, the controls should be representative of the population from which the study cases came (Bertolli et al., 1992; Kleinbaum et al., 1982; Leventhal, 1982). This design is far more efficient than prospective cohort studies for studying statistically rare outcomes like abuse and neglect but it is subject to measurement error because exposure variables are measured after the outcome of interest has occurred.

The last study design is considerably different from the other designs in that the areas of analyses are not individuals but rather geopolitical areas (e.g., census tracts). In this type of design the investigator does not know the joint distribution of exposure and outcomes but simply the number of exposed and unexposed cases and noncases. These studies are quick and inexpensive but commonly subject to a problem called ecologic bias (Morgenstern, 1982), whereby correlations between outcomes and observed characteristics of the area may be the spurious result of unmeasured characteristics. Furthermore, because they employ routinely collected data, they may be subject to problems resulting from the use of administrative data.

Measurement

Research on child abuse and neglect has been severely hampered by the lack of instruments to measure the phenomena. Relatively few instruments have reported reliability and validity.[7] The lack of instrumentation, whether on a state or an individual level, leads to misclassification bias, a systematic error introduced into studies through mistakes in measuring or classifying subjects on variables to be used in the analysis of the study (Bertolli et al., 1992; Cicchetti and Barnett, 1991; Eckenrode et al., 1988a,b). Furthermore, inconsistency in the design of questions about sensitive social topics (such as child sexual abuse) contributes to extreme differences in estimates of the problem (Peters et al., 1986).

One recent study of methodological issues in the measurements used in U.S. programs for tracking the use of licit and illicit drugs concluded that nonsampling components of error and bias in measurements can dwarf the sampling variance in research on socially sensitive topics (Turner et al., 1992). This same study noted that significant improvements in survey instruments can be achieved by focusing on the cognitive demands that individual survey questions make on respondents, and by relying more extensively on self-administered forms rather than interviewer-administered formats when research subjects can complete self-report questionnaires (Turner et al., 1992).

Effect of Mandatory Reporting

In some cases, previously undetected or imminent incidents of abuse or neglect may be detected during an investigation. As part of the informed consent procedure required in federally supported studies, participants in most child maltreatment studies should be informed of their rights and duties as research subjects (see Chapter 9 for a full discussion of ethical issues in child maltreatment research). In addition, every state has adopted legislation that requires research investigators (and other professionals who have contact with children) to disclose to child welfare officials reports of suspected child abuse or neglect that have not been recorded.[8] The basic requirement is that professionals must report any cases in which there is "reason to believe" or "reasonable cause to suspect" that child abuse, past or present, has occurred. Whether such "reason to believe" refers to a clinical hunch or firm evidence is open to conjecture, but a professional who fails to disclose suspected child maltreatment may be charged with criminal action (Sieber, 1992).

The requirements of mandatory reporting vary from state to state; in some cases, disclosure to child welfare authorities is not required if the individual who makes the disclosure is receiving therapeutic services (such as family counseling). There are also variations in the level of endangerment that constitute child maltreatment, as well as variations in evidentiary standards that warrant a report to child welfare authorities.

Empirical research studies on the conditions and circumstances that affect professional reports of privately disclosed incidents of child maltreatment are rare. But one survey study has indicated that a significant amount of "discretionary reporting" occurs, whereby professionals who come into contact with children may report some suspected cases of child maltreatment but not others (Zellman, 1990). Professionals who have made reports of child maltreatment cite various reasons for doing so, including stopping maltreatment, getting help for the family, helping the family to recognize the seriousness of their problems, and complying with legal requirements (Zellman, 1990).

Estimates of failure to report cases of suspected abuse range from about a third of practicing psychologists (Borsig and Kalichman, in press) to 22 percent of a sample of professionals that included general and family practitioners, pediatricians, child psychiatrists, clinical psychologists, social workers, principals of public schools, and heads of child care centers (Zellman, 1990). The issue of failure to report needs to be examined in light of its impact on incidence and prevalence estimates of child maltreatment as well as its significance for the conduct of research in this area. For example, some potential research subjects may decide not to participate in the research project because of mandatory reporting requirements, while others may falsify or distort responses revealing reportable child maltreatment activity (Sieber, 1992).

The interests and safety of the child are obviously paramount to any research objectives. The primary reasons provided by professionals who have indicated failure to report include the lack of sufficient evidence to justify a report, treatment-related concerns (i.e., "I can do better than the system"), and the costs of reporting to professionals (e.g., reports too time-consuming or fear of lawsuit for reporting) (Zellman, 1990).

The impact of mandatory reporting requirements on research projects has not been studied. Many research investigators believe that the requirements of mandatory reporting may conflict with other fundamental principles in the informed consent process, which assure subjects of complete confidentiality of their responses. The dilemma, from the scientist's perspective, is tantamount to saying, "If you respond truthfully, I may report you to the appropriate authority" (Sieber, 1992). Many research scientists are reluctant to report disclosures of child abuse and neglect that occur in a research investigation unless the child is endangered. In the case of prior abuse incidents, research investigators sometimes believe that little benefit will be gained by recording earlier cases of abuse that may be quite dated, especially if the family or the offender is already in treatment for other reported cases, if the child does not want the incident reported, or if the perpetrator is not alive or not in contact with children.

CONCLUSIONS

The panel concludes that much of the methodology for prevalence and incidence research in the area of child abuse and neglect is seriously flawed. Definitional variations, variations in state cooperation with national data collection efforts, legal requirements for mandated reporting, scarce funding for methodological work (specifically instrument development), and the paucity of rigorous epidemiologic investigations have retarded progress in this field. However, the limited available evidence suggests that child abuse and neglect is an important, prevalent problem in the United States, involving more than 1 million children each year in case reports and 2,000 child deaths annually. Child abuse and neglect are particularly important compared with other critical childhood health and mental health problems because the consequences of child maltreatment are often directly associated with adverse health and mental outcomes in children and families (Institute of Medicine, 1989). Furthermore, given the prevalence of childhood maltreatment, the level of federal funds expended in this research area is extremely small when compared with the resources allocated for less prevalent childhood mental disorders, such as autism and childhood schizophrenia.[9]

Specifically, the panel concludes:

• Much of the tremendous increase in maltreatment rates is probably the result of increased reporting rather than significant changes in actual rates of occurrence. However, the possibility that rates of occurrence have increased as well needs consideration, given the large numbers of children now living in adverse circumstances.

• Neglect is more common than any individual type of child maltreatment and has consistently accounted for approximately half of the cases of maltreatment (NCCAN, 1992). Although reports of physical or sexual abuse of childhood significantly increased between 1980 and 1986, reports of child neglect still account for a large majority (63 percent) of the cases reported in the 1986 National Incidence Study. Reported cases of child neglect involved 14.6 per 1,000 countable neglected children, or 917,200 children nationwide, identified in the 1986 study of National Incidence and Prevalence of Child Abuse and Neglect (Sedlak, 1990; NCCAN, 1988).

However, these figures may underestimate the prevalence of neglect because cases involving multiple forms of child maltreatment are likely to be reported as abuse rather than neglect; siblings of reported children may experience the same family conditions; and many children in both poor and affluent families are probably underreported (Crittenden, 1992). In addition to unreported cases of physical neglect, the incidence of psychological or emotional neglect (which includes verbal battering, belittling, and terrorism) is probably much greater than that reflected in the NIS reports, since such cases are rarely reported in the absence of other forms of child maltreatment.

The chronicity of child neglect cases needs to be considered in discussions of incidence and prevalence. Incidence figures are more suited to the measurement of maltreatment cases that are specific and short-lived, and prevalence measures may be more appropriate for child neglect cases, since they tend to be chronic and long-term (Polansky et al., 1981).

• Total reports of physical abuse increased 58 percent between 1980 and 1986 (NCCAN, 1988), although severe forms of physical abuse may actually have decreased (Straus and Gelles, 1986).

• Sexual abuse reported to child protective services has shown the largest reported increase of any form of abuse or neglect, rising from 0.7 per 1,000 children to 2.2 per 1,000 children per year in the National Incidence Studies (1980-1986) (NCCAN, 1988). Using different definitions of sexual abuse and data from community respondents, estimates of prevalence range from a low of 20-24 percent (Hamilton, 1929; Institute for Sex Research, 1953) to a high of 54-62 percent (Russell, 1983; Wyatt, 1985). The high estimates included noncontact exposure.

• Emotional abuse is the least studied of all types of abuse. Emotional abuse, across the 1990 Annual Fifty States Survey, the 1986 Second National Incidence Study, and the 1990 NCANDS accounts for approximately 7 percent of the reported cases of maltreatment.[10] However, in the absence of operational definitions and standards of severity, the true extent of occurrence of emotional maltreatment is unknown. In addition to existing in its own discrete forms, emotional abuse may be inherent in many reported cases of child abuse and neglect but it may not be recorded as a specific form of maltreatment (American Association for Protecting Children, 1986). No population surveys of emotional maltreatment have been conducted (Knudsen, 1992).

RESEARCH RECOMMENDATIONS

Recognizing that incidence and prevalence data comprise the cornerstone of good etiologic, treatment, and prevention work, the panel proposes strategies for improving research on the occurrence of child abuse and neglect. Although many of the following recommendations can be achieved with little additional expenditure of funds, a well-designed, multiyear plan with appropriate guidance to the states is needed.

Recommendation 3-1: State data systems should be improved so that high-quality research on service systems can be conducted. The range of variation in state definitions of child abuse and neglect as well as verification procedures seriously undermine the quality of existing data. Effort is needed on a national level to:

• mandate state compliance with data acquisition and reporting efforts as in other federal efforts like Medicaid and Medicare;
• develop uniform case definitions with measurable criteria;
• generate risk assessment tools that are sensitive to complex professional and ethical problems to guide protective services workers' decisions;
• identify potential sources of bias in current procedures for reporting and investigation of reported cases;
• redesign state data processing systems so that uniform individual-level data are available and unduplicated counts of children affected by abuse and neglect are easily obtainable;
• establish an expert panel to periodically review the data system, establish quality indicators, and identify key areas for services systems investigation;
• make available state-level data as public use data tapes;
• conduct ethnographic studies to identify the systems level features that affect reporting and case verification; and
• provide sufficient incentive for state child welfare agencies to become equal partners in the research process while acknowledging the problems (e.g., understaffing, management emphasis) of state-level research.

Recommendation 3-2: Standardized measures and methodological research should be developed for use in epidemiologic studies of child abuse and neglect. Unlike the National Institute of Mental Health, the National Center for Child Abuse and Neglect has not mounted an extensive multiyear effort to develop valid and reliable instruments to identify child abuse and neglect in population-based studies. While a few good measures have been developed over time (such as the Conflict Tactics Scales, the Trauma Symptom Checklist, and the Wyatt Sex History Questionnaire), more attention must be paid to instrumentation and methodological issues to improve the scientific quality of child abuse and neglect research. The panel recommends:

• development of field-tested instruments and interview techniques for identifying physical, sexual and emotional abuse, and neglect. We recognize that many different types of instruments need to be developed, including observational protocols and child self-report instruments, and we encourage the representation of a diversity of perspectives in this process.

• dedication of funds to undertake psychometric work to ensure instruments that are both reliable and valid. Instruments should be tested to ensure that they are useful in diverse ethnic groups and incorporate strategies for eliciting information about a sensitive topic. Development of child as well as parent report instruments is needed.

• encouragement of methodological studies to improve the quality of child maltreatment research. Such studies should focus on problems in defining populations of interest to be sampled in studies of child abuse and neglect, choosing sources of information, and deciding the time frame to be covered.

Recommendation 3-3: Data collection efforts should capitalize on future national survey efforts to include questions on child abuse and neglect. Currently, little information is gathered about child abuse or neglect in many national surveys (such as the National Health Interview Survey on Child Health, the National Survey of Children, and the Child Supplement to the National Longitudinal Survey of Youth)[11]. Although the inclusion of questions on child maltreatment may raise issues of cost and administrative burdens, past surveys and secondary analyses of existing data sets represent research opportunities that could provide further insights into the nature and frequency of child abuse and neglect.
The panel recommends:

• establishing an expert panel to resolve issues around mandatory reporting requirements and the legal status of certificates of confidentiality.

• including questions on child abuse and neglect and key covariates, such as family violence, on national survey efforts such as the National Survey of Children.

Recommendation 3-4: Research should encourage secondary analyses of existing data available from multiple national surveys for questions about abuse and neglect. Specifically, the panel suggests:

• funding secondary analysis of already existing data sets that do not specifically apply to maltreatment but may reveal important information.

• expanding the data archives to include studies about children with questions potentially pertaining to child maltreatment.

Recommendation 3-5. After considerable work on instrumentation, including investigations into the most effective questioning strategies, the panel recommends the funding of a series of full scale epidemiologic studies on the incidence and prevalence of child abuse and neglect. Once the methodological work is complete, large scale epidemiologic investigations are feasible. These investigations would provide solid information on the occurrence of these important problems as well as on key etiologic agents. This series should be:

• multisite and competitively awarded to ensure that the most qualified investigators participate in the effort.

• of sufficient size to characterize families from a variety of communities. Sites must be chosen to: (1) permit adequate representation of all segments of the U.S. population; (2) ensure samples enriched in key predisposing features through the use of multistage probability sampling schemes; and (3) exemplify state-of-the-art field study procedures including skilled and well-supervised interviewers, concurrent data entry, and structured protocols for follow-up of refusals.

• inclusive of all ethnic groups represented in the United States. Studies should be undertaken that include ethnic subgroups (e.g., Cambodians, Samoans) rather than large groupings (e.g., Asian/Pacific Islanders).

• continued as a cohort study where subsamples of families thought to be at high and low risk for maltreatment are followed over time and assessed at specified intervals to determine the incidence of new cases of abuse and neglect.

• mandated to use multiple data sources to verify reports of abuse and neglect, particularly when parents report either medically attended injuries or social services interventions as a result of the maltreatment. These strategies would serve not only as case ascertainment but would also allow the development of realistic indicators of what portion of these problems are brought to the attention of child protective services.

NOTES

1. This figure is the corrected estimate, revising an earlier 16.3 figure reported in the initial report of the NIS-II survey (see Sedlak, 1990). Technical amendments to the study findings—National incidence and prevalence of child abuse and neglect: 1988. May 23, 1990.

2. This figure is the corrected estimate, revising an earlier 25.2 figure reported in the initial report of the NIS-II survey (see Sedlak, 1990). Technical amendments to the study findings—National incidence and prevalence of child abuse and neglect: 1988. May 23, 1990.

3. The NIS-II survey also had a category of "emotionally neglected," which is included in the neglect rather than abuse incidence estimates.

4. This figure compares to about 8,000 deaths per year for children ages 1 to 4 (4 million births per year x 4 years x 50/100,000 death rate for 1-4-year-olds).

5. Broad racial categories often do not accurately reflect cultural or ethnic affiliation. There are multiple types of Hispanics/Latinos (e.g., Puerto Ricans, Mexicans, Mexican-Americans, Guatemalans, Cubans); blacks (e.g., African-Americans; Haitians, West Indians); Asians (e.g., Chinese, Japanese, Koreans, Thais, Cambodians); Native American Indians (e.g., Navaho, Sioux); Pacific Islanders (e.g., Hawaiians, Samoans); and European-Americans (e.g., Italians, British, Germans). Furthermore, within any of these populations, there is substantial intracultural diversity along such dimensions as socioeconomic status, acculturative status, education, and gender.

6. Child deaths are classified according to the *International Classification of Diseases,* 9th revision, known as ICD-9 (World Health Organization, 1977). ICD-9 includes several categories (E967, E968.4, and E904.0) that explicitly note child abuse and neglect, including child battering and other maltreatment, criminal neglect, abandonment and neglect of infants and the child maltreatment syndrome (McClain et al., 1993). However, other categories in the ICD-9 system may also include deaths from child abuse and neglect, including some deaths recorded as the following: child homicide, undetermined origin, accidental fatalities, or Sudden Infant Death Syndrome.

7. Examples of such instruments include the Conflict Tactics Scales (Straus and Gelles 1986; Straus 1990a,b), the Trauma Symptom Checklist (Briere and Runtz, 1987), the Wyatt Sex History Questionnaire (Wyatt, 1985; Wyatt et al., in press), the Childhood History Questionnaire (Milner, J.S., Robertson, K.R., and D.L. Rogers, 1990), and the Child Abuse Potential Inventory (Milner and Wimberley, 1979; Milner, J.S., Gold, R.G., Ayoub, C., and M.M. Jacewitz, 1984; Milner, J.S., Gold, R.G., and R.C. Wimberley, 1986; Milner, J.S., Robertson, K.R., and D.L. Rogers, 1990).

8. By 1967, all states had adopted mandatory reporting laws, largely in response to the widely publicized cases of child maltreatment following the publication of "The Battered Child" paper by Kempe and colleagues (1962).

9. For example, officials at the National Institute on Mental Health estimate that that agency alone spent $4 million in FY 1992 on research on childhood autism and pervasive developmental disorders.

10. Although most state statutes include some reference to the concept of child maltreatment, emotional maltreatment is seldom defined and few cases are processed as such (Hart et al., 1987).

The validity of the figures in the National Incidence Study are difficult to assess, given the ambiguous diagnostic criteria and the large number of agencies asked to report. In the 1986 National Incidence Study 3.4 per 1,000 children per year were estimated to be victims of emotional abuse or in danger of emotional abuse. These rates are higher than those for sexual abuse and they may reflect the sources of data for the study: schools, day care, and social service agencies (Knudsen, 1992). An analysis of official reports to child protection agencies in 1986 by the American Humane Association indicated that 8.3 percent of all reported cases included emotional abuse or neglect (1.1 per 1,000 children per year were victims of emotional maltreatment). Differences in estimates between the incidence of emotional maltreatment in the National Incidence Study (which suggests that 435,000 children were victims of child maltreatment) and the American Humane Association analysis of reports (which suggests that 28,000 children were identified as victims of emotional maltreatment) primarily reflect the problems with definitions and diagnosis. The differences in these rates may demonstrate, in part, that only a fraction of the cases of emotional maltreatment are reported. Unless it co-occurs with other forms of severe abuse, emotional maltreatment is less likely to be documented, and less likely to receive intervention, than other forms of child maltreatment (Hart and Brassard, 1991).

11. For further information about these and other national child surveys see the following references (Zill and Coiro, 1992):
1) National Health Interview Survey on Child Health (National Center for Health Statistics, 1989; Dawson, 1991; and Zill, Moore, Smith, Stief, and Coiro, 1991);
2) National Survey of Children (Peterson and Zill, 1986; Allison and Furstenburg, 1989); and
3) Child Supplement to the National Longitudinal Survey of the Labor Market Experience of Youth (Baker and Mott, 1989).

REFERENCES

Abel, G., J. Becker, J. Cunningham-Rathner, and M. Mittelman
1988   Multiple paraphiliac diagnosis among sex offenders. *Bulletin of the American Academy of Psychiatry and the Law* 16(2):153-68.
Aber, J.L., and E. Zigler
1981   Developmental considerations in the definition of child maltreatment. *New Directions for Child Development* 11(1):1-29.
Allison, P.D., and F.F.Furstenburg, Jr.
1989   How marital dissolution affects children: Variations by age and sex. *Developmental Psychology* 25:540-549.
American Humane Association
1979   Annual Statistical Report: National Analysis of Child Neglect and Abuse Reporting, 1978. Englewood, Colorado.
1981   National Analysis of Official Child Neglect and Abuse Reporting, 1979. Englewood, Colorado.
American Association for Protecting Children
1986   *Highlights of Official Child Neglect and Abuse Reporting, 1984.* Englewood, Colorado: American Humane Association.
1987   *Highlights of Official Child Neglect and Abuse Reporting, 1985.* Denver, Colorado: American Humane Association.
Baker, P.C., and F.L.Mott
1989   *A Guide and Resource Document for the National Longitudinal Survey of Youth 1986, Child Data.* Columbus: The Ohio State University, Center for Human Resource Research.
Becker, J.
1991   Treatment Methods for Perpetrators of Child Sexual Abuse. Background paper for the Child Abuse Treatment Working Group of the American Psychological Association.
Berger, A.M., J.F. Knutson, J.G. Mehm, and K. Perkins
1988   The self-report of punitive childhood experiences of young adults and adolescents. *Child Abuse and Neglect* 12:251-262.
Bertolli, J., H. Morganstern, and S. Sorenson
1992   The Occurrence of Child Abuse and Neglect: Issues, Findings, and Directions. Background Paper prepared for the National Research Council's Panel on Research on Child Abuse and Neglect.
Borsig, C., and S. Kalichman
in press Clinicians reporting of suspected abuse: A review of the empirical literature. *Clinical Psychology Review.*
Briere, J.
1992   Methodological issues in the study of sexual abuse effects. *Journal of Consulting and Clinical Psychology* 60(2):196-203.

Briere, J., and M. Runtz
    1987   Post sexual abuse trauma: Data and implications for practice. *Journal of Interpersonal Violence* 2:367-379.
Cicchetti, D., and D. Barnett
    1991   Toward the development of a scientific nosology of child maltreatment. Pp. 346-377 in D. Cicchetti and W. Grove, eds., *Thinking Clearly about Psychology: Essays in Honor of Paul E. Meehl.* Minneapolis: University of Minnesota Press.
Crittenden, P.M
    1992   *Preventing Child Neglect.* Chicago: National Committee for Prevention of Child Abuse.
Daro, D., and K. McCurdy
    1991   *Current Trends in Child Abuse Reporting and Fatalities: The Results of the 1990 Annual Fifty State Survey.* Chicago: National Committee for Prevention of Child Abuse.
Daro, D., K. Casey, and N. Abrahams
    1990   Reducing Child Abuse 20% by 1990: Preliminary Assessment. National Committee for Prevention of Child Abuse. Working Paper No. 843.
Dawson, D.
    1991   Family structure and children's health and well-being: Data from the 1988 national health interview survey on child health. *Journal of Marriage and the Family* 53:573-584.
Della Femina, D., C.A. Yeager, and D.O. Lewis
    1990   Child abuse: Adolescent records vs. adult recall. *Child Abuse and Neglect* 14:227-231.
Division of Injury Control, Centers for Disease Control
    1990   Childhood injuries in the United States. *American Journal of Diseases of Children* 144:627-646.
Eckenrode, J., and J. Doris
    1987   *Unreliable Child Maltreatment Reports: Variations Among Professional and Nonprofessional Reporters.* Washington, DC: National Center on Child Abuse and Neglect.
Eckenrode, J., J. Powers, J. Doris, J. Munsch, and N. Bolger
    1988a   Substantiation of child abuse and neglect reports. *Journal of Consulting and Clinical Psychology* 56(1):9-16.
Eckenrode, J., J. Munsch, J. Powers, and J. Doris
    1988b   The nature and substantiation of official sexual abuse reports. *Child Abuse and Neglect* 12: 311-319.
Ewigman, B., C. Kivlahan, and G. Land
    1993   The Missouri child fatality study: Underreporting of maltreatment fatalities among children younger than five years of age, 1983 through 1986. *Pediatrics* 91(2):330-337.
Fehrenbach, P.A., W. Smith, C. Monastersky, and R.W. Deisher
    1986   Adolescent sex offenders: Offender and offense characteristics. *American Journal of Orthopsychiatry* 56: 225-233.
Frischholz, E.J.
    1985   The relationship among dissociation, hypnosis, and child abuse in the development of multiple personality disorder. Pp. 100-126 in R.P. Kluft, ed., *Childhood Antecedents of Multiple Personality.* Washington, DC: American Psychiatric Press, Inc.
Fromuth, M.E., and B.R. Burkhart
    1987   Childhood sexual victimization among college men: Definitional and methodological issues. *Violence & Victims* 2(4):241-252.

Garbarino, J.
    1987   The abuse and neglect of special children: An introduction to the issues. Chapter
            in Garbarino, J. et al., eds., *Special Children—Special Risks.* New York: Aldine
            De Gruyter.
Gelles, R.J.
    1978   Violence towards children in the U.S. *American Journal of Orthopsychiatry* 48:580-
            592.
    1982   Problems in defining and labeling child abuse. Pp. 1-30 in R.H. Starr, ed., *Child
            Abuse Prediction: Policy Implications.* Cambridge, MA: Ballinger.
Gil, D.
    1970   *Violence Against Children: Physical Child Abuse in the United States.* Cam-
            bridge, MA: Harvard University Press.
Giovannoni, J.
    1989   Substantiated and unsubstantiated reports of child maltreatment. *Child Youth Ser-
            vice Review* 11:299-318.
Giovannoni, J.M., and A. Billingsley
    1970   Child neglect among the poor: A study of parental adequacy in families of 3 ethnic
            groups. *Child Welfare* 49(April):196-204.
Groce. N.E.
    1988   Special groups of children at risk of abuse: The disabled. Pp. 223-239 in M.
            Straus, ed., *Abuse and Victimization Across the Life Span.* Baltimore: Johns Hopkins
            University Press.
Hamilton, G.V.
    1929   *A Research in Marriage.* New York: Albert and Charles Boni.
Hampton, R.L., and E.H. Newberger
    1985   Child abuse incidence and reporting by hospitals: Significance of severity, class,
            and race. *American Journal of Public Health* 75(January):56-60.
Hart, S.N., and M.R. Brassard
    1991   Developing and Validating Operationally Defined Measures of Emotional Mal-
            treatment. Report supported by the National Center on Child Abuse and Neglect
            Grant 90CA1216.
Hart, S.N., R. Germain, and M.R. Brassard
    1987   The challenge: To better understand and combat the psychological maltreatment of
            children and youth. In M.R. Brassard, R. Germain, and S.N. Hart, eds., *Psycho-
            logical Maltreatment of Children and Youth.* New York: Pergamon Press.
Haugaard, J.J., and R.E. Emery
    1989   Methodological issues in child sexual abuse research. *Child Abuse and Neglect*
            13:89-100.
Helfer, R.E.
    1987   The litany of the smoldering neglect of children. Pp. 301-311 in R.E. Helfer and
            R.S. Kempe, eds., *The Battered Child, Fourth Edition, Revised and Expanded.*
            Chicago: University of Chicago Press.
Herzberger, S.D., and H. Tennen
    1983   Coping with abuse: Children's perspectives on their abusive treatment. In D.
            Finkelhor, ed., *The Dark Side of Families.* Beverly Hills, CA: Sage.
Hoaglin, D.C., R.J. Light, B. McPeek, F. Mosteller, and M. Stoto
    1982   *Data for Decisions: Information Strategies for Policymakers.* Cambridge, MA:
            Abt Books.
Horowitz, B., and I. Wolock
    1981   Maternal deprivation, child maltreatment, and agency interventions among poor

families. Pp 137-184 in L. Pelton, ed., *The Social Context of Child Abuse and Neglect.* New York: Human Sciences Press.

Institute for Sex Research
1953   *Sexual Behavior in the Human Female.* Philadelphia: W.B. Saunders.

Institute of Medicine
1989   *Research on Children and Adolescents with Mental, Behavioral, and Developmental Disorders.* Washington, DC: National Academy Press.

Jason, J., N.D. Andereck, J. Marks, and C.W. Tyler, Jr.
1982   Child abuse in Georgia: A method to evaluate risk factors and reporting bias. *American Journal of Public Health* 72(December):1353-1358.

Kleinbaum, D.G., L.L. Kupper, and H. Morgenstern
1982   *Epidemiologic Methods: Principles and Quantitative Methods.* New York: Van Nostrand Reinhold Co.

Knudsen, D.
1992   *Child Maltreatment: Emerging Perspectives.* Dix Hills, NY: General Hall, Inc.

Korbin, J.E.
1987   Child abuse and neglect: The cultural context. Pp. 23-41 in R. Helfer and R. Kempe, eds., *The Battered Child.* Chicago: University of Chicago Press.

Lauderdale, M., A. Valiunas, and R. Anderson.
1980   Race, ethnicity, and child maltreatment: An empirical analysis. *Child Abuse and Neglect* 4:163-169.

Leventhal, J.M.
1982   Research strategies and methodologic standards in studies of risk factors for child abuse. *Child Abuse and Neglect* 6(1):113-123.

1988   Have there been changes in the epidemiology of child abuse during the 20th century? *Pediatrics* 82(5): 766-773.

1990   Epidemiology of child sexual abuse. Pp. 18-41 in R.M. Oates, ed., *Understanding and Managing Child Sexual Abuse.* Sydney, Australia: Harcourt Brace Jovanovich.

Leventhal, J., S. Horwitz, C. Rude, and D. Stier
1993   Maltreatment of children born to teenage mothers: A comparison between the 1960s and the 1980s. *Journal of Pediatrics* 122:314-319.

Lewis, D.O., C.A. Yeager, C.S. Cobham-Portorreal, N. Klein, C. Showalter, and A. Anthony
1991   A follow-up study of female delinquents: Maternal contributions to the perpetuation of delinquency. *Journal of the American Academy of Child and Adolescent Psychiatry* 30(2):197-201.

Light, R.
1973   Abused and neglected children in America: A study of alternative policies. *Harvard Educational Review* 43:556-598.

Mash, E.J., and D.A. Wolfe
1991   Methodological issues in research on physical child abuse. *Criminal Justice and Behavior* 18(1)(March):8-29.

McClain, P.W., J.J. Sacks, R.G. Froehlke, and B.G. Ewigman
1993   Estimates of fatal child abuse and neglect, United States, 1979 through 1988. *Pediatrics* 91(2):338-343.

Milner, J.S., and R.C. Wimberley
1979   An inventory for the identification of child abusers. *Journal of Clinical Psychology* 35(1)(January):95-100.

Milner, J.S., Gold, R.G., Ayoub, C., and M.M. Jacewitz
1984   Predictive validity of the Child Abuse Potential Inventory. *Journal of Consulting and Clinical Psychology* 52:879-884.

Milner, J.S., Gold, R.G., and R.C. Wimberley
1986   Prediction and explanation of child abuse: Cross-validation of the Child Abuse
         Potential Inventory. *Journal of Consulting and Clinical Psychology* 54:865-866.
Milner, J.S., Robertson, K.R., and D.L. Rogers
1990   Childhood history of abuse and adult child abuse potential. *Journal of Family
         Violence* 5(1):15-34.
Morgenstern, H.
1982   Uses of ecologic analysis in epidemiologic research. *American Journal of Public
         Health* 72:1336-44.
Nagi, R.
1975   Child abuse and neglect programs: A national overview. *Children Today* (May/
         June):13-17.
National Center for Child Abuse and Neglect
1981   *National Study of the Incidence and Severity of Child Abuse and Neglect.* 81-
         30325. Washington, DC: U.S. Department of Health and Human Services. [NIS 1]
1988   *Study Findings: Study of National Incidence and Prevalence of Child Abuse and
         Neglect.* Washington, DC: U.S. Department of Health and Human Services. [NIS
         2]
1992   *Na*tional Child Abuse and Neglect Data System, Working Paper 1, 1990 Summary
         Data Component. April. Washington, DC: U.S. Department of Health and Human
         Services.
National Center for Health Statistics
1989   *Vital Statistics of the United States, 1987, Vol. 1, Natality.* Washington, DC:
         Government Printing Office, DHHS Publication No(PHS)89-1100.
National Commission on Children
1991   *Beyond Rhetoric: A New American Agenda for Children and Families.* Washing-
         ton, DC: Government Printing Office.
Newberger, E., R. Reed, J. Daniel, J. Hyde, and M. Kotelchuck
1977   Pediatric social illness: Toward an etiologic classification. *Pediatrics* 60:178-185.
Peters, S.D., G.E. Wyatt, and D. Finkelhor
1986   Prevalence. In D. Finkelhor, ed., *A Sourcebook on Child Sexual Abuse.* Beverly
         Hills, CA: Sage Publishers.
Peterson, J.L., and N. Zill
1986   Marital disruption, parent-child relationships, and behavioral problems in children.
         Journal of Marriage and the Family 48:295-307.
Polansky, N.A., M.A. Chalmers, E. Buttenweiser, and D.P. Williams
1981   *Damaged Parents: An Anatomy of Child Neglect.* Chicago: University of Chicago
         Press.
Russell, D.
1983   The incidence and prevalence of intrafamilial and extrafamilial sexual abuse of
         female children. *Child Abuse and Neglect* 7:133-146.
Sedlak, A.J.
1990   Technical Amendments to the Study Findings—National Incidence and Prevalence
         of Child Abuse and Neglect. [NIS 2] 1988. May 23, 1990.
Sieber, J.E.
1992   Issues Presented by Mandatory Reporting Requirements. Paper prepared for the
         National Research Council, Commission on Behavioral, and Social Sciences, and
         Education, Panel on Research on Child Abuse and Neglect.
Stein, A., and D.O. Lewis
1992   Discovering physical abuse: Insights from a follow-up study of delinquents. *Child
         Abuse and Neglect* 16:523-531.

Straus, M.A.
1979   Family patterns and child abuse in a nationally representative sample. *Child Abuse and Neglect* 3: 23-25.
1980   Stress and physical child abuse. *Child Abuse and Neglect* 4:75-88.
1990a   Measuring Psychological and Physical Abuse of Children with the Conflict Tactics Scales. Family Research Laboratory, University of New Hampshire.
1990b   The Conflict Tactics Scales and its critics: An evaluation and new data on validity and reliability. In M.A. Straus and R.J. Gelles, Ph*ysical Violence in American Families: Risk Factors and Adaptations to Violence in 8145 Families.* New Brunswick, NJ: Transaction Publications.
Straus, M.A., and R.J. Gelles
1986   Societal change in family violence from 1975 to 1985 as revealed by two national surveys. *Journal of Marriage and the Family* 48(August): 465-479.
Sullivan, H.S.
1956   *Clinical Studies in Psychiatry.* New York: W.W. Norton.
Turner, C.F., J.T. Lessler, and J.C. Gfroerer, eds.
1992   *Survey Measurement of Drug Use: Methodological Studies.* Washington, DC: National Institute on Drug Abuse. Division of Epidemiology and Prevention Research.
U.S. Advisory Board on Child Abuse and Neglect
1990   *Child Abuse and Neglect: Critical First Steps in Response to a National Emergency.* Washington, DC: U.S. Department of Health and Human Services.
Widom, C.S.
1988   Sampling biases and implications for child abuse research. *American Journal of Orthopsychiatry* 58(2):260-270.
1989   Does violence beget violence? A critical examination of the literature. *Psychological Bulletin* 106(1):3-28.
Wilbur, C.B.
1985   The effect of child abuse on the psyche. Pp. 22-35 in R.P. Kluft, ed., *Childhood Antecedents of Multiple Personality.* Washington, DC: American Psychiatric Press.
Williams, B.C., and J.B. Kotch
1990   Excess injury mortality among children in the United States: Comparison of recent international statistics. *Pediatrics* 86(6):982-987.
Wolfe, D.A., and M.D. Mosk
1983   Behavioral comparisons of children from abusive and distressed families. *Journal of Consulting and Clinical Psychology* 51:702-708.
Wolock, I., and B. Horowitz
1979   Child maltreatment and material deprivation among AFDC-recipient families. *Social Service Review* 53:175-194.
World Health Organization
1977   *World Health Classification: Manual of the International Statistical Classification of Diseases, Injuries, and Causes of Death.* 9th revision. Geneva, Switzerland: World Health Organization.
Wyatt, G.E.
1985   The sexual abuse of Afro-American and white American women in childhood. *Child Abuse and Neglect* 9:507-519.
Wyatt, G.E., and S.D. Peters
1986a   Issues in the definition of child sexual abuse in prevalence research. *Child Abuse and Neglect* 10:231-240.
1986b   Methodological considerations in research on the prevalence of child sexual abuse. *Child Abuse and Neglect* 10:241-251.

Wyatt, G.E., L. Lawrence, A. Vodounon, and M.R. Mickey
   1993   The Wyatt Sex History Questionnaire: A structured interview for sexual history taking. *Journal of Child Sexual Abuse* 48(4) (Summer):51-68.
Zellman, G.L.
   1990   Child abuse reporting and failure to report among mandated reporters. *Journal of Interpersonal Violence* 5(1):3-22.
Zill, N., and M.J. Coiro
   1992   Assessing the condition of children. *Children and Youth Services Review* 14:119-136.
Zill, N., Moore, K.A., Smith, E.W., Stief, T., and M.J.Coiro
   1991   *Life Circumstances and Development of Children in Welfare Families: A Profile Based on National Survey Data.* Washington, DC: Child Trends.

4

Etiology of Child Maltreatment

Certain characteristics of child maltreatment complicate research into its etiology. These characteristics include: (1) the extreme socially deviant nature of the behavior, (2) its low prevalence, (3) the presence of multiple factors in the context of child maltreatment, such as poverty and violence, (4) changing political and historical definitions of the behavior, and (5) the troubling and complex nature of the behavior that requires a rethinking of conventional wisdom about human nature and parenting.

Variation in operational definitions and theoretical concepts of child maltreatment is a major problem in reviewing the etiology of child maltreatment. Although this chapter sometimes distinguishes among the etiologies of different kinds of maltreatment, the necessary data to support these distinctions are generally unavailable. The panel believes that, rather than separating research on subpopulations divided by types of maltreatment, it is more useful to review research within a framework that focuses on the range of factors associated with child maltreatment as a general phenomenon. The panel recognizes that some factors are more closely linked with certain forms of child abuse and neglect (such as the relationship between poverty and child neglect). However, as noted in Chapter 2, similarities and differences in the etiologies of physical abuse, physical punishment, sexual abuse, emotional abuse, and neglect have not been well articulated in the scientific literature. In many cases research has not differentiated the etiologies and outcomes associated with multiple forms of maltreatment especially when various forms co-occur in one individual, either within the same contemporaneous period or during a lifetime. Comparative studies of the origins and correlates of different kinds of abuse are rare. Most forms of maltreatment are part of a pattern of maladaptive behavior that emerges over time, but research evidence regarding the origins and maintenance of this pattern of behavior is not clear. Investigators disagree about whether child maltreatment is a continuum of behaviors (ranging from mild physical discipline to severe forms of physical or sexual abuse) or a set of unique behavioral problems with distinctive etiologies (Gelles, 1991). Since studies of multiple forms of maltreatment are rare and researchers generally deal with one type of maltreatment in their work, such disagreement may result from the manner in which research projects have been organized.[1] More recently, researchers are giving more attention to factors such as the severity and chronicity of abuse and neglect and the co-occurrence of multiple forms of maltreatment. With few exceptions (Wolfe, 1991), most etiological models lack a vocabulary for understanding the temporal organization of child maltreatment or demonstrating potential connections between maladjustments (including attitudes and beliefs) and abusive behaviors of the perpetrators. The existing models also do not resolve uncertainties about the continuum that may or may not exist between physical punishment and physical abuse, or between inadequate care giving and parental neglect. As a result, we currently know very little about the significant causes and pathways that influence risk factors in the etiology of child maltreatment.

OVERVIEW OF ETIOLOGICAL MODELS

Etiological models of child maltreatment are beginning to evolve from isolated cause-and-effect models to more sophisticated approaches that consider multiple pathways and interactive effects among factors that contribute to child maltreatment.[2] In the early 1970s, recognizing the limitations of focusing on only parent or only child characteristics, researchers started to emphasize interactions among child, parent, and environmental risk factors. Gil (1970), for example, was one of the first to document the role of poverty and family disadvantage on the rates of child abuse. His work was followed by investigations by Garbarino (1977), who noted that isolation from social support systems was a significant, but not a sufficient, condition of child maltreatment (Wolfe, 1991).

The recognition of the role of ecological or "situational" factors gradually led to the development of contemporary multicausal interactive models, which emphasize the importance of the sociocultural context of child maltreatment. Current theoretical models include: (a) the ecological models of Belsky and Garbarino, based on the conceptions of Urie Bronfenbrenner (Belsky, 1980, Garbarino, 1977; Lutzker, 1984); (b) the transitional model of Wolfe, which views child maltreatment as an escalating process and as one end of the continuum of maladaptive parenting (Wolfe, 1991); and (c) the transactional model of Cicchetti (Cicchetti and Carlson, 1989), based on Sameroff and Chandler's (1975) formulations.

Although simple models identified key variables associated with child maltreatment—often termed "risk factors"—they did not establish a firm etiology of child maltreatment or specify causal relationships or sequences between the associated variables. Furthermore, results across these studies are often conflicting, and the predictive power of single variables, such as the individual characteristics of the parent, child, or environment alone, is limited. The emerging social interactional models emphasize the importance of viewing child maltreatment in the context of the family, community, and society rather than emphasizing only individual parental psychopathology or individual stressors (Belsky, 1980, 1992; Cicchetti and Carlson, 1989; Garbarino, 1977; Parke and Collmer, 1975; Wolfe, 1991). The phenomenon of child abuse and neglect has thus been moved away from the conception of an individual disorder or psychological disturbance, toward the conception of a symptom of an extreme disturbance of childrearing, often part of a context of other serious family problems, such as poverty, alcoholism, or antisocial behavior (Burgess, 1979; Pelton, 1989; Starr, 1979; Wolfe, 1991). New empirical findings invoking interaction models suggest that, although studies of abusive and nonabusive parents have not detected important significant differences in terms of personality dimensions, studies of the interactions of abusive and nonabusive family processes have yielded important distinctions, including unrealistic expectations of their children, the tendency to view their own children's behavior as extremely stressful, and their view of themselves as inadequate or incompetent in the parenting role (Wolfe, 1991).

As a result of these shifting paradigms, the panel has observed that terms in the research literature on the origins of child maltreatment are often confused in discussions of cause and effect and risk relationships. The use of terms in child maltreatment studies such as *risk factors, intermediate or moderator variables, mitigators, mediators, confounding variables*, and so forth lacks the precision found in fields that have more developed sources of statistical and epidemiological data to test theories.[3] Furthermore, theoretical terms used in child maltreatment discussions are generally not matched by empirical data, and factors that are hypothesized as significant correlates have often not been tested in rigorous controlled studies. Much of the data base relies on anecdotal material derived from clinical research. As a result, many variables are hypothesized as acting in multiple ways, sometimes as antecedents to child maltreatment, sometimes as consequences, sometimes as factors that are present with or without a modifying effect on the causal relationships that result in child maltreatment.

For example, a strong association has been shown between the role of poverty in generating stressful experiences and the anger that become precipitating factors in child abuse and neglect (Gil, 1970; Pelton, 1978, 1989). Yet the relationship between poverty and child maltreatment is complex— most poor parents clearly are not abusive and poverty alone is not a sufficient or necessary antecedent for child maltreatment. In addition, the effects of parent and family characteristics on the etiology of child maltreatment may vary significantly with social class (Trickett et al., 1991).

Interactive models generally build on a probabilistic risk assessment process, assuming that child maltreatment occurs when multiple risk factors outweigh protective, compensatory, and buffering factors (Cicchetti and Carlson, 1989). Some factors may be relatively enduring and others transient. Some factors may play important roles in instigating maltreatment, while others may help sustain patterns of abuse and neglect. A factor may be protective in some combinations or increase the potential for abuse (potentiating) in others. It is the combination of risk potentiating and protective factors in all levels of the system that determine the likelihood of maltreatment, rather than a single factor serving as a causal influence in isolation from the others (Cicchetti and Carlson, 1989). In reviewing potentiating and contributing factors, researchers often focus on risk factors that appear to be malleable, that is, that can be changed as a result of a treatment or preventive interventions.

This perspective suggests that maltreatment results from complex constellations of correlated variables whose influence may increase or decrease during different developmental and historical periods. The combined effects of multiple variables provide diverse possible pathways to maltreatment. Furthermore, interactive models recognize that risk and protective factors are not static, but change over time as individuals, their life circumstances, and the society in which they live change. The interactive models, although relatively new, show promise and suggest issues that need to be addressed in research on the etiology of child maltreatment. However, the complexity of analysis associated with interactive models and the difficulties of distinguishing causal effects from observational data have inhibited their testing and application.

The panel has selected a developmental/ecological/transactional model of the etiology of child maltreatment as the basis for reviewing the key literature relevant to this chapter (Belsky, 1980; Cicchetti and Lynch, in press; Garbarino, 1977). As summarized in Figure 4.1, this model was selected for its breadth and advantages in organizing the large and often conflicting literature on the etiology of child maltreatment. Although the selected model identifies promising strategies or questions that should be addressed in future research, it is not intended to exclude others in research on child maltreatment.

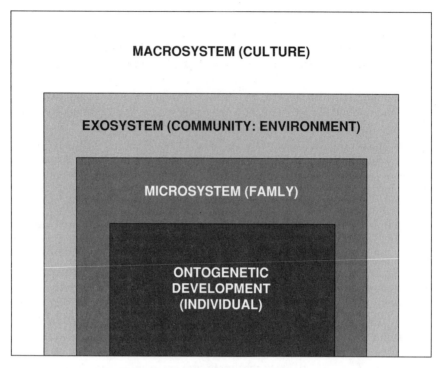

FIGURE 4.1   Diagram of Belsky's (1980) ecologically integrative model of child abuse. SOURCE: Hamilton, Stiles, Melowsky, and Beal (1987).

The selected model views maltreatment within a system of risk and protective factors interacting across four levels: (1) the individual or ontogenic level, (2) the family microsystem, (3) the exosystem, and (4) the social macrosystem. The ontogenic level involves individual characteristics and the changing developmental status of family members. The family microsystem includes the family environment, parenting styles, and interactions among family members. The exosystem consists of the community in which the family lives, the workplace of the parents, school and peer groups of the family members, formal and informal social supports and services available to the family, and other factors such as family income, employment, and job availability. Finally, the social macrosystem consists of the overarching values and beliefs of the culture.

The ecological/developmental framework indicated in Figure 4.1 begins with an analysis of individual factors at the individual level and proceeds through the other ecological levels. This approach follows the conception of human development as being nested within a set of transacting ecological systems. This conceptual framework is presented by the panel to highlight emerging research priorities in the field of child maltreatment.

INDIVIDUAL ONTOGENIC FACTORS

The influence of ontogenic factors such as adult[4] and child characteristics in contributing to child maltreatment is often moderated by interactions with other factors. Attempts to identify adult or child characteristics related to maltreatment have produced an inconsistent and contradictory research literature. Consequently, the effects of individual factors need to be studied in conjunction with other factors and not studied in isolation.

Adult Personality Characteristics

Early studies of the etiology of child maltreatment assumed that a distinct psychiatric syndrome or disorder would be found to characterize parents or other caretakers (such as stepparents, grandparents, and foster parents) who maltreat children under their supervision and care. Although a small percentage of parents involved in child maltreatment could be diagnosed with a psychotic disorder, most individuals were identified as troubled or anxious persons who rarely exhibited extreme psychopathology (Steele and Pollock, 1968). A consistent profile of parental psychopathology or a significant level of mental disturbance has not been supported (e.g., Melnick and Hurley, 1969; Polansky et al., 1981, 1992; Spinetta and Rigler, 1972). However, certain types of psychiatric disorders can be important factors in determining outcomes for the maltreated child—children reported as maltreated are less likely to remain with their biological family if evidence of a parental psychiatric disorder is obtained (Runyan et al., 1981; Widom, 1991).

Physical Abuse

Early psychiatric studies stimulated a search for parental characteristics and a personality profile of abusing parents (Milner and Chilamkurti, 1991).[5] Recent prospective studies (e.g., Pianta et al., 1989) have identified a set of parental personality attributes associated with child maltreatment that have emerged with sufficient frequency to warrant attention. These attributes are low self-esteem, external locus of control, poor impulse control, negative affectivity (including depression and anxiety), and antisocial behavior (including aggression and substance abuse) (for reviews, see Baumrind, 1992; Belsky, 1992; Cicchetti and Lynch, in press). Central in these attributes is a triad of highly correlated personality characteristics, involving depression, anxiety, and antisocial behavior.

Depression, anxiety, and antisocial behavior are associated with disrupted social relations, social isolation, unavailability or lack of utilization of social supports, and an inability to cope with stress (Crittenden, 1985; Wolfe, 1985). Disruptions in social relations are also found in studies of maltreating parents who are described as insular, alienated, unhappy and dissatisfied in relationships with friends, neighbors, spouses, and children. This pervasive discontent and lack of skill in social relations can be exacerbated by additional stressors (Belsky, 1980; Cicchetti and Lynch, in press; Garbarino, 1977). Furthermore, these attributes and attitudes are likely to increase the probability of encountering stressful life experiences and inhibit the development of supportive relationships with a spouse, friends, and family that could help buffer the affected individual from the effects of stress.

Neglect

Polansky et al. (1981) have proposed that parental characteristics help explain the origins of neglect, particularly chronic neglect. Early studies of neglectful families have suggested that child neglect is only one expression of pervasive and deeply rooted inadequacies in the life of a parent that sometimes appear early in adolescence. This condition has been termed as a character disorder of neglectful parents, usually expressed as the "apathy-futility syndrome" and the "impulse-ridden character" (Polansky et al., 1972, 1981, 1992). Although neglectful parents appear to be less depressed, anxious, angry, and confused than physically abusive parents (Pianta et al., 1989), such parents have been termed *childlike* or *infantile*, revealing an absence of self-esteem and an inability to plan important life choices such as marriage, having children, or getting a job. Impulse-ridden behaviors can result from early deprivations in the parent's own life, usually involving the absence of mature adults with whom the child may identify.

Sexual Abuse

The literature on adult personality characteristics associated with child sexual abuse is more extensive than that of other forms of child maltreatment, since the primary etiology of child sexual abuse has been sought in the profile of the adult offender in contrast to other forms of child maltreatment, which often focus on parent-child interactions. Although no specific syndrome or diagnostic category has been associated with child sexual abuse, personality characteristics frequently found in child molesters have contributed to various etiological theories of pedophilia (DSM-III-R, 1987). Some child molesters are reported to be timid, unassertive and awkward; others exhibit conduct disorder and poor impulse control; others are successful community leaders who have achieved professional respect. Empirical evidence clarifying the role of psychological and psychosexual development and maturity levels of child molesters is needed (Araji and Finkelhor, 1986).

Psychiatric profiles used to classify sex offenders frequently report the presence of an antisocial personality disorder among child molesters, but sex offenders have a heterogeneous range of psychopathology and personality disorders and an accepted system for sexual offender classification and the contribution of perpetrator characteristics has not been established[6] (Conte, 1984; Hartman and Burgess, 1989; Lanning, 1992; Prentky, 1990).

Currently, Faller has suggested an incest-assault continuum, noting that, although contributing factors from the cultural, environmental, individual, and family context will vary from case to case, sexual abuse requires "an adult who has sexual desires toward children and the willingness to act upon them" (Faller, 1988:115). Efforts to classify pedophiles and incest offenders have also focused on the style of abuse, drawing on information obtained from offender self-reports, criminal investigative reports, and victim reports (Hartman and Burgess, 1989). A series of research studies have sought to highlight critical factors in the style of sexual abuse, such as the degree of violence (Finkelhor, 1984; Wyatt and Newcomb, 1990), the relationships among sexual stimuli and violence stimuli and their respective arousal components (Hartman and Burgess, 1989); the offender-victim relationship (Panton, 1978; Wyatt and Newcombe, 1990), the victim's and offender's age (Armentrout and Hauer, 1978); and the offender's level of education and mediators to negative outcomes (Knight, 1985; Wyatt and Newcombe, 1990).

Although the large majority of adult offenders in reported child sexual abuse cases are male, the increasing number of reports of female offenders suggests an unexplored pathway in examining the dynamics and origins of child sexual abuse (Finkelhor, 1987). Although women have been reported in a smaller number of cases (Finkelhor, 1987), concerns about detection bias, general research inattention to women, and the significance of maternal-child relations suggest that the role of female sexual offenders has been underestimated in research on child sexual abuse. Clinical studies of child victims of sexual abuse as well as adult offenders (based on retrospective studies) indicate that behavioral and perceptual disorders resulting from childhood sexual victimization may contribute to subsequent assault behavior (Becker, 1988; Hartman and Burgess, 1989).

One promising area of research inquiry has examined outcomes—such as power, control, sadistic pleasure, or displaced anger—that offenders seek to achieve in the sexual victimization of a child (Knight et al., 1985). Finkelhor (1987) has proposed four major theories, often presented as competing explanations, to explain child sexual abuse:

- Abusers obtain powerful, developmentally induced emotional gratification from the acts;
- Abusers have deviant physiological sexual arousal patterns;
- Abusers are blocked by arrested psychosexual development and emotional immaturity in their capacity to meet their sexual needs in more conventional ways; and
- Abusers have problems in their capacity for behavioral inhibition (Finkelhor, 1987).

The search for a biological basis for child sexual abuse has also not been successful. Although mental retardation or physiological abnormalities sometimes provoke arousal and disinhibition in sexual abusers, such abnormalities have not been substantiated as a major cause of sexual abuse (Araji and Finkelhor, 1986; Kelly and Lusk, 1992; Langevin, 1983). Hormone levels and chromosomal makeup have been studied extensively, but definitive evidence of these factors accounting for specific sexual interest toward children has not emerged (Goy and McEwen, 1977; Kelly and Lusk, 1992). The disinhibiting contribution of alcohol and alcoholism is the most frequent and well-established biologic agent often associated with sexual abuse, ranging from 19 to 70 percent of reported cases (Aarens et al., 1978; Finkelhor, 1987; Morgan, 1982). Other potent psychoactive agents, such as opiates (including heroin), amphetamines, and cocaine, may be additional pharmacological contributors to abuse.

However, the nature of the relationship of substance use and abuse, different types of substance abuse situations, and the use of violence against children is not well understood. Empirical studies have been biased by a reliance on reported incidents of drunkenness or drug use rather than studying the emerging relationship between such phenomena and child maltreatment as they occur (Pernanen, 1991). Cultural acceptance of the disinhibiting effects of alcohol (MacAndrew and Edgerton, 1969) or drugs has been proposed as one theory that provides an explanation for the breach of social norms and standards involved in child sexual abuse, but theoretical work in this area is in a very early stage of development.

Emotional Maltreatment

The etiology of emotional abuse and neglect is less developed than that of the other three forms of maltreatment discussed above. However, emotional maltreatment appears to be more prevalent, and some investigators believe that its consequences are more destructive than other forms of child abuse and neglect (Garbarino and Vondra, 1987; Hart and Brassard, 1987; Hart et al., 1987). The relationship between the etiology of emotional maltreatment and other forms of child abuse and neglect is currently not known.

Summary

Although we have limited knowledge about processes that link adult and child characteristics and child maltreatment, a considerable research literature on child maltreatment, stress and coping, developmental psychopathology, and normal child development indicates that parental personality characteristics influence child development primarily through the interactive process of parenting. Disrupted parenting can occur in a variety of ways, especially when a parent's personality attributes (such as anger, anxiety, etc.) are compounded by additional stressors such as marital conflict, poverty, unemployment, and having a difficult child (Conger et al., 1984; Hetherington, 1991; Patterson et al., 1992). It is vital, therefore, that scientists examine individual or psychological factors in combination with each other to develop a more comprehensive understanding of their contributions to child maltreatment.

Adult Attitudes, Attributions, and Cognition

Cognitive factors in adults who maltreat children, including negative attitudes and attributions about their children's behavior and inaccurate knowledge and expectations about child development, also play a contributing role in child maltreatment, especially neglect (Holden et al., 1992; Zuravin, 1987). Attitudes held before the birth of the child, such as negative maternal attitude toward an unwanted or unplanned pregnancy, have also been associated with later maltreatment (Altmeier et al., 1982; Brunquell et al., 1981; Egeland and Brunquell, 1979; Murphy et al., 1985; Zuravin, 1987).

Abusive parents may have incomplete or distorted knowledge and understanding of normal child development or their own children's behaviors. The tendency of physical abusers to impart negative attributes to others, including their own children and interpersonal relationships, is associated both with differences in abusive parents' expectations and attributions about children's behavior and with psychophysiological hyperresponsiveness to stimuli. In comparison to nonabusive parents, abusive parents show greater physiological reactivity as well as irritation and annoyance in response to children's positive and negative affective states and behavior (Casanova et al., 1992).

For example, abusive parents, in comparison with nonabusive parents, sometimes perceive their children as more aggressive and intentionally disobedient, annoying, and less intelligent, although other observers fail to detect such differences in the children's behavior (Mash et al., 1983; Reid et al., 1987). In addition, physically abusive mothers perceive their children's negative behavior as a result of stable internal factors such as a personality trait, but their positive behaviors as a result of unstable external factors. The reverse is true for nonabusive mothers (Larrance and Twentyman, 1983).

Research has been contradictory on abusive parents' knowledge of normal child development as a contributing factor to maltreatment. While some studies have pointed to abusive parents' limited understanding of child development (Disbrow et al., 1977; Spinetta and Rigler, 1972), others have found no significant differences from nonabusive parents (Starr, 1982). Starr (1992) suggests that, even if abusive parents have adequate child development knowledge, they may not apply such knowledge to their childrearing practices.

The absence of studies on how transactions between fathers' and children's characteristics and life circumstances promote or buffer children from the risk of maltreatment is a major gap in the research literature. With the exception of studies of sexual abuse, researchers generally exclude analysis of fathers' attributes or roles within the family or rely on maternal reports of such information, which is a major methodological limitation (Holden et al., 1992). This exclusion results from the difficulties of recruiting fathers into child maltreatment studies.

Intergenerational Transmission of Abusive Parenting

The notion that abused children become abusing parents has received significant attention and has been one of the most pervasive and popular themes in the literature over the past several decades (Cicchetti and Aber, 1980; Kaufman and Zigler, 1987; Kempe and Kempe, 1978; Steele and Pollack, 1968; Widom, 1989).

Two clinicians at the forefront of child maltreatment research in the 1970s observed that "the most constant fact (concerning child abusers) is that parents themselves were nearly always abused or battered or neglected as children" (Fontana, 1973:74, quoted in Belsky, 1992) and that "we see an unbroken line in the repetition of parental abuse from childhood into the adult years" (Steele, 1976:15, quoted in Belsky, 1992).[7]

The intergenerational hypothesis is controversial because it is supported largely by retrospective analyses. Retrospective studies suggest that the rate of intergenerational transmission is high and that the vast majority of abusing parents were abused as children. For example, Steele and Pollack (1968), in a study evaluating clinical data, found that *all* 60 abusing parents had been abused during childhood. Retrospective studies indicate a range between 7 percent (Gil, 1970) and 70 percent (Egeland and Jacobvitz, 1984) in the intergenerational transmission of child maltreatment. Kaufman and Zigler's (1987) partial review of the literature estimated a 30 percent rate (plus or minus 5 percent) of intergenerational transmission.

However, retrospective studies of intergenerational transmission are limited by methodological difficulties of definition, design, and reliance on reports of offenders already labeled as maltreaters (Belsky, 1992).[8] Inherent limitations of the retrospective approach include the impossibility of determining the proportions of adults who were maltreated as children who have provided adequate care for their children. In addition, the studies do not indicate the extent to which past and current concepts of abuse are in agreement. It is also difficult to assess whether abusive parents may provide distorted reports of their childhood. These factors may lead to an overestimate of the rate of intergenerational transmission.

Other theoretical paradigms (e.g., attachment, social learning) have been generally overlooked in the discussions of the intergenerational hypothesis, with some exceptions (Zeanah and Zeanah, 1989). Such theoretical explanations deserve closer examination in linking types of maltreatment in childhood and the multiple possible pathways to abusive parenting.

The methodological and measurement problems of retrospective studies emphasize the importance of testing the intergenerational hypothesis with longitudinal prospective studies that examine the ongoing caretaking practices of samples of adults who were abused as children (Cicchetti and Aber, 1980; Aber and Cicchetti, 1984). A few prospective studies document a linkage between a reported history of childhood maltreatment and the perpetration of maltreatment but prospective studies generally have significantly smaller rates of transmission associated with the intergenerational hypothesis (Hunter et al., 1978; Egeland et al., 1987). Hunter and Kilstrom's (1979) one-year prospective study of premature infants yielded an intergenerational transmission rate of 18 percent when examined from a prospective vantage point, in contrast to a transmission rate of 90 percent when the same data were examined from a retrospective position.[9] Since some studies have shown that "antisocial behavior patterns are passed from one generation to the next at a rate well beyond chance," particularly when controls for confounding factors such as family size, area of residence, or rates of criminal behavior have been established, the relationship between antisocial behavior and child maltreatment deserves further exploration in intergenerational studies (Huesmann et al., 1984; Wahler and Dumas, 1986:50, quoted in Belsky, 1992).

Several investigators have tentatively identified protective factors that break the cycle of abuse (Egeland, 1988; Egeland et al., 1988; Hunter and Kilstrom, 1979). In retrospective studies, parents with reported histories of childhood maltreatment who do not maltreat their own children are more likely than those who perpetuate the intergenerational cycle to have: (a) better current social support, including a supportive spouse; (b) a positive relationship with a significant adult in childhood or the experience of therapy as an adolescent or an adult; (c) an ability to provide a clear account of their childhood trauma with anger and responsibility for that abuse directed toward the perpetrator and not themselves.[10]

In studying why some individuals do or do not perpetuate a cycle of violence, all possible outcomes need to be examined: (1) the maltreated child who maltreats his or her own children; (2) the maltreated child who does not maltreat his or her own children; (3) the nonmaltreated child who maltreats his or her own children; and (4) the nonmaltreated child who does not maltreat his or her own children. Examining the processes and mechanisms of continuity in the first and fourth cells, and of discontinuity in the second and third cells, are important research priorities.

Prospective research on the intergenerational transmission of abuse has not adequately considered the interaction of parental characteristics and children's age and developmental stage (Hunter and Kilstrom, 1979). The one-year duration of the Hunter and Kilstrom prospective study, for example, encompasses only parents who display difficulties in the parenting of infants. Since child maltreatment is not limited to onset in infancy, additional abuse or neglect may be identified at later stages, such as toddlerhood or adolescence (Belsky, 1992).

Research has not demonstrated the transmission of specific types of abuse. For example, mothers who were physically abused as children increase the risk of both physical and sexual abuse for their children (Goodwin et al., 1981). The current studies emphasize the importance of examining factors related to breaking the cycle of abuse in the context of prospective investigations.

Alcohol and Drugs

The often noted association between substance use or abuse and aggression has suggested that the use of alcohol and drugs may be a significant risk factor in abusive families, but the associations among alcoholism, drug use, and child maltreatment are not well understood (for reviews see Hamilton and Collins, 1982; Orme and Rimmer, 1981; Widom, 1992). In particular, the severity and chronicity of intoxication and substance abuse remains poorly documented in studies of child maltreatment (Widom, 1992). Studies of alcoholism among maltreating parents have consistent methodological problems resulting from sample selection and research design.

Hamilton and Collins (1982) concluded that the results were contradictory, with some studies finding a significant relationship and others not (Widom, 1992). A second review published about the same time also found "no empirical data to support an association between alcoholism and child abuse" (Orme and Rimmer, 1981: 273).

More recent studies are based on improved methodologies, but their results are also contradictory. Estimates of the extent of alcoholism among maltreating parents range from 18 to 38 percent compared with estimates of 6 to 16 percent in the general population (Harford and Parker, 1985; Robins et al., 1984; Widom, 1992). Reports of parental alcohol use by abused psychiatric patients ranged from 30 to 51 percent (Widom, 1992). Only one study has offered strong evidence of a connection between child abuse and alcohol use (Famularo et al., 1986), but authors of this report have noted that limitations in their study design may have affected the incidence of reported alcoholism in their groups (Widom, 1992). One prospective study that compared matched groups of sons of alcoholic and nonalcoholic fathers found no significant differences in the extent of childhood physical abuse (Pollock et al., 1990; Widom, 1992).

Although alcohol often is cited as a principal risk factor in the etiology of child maltreatment, its relationship to child abuse and neglect remains uncertain (Widom, 1992). More needs to be known about the unique and immediate effects of alcohol, its co-occurrence with other problem behaviors such as antisocial personality disorder and substance abuse, the circumstances under which different types of drinking situations lead to or sustain violence against children, and cultural factors that mitigate or exacerbate connections between substance use or abuse and aggression (Abram, 1990; Fagan, 1990; Pernanen, 1991; Robins and Regier, 1991).

The use of drugs during pregnancy, especially cocaine, and their effects on fetal development and the care of infants, has prompted some researchers to examine the relationships among substance use, abuse, and child maltreatment. Such studies are often complicated, however, by the presence of other social and economic variables, such as poverty, that confound the analysis of the contributing role of drugs themselves. At this time the scientific literature on substance abuse and child maltreatment is not well enough developed to allow for inferences by the panel.

Biology and Child Maltreatment

There is no direct evidence that biological factors contribute to child maltreatment, and social and biological scientists tend to agree that the most important influences on aggressive behavior are experiential or environmental. However, efforts to understand biological aspects of aggression, and the role of experience and environment in enhancing or modifying these factors, may contribute to the identification of specific variables and interactive processes that affect the maltreatment of children.

Several studies have examined aspects of child maltreatment and aggression involving both human subjects and animal analogues—most important, perhaps, rhesus monkeys and other species of monkeys and apes that resemble human behavior in the development of mother-infant and other social relationships (Suomi, 1978). Biological studies have generally focused on physiological consequences and reactive mechanisms by which childhood victimization can lead to dysfunctional behavior (Lewis, 1992), a topic that is discussed in Chapter 6. Some studies, however, have focused on examples of primate behavior in both field and laboratory environments that demonstrate cases of infant neglect and abuse. Other studies have examined the role of hormones, neurotransmitters, noxious substances (e.g., drugs, alcohol), diet, and abnormalities of brain functions in aggression research in both human and animal models.

Primate studies by Suomi and colleagues suggest that, although some species of monkeys and apes have a capacity to neglect or abuse their young, a valid and useful primate model of human child abuse has not been identified (Suomi, 1978; Suomi and Ripp, 1983). The most extensive data on infant maltreatment by nonhuman primates comes from laboratory settings (Suomi, 1978). The incidence of infant neglect or abuse by biological primate parents in feral environments is relatively rare (Hrdy, 1976).

Stress and social isolation, in particular, show negative effects on primate maternal-child interactions, particularly if stress or isolation occurs during critical periods of development such as the mother's own infancy or birth of her offspring (Suomi, 1978). Rearing experiences may be associated with changes in central nervous system neurotransmitter activity, affecting norepinephrine and serotonin monamine systems (Higley and Suomi, 1989). Primates reared in isolation from their own mothers and peers exhibited inadequate care as well as excessive and inappropriately directed aggression toward their own offspring, especially their first born and male offspring (Suomi, 1978). However, mothers reared in isolation who were given limited exposure (even a minimum of two weeks) to stable social groups during their pregnancy and postnatal period improved their care for subsequent infants, suggesting that socialization can improve the quality of parental care (Suomi, 1978).

The absence of a valid animal model for studies of child maltreatment may be an important barrier to research interventions that would be ethically unacceptable for human subjects. Some causal factors suggested but not proven by the monkey data could be explored in further research, such as the relationship between elevated levels of testosterone in the mother and the increased risk of abuse for male offspring (Suomi, 1978). The contribution of the infant's behavior to its treatment by an inadequate or abusive mother could also be tested experimentally by studies of nonhuman primates through the use of stimulants or depressants. Suomi has noted (1978), however, that the rarity of infant abuse among primates in their natural environments, and the sharply decreasing availability of animal research subjects, suggest that extended experimental studies of infant abuse involving nonhuman primates will not occur unless justified by researchers who believe that the animal data present important insights into human phenomena.

Beyond the studies of infant maltreatment, the results of aggression research involving both human and animal models are contradictory and inconsistent. No known biological factor in and of itself causes aggression. A changing reciprocity between biological and environmental factors appears to determine whether or not an individual will behave aggressively. As a result, an aggressive temperament may be the reflection of a passing physiological state induced and reinforced by environmental stressors.

Studies of both humans and animals indicate that aggressive behaviors engendered by environmental conditions are often mediated at least in part by physiology. Different parts of the brain continuously interact with each other, and violent or abusive behaviors represent a combination of stimulation and suppression of particular brain areas, past experience and learning, and immediate environmental stimuli or stressors.

Results of studies regarding the relationship between testosterone levels and aggression in humans are equivocal (Ehrenkraz et al., 1974; Kreuz and Rose, 1972; Meyer-Bahlberg, 1974; Monti et al., 1977; Rada et al., 1976). The relationship of endocrine status to behavior is extremely complex and poorly understood, in part because the effects of hormones and their interactions differ from species to species and extrapolations from animal studies are controversial.[11] Neurotransmitters, especially norepinephrine, dopamine, and serotonin are involved in both the genesis and suppression of aggressive behaviors.

Clinical data and data from experimentation with animals have shown that aggressive behaviors can be elicited or suppressed, depending on which parts of the brain (the hypothalamus, the amygdala, or the orbital prefrontal cortex) are stimulated or ablated (Bard, 1928; Floody and Pfaff, 1972; MacLean, 1985; Weiger and Bear, 1988). Acetylcholine has been shown to be an important neurotransmitter in the hypothalamus (Bandler, 1970; Bear et al., 1986; Smith et al., 1970).

None of the neuroanatomical or physiological factors considered above, in and of themselves, results in violence or abusiveness. Studies of young offenders (Lewis et al., 1980, 1988, 1989) and follow-up studies of delinquents (Lewis et al., 1989), however, suggest that, when neuropsychiatric vulnerabilities to irritability, oversuspiciousness, impulsivity, and extreme emotionality exist, then parental maltreatment may be a potent catalyst for the child's aggressive behavior.

Children whose ability to function is compromised by virtue of brain dysfunction, brain damage, or psychiatric illness may have difficulty in controlling impulses, distinguishing fantasy from reality, and modulating behavior in response to abusive treatment. Extrapolating from research on animals, maltreatment may modify the physiology of the child, diminish concentrations in the brain of substances such as serotonin that ordinarily help to modulate feelings, and increase substances such as dopamine and testosterone that enhance hypervigilance and retaliatory aggression in animals.

For these reasons the neurophysiological consequences of maltreatment deserve further study. Furthermore, the biological factors that affect parenting behaviors, especially in primates and other animals closely related to humans, deserve further study.

Evolutionary theory in the form of sociobiology has been applied to studies of child maltreatment (Belsky, 1992; Burgess and Draper, 1989; Daly and Wilson, 1983). Sociobiology holds that parental behavior is influenced by genetic factors and strategies of investment or disinvestment in offspring to enhance the chances of survival of the species (Hrdy, 1976). According to this theory, conditions that amplify biological conflicts of interest between parent and child contribute to child maltreatment; conditions that reduce such conflict prevent its occurrence (Belsky, 1992:47). Although primate studies have documented reproductive and parenting strategies that enhance survival of the species (Hrdy, 1976), the evidence for human behavior is less compelling because the contributions of culture and biology are extremely difficult to disentangle.

Demographic Factors

Although research on characteristics of maltreating parents has focused on their personality and cognitive features, the risk of maltreatment varies by demographic factors as well. Demographic variables are often of less interest to researchers because evidence of their significance in the etiology of child maltreatment is conflicting, their contribution to child maltreatment can be understood only by analyzing the interaction of individual characteristics and circumstances with other factors, and they cannot be manipulated through treatment or other intervention programs. As a result, demographic variables often acquire importance only in sociological models that require fundamental social reforms (such as reducing the incidence of teen pregnancy) as a basis for intervention.

Reports of specific demographic factors associated with child maltreatment are derived primarily from clinical research, which is subject to reporting and labelling bias. Such reports are inconsistent. For example, some studies associated young maternal age with maltreatment (Benedict et al., 1985; Creighton, 1985; Egeland and Brunquell, 1979; Leventhal, 1981; Leventhal et al., 1993; Whipple and Webster-Stratton, 1991; Zuravin, 1988). Others find no such relationship or suggest that maternal age is confounded by social class (Altmeier et al., 1982; Earp and Ory, 1980; Hunter et al., 1978; Kinard and Klerman, 1980; Leventhal et al., 1993; Murphy et al.,

1985; Oates, 1986). However, when age is operationalized as mother's age at time of abuse there is no relationship, but when age is operationalized as mother's age at time of birth of the abused child, then younger mothers appear to have higher rates of physical abuse (Kinard and Klerman, 1980; Connelley and Straus, 1992). This example illustrates how seemingly small differences in conceptualization and operationalization of etiologic variables can account for discrepancies in the literature.

Abusive and neglectful parents are more likely to be single (Caplan et al., 1984; Holden et al., 1992; Zuravin, 1988), to have a large number of closely spaced children (Belsky, 1992; Holden et al., 1992), and to have a larger family size (Belsky, 1992; Creighton, 1985; Polansky, 1981). They have also been reported to be less educated, but not less intelligent, than nonmaltreating parents (Dubowitz, 1987; Egeland and Brunquell, 1979; Starr, 1982). As discussed below, they are more likely than nonabusive parents to be poor and unemployed (Holden et al., 1992).

Child Characteristics

Attention to child characteristics associated with maltreatment was stimulated by the recognition that some abused children were abused again in foster homes. Since the prevailing etiological model was a parental pathology model, the abuse of children in foster care directed attention toward characteristics of the child that might provoke anger from both adults at risk of abuse and previously nonabusive adults.

Research on child risk factors associated with maltreatment have included prematurity, temperament, age, and gender. Retrospective research has suggested that factors such as prematurity, low birthweight, and illness or handicapping conditions in the infant or child interfere with attachment and bonding, making the child more vulnerable to maltreatment (Lynch and Roberts, 1977; Oates et al., 1979). Others have found this not to be true and suggest that such findings are more likely due to methodological flaws in study design (Leventhal, 1981).

The identification of child risk factors associated with abuse sometimes generates controversy as to whether child behaviors and characteristics contribute to or are consequences of maltreatment. A focus on the abused child has been thought to be a victim-blaming strategy. Researchers have sought to distinguish between child characteristics that may be causal and those that maintain or perpetuate maltreatment (Ammerman, 1991; Drotar, 1992). In general, little is known about the processes and interactions through which child characteristics and behaviors become risk factors, either as contributing to or maintaining abusive situations.

Child factors are viewed as ones that increase the potential for abuse only if other causal or predictive factors are present—such as parental factors and societal/environmental factors—in a transactional model (Starr, 1992). Both prospective studies (e.g., Egeland, 1988; Hunter et al., 1978) and retrospective studies (e.g., Leventhal et al., 1981) indicate that when researchers control for parental and societal variables (such as social isolation, poverty, substance abuse, or socioeconomic status), child variables such as prematurity and low birthweight do not appear to be major risk factors for child maltreatment, even though such factors have been linked with abuse in some studies involving retrospective designs (e.g., Hunter et al., 1978; Lynch and Roberts, 1977; Oates et al., 1979).

Mothers of low-birthweight infants usually have higher anxiety and depression, negative parenting styles, and less positive interactions with their infants than full-birthweight infants (Beckwith and Cohen, 1984; Brooten et al., 1988; Shosenberg, 1980). Low-birthweight infants are often less soothable, are less responsive, are often perceived as less attractive, and often demand a great deal of care (DiVitto and Goldberg, 1979; Klein and Stern, 1971; Meisels and Plunkett, 1988; Parmelee, 1975). Maternal anxiety and distress, high caretaking demands, and difficulty in soothing low-birthweight infants may account for some abusive treatment (Maccoby and Martin, 1983; Parke and Collmer, 1975). However, since low birthweight is often associated with poverty and low parental education, it may simply represent confounded effects of the cycle of inadequate parenting rather than an independent causal effect.

Infants with difficult temperaments are characterized by high levels of irritability and negative mood, fearfulness, rapid arousal but difficulty in soothing, lack of rhythm in sleep and feeding patterns, and lack of adaptability. In view of these characteristics, it is not surprising that mothers with temperamentally "difficult" children are likely to report more childrearing stress. When mothers of difficult infants experience multiple life stressors and few social supports, both parenting and the bonds of attachment are likely to be disrupted (Goldberg, 1983). What is surprising is that research has not demonstrated that either nurses' or mothers' ratings of infant temperament are associated with maltreatment of infants (Egeland, 1988).

Older children with difficult temperaments, especially boys, are more likely than easy children to be the target of mothers' coercive punitive discipline (Rutter, 1987), especially when the mother is depressed or antisocial, stressed, and has few available supports (Hetherington, 1989, 1991).[12]

Studies that consider developmental status often focus on the outcomes of abuse at various ages rather than developmental level as a cause of child abuse. However, some parents may be better able to deal with the dependency of an infant than with the combativeness of a toddler or adolescent. Children under age 3, perhaps because of their physical vulnerability, are the most likely to suffer from fatal child abuse (Belsky, 1992). Straus and colleagues (1986) found that toddlers and adolescents were subjected to the most serious acts of violence and postulated a connection with increased oppositionality in both of these age groups. It is unclear whether there is an onset of abuse at adolescence or whether it represents an ongoing pattern of violence (Farber and Joseph, 1985). More attention needs to be directed to age and gender, and their combination, in increasing or decreasing the vulnerability of children to maltreatment.

Child characteristics may play only a minor role in the initiation of child maltreatment, but they may be important in the maintenance or persistence of abusive relationships or the escalation of at-risk relationships (Ammerman, 1991; Wolfe, 1985). Child characteristics also may be important in reabuse or revictimization. Sexually abused children may develop or learn sexualized behaviors that put them at risk of continued abuse by the original and/or other perpetrators (Frederich, 1988). Similarly, they may engage in sexual intercourse at earlier ages and, if abused by a family member, be poor contraceptors and be more likely to engage in unprotected, high-risk sexual behaviors (Wyatt et al., in press). Toddlers who have been physically abused exhibit aggressive, provocative, and approach-avoidant behaviors with teachers and peers (George and Main, 1979; Main, 1983), characteristics associated with provoking irritability, rejection, aggression, and abuse in others. Indeed, abused children may have learned distorted interaction patterns so well that they evoke similar interactions from both their parents and other social contacts such as teachers (Sroufe, 1983; Dodge et al., 1990).

Factors that trigger child neglect also should be separated from factors that maintain this behavior, especially in the development of infants. In early periods of neglectful behavior, the child may exhibit stressful behaviors in the forms of feeding problems, irritability, or deficits in social responsiveness that place increased demands on the parent's caretaking duties (Powell and Low, 1983; Powell et al., 1987). In some cases, nutritional deprivation, combined with increased maternal detachment, results in nonorganic failure to thrive and sets into motion a "vicious cycle of cumulative psychological risk" (Drotar, 1992:121). Eventually, the parent may begin to perceive the child as quiet, sickly, or not very competent, perceptions that may not be shared by others who observe the child (Ayoub and Milner, 1985; Kotelchuck, 1982).

Child characteristics may be contributing factors rather than independent causes for abuse or neglect. Certain child characteristics, such as low birth weight, prematurity, or non-organic failure to thrive, represent targets for intervention if they are found to be associated with increased maltreatment after the effects of confounding variables have been controlled. However, other factors associated with parental behavior or parent-child interactions appear much more promising sites for intervention at this time.

THE FAMILY MICROSYSTEM

Building on this review of ontogenic factors within the child, the parent, and the extra-familial offender, we now move to an analysis of significant factors in the family functioning of maltreating families.

Family Functioning in Maltreating Families

Disruptions in all aspects of family relations, not just parent-child interactions, are often present in the families of maltreated children, although it is not clear if such disruptions contribute to or are consequences of child maltreatment. Anger and conflict are pervasive features of maltreating families, although conflict may be more characteristic of abusive families and social isolation may be more associated with neglectful families (Crittenden, 1985). Husbands and wives in maltreating families are less warm and supportive, less satisfied in their conjugal relationships, and more aggressive and violent than those in nonabusive families (Fagan and Browne, 1990; Rosenbaum and O'Leary, 1981; Rosenberg, 1987; Straus, 1980).[13] Furthermore, sibling relationships are more conflicted and less supportive in families characterized by high marital conflict or coercive punitive parenting, and tolerance of sibling violence sets the stage for later family violence (Hetherington, 1991; Hetherington and Clingempeel, 1992; Patterson et al., 1992; Straus, 1980). In many cases of maltreatment, there often is not a single maltreated child, but multiple victims (Faller, 1988). Thus, maltreated children may be exposed to considerable violence involving other family members as well as violence directed toward them (Rosenberg, 1987).

In addition, violence and maltreatment are often not confined to the boundaries of the family. Parents with violent, antisocial, or criminal records or those who are aggressive outside the family are more likely to be aggressive in family relations (Patterson, 1982). Similarly, many incestuous offenders do not limit their activities to children within the family. One study indicated that 49 percent of incestuous fathers and stepfathers abuse children outside the family at the same time they are abusing their own children (Abel et al., 1988). The deviant behavior exhibited toward children by maltreating parents is often part of a network of disrupted relationships within the family and in extrafamilial relationships.

Single-parent, particularly female-headed, families are inextricably linked with poverty (Coulton et al.. n.d., 1990a,b), and the contribution of family structure to abuse and neglect is difficult to disentangle from conditions of poverty. Poor, young, single mothers with young children are at the greatest risk of reporting that they use violent behaviors toward their children (Gelles, 1992).

Family structure has been implicated in child sexual abuse in that step-fathers are more likely perpetrators than are biological fathers, and children who have had a stepfather are at greater risk of abuse. The potential for role confusion in reconstituted families and the greater exposure of children to unrelated men as the mother seeks a new relationship have been postulated as contributing to this increased risk (Faller, 1990; Finkelhor et al., 1986; Russel, 1986).

A distinctive feature associated with chronically neglecting families is the chaotic and unpredictable character of the family system.[14] One recent examination of the family dynamics and structures of neglectful families concluded that the changeable membership of a neglectful household pre-sents unique challenges for the application of basic principles of family therapy to child neglect (Polansky et al., 1992). Rather than the two-parent family living in a stable location with two or three small children, the neglectful household is often characterized by a shifting constellation of adult and child figures, representing at times desperate efforts by the parent to keep the family together during times of economic and other social crisis. During periods of change, the household of the neglectful mother and her children becomes increasingly fragile, isolated, and detached from adult figures in the neighborhood, church, or other community structures that could offer assistance and support during times of unusual stress or depriva-tion. The family also may eventually be rejected by relatives and friends, who may show increasing disapproval of the mother's or children's behav-iors, especially if substance abuse, delinquency, or other forms of addiction or dysfunctional behaviors are present. The effect on children of repeated fluctuations in the makeup of their household, in addition to child neglect, has not been examined in the research literature, although such changes are suspected to contribute to unrelatedness and detachment (Polansky et al., 1992).

Family relationships that affect the quality of parent-child interactions have also been considered in developing the context for understanding child sexual abuse (Finkelhor, 1984; Hartman and Burgess, 1989). Such factors include an estranged family; one in which the victim is closest to no one individual (Wyatt et al., in press); a mother who is absent, ill, or otherwise not protective of the child; social isolation of the family; lack of supervi-sion of the child; unusual sleeping or rooming conditions; the erosion of social networks; and the lack of social supports for the mother (Finkelhor, 1984). Factors in the child's behavior, education, and relationships have also been considered, including the emotional security or social isolation of the child; knowledge about sexual abuse (which may be affected by school sex education programs); the relationship of trust between the offender and the child; and coercion.

Parenting Styles

Although a substantial research literature describes the effects of parenting styles on child adjustment, few attempts have been made to link this body of knowledge with child maltreatment research (Baumrind, 1992). Research on parenting styles (Baumrind, 1989, 1991; Dornbusch et al., 1987) has identified two styles that have relevance for studies of maltreatment: (1) a neglecting/disengaged style involving low involvement, nurturance, warmth, control, and monitoring, and (2) an authoritarian style involving punitiveness, coercion, restrictiveness, and low warmth and support. The first appears to be related to child neglect and the second to child abuse (Maccoby and Martin, 1983). Although most studies of parenting styles have not been based on clinical samples of parents or of parents identified as maltreating, the outcomes reported for children who experience these types of parenting styles are similar to those reported for maltreated children—high rates of aggression, antisocial behavior, depression and anxiety, and problems with peers, in school, and in intimate relations. These observations suggest that parenting dysfunction is directly related to maltreatment and that examinations of different levels of parental dysfunction would be beneficial, particularly when certain behaviors have adverse effects on the well-being of children. This issue is directly relevant to the next section on the relationship between physical punishment and maltreatment.

Few comparative studies have examined variations in parenting styles and dysfunctional parenting patterns (including abuse and neglect) and their effects on children in different cultural or ecological settings. For example, authoritative parenting styles—involving high levels of responsiveness, warmth, control, monitoring, communication, and demands for mature, responsible behavior—are most accepted and successful in promoting competence in white middle-class children. But the authoritative parenting style may not be equally advantageous for other groups (e.g., poor families) and in other situations, especially for families that live in communities characterized by violence.

An important gap in the literature on child maltreatment is the lack of comparative analysis of risk factors for child maltreatment for families in different social, ethnic, and cultural groups. One study has investigated social class differences in the etiology and consequences of child maltreatment (Trickett et al., 1991). Such research could identify different cultural patterns of transactions between risk potentiating and protective factors in the etiology and outcome of child maltreatment. For example, some Latin-American and Asian communities value close adult supervision into late adolescence, a cultural practice that might serve an important protective role while also being viewed as dysfunctional or intrusive by other ethnic groups (Brown et al., 1992). Standards of parental control and discipline may also be conditioned by cultural factors, especially in environments characterized by danger and violence.

The few existing studies on parenting styles and child maltreatment identify important distinctions between maltreating and nonmaltreating parents, but within maltreating samples the behavior of neglectful and abusive parents indicates that the etiology of physical abuse and neglect shares more similarities than differences (Pianta et al., 1989).

Observational studies have indicated that in comparison to nonabusing parents, physically abusing parents have less pleasant interactions with their children even if not always more negative.[15] Abusing parents are less supportive, affectionate, playful, and responsive with their children (Burgess and Conger, 1978; Egeland et al., 1980; Kavanaugh et al., 1988; Reid et al., 1987; Trickett and Susman, 1988; Twentyman and Plotkin, 1982). Even with infants, abusive parents are more controlling, interfering, and covertly, if not overtly, hostile (Crittenden, 1981, 1985).

Moreover, aversive behavior in abusive families is more likely to be reciprocated (Lorber et al., 1984), with escalating acrimonious exchanges of longer duration than those in nonabusive families, described as a coercive cycle by Patterson (1982). Abused children, as a consequence of abusive and inept parenting, may eventually develop characteristics (including brain damage) that make them disagreeable and difficult to manage, resulting in greater involvement in hostile, coercive cycles and an increased risk of abuse.

For chronically neglectful families, child neglect is not a single form of poor hygiene or inadequate nutrition in an otherwise well-ordered family unit, but it exists as a broader aspect of household disorganization, insularity, and lack of cognitive stimulation and emotional nurturance in the household (Polansky et al., 1992). Neglectful parents are unresponsive both with infants (Crittenden, 1981, 1985) and with older children (Burgess and Conger, 1978). They tend not to initiate interactions and not to respond to the initiations of their children; they exhibit little prosocial behavior toward their children; and, under some circumstances, they may actually exhibit more negative behavior than abusive parents (Burgess and Conger, 1978).

Abusive and nonabusive parents usually, but not consistently, exhibit differences in control and disciplinary practices. Abusive parents are more likely to use punishment, threats, coercion, and power and they are less likely to use reasoning and affection in controlling their children (Lorber et al., 1984; Trickett and Sussman, 1988). Moreover, their discipline is less likely to be contingent on the type of behavior exhibited by the child (Crittenden, 1981; Trickett and Kuczynski, 1986). The more frequent use of coercive, physical, punitive disciplinary techniques by abusive parents appears to reflect their negative perceptions of their children's behavior and their belief in the effectiveness of power assertion in controlling it (Milner and Chilamkurti, 1991).

Physical Discipline

The relationship between physical discipline and child abuse is one that elicits strong beliefs and opinions, but few definitive conclusions. Societal tolerance and use of physical discipline have been suggested as risk factors in child maltreatment (Gil, 1970; Kadushin and Martin, 1981; Straus, 1980; Zigler and Hall, 1989). Acceptance of physical discipline or punishment of children, including infants, is widespread among lay persons (Carson, 1986; Gelles and Straus, 1988; Gil, 1970) and physicians (McCormick, 1992).

Physical discipline has been viewed as one end of a continuum of abusive behavior, but the linkage between physical discipline and abuse has not been established (Gelles, 1991). International and cross-cultural comparisons also do not support an inevitable tie between physical discipline and physical abuse. Sweden, which has laws prohibiting physical punishment, was significantly lower than the United States on self-reports of physical punishment on the Conflict Tactics Scales (Gelles and Edfeldt, 1986). However, there was no significant difference between the United States and Sweden in severe, or abusive, violence against children. Kadushin and Martin (1981) have pointed out that, while most discipline does not become abuse, retrospective reports suggest that most abuse begins with parental intentions to discipline the child. At least two studies also show that severe punishment that falls below the threshold of reported abuse appears to occur at the same rates as child maltreatment (Egeland, 1988; Straus and Yodanis, 1994).

Parke and Collmer (1975) suggest that physical discipline may be most dangerous among parents who disapprove of its use, since it is then used as a method of last resort, when parental anger is highest. They speculate that "As a result of this cultural shift in attitude [away from the use of physical discipline], the manner in which physical punishment is employed makes the contemporary use of this type of discipline potentially more dangerous than in the past." (p. 27).

Physical discipline, or at least harsh discipline, may be involved in the intergenerational transmission of abusive parenting. Harsh disciplinary practices have been causally related to a maladaptive style of processing social information that then leads to aggression, suggesting that severe discipline fosters more aggressive behavior by the child (Weiss et al., 1992).

The evidence on cultural differences in the use of physical discipline, and its relationship to abuse, is mixed. Self-report data on the Conflict Tactics Scale (CTS) did not exhibit a significant difference between blacks and whites, although parents in an "other category" (including Native American

Indians, Asians, and "other" cultural groups) were most likely to exhibit violent acts toward children (Straus, 1980). The lack of black-white differences supported earlier literature that blacks are not more violent toward children than whites (Billingsley, 1969), and that blacks and whites do not differ in self-reports of spanking (Stark and McElvoy, 1970). Weller et al. (1987) also found that Anglo and Hispanic adolescents did not differ in the proportion of each group reporting the experience of physical punishment.

Stressful Life Events and Child Maltreatment

Several investigators have examined the relationship between stressful life events and parenting outcomes, including quality of mother-infant attachment (Crockenberg, 1981) and child maltreatment (Egeland et al., 1980; Straus, 1980).[16] Most research has compared maltreating and nonmaltreating families on a scale that typically consists of a checklist of stressful life events, such as loss or reduction in family income, sickness in family, moves, and death or loss of family member.

The relationships among stressful life events, the characteristics of people affected by them (particularly anger, hostility, and depression), and the role of stress as an etiological factor in child maltreatment are not well understood. Traits of negative affectivity may help generate or exacerbate stressful life events themselves, thereby contributing to the maltreatment process. Stress seems to aggravate the level of conflict among family members. The effects of stressors on parental abilities depend on their overall coping strategies, the availability of support, and other buffering factors. One study has suggested that mothers who were subjected to high rates of stressful events were inconsistent in matching their disciplinary actions to the behavior of their children, in contrast to mothers experiencing low levels of stress (Dumas and Wahler, 1985).

In a prospective study of the antecedents of child maltreatment, Egeland et al. (1980) compared families who had been reported for maltreatment with a subsample of high-risk mothers who provided adequate care. They found a significant difference between stressful life event scores, although the relationship between stress and child maltreatment was far from perfect. Comparing the predictive value of family stressful life events with other variables, a number of interactional and maternal characteristics were better predictors than family stress of membership in the maltreatment and nonmaltreatment groups. Egeland et al. (1980) found that many high-stress mothers were providing adequate care, and that many mothers experiencing low stress were maltreating their children. The high-stress mothers who maltreated their child were often more angry, suspicious of others, and highly anxious compared to high-stress mothers who had low scores on these variables. Abuse was also more likely to occur among high-stress mothers who had poor quality interaction with their child than among high-stress mothers with good-quality interaction.

The complex relation between stressors and parenting outcomes, including child maltreatment, needs more attention. The exceptions to predicted outcomes, such as why some high-stress parents provide adequate caregiving and why some families experiencing low levels of stress maltreat their children, are fertile areas for future research. The relationships between stress, poor parenting outcomes, family dysfunction, and child maltreatment also need to be clarified.

Summary

Family functioning in maltreating families is affected by combinations of factors that are present in many families that do not maltreat their children. Different levels of parental dysfunction need to be studied over time in order to identify conditions that give rise to the emergence of child maltreatment. Although a parent's own history of victimization during childhood is thought to be highly correlated with child maltreatment, this association is based on retrospective studies that are methodologically flawed. The relationship between physical discipline and child maltreatment is also largely unknown, particularly in terms of cultural differences and practices. Finally, stressful life events are thought to play an important role on individuals, abilities to parent, but relations between stressors and parenting outcomes are complex and poorly understood at this time.

THE EXOSYSTEM

Individual and family characteristics do not function in isolation from the larger community that surrounds both maltreating and nonmaltreating families. Although research on exosystem factors has concentrated on neighborhood and community environments, other factors may affect individual or family functioning as well, including the workplace, the media, the school, the church, and peer groups.

One of the most significant research developments in the past decade has been the recognition of the importance of viewing family functioning in the context of various social institutions and external forces that govern family and parent-child behaviors. We now examine the interactions and experiences between families and family members with networks of these extrafamilial social systems, termed the "exosystem."

Family Income/Poverty

In 1990, one in five of all American children, approximately 13.4 million, lived in families with total incomes below the poverty level (e.g., $13,254 for a family of four, U.S. Bureau of the Census, 1991). The rates are higher in families with children age six and under than in those whose children are ages 7-16 (23 percent versus 19 percent), indicating that almost one in four preschoolers lives in a poor household at any point in time. Research has shown that living in poverty exacts a toll on children's well-being (Chase-Landale and Brooks-Gunn, in press; Chase-Landale et al., in press; Huston, 1991).

Discussion of the relationship of poverty to child maltreatment has persisted since publication of the early professional papers on child abuse (e.g., Gil, 1970; Gelles, 1983, 1992; Kadushin, 1976; Kempe et al., 1962; Pelton, 1978; Steele and Pollock, 1968). Although child maltreatment is reported across the socioeconomic spectrum, it is disproportionately reported among poor families. Further, child maltreatment—especially child neglect—is not simply concentrated among the poor, but among the poorest of the poor (Giovannoni and Billingsley, 1970; Pelton, 1981; Wolock and Horowitz, 1979, 1984). Whether this association results from greater stress due to poverty-related conditions that precipitate abuse or from greater scrutiny by public agencies that results in overreporting continues to be debated. Nevertheless, the deleterious effects of poverty on children and their families is well documented (Baumrind, 1992).

Self-reports on the Conflict Tactics Scales indicate that lower socioeconomic status is a risk factor for violent behaviors toward children (Straus, 1980; Gelles and Straus, 1988). Although violence toward children occurs in all social strata, violent behaviors toward children, particularly severe violence, is more likely in poor families. Furthermore, although maternal age by itself is not a significant risk factor for child maltreatment, mothers with young children living below the poverty line are at the greatest risk of violent behavior toward children (Connelly and Straus, 1992; Gelles, 1992).

Poverty has been highly correlated with both physical abuse and neglect. Polansky et al. (1981), however, argue that, although poverty often pervades the lives of neglectful families, it is not the major cause of neglect. In contrast, reported cases of child sexual abuse do not seem to occur disproportionately among the poor, but appear to be concentrated in the middle-class (Finkelhor, 1986). However, this finding may be flawed by the selection of samples for study, since poor children may have limited access to the treatment services that often provide the pool of subjects for this kind of research.

Despite general agreement in the literature on a linkage between poverty and maltreatment (both official reports and self-reports), the processes and mechanisms involved in this association require further research. Why are all poor families not equally at risk for maltreatment? Why does maltreatment occur in families that are not poor? How does economic deprivation translate into child abuse and neglect?

Unemployment

The link between unemployment and maltreatment is significant in understanding the relationship between poverty and maltreatment. While Gil (1970) found child maltreatment to be highly linked with poverty, Light's (1973) reanalysis of Gil's data found unemployment to be the most powerful predictor of child abuse and neglect. The relationship between unemployment and maltreatment has been documented in several research studies (e.g., Gabinet, 1983; Gelles and Hargreaves, 1981; Krugman et al., 1986; Whipple and Webster-Stratton, 1991). Steinberg et al. (1981) used an aggregate longitudinal approach, replicated in two distinct metropolitan communities, to demonstrate that increases of child abuse are preceded by periods of high job loss, consistent with the hypothesis that unemployment can cause family stress, subsequently resulting in child abuse.

The relationship between unemployment and violent behaviors toward children is strongest for fathers, and for fathers employed part time, possibly due to higher frustration than the totally unemployed (Straus, 1980). The association between unemployment and maltreatment has also been documented in studies of individuals (Gabinet, 1983; Krugman et al.,1986; Whipple and Webster-Stratton, 1991) and communities (Bycer et al., 1984; Lichtenstein, 1983; Steinberg et al., 1981). Although these studies have demonstrated such an association, the mechanisms (such as stress) by which a job loss or lack of employment may stimulate child maltreatment have not been identified.

Neighborhood Impact

Poor neighborhoods differ in their social and physical conditions and in their ability to influence the specific risks posed to children by poverty, unemployment, drugs, and community violence (Coulton et al., 1990a,b; Coulton and Pandey, 1992; Duncan and Aber, in press).[17] Garbarino and colleagues found that, although socioeconomic conditions have predictive value for explaining child maltreatment rates, some neighborhoods have higher child abuse rates than would be expected (high-risk neighborhoods) and some have lower rates than would be expected (low-risk neighborhoods) based on socioeconomic conditions alone. Child abuse rates were found to be higher in poor neighborhoods with fewer social resources than in equally economically deprived neighborhoods where social resources were perceived to be higher. Parents in the high-risk neighborhoods did not use resources in a preventive fashion, but in response to crises; did not use informal resources such as scouting or youth groups; and often fell back on formal public agencies when intervention was necessary. Parents tended not to exchange services and, when such exchanges occurred, abusive parents attempted to exploit others. Residents in poor but low-risk neighborhoods built better environments, made constructive use of resources, and perceived quality of life and goodness of the neighborhood as a place to rear children more positively than those in high risk neighborhoods (Garbarino and Crouter, 1978; Garbarino and Sherman, 1980). While arguments for neighborhood impact on child abuse and child neglect are compelling, Polansky (1981) notes that neglectful families often are socially isolated and their perceptions of themselves, their children, and others do not reflect attitudes prevalent in their neighborhoods.

Although neighborhoods are recognized as important in the ecology of child maltreatment, more insight is needed into the processes by which neighborhood conditions and factors affect family processes in general and child maltreatment in particular. Why do some maltreating families remain socially isolated, yet others can be motivated to take advantage of community or neighborhood resources? What neighborhood resources reaffirm or weaken destructive beliefs about empathy, trust, and self-esteem? What key neighborhood factors have the ability to mitigate the contributions of poverty, unemployment, and young maternal age toward child maltreatment?

Social isolation has been identified as an important etiological risk factor in child maltreatment, but its role as a consequence or cause of maltreatment is uncertain (Polansky et al., 1981, 1992). Abusive parents have been reported to isolate themselves from others, and also to isolate their children from friendship networks (Young, 1964). The presence and use of social networks has generally been regarded as a protective factor against child maltreatment (e.g., Garbarino, 1977). Two important issues require further research attention. First, abusive parents may be isolated by those around them as a consequence of deviant parenting attitudes and behaviors of abusive families that cause neighbors and acquaintances to avoid the family. Second, research attention needs to be directed toward maladaptive qualities of networks. Abusive parents may select networks of individuals who condone their maladaptive parenting styles, and the networks thereby increasing the likelihood of continued abuse rather than acting as a protective factor.

The relationship between child maltreatment and the social networks of organized religion is not well understood. On an individual level, parental religious preference has not demonstrated a clear relationship with physical (Straus, 1980) or sexual abuse. Little is known about the relationship of religion to either neglect or emotional abuse. Although religious beliefs favoring harsh discipline of children have been suggested to contribute to physical abuse, religious affiliation and participation have been identified as countering the social isolation associated with maltreatment (Garbarino, 1977) and as an important influence in protecting against child maltreatment, particularly among African-Americans (Giovannoni and Billingsley, 1970).

Summary

The influence of family ties and organizational affiliations (including employment and education) are poorly understood but increasingly recognized as powerful forces in shaping parenting styles and family functioning. Financial stability, employment, alcohol and drugs, and neighborhoods can create a context that either supports a family during periods of stress or enhances the potential for abuse. Families reported for abuse often have multiple problems; and the abuse may simply be a part—or a consequence— of a broader continuum of social dysfunctions.

THE MACROSYSTEM

The last system in our framework of analysis is the set of cultural and social values that pervade and support individual and family life styles and community services in today's society. The macrosystem is the often invisible layer in theoretical models of child maltreatment, yet its influence is increasingly recognized as important in understanding the hidden forces that govern personal and institutional behaviors.

Social and cultural factors can foster or mitigate stress in family life and such factors have achieved new importance in emerging theoretical models of child maltreatment. These values are thought to play a significant role in affecting adult reliance on coercion and violence to control the irritating daily events associated with family stress (Wolfe, 1991).

Cultural and Social Values

The macrosystem encompasses broader cultural and societal values that contribute to our understanding of the etiology of child maltreatment. Two primary topics have attracted research interest in this fourth level of our conceptual model. First, are broader societal and cultural values in American society—such as the privacy of the family or a cultural preoccupation with violence—contributing to child maltreatment? And second, how does culture influence the causes of or responses to child maltreatment, especially in a multicultural society such as the United States? Although the relationship of these factors is not well understood, some cultural and societal values in American society may contribute to child maltreatment. Racism, for example, can lead to an inequitable distribution of resources, education, and employment that undermines many ethnic minority families' abilities to support their children financially and emotionally and to provide parental care. The term societal neglect has been suggested to characterize American tolerance for a situation in which one-fifth of all preschool children live below the poverty line, with a substantially higher rate among ethnic minorities (Baumrind, 1992; Children's Defense Fund, 1991). Societal fascination with violence, including violence toward children, also has been suggested as a risk factor for physical abuse (Gil, 1970; Gelles and Straus, 1988). The lack of coherent family leave and family support policies, such as those in place in many European countries, increases the difficulties faced by many parents (National Research Council, 1990; Ferber and O'Farrell, 1991). In particular, the absence of preventive health care for infants and children increases the risk that abused children will remain undetected or that health problems will contribute to maltreatment. These broader societal and cultural factors should be considered in cross-national and cross-cultural comparisons.

The disproportionate representation of reports of maltreatment of children in ethnic minorities stimulated a search for cultural practices that contribute to abuse and neglect. A major problem with the research literature is that specific cultural practices have not been linked to differential rates or types of maltreatment, but instead post hoc explanations have been sought in cultural patterns. Pathways and mechanisms for a relationship between culture and maltreatment are thus left unclear.

Parents who abuse children are generally behaving outside their culture's acceptable continuum rather than exercising abusive behavior toward children that is culturally sanctioned. In assessing methods of health care, discipline, spiritual beliefs about health, and other aspects of life that are culturally determined, researchers need to obtain information about which practices the populations under study perceive as acceptable due to their culture, their current life circumstances, or the behaviors of the child. Some behaviors that are thought to be cultural from an outsider's perspective are familial practices or are artifacts of circumstances encountered by the families. The continuum of cultural acceptability within and across populations and the reasons for individual violation of these norms have not yet been determined. Greater effort must be directed at differentiating culturally acceptable behaviors from individually deviant behavior, and toward determining whether the interaction of causal factors varies across population groups.

In exploring the relationship between culture/ethnicity and child maltreatment, the cultural variable must be "unpacked" (Tharp, 1991). Since culture is not monolithic, it does not have a uniform impact on all members. The few studies that have considered intracultural variability have identified factors of interest for future research, such as extended family involvement (Dubanoski, 1981), and rural-urban residence (Lauderdale et al., 1980).

Child sexual abuse does not appear to be disproportionately represented in any cultural/ethnic group. In earlier studies of child sexual abuse, ethnic minority families were overrepresented (DeFrancis, 1969; Peters, 1976). However, these studies employed clinical samples from medical or social service settings in which poor and ethnic minority children were likely to be overrepresented. Survey research on the prevalence of child sexual abuse has not supported the existence of racial or ethnic differences in intrafamilial child sexual abuse (Finkelhor, 1984; Russell, 1986; Wyatt, 1985). Furthermore, the two National Incidence Studies have not found a relationship between race and sexual abuse (NCCAN, 1981, 1988).

The causal relationship of cultural factors and child sexual abuse requires further research within and across populations. For example, the practice of parent and child sleeping together may be viewed as a potentiating factor in some populations, according to the preconditions model set for by Finkelhor (1984), but this custom may prevent child sexual abuse in others. Anecdotal evidence suggests that some Native American groups believe that sexual abuse increased when families stopped sleeping together. The dispersal of children to their own rooms provided the conditions of secrecy conducive to abuse that would have been prevented if all adults had been present (Scheper-Hughes, 1987).

Searching for transactions or pathways that cause maltreatment across and within cultural groups has significant potential to improve understanding of the etiology of maltreatment. More punitive or restrictive approaches may be necessary under some circumstances to promote competencies and to protect children from danger in settings such as inner cities (Ogbu, 1981). Moreover, effective parenting styles may differ for different domains of adjustment in different groups. Studies by Steinberg, Dornbusch, and their colleagues have demonstrated that, although authoritative parenting is associated with low levels of problem behavior in all ethnic groups, it is associated with academic competence in white but not black children; in addition, restrictive authoritarian childrearing is associated with low academic competence in white but not Asian children (Dornbusch et al., 1987; Steinberg et al., 1990a,b).

Pornographic Materials

The relationship between pornography and child maltreatment, particularly child sexual abuse, has been examined only sporadically in the research literature. Most of the research has focused on the relationship between pornography and adult sexual behavior. Pornography is rarely a primary or direct motivator of violent sexual acts, although it may indirectly influence child sexual maltreatment (Knudsen, 1988). The 1970 report of a presidential commission declared that pornography does not have any significant, harmful social effects (Mason, 1989). In 1986, however, the attorney general's Commission on Pornography identified several areas of "pronounced harm" due to pornography, including a link between pornography, sexual violence, and child abuse (Mason, 1989), but did not support these findings with empirical evidence.

The fascination of pedophiles with child pornography and erotica is documented by many arrests of pedophiles who possess large amounts of sexually explicit materials involving children (Schetky, 1988; U.S. Senate, Committee on Governmental Affairs, 1986; West et al., 1978). Children who are sexually abused are sometimes further victimized by their involvement in child pornography. Although individual reactions to pornography are highly varied, adolescents may be particularly impressionable viewers of pornography (Marshall, 1989). Pornography has been reported to increase interest in deviant sexual practices in more than 39 percent of offenders (Abel, 1985, cited in Marshall, 1989). Repeated exposure to pornographic materials can alter perceptions toward sexuality and relationships, increase acceptance of physical force, and lessen compassion for victims (Knudsen, 1988). Yet the temporal sequence is unknown—a sexual interest in children or repeated victimization experiences may stimulate interest in sexually explicit materials, and an interest in child pornography may follow rather than precede a sexual interest in children (Crewdson, 1988).

SUMMARY OF ETIOLOGICAL FACTORS

Many factors have been identified as contributing to the occurrence of child maltreatment, but single-factor or unicausal theories of child maltreatment have not been able to identify specific mechanisms that influence the etiology of child maltreatment. Environmental factors such as poverty or unemployment and individual characteristics such as a prior history of abuse, social isolation, or low self-esteem have been significantly associated with child maltreatment offenders, but the relationships among such factors are not well understood in determining the origins of child maltreatment. The panel believes that the etiology of maltreatment involves a complex interactive process, one that includes constellations of variables that interact along various dimensions of a child's ecological/transactional system. Potentiating factors that increase risk for maltreatment and protective factors that decrease the likelihood for maltreatment are found at all ecological levels and interact to produce child maltreatment. Although theoretical models that describe the etiological complexity of maltreatment have been developed, they have not been subjected to testing and adequate research. Our recommendations seek to address these limitations.

RESEARCH RECOMMENDATIONS

Recommendation 4-1: Research using multivariate models and etiological theories that integrate ecological, transactional, and developmental factors will improve our understanding of the causes of child maltreatment. Rather than focusing on specific factors (such as depression, unemployment, or history of abuse), the interactions of variables at multiple ecological levels should be examined.

Although considerable research has focused on single-risk factors that contribute to child maltreatment, we know very little about mechanisms or processes by which these factors lead to maltreatment. Research designs and analytic strategies should focus on the multidimensional character of child maltreatment using a framework that accommodates risk and protective factors in an interactive model, examining possible etiological factors in child maltreatment in combination with other contributing agents. Continued reliance on univariate models or isolated risk factors in future research will not be productive. Process-oriented studies are needed to identify mechanisms by which factors interact in promoting or moderating child maltreatment.

Rather than endorsing one approach, the panel recommends that diverse theoretical models and research strategies be developed at this juncture. The capabilities of emerging multisystem interactional models offer significant promise in the study of child maltreatment that deserve to be supported.

In recommending the development of complex models and etiological theories, the panel has identified several key factors that deserve further emphasis at this time:

• Research should clarify distinctions between long-term chronic factors and immediate precipitating factors associated with maltreatment. There is a need to support research that would distinguish between factors associated with the initiation of child maltreatment and factors that sustain or escalate it.

• The intergenerational transmission of child maltreatment is an issue that deserves explicit analysis to determine the circumstances under which high- and low-risk circumstances will lead to child abuse and neglect. Prospective studies are needed to identify not only which parents do or do not maltreat children under conditions of high risk (based on their own histories of child maltreatment), but also those that do or do not maltreat under conditions of low risk. Exceptions to expectations under high- and low-risk conditions will improve our understanding of protective and risk potentiating factors. In addition, evaluations of samples of mothers from abusive and nurturing backgrounds should be conducted to determine the conditions that contribute to supportive parenting. Future research should explore the interaction of risk factors based on the concepts of contemporary attachment theory and inner working models as well as models based on cognitive learning skills and other approaches.

• Problems experienced by families characterized by multiple problems (such as poverty, unemployment, and violent neighborhoods) need to be better understood in clarifying the role of specific factors, such as alcohol or substance abuse, in the etiology of child maltreatment. We currently know very little about the conditions under which these factors interact with different individual and ecological factors to produce maltreatment. In particular, the role of alcohol as a mitigating factor (including cultural tolerance of drunkenness as an excuse of violence against family members) requires substantial exploration in child maltreatment studies. Relationships between acute intoxication, chronic alcoholism, and various forms of child maltreatment, including physical and sexual abuse, neglect, and emotional maltreatment, require systematic examination and analysis.

• The operation of social relationships and social networks is a critical feature in the etiology of child maltreatment. Research that seeks to clarify the conditions under which social networks can serve as risk or protective factors in child maltreatment should be supported. In particular, the roles of fathers and other male figures as offenders and protectors need more clarification and analysis. With the exception of sexual abuse, most research on child maltreatment focuses on mothers as agents of maltreatment. More information is needed on the role that fathers, siblings, grandparents, stepparents, and other household members play as risk or protective factors in child maltreatment.

Recommendation 4-2: Similarities and differences among the etiologies of different forms of child maltreatment should be clarified in order to improve the quality of future prevention and intervention efforts.

Studies that identify the etiologies of different types of maltreatment, and studies that explore diverse patterns of risk and protective factors and pathways leading to the same and different forms of maltreatment, should be supported. Multiple forms of maltreatment often co-occur in various combinations (physical abuse and neglect, sexual abuse and emotional maltreatment, and so forth), so it is particularly important at this time to emphasize key pathways for child victimization that may be amenable to prevention or other forms of intervention. Research is needed to clarify the most common types of maltreatment with some degree of specificity and then examine these types along a broad continuum of severity. For example, being a victim of physical abuse or emotional maltreatment may be a significant risk factor for child sexual abuse (or vice versa), but the relationships among multiple forms of maltreatment remain unexamined.

The serious and destructive nature of emotional maltreatment has not been fully recognized by researchers and practitioners in child maltreatment studies. Links among verbal abuse, physical punishment, and physical abuse are not well understood. It is not yet known whether physical punishment and emotional maltreatment are part of a progression leading to other forms of maltreatment. We also do not know if the origins of mild, moderate, and severe forms of abuse are similar or different. Continuity or discontinuity in the emergence of emotional maltreatment, physical abuse, and sexual abuse deserves examination.

Recommendation 4-3: Studies of similarities and differences in the etiologies of various forms of maltreatment across various social class, cultural, and ethnic populations should be supported.

The effects of risk-potentiating and protective factors on child maltreatment in diverse social class, cultural, and ethnic populations have not been adequately explored. Researchers have often relied primarily on clinical populations or subjects who have already been identified as offenders as representatives of entire cultural groups. Samples that are more representative of the diversity of contemporary American society are necessary to improve research quality. More needs to be known about "normal" forms of physical discipline, sexual behavior, and parenting styles within various social class, cultural, ethnic, and residential subgroups, because cultural norms have an impact on child maltreatment. Research is also needed to identify culturally acceptable behaviors that may inhibit the healthy development of the child. Research must address both commonalities and diversity among populations in the pathways and transactions of variables that promote or prevent various forms of maltreatment.

NOTES

1. A comparison might be made with other fields of study. Research on child maltreatment has often been grouped collectively because of the child status of the victim. Many research sponsors and investigators assume that child physical and sexual abuse, emotional maltreatment, and neglect have more similarities than differences. However, this organizational principle has not been rigorously tested. One could argue, for example, that comparing the etiology of child physical and sexual abuse is similar to comparing the etiology of burglary and rape of adult women. There may in fact be more differences than similarities in the origins of the offending behavior. The four categories of child maltreatment may have quite distinct etiologies and consequences and thus require distinct treatment and prevention efforts.

2. These models were derived from retrospective studies, including early psychiatric models focused on psychopathology, deviance, or psychological or behavioral deficits in abusive parents. Contrasting sociological models soon appeared that emphasized contributions of the social and physical environment. Models based on child attributes also emerged following reports of abuse of children placed in foster care.

3. See, for example, the definitions of terms as presented in *A Dictionary of Epidemiology* (Last, 1988).

4. Discussions of adult characteristics often focus on factors associated with the parent or caretaker, often the mother. In this framework of analysis the panel uses the term *adult,* but it should be recognized that the adult usually has a special relationship with the child, either as a parent, caretaker, or trusted authority figure. In cases of sexual abuse, however, the adult may be someone unrelated or unknown to the child.

5. Predictive instruments based on parental personality profiles have been characterized by limited sensitivity and specificity as well as an inadequately validated profile of personality characteristics or perpetrator typology (Wolfe, 1985).

6. Classifications of sex offenders include: preferential versus situational, incest versus pedophilia, and homosexual versus heterosexual. The distinction between preferential (or fixated) molesters and situational (or regressed) molesters (Groth et al., 1982), based on a prison population, is the classification generally regarded as significant (Prentky, 1990; Lanning, 1987), although community-based therapists often find that many offenders have combined features from both categories (Hartman and Burgess, 1989).

Incest is generally defined as sexual contact between people who are biologically related. Distinctions between *incest offenders* and *pedophiliacs* are based on certain core assumptions: (1) that incestuous fathers do not act sexually outside the home; (2) that incest is an expression of nonsexual needs; and (3) that other family members contribute psychologically to the development and maintenance of sexual abuse (Conte, 1991; Hartman and Burgess, 1989). However, increasing research evidence challenges the separate classification of incest offenders and pedophiles, suggesting that many incest offenders are sexually aroused by children, that many incestuous fathers are abusing children outside the family, that sexual and nonsexual dimensions are present in all sexuality; and that consistent profiles of incest families do not emerge from empirical studies (Conte, 1985; Conte et al., 1986). For example, one study indicated that 49 percent of a group of incestuous fathers and stepfathers referred for outpatient treatment abuse children outside the family at the same time they are abusing their own children (Abel et al., 1988).

The distinction between *homosexual* and *heterosexual* child molesters relies on the premise that male molesters of male victims are homosexual in orientation. Most molesters of boys do not report sexual interest in adult men, however (Conte, 1991).

7. Steele, a prominent and early proponent of the intergenerational hypothesis, did not claim that the cycle was inevitable, even though present in the history of virtually all identified maltreating parents in his clinical samples. Protective factors, particularly a supportive adult in the life of the child, could break the cycle (Steele, 1976).

8. A retrospective approach examining the intergenerational hypothesis is limited by its reliance on autobiographical memory (Bradburn et al., 1987). As adults, children who were abused may have repressed memories of childhood abuse, may be unwilling to talk about such painful memories, or may have accepted their mistreatment as normal, and even acceptable, childrearing behavior.

9. The low figure may have been affected by following the families for only one year.

10. Egeland et al. (1988) interpret the relationship differences between the continuity group and those who broke the cycle of abuse within a framework of contemporary attachment theory. Their analysis stated that the early caretaker-infant attachment relationship is a prototype of an individual's later relationships and influences the capacity for later affectionate bonds. The inner working models of abused individuals, who did not have a supportive adult figure, may be vastly different from the relationship expectations of the exception group, who appear to have experienced a positive, emotional attachment to an adult figure.

11. Some animal studies have indicated, for example, that bright lights can increase serum testosterone levels in pregnant rats as well as in their male fetuses (Rines and vom Saal, 1984). Episodic elevations of testosterone have been associated not only with increased maternal aggressiveness but also with increased postnatal aggressiveness of offspring. Androgens also contribute to hypervigilance and are thought to sensitize the parts of the fetal brain that mediate aggression. Sensitized animals subsequently are able to respond rapidly and aggressively to stimuli that elicit surges of testosterone (Kamel et al., 1975).

12. Although many aspects of the punitiveness measured in these studies, such as criticism, threats, physical punishment, coerciveness, and guilt-inducing behaviors, fall within definitions of maltreatment used by many investigators, the studies of older children dealt with punitiveness and not specifically abuse.

13. Since a supportive spouse can moderate the disruptive effects of other stressors on parenting, such couples lack a salient buffer (Rutter, 1987).

14. For example, the mother may live alone with her children, then live with the father of some of the children (and perhaps conceiving another during this time), then move in with her own mother, then live on her own again (perhaps in a shelter program), then reside with the mother's sister and her own children in a small apartment.

15. Studies using parental reports and observations of parent-child interactions do not consistently demonstrate greater negative or aversive behaviors such as criticizing, slapping, and teasing, but this may result from reactions being observed or a reluctance to report harsh behavior. However, a greater proportion of negative relative to positive parent-child exchanges is found, even in studies that do not report more frequent aversive parental behavior (Burgess and Conger, 1978; Mash et al., 1983).

16. Despite the popularity of this approach, many problems remain in studying the effects of stress, including the failure to consider the significance of a specific stressful event for an individual. Most researchers do not consider the individual's coping strategy, which may alter the impact of stress (Pianta and Egeland, 1990).

17. Neighborhoods may also be a source of reporting bias. Child protection workers in poverty areas with more severe abuse and neglect caseloads tended to judge maltreatment vignettes less seriously, while workers in socioeconomically advantaged areas had a lower threshold in judging the severity of abuse vignettes (Wolock, 1982).

REFERENCES

Aarens, M. et al.
1978   *Alcohol, Casualties and Crime.* Berkeley, CA: Social Research Group.
Abel, G.G.
1985   Use of Pornography Erotica by Sex Offenders. Paper presented at the United States Attorney General's Commission on Pornography, Houston, TX.
Abel, G.G., J. Becker, J. Cunningham-Rathner, M. Mittelman, and J.L. Rouleau
1988   Multiple paraphiliac diagnosis among sex offenders. *Bulletin of the American Academy of Psychiatry and the Law* 16(2):153-168.
Aber, J.L., and D. Cicchetti
1984   The socio-emotional development of maltreated children: an empirical and theoretical analysis. Pp. 147-205 in Fitzgerald, B. Lester, and M. Yogman (eds.) *Theory and Research in Behavioral Pediatrics.* Vol. II. New York: Plenum Press.
Abram, K.
1990   The problem of co-occurring disorders among jail detainees: Antisocial disorder, alcoholism, drug abuse, and depression. *Law and Human Behavior* 14:333-345.
Altemeier, W.A., S. O'Connor, P.M. Vietze, H. Sandler, and K.B. Sherrod
1982   Antecedents of child abuse. *Journal of Pediatrics* 100 (May):823-829.
Ammerman, R.T.
1991   The role of the child in physical abuse: A reappraisal. *Violence and Victims* 6(2):87-100.
Araji, S., and D. Finkelhor
1986   Abusers: A review of the research. Pp. 89-118 in D. Finkelhor, ed., *A Sourcebook on Child Sexual Abuse.* Beverly Hills, CA: Sage.
Armentrout, J.A., and A.L. Hauer
1978   MMPIs of rapists of adults, rapists of children, and non-rapist sex offenders. *Journal of Clinical Psychology* 34(2):330-332.
Ayoub, C.C., and S.S. Milner
1985   Failure to thrive parental indicators, types, and outcome. *Child Abuse and Neglect* 9:491-499.
Bandler, R.J.
1970   Cholinergic synapses in the lateral hypothalamus for the control of predatory aggression in the rat. *Brain Research* 20:409-424.
Bard, P.
1928   A diencephalic mechanism for the expression of rage with special reference to the sympathetic nervous system. *American Journal of Physiology* 84:490-515.
Baumrind, D.
1989   Rearing competent children. Pp. 349-378 in W. Damon (ed.), *Child Development Today and Tomorrow.* San Francisco: Jossey-Bass.
1991   The influence of parenting style on adolescent competence and substance abuse. *Journal of Early Adolescence* 11(1):56-94.
1992   Family Factors Applied to Child Maltreatment. Background paper prepared for the Panel on Research on Child Abuse and Neglect. Washington, DC: National Research Council.
Bear, D.M., J.F. Rosenbaum, and R. Norman
1986   Aggression in cat and man precipitated by a cholesterase inhibitor. *Psychosomatics* 26:535-536.
Becker, J.V.
1988   The effects of child sexual abuse on adolescent sexual offenders. Pp. 193-207 in G.E. Wyatt and G.J. Powell, eds., *The Lasting Effects of Child Sexual Abuse.* Newbury Park, CA: Sage.

Beckwith, L., and S.E. Cohen
    1984   Home, environmental, and cognitive competence in preterm children during the
            first 5 years. Pp. 235-271 in A. Gottfried, ed., *Home Environmental and Early
            Cognitive Development.* New York: Academic Press.
Belsky, J.
    1980   Child maltreatment: An ecological integration. *American Psychologist* 35:320-
            335.
    1992   The Etiology of Child Maltreatment: An Ecological-Contextual Analysis. Paper
            prepared for the Panel on Research on Child Abuse and Neglect. Washington,
            DC: National Research Council.
Benedict, M.I., R.B. White, and D.A. Cornely
    1985   Maternal perinatal risk factors and child abuse. *Child Abuse and Neglect* 9:214-
            224.
Billingsley, A.
    1969   Family functioning in the low-income black community. *Social Casework* 50(10):563-
            572.
Bradburn, N.M., L.J. Ripps, and S.K. Shevall
    1987   Answering autobiographical questions: The impact of memory and inference on
            surveys. *Science* 236(4798):158-61.
Brooten, D., S. Gennaro, L.P. Brown, P. Butts, A.L. Gibbons, S. Bakewell-Sachs, and S.P.
Kumar
    1988   Anxiety, depression, and hostility in mothers of preterm infants. *Nursing Re-
            search* 37:213-217.
Brown, E., P. Martinez, and M. Radke-Yarrow
    1992   Diversity: Research with diverse populations. *Society for Research on Child
            Development Newsletter* (Fall).
Brunquell, D., L. Crichton, and B. Egeland
    1981   Maternal personality and attitude in disturbances of child rearing. *American Journal
            of Orthopsychiatry* 51:680-691.
Burgess, R.L
    1979   Child abuse: A social interactional analysis. Pp. 142-172 in B.B. Lahey and A.
            Kazdin, eds., *Advances in Clinical Child Psychology* 2. New York: Plenum.
Burgess, R.L., and R.D. Conger
    1978   Family interaction in abusive, neglectful, and normal families. *Child Development*
            49:1163-1173.
Burgess, A., and P. Draper
    1989   The explanation of family violence: The role of biological, behavioral, and cul-
            tural selection. Pp 59-116 in L. Ohlin and M. Tonry, eds., *Family Violence.*
            Chicago: University of Chicago Press.
Bycer, A., L.D. Breed, J.E. Fluke, and T. Costello
    1984   *Unemployment and Child Abuse and Neglect Reporting.* Denver: American Hu-
            mane Association.
Caplan, P.J., J. Watters, G. White, R. Parry, and R. Bates
    1984   Toronto multiagency child abuse research project: The abused and the abuser.
            Child Abuse and Neglect 8:343-351.
Carson, B.
    1986   Parents Who Don't Spank: Deviation in the Legitimation of Physical Force.
            Unpublished doctoral dissertation, University of New Hampshire.
Casanova, G.M., J. Domanic, T.R. McCanne, and J.S. Milner
    1992   Physiological responses to non-child-related stressors in mothers at risk for child
            abuse. *Child Abuse and Neglect* 16(1):31-44.

Chase-Lansdale, P.L., and J. Brooks-Gunn, eds.
  in press *Escape from Poverty: What Makes a Difference for Poor Children.* New York: Cambridge University Press.
Chase-Lansdale, P.L., J. Brooks-Gunn, and E. Zamsky
  in press Young multigenerational families in poverty: Quality of mothering and grandmothering. *Child Development.*
Children's Defense Fund
  1991 *The State of America's Children.* Washington, DC: Children's Defense Fund.
Cicchetti, D., and J.L. Aber
  1980 Abused children - abusive parents: An overstated case? *Harvard Educational Review* 50(2):244-255.
Cicchetti, D., and V. Carlson, eds.
  1989 *Child Maltreatment: Theory and Research on the Causes and Consequences of Child Abuse and Neglect.* New York: Cambridge University Press.
Cicchetti, D., and M. Lynch
  in press Toward an ecological/transactional model of community violence and child maltreatment: Consequences for children's development. *Psychiatry.*
Conger, R., J. McCarty, R. Yang, B. Lahey, and J. Kropp
  1984 Perception of child, childrearing values, and emotional distress as mediating links between environmental stressors and observed maternal behavior. *Child Development* 54:2234-2247.
Connelley, C.D., and M.A. Straus
  1992 Mothers' age and risk for physical abuse. *Child Abuse and Neglect* 16:703-712.
Conte, J.R.
  1984 Research on the Prevention of Sexual Abuse of Children. Paper presented at the Second National Conference for Family Violence Researchers, Durham, NH.
  1985 Clinical dimensions of adult sexual abuse of children. *Behavioral Sciences and the Law* 3(4):341-354.
  1991 The nature of sexual offenses against children. Pp. 11-34 in C.R. Hollin and K. Howells, eds., *Clinical Approaches to Sex Offenders and their Victims.* New York: John Wiley.
Conte, J.R., C. Rosen, and L. Saperstein
  1986 An analysis of programs to prevent the sexual victimization of children. *Journal of Primary Prevention* 6(3):141-155.
Coulton, C., J. Chow, and S. Pandey
  1990a An Analysis of Poverty and Related Conditions in Cleveland Area Neighborhoods. Case Western Reserve University, Center for Urban Poverty and Social Change.
Coulton, C., J. Korbin, M. Su, and J. Chow
  (n.d.) Community Level Factors and Child Maltreatment Rates. Unpublished manuscript.
Coulton, C.J., and S. Pandey
  1992 Geographic concentration of poverty and risk to children in urban neighborhoods. Special Issue: The impact of poverty on children. *American Behavioral Scientist* 35(3):238-257.
Coulton, C., S. Pandey, and J. Chow
  1990b Concentration of poverty and the changing ecology of low-income urban neighborhoods: An analysis of the Cleveland area. *Social Work Research and Abstracts* 26(4):5-16.
Creighton, S.J.
  1985 An epidemiological study of abused children and their families in the United Kingdom between 1977 and 1982. *Child Abuse and Neglect* 9:441-448.

Crewdson, J.
  1988   *By Silence Betrayed: Sexual Abuse of Children in America.* New York: Harper and Row.
Crittenden, P.M.
  1981   Abusing, neglecting problematic, and adequate dyads: Differentiating by patterns of interaction. *Merrill-Palmer Quarterly* 27:201-208.
  1985   Social networks, quality of child rearing, and child development. *Child Development* 56(October):1299-1313.
Crockenberg, S.B.
  1981   Infant irritability, mother responsiveness, and social influences on the security of infant-mother attachment. *Child Development* 52:857-865.
Daly, M., and M. Wilson
  1983   *Sex Evolution and Behavior. Adaptations for Reproduction.* 2nd edition. Boston: Willard Grant Press.
DeFrancis, V.
  1969   *Protecting the Child Victim of Sex Crimes Committed by Adults.* Englewood, CO: American Humane Association.
Disbrow, M.A., H. Doerr, and C. Caulfield
  1977   Measuring the components of parents potential for child abuse and neglect. *Child Abuse and Neglect* 1:279-296.
DiVitto, B., and S. Goldberg
  1979   The effects of newborn medical status on later parent-infant interaction. Pp. 311-356 in T.M. Field, S.M. Sostek, S. Goldberg, and H.H. Shuman, eds., *Infants Born at Risk: Behavior and Development.* New York: Spectrum Publication.
Dodge, K.A., J.E. Bates, and G.S. Pettit
  1990   Mechanisms in the cycle of violence. *Science* 250 (December 21):1678-1683.
Dornbusch, S.M., P.L. Ritter, P.H. Leiderman, D.J. Roberts, and M.J. Fraleigh
  1987   The relation of parenting style to adolescent performance. *Child Development* 58:1244-1257.
Drotar, D.
  1992   Prevention of neglect and nonorganic failure to thrive. Pp. 115-149 in D.J. Willis, E.W. Holden, and M. Rosenberg, eds., *Prevention of Child Maltreatment: Developmental and Ecological Perspectives.* New York: John Wiley.
DSM-III-R
  1987   *Diagnostic and Statistical Manual of Mental Disorders.* 3rd ed., rev. Washington, DC: American Psychiatric Association.
Dubanoski, R.
  1981   Child maltreatment in European and Hawaiian Americans. *Child Abuse and Neglect* 5(4):457-466.
Dubowitz, H.
  1987   Child maltreatment in the United States: Etiology, impact, and prevention. In *Healthy Children: Investing in the Future.* Health Program, Office of Technology Assessment, U.S. Congress, Washington, DC.
Dumas, J., and R.G. Wahler
  1985   Indiscriminate mothering as a contextual factor in aggressive-oppositional child behavior: "Damned if you do, damned if you don't." *Journal of Abnormal Child Psychology* 13:1-17.
Duncan, G., and J.L. Aber
  In press Neighborhood conditions and structure. In G. Duncan and J. Brooks-Gunn (eds.) *Neighborhoods, Families, and Poverty: These Effects on Children and Youth.*

Earp, J., and M.G. Ory
1980   The influence of early parenting on child maltreatment. *Child Abuse and Neglect* 4:237-245.
Egeland, B.
1988   Breaking the cycle of abuse: Implications for prediction and intervention. Pp. 87-99 in K.D. Browne, C. Davies, and P. Stratton, eds., *Early Prediction and Prevention of Child Abuse*. New York: John Wiley.
Egeland, B., and D. Brunquell
1979   An at-risk approach to the study of child abuse: Some preliminary findings. *Journal of the American Academy of Psychiatry* 18:219-235.
Egeland, B., and D. Jacobvitz
1984   Intergenerational Continuity in Parental Abuse: Causes and Consequences. Paper presented at the Conference on Biosocial Perspectives in Abuse and Neglect, York, ME.
Egeland, B., M. Breitenbucher, and D. Rosenberg
1980   A prospective study of the significance of life stress in the etiology of child abuse. *Journal of Clinical and Consulting Psychology* 48:195-205.
Egeland, B., D. Jacobvitz, and K. Papatola
1987   Intergenerational continuity of abuse. Pp 255-276 in R.J. Gelles and J. Lancaster, eds., *Child Abuse and Neglect: Biosocial Dimensions*. New York: Aldine.
Egeland, B., D. Jacobvitz, and L.A. Sroufe
1988   Breaking the cycle of abuse. *Child Development* 59(4):1080-1088.
Ehrenkranz, J., E. Bliss, and M.H. Sheard
1974   Plasma testosterone: Correlations with aggressive behavior and social dominance in man. *Psychosomatic Medicine* 36:469-475.
Fagan, J.
1990   Intoxication and aggression. Pp. 241-320 in M. Tonry and J.Q. Wilson, eds., *Drugs and Crime*. Chicago: University of Chicago Press.
Fagan, J., and A. Browne
1990   Marital Violence: Physical Aggression Between Men and Women in Intimate Relationships. Background paper prepared for the Panel on the Understanding and Control of Violent Behavior. Washington, DC: National Research Council.
Faller, K.C.
1988   *Child Sexual Abuse*. New York: Columbia University Press.
Faller, K.
1990   *Understanding Child Sexual Maltreatment*. Newbury Park, CA: Sage.
Famularo, R., K. Stone, R. Barnum, and R. Wharton
1986   Alcoholism and severe child maltreatment. *American Journal of Orthopsychiatry* 56:481-485.
Farber, E.D., and J.A. Joseph
1985   The maltreated adolescent: Patterns of physical abuse. *Child Abuse and Neglect* 9(2):201-206.
Ferber, M.A., and B. O'Farrell
1991   *Work and Family: Policies for a Changing Work Force*, Panel on Employer Policies and Working Families. Washington, DC: National Academy Press.
Finkelhor, D.
1984   *Child Sexual Abuse*. New York: Free Press.
1987   The sexual abuse of children: Current research reviewed. *Psychiatric Annals* 17(4)(April):233-241.
Finkelhor, D., S. Araji, L. Baron, A. Growne, S.D. Peters, and G.E. Wyatt
1986   *A Sourcebook on Child Sexual Abuse*. Newbury Park, CA: Sage.

Floody. O.R., and D.W. Pfaff
   1972   Steroid hormones and aggressive behavior: Approaches to the study of hormone-
           sensitive brain mechanisms for behavior. *Aggression* 149-185.
Fontana, V.
   1973   The diagnosis of the maltreatment syndrome in children. *Pediatrics* 51:780-782.
Friederich, W.N.
   1988   Behavior problems in sexually abused children. Pp. 171-191 in G.E. Wyatt and
           G.J. Powell, eds., *The Lasting Effects of Child Sexual Abuse*. Newbury Park, CA:
           Sage Publications.
Gabinet, L.
   1983   Child abuse treatment failures reveal need for redefinition of the problem. *Child
           Abuse and Neglect* 7:395-402.
Garbarino, J.
   1977   The human ecology of child maltreatment: A conceptual model for research.
           Journal of Marriage and the Family 39:721-735.
Garbarino, J., and A. Crouter
   1978   Defining the community context for parent-child relations: The correlates of child
           maltreatment. *Child Development* 49:604-616.
Garbarino, J., and D. Sherman
   1980   High-risk neighborhoods and high-risk familes: The human ecology of child
           maltreatment. *Child Development* 51:188-198.
Garbarino, J., and J. Vondra.
   1987   Psychological maltreatment: Issues and perspectives. Pp. 24-44 in M.R. Brassard,
           R. Germain, and S.N. Hart, eds., *Psychological Maltreatment of Children and
           Youth*. New York: Pergamon Press.
Gelles, R.J.
   1983   International perspectives on child abuse and neglect. *Child Abuse and Neglect*
           7(4):375-386.
   1991   Physical violence, child abuse, and child homicide: A continuum of violence or
           distinct behaviors. *Human Nature* 2(1):59-72.
   1992   Poverty and violence toward children. *American Behavioral Scientist* 35(3):258-
           274.
Gelles, R.J., and A.W. Edfeldt
   1986   Violence towards children in the United States and Sweden. *Child Abuse and
           Neglect* 10:501-510.
Gelles, R.J., and E.F. Hargreaves
   1981   Maternal employment and violence toward children. *Journal of Family Issues*
           2:509-530.
Gelles, R.J., and M.A. Straus
   1988   *Intimate Violence*. New York: Simon and Schuster.
George, C., and M. Main
   1979   Social interactions of young abused children: Approach, avoidance, and aggres-
           sion. *Child Development* 50:306-318.
Gil, D.G.
   1970   *Violence Against Children: Physical Child Abuse in the United States*.   Cam-
           bridge, MA: Harvard University Press.
Giovannoni, J.M., and A. Billingsley
   1970   Child neglect among the poor: A study of parental adequacy in families of three
           ethnic groups. *Child Welfare* 49(April):196-204.
Goldberg, S.
   1983   Parent-infant bonding: Another look. *Child Development* 54:1355-1382.

Goodwin, J., T. McCarthy, and P. Divasto
    1981   Prior incest in mothers of abused children. *Child Abuse and Neglect* 5:87-96.
Goy, R., and B. McEwen
    1977   *Sexual Differentiation and the Brain.* Cambridge, MA: MIT Press.
Groth, N.A., W.F. Hobson, and T.S. Gary
    1982   The child molester: Clinical observations. *Journal of Social Work and Human Sexuality* 1(1-2):129-144.
Hamilton, A., W.B. Stiles, F. Melowsky, and D.G. Beal
    1987   A multilevel comparison of child abusers with nonabusers. *Journal of Family Violence* 2(3):215-225.
Hamilton, C.J., and J.J. Collins
    1982   The role of alcohol in wife beating and child abuse: A review of the literature. Pp. 253-287 in J.J. Collins, ed., *Drinking and Crime: Perspectives on the Relationships Between Alcohol Consumption and Criminal Behavior.* London: Guilford Press.
Harford, T.C., and D.A. Parker
    1985   Alcohol dependence and problem drinking in a national sample. Pp. 29-31 in *Alcohol, Drugs and Tobacco: An International Perspective for the Future*, Volume II. Proceedings of the 34th International Congress on Alcoholism and Drug Dependence, Calgary, Alberta.
Hart, S.N., and M.R. Brassard
    1987   A major threat to children's mental health: Psychological maltreatment. *American Psychologist* 42(2):160-165.
Hart, S.N., R., Germain, and M.R. Brassard.
    1987   The challenge: To better understand and combat the psychological maltreatment of children and youth. Pp. 3-234 in M.R. Brassard, R. Germain, and S.N. Hart, eds., *Psychological Maltreatment of Children and Youth.* New York: Pergamon Press.
Hartman, C.R., and A.W. Burgess
    1989   Sexual abuse of children: Causes and consequences. Pp. 95-128 in D. Cicchetti and V. Carlson, eds., *Child Maltreatment: Theory and Research on the Causes and Consequences of Child Abuse and Neglect.* New York: Cambridge University Press.
Hetherington, E.M.
    1989   Coping with family transitions: Winners, losers and survivors. *Child Development* 60:1-15.
    1991   The role of individual difference in family relations in coping with divorce and remarriage. In P. Cowan and E.M. Hetherington, eds., *Advances in Family Research: Vol. 2 Family Transitions.* Hillsdale, NJ: Lawrence Erlbaum Press.
Hetherington, E.M., and W.G. Clingempeel
    1992   Coping with marital transitions: A family systems perspective. *Monographs of the Society for Research in Child Development* 57(no. 2-3).
Higley, J.D., and S.J. Suomi
    1989   Temperamental reactivity in non-human primates. Pp 153-167 in G.A. Kohnstamm, J.E. Bates, and M.K. Rothbart, eds., *Temperament in Childhood.* New York: John Wiley.
Holden, E.W., D.J. Willis, and M. Corcoran
    1992   Pp. 17-46 (Chapter 2) in D.J. Willis, E.W. Holden, and M. Rosenberg, eds., *Prevention of Child Maltreatment: Developmental and Ecological Perspectives.* New York: John Wiley.

Hrdy, S.B.
    1976   Care and exploitation of nonhuman primate infants by conspecifics other than the
            mother. In D. Lehrman, R.A. Hinde, and E. Shaw, eds., *Advances in the Study of
            Behavior* Vol 4. New York: Academic Press.
Huesmann, L.R., L.D. Eron, M.M. Lefkowitz, and L.O. Walder
    1984   Stability of aggression over time and generations. *Journal of Abnormal Psychol-
            ogy* 20:1120-1134.
Hunter, R.S., and N. Kilstrom
    1979   Breaking the cyle in abusive families. *American Journal of Psychiatry* 36(Octo-
            ber):1320-1322.
Hunter, R.S., N. Kilstrom, E.N. Kraybill, and F. Loda
    1978   Antecedents of child abuse and neglect in premature infants: A prospective study
            in a newborn intensive care unit. *Pediatrics* 61:629-635.
Huston, A.C.
    1991   *Children in Poverty: Child Development and Public Policy.* Cambridge: Cam-
            bridge University Press.
Kadushin, A.
    1976   Child welfare services. *Children Today* (May/June) 5(3):16-23.
Kadushin, A., and J.A. Martin
    1981   *Child Abuse: An Interactional Event.* New York: Columbia University Press.
Kamel, F., E. Mock, W. Wright, and A. Frankel
    1975   Alterations in plasma concentrations of testosterone, LH, and prolactin associated
            with mating in the male rat. *Hormones and Behavior* 6(3):277-288.
Kaufman, J., and E. Zigler
    1987   Do abused children become abusive parents? *American Journal of Orthopsychiatry*
            57:186-192.
Kavanaugh, K., L. Youngblade, J. Reid, and B. Fagot
    1988   Interactions between children and abusive control parents. *Journal of Clinical
            Child Psychology* 17:137-142.
Kelly, R.J., and R. Lusk
    1992   Theories of pedophilia. In W. O'Donohue and J.H. Geer, eds., *The Sexual Abuse
            of Children: Theory and Research, Volume 1.* Hillsdale, NJ: Lawrence Erlbaum
            Press.
Kempe, C.H., F.N. Silverman, B. Steele, W. Droegemueller, and H.R. Silver.
    1962   The battered child syndrome. *Journal of the American Medical Association* 181(1):17-
            24.
Kempe, R.S., and C.H. Kempe
    1978   *Child Abuse.* Cambridge, MA: Harvard University Press.
Kinard, E.M., and L.V. Klerman
    1980   Teenage parenting and child abuse: Are they related? *American Journal of
            Orthopsychiatry* 50(3):481-488.
Klein, M., and L. Stern
    1971   Low birth weight and the battered child syndrome. *American Journal of Diseases
            of Childhood* 122:15-18.
Knight, R.A.
    1985   A taxonomic analysis of child molesters. Pp. 2-20 in R.A. Prentky and V.L.
            Quinsey, eds., *Human Sexual Aggression: Current Perspectives.* Annals of the
            New York Academy of Sciences 528. New York: The New York Academy of
            Sciences.
Knudsen, D.D.
    1988   Child sexual abuse and pornography: Is there a relationship? *Journal of Family
            Violence* 3(4):253-267.

Kotelchuck, M.
1982   Child abuse and neglect: Prediction and misclassification. Pp. 67-104 in R.H. Starr, ed., *Child Abuse Prediction: Policy Implications*. Cambridge, MA: Ballinger.

Kreuz, L.E., and R.M. Rose
1972   Assessment of aggressive behavior and plasma testosterone in a young criminal population. *Psychosomatic Medicine* 34:321-332.

Krugman, R.D., M. Lenherr, L. Betz, and G.E. Fryer
1986   The relationship between unemployment and physical abuse of children. *Child Abuse and Neglect* 10:415-418.

Langevin, R.
1983   *Sexual Strands: Understanding and Treating Sexual Anomalies in Men*. Hillsdale, NJ: Lawrence Erlbaum Press.

Lanning, K.V.
1987   Child Molesters: A Behavioral Analysis. December. National Center for Missing and Exploited Children, Arlington, VA.
1992   Investigators' Guide to Allegations of Ritual Abuse. January. National Center for the Analysis of Violent Crime. Quantico, VA.

Lanyon, R.I.
1986   Theory and treatment in child molestation. *Journal of Consulting and Clinical Psychology* 54(2):176-182.

Larrance, D.T., and C.T. Twentyman
1983   Maternal attribution and child abuse. *Journal of Abnormal Psychology* 92:449-457.

Last, J.M.
1988   *A Dictionary of Epidemiology*. 2nd ed. New York: Oxford University Press.

Lauderdale, M., A. Valiunas, and R. Anderson
1980   Race, ethnicity, and child maltreatment: An empirical analysis. *Child Abuse and Neglect* 4:163-169.

Leventhal, J.M.
1981   Risk factors for child abuse: Methodologic standards in case-control studies. *Pediatrics* 68(November):684-690.

Leventhal, J.M., S. Horwitz, C. Rude, and D. Stier
1993   Maltreatment of children born to teenage mothers: A comparison between the 1960s and the 1980s. *Journal of Pediatrics* 122:314-319.

Lewis, D.O.
1992   From abuse to violence: Psychophysiological consequences of maltreatment. *Journal of the American Academy of Child and Adolescent Psychiatry* 31(3):383-391.

Lewis, D.O., J.H. Pincus, B. Bard, and E. Richardson
1988   Neuropsychiatric, psycho-educational, and family characteristics of 14 juveniles condemned to death in the United States. *American Journal of Psychiatry* 145(5):584-589.

Lewis, D.O., S.S. Shanok, J.H. Pincus, and G.H. Glaser
1980   Violent juvenile delinquents. *Annual Progress in Child Psychiatry and Child Development:Psychiatric, Neurological, Psychological Abuse Factors*:591-603.
1989   Toward a theory of the genesis of violence: A follow-up study of delinquents. *American Academy of Child and Adolescent Psychiatry* 28(3):431-436.

Lichtenstein, K.
1983   Prediction Based on Census Data and Economic Indicators. Paper presented at the 3rd National Conference on Research, Demonstration, and Evaluation in Social Services, American Public Welfare Association, Washington, DC.

Light, R.
1973   Abused and neglected children in America: A study of alternative policies. *Harvard Educational Review* 43:556-598.
Lorber, R., D.K. Felton, and J.B. Reid
1984   A social learning approach to the reduction of coercive processes in child abusive families: A molecular analysis. *Advances in Behavior Research and Therapy* 6:29-45.
Lutzker, J.R.
1984   Project 12-Ways: Treating child abuse and neglect from an ecobehavioral perspective. Pp. 260-295 in R.F. Dangel and R.A. Polster, eds., *Parent Training: Foundations of Research and Practice*. New York: Guilford Press.
Lynch, M.A., and J. Roberts
1977   Predicting child abuse: Signs of bonding failure in the maternity hospital. *British Medical Journal* 1:624-626.
MacAndrew, C., and R.B. Edgerton
1969   *Drunken Comportment: A Social Explanation*. Chicago, IL: Aldine.
Maccoby, E.E., and J.A. Martin
1983   Socialization in the context of the family: Parent-child interaction. Pp. 1-102 in P.H. Mussen and E.M. Hetherington, eds., *Handbook of Child Psychology: Socialization, Personality, and Social Development*. New York: John Wiley and Sons.
MacLean, P.
1985   Brain evolution relating to family, play and the separation call. *Archives of General Psychiatry* 42:405-417.
Main, M.
1983   Exploration, play, and cognitive functioning related to infant mother attachment. *Infant Behavior and Development* 6:167-174.
Marshall, W.L.
1989   Pornography and sex offenders. Pp. 185-214 in D. Zillmann and J. Bryant, eds., *Pornography: Research Advances and Policy Considerations*. Hillsdale, NJ: Lawrence Erlbaum Press.
Mash, E.J, C. Johnston, and K. Kovitz
1983   A comparision of the mother-child interactions of physically abused and nonabused children during play and task situations. *Journal of Clinical Child Psychology* 12:337-346.
Mason, J.O.
1989   The Harm of Pornography. Address to the Religious Alliance Against Pornography. October 26.
McCormick, K.F.
1992   Attitudes of primary care physicians toward corporal punishment. *Journal of the American Medical Association* 267(23)(June 17):3161-3165.
Meisels, S.J., and J.W. Plunkett
1988   Developmental consequences of preterm birth: Are there long-term effects? Pp. 87-128 in P.B. Baltes, D.L. Featherman, and R.M. Lerner, eds., *Life-span Development and Behavior*. Hillsdale, NJ: Lawrence Erlbaum.
Melnick, B., and J.R. Hurley
1969   Distinctive personality of child-abusing mothers. *Journal of Consulting and Clinical Psychology* 33(December):746-749.
Meyer-Bahlburg, H.F.L.
1974   Aggression, and androgens, and the XYY syndrome. Pp. 433-453 in R.C. Friedman, R.M. Richart, and R. Vande Wiele, eds., *Sex Differences in Behavior*. New York: John Wiley.

Milner, J.S., and C. Chilamkurti
    1991   Physical child abuse perpetrator characteristics: A review of the literature. *Journal of Interpersonal Violence* 6(3)(September):345-366.
Monti, P.M., W.A. Brown, and M.A. Corriveau
    1977   Testosterone and components of aggressive and sexual behavior in man. *American Journal Psychiatry* 134:692-694.
Morgan, P.
    1982   Alcohol and family violence: A review of the literature. In National Institute of Alcoholism and Alcohol Abuse, Alcohol Abuse, Alcohol Consumption and Related Problems. (Alcohol and Health Monograph 1) Washington, DC: Department of Health and Human Services.
Murphy, S., B. Orkow, and R.M. Nicola
    1985   Prenatal prediction of child abuse and neglect: A prospective study. *Child Abuse and Neglect* 9(2):225-235.
National Center for Child Abuse and Neglect
    1981   *National Study of the Incidence and Severity of Child Abuse and Neglect*. 81-30325. Washington, DC: U.S. Department of Health and Human Services. [NIS-1]
    1988   *Study Findings: Study of National Incidence and Prevalence of Child Abuse and Neglect*. Washington, DC: U.S. Department of Health and Human Services. [NIS-2]
National Research Council
    1990   *Who Cares for America's Children?* Panel on Child Care Policy, Committee on Child Development Research and Public Policy, Commission on Behavioral and Social Sciences and Education. Washington, DC: National Academy Press.
Oates, K.
    1986   *Child Abuse and Neglect: What Happens Eventually?* New York: Brunner Mazel.
Oates, R.K., A.A. Davis, M.G. Ryan, and L.F. Stewart
    1979   Risk factors associated with child abuse. *Child Abuse and Neglect* 3:547-553.
Ogbu, J.
    1981   Origins of human competence: A cultural-ecological perspective. *Child Development* 52:413-429.
Orme, T.C., and J. Rimmer
    1981   Alcoholism and child abuse. *Journal of Studies on Alcohol* 42:273-287.
Panton, J.H.
    1978   Personality differences appearing between rapists of adults, rapists of children, and non-violent sexual molesters of children. *Research Communications in Psychology, Psychiatry, and Behavior* 3(4):385-393.
Parke, R.D., and C.W. Collmer
    1975   Child abuse: An interdisciplinary analysis. Pp. 509-590 in E.M. Hetherington, ed., *Review of Child Development Research* 5. Chicago: University of Chicago Press.
Parmalee, A.H., Jr.
    1975   Neurophysiological and behavioral organization of premature infants in the first months of life. *Biological Psychiatry* 10:501-512.
Patterson, G.R.
    1982   *Coercive Family Processes.* Eugene, OR: Castalia Publishing Co.
Patterson, G.R., J.B. Reid, and T.J. Dishion
    1992   *Antisocial Boys.* Eugene, OR: Castalia Publishing Co.

Pelton, L.H.
1978   Child abuse and neglect: The myth of classlessness. *American Journal of Orthopsychiatry* 48:608-617.
1981   *The Social Context of Child Abuse and Neglect.* New York: Human Sciences Press.
1989   *For Reasons of Poverty.* New York: Praeger.
Pernanen, K.
1991   *Alcohol in Human Violence.* New York: Guilford Press.
Peters, J.J.
1976   Children who are victims of sexual assault and the psychology of offenders. *American Journal of Psychotherapy* 30(3):395-421.
Pianta, R.C., and B. Egeland
1990   Life stress and parenting outcomes in a disadvantaged sample: Results of the Mother-Child Interaction project. Special Issue: The stresses of parenting. *Journal of Clinical Child Psychology* 19(4):329-336.
Pianta, R., B. Egeland, and M.F. Erickson
1989   The antecedents of maltreatment: Results of the Mother-Child Interaction Research Project. Pp. 203-253 in D. Cicchetti and V. Carlson, eds., *Child Maltreatment: Theory and Research on the Causes and Consequences of Child Abuse and Neglect.* New York: Cambridge University Press.
Polansky, N.A., R. Borgman, and C. DeSaix
1972   *Roots of Futility.* San Francisco: Jossey-Bass.
Polansky, N.A., M.A. Chalmers, E. Buttenweiser, and D.P. Williams
1981   *Damaged Parents: An Anatomy of Child Neglect.* Chicago: University of Chicago Press.
Polansky, N.A., J.M. Gaudin, and A.C. Kilpatrick
1992   Family radicals. *Children and Youth Services Review* 14:19-26.
Pollock, V.E., J. Briere, L. Schneider, J. Knop, S.A. Mednick, and D.W. Goodwin
1990   Childhood antecedents of antisocial behavior: Parental alcoholism and physical abusiveness. *American Journal of Psychiatry* 147:1290-1293.
Powell, G.F., and J.L. Low
1983   Behavior in non-organic failure to thrive. *Journal of Developmental and Behavioral Pediatrics* 4:26-33.
Powell, G.F., J.L. Low, and M.A. Spears
1987   Behavior as a diagnostic aid in failure to thrive. *Journal of Developmental and Behavioral Pediatrics* 8:18-24.
Prentky, R.A.
1990   Sexual Violence. Paper prepared for the Panel on the Understanding and Control of Violent Behavior. Washington, DC: National Research Council.
Rada, R.T., D.R. Laws, and R. Kellner
1976   Plasma testosterone levels in the rapist. *Psychosomatic Medicine* 38:257-268.
Reid, J.B., K. Kavanagh, and D.V. Baldwin
1987   Abusive parents' perceptions of child problem behaviors: An example of parental bias. *Journal of Abnormal Child Psychology* 15:457-466.
Rines, J.P., and F.S. Vom Saal
1984   Fetal effects on sexual behavior and aggression in young and old female mice treated with estrogen and progesterone. *Hormones and Behavior* 18(2):117-129.
Robins, L.N., and D.A. Regier, eds.
1991   *Psychiatric Disorders in America: The Epidemiological Catchment Area Study.* New York: Free Press.

Robins, L.N., J.E. Helzer, M.M. Weissman, H. Orvaschel, E. Gruenberg, J.D. Burke, and D.A. Regier
1984   Lifetime prevalence of specific psychiatric disorders in 3 sites. *Archives of General Psychiatry* 41(10):949-958.
Rosenbaum, A., and K.D. O'Leary
1981   Children: The unintended victims of marital violence. *American Journal of Orthopsychiatry* 51:692-699.
Rosenberg, M.S.
1987   New directions for research on the psychological maltreatment of children. *American Psychologist* 42:166-171.
Runyan, D.K., C.L. Gould, D.C. Trost, and F.A. Loda
1981   Determinants of foster care placement for the maltreated child. *American Journal of Public Health* 71(July):706-711.
Russell, D.E.H.
1986   *The Secret Trauma: Incest in the Lives of Girls and Women*. New York: Basic Books.
Rutter, M.
1987   Psychosocial resilience and protective mechanisms. *American Journal of Orthopsychiatry* 57(3):316-331.
Sameroff, A.J., and M. Chandler
1975   Reproductive risk and the continuum of caretaking casualty. Pp. 187-244 in F. Horowitz, ed., *Review of Child Development Research* 4. Chicago: University of Chicago Press.
Scheper-Hughes, N., ed.
1987   *Child Survival: Anthropological Perspectives on the Treatment and Maltreatment of Children*. Boston: Kluwer.
Schetky, D.H.
1988   Child pornography and prostitution. Pp. 153-165 in D.H. Schetky and A.H. Green, eds., *Child Sexual Abuse: A Handbook for Health Care and Legal Professionals*. New York: Brunner/Maxel.
Shosenberg, N.
1980   Self-help groups for parents of premature infants. *Canadian Nurse* (July-August):30-33.
Smith, D.E., M.D. King, and B.G. Hoebel
1970   Lateral hypothalamic control of killing: Evidence for a cholinoceptive mechanism. *Science* 167:900-901.
Spinetta, J.J., and D. Rigler
1972   The child abusing parent: A psychological review. *Psychological Bulletin* 77:296-304.
Sroufe, L.A.
1983   Infant-caregiver attachment and patterns of adaptation in preschool: The roots of maladaptation and competence. Pp. 41-83 in M. Perlmutter, ed., *Minnesota Symposium in Child Psychology* 16. Hillsdale, NJ: Lawrence Erlbaum Press.
Stark, R., and J. McElvoy, III
1970   Middle class violence. *Psychology Today* 4:52-65.
Starr, R.H., Jr., ed.
1979   Child abuse. *American Psychologist* 34(10):872-878.
1982   *Child Abuse Prediction: Policy Implications*. Cambridge, MA: Ballinger.
1992   Physical abuse of children. In V.B. Van Hasselt et al., eds., *The Handbook of Family Violence*. New York: Plenum Press.

Steele, B.
    1976   Violence within the family. Pp. 3-24 in C.H. Kempe and A.E. Helfer, eds., *Child Abuse and Neglect: The Family and the Community*. Cambridge, MA: Ballinger.

Steele, B.F., and C.B. Pollock
    1968   A psychiatric study of parents who abuse infants and small children. Pp. 89-133 in R.E. Helfer and C.H. Kempe, eds., *The Battered Child*. Chicago: University of Chicago Press.

Steinberg, L., R. Catalano, and D. Dooley
    1981   Economic antecedents of child abuse and neglect. *Child Development* 52:975-985.

Steinberg, L., S.M. Dornbusch, and B. Brown
    1992a   Ethnic differences in adolescent achievement: An ecological perspective. *American Psychologist*.

Steinberg, L., S.D. Lamborn, S.M. Dornbusch, and N. Darling
    1992b   Impact of parenting practices on adolescent achievement: Authoritative parenting, school involvement, and encouragement to succeed. *Child Development* 63:1266-1281.

Straus, M.A.
    1980   Stress and physical child abuse. *Child Abuse and Neglect* 4:75-88.

Straus, M.A., and R.J. Gelles
    1986   Societal change in family violence from 1975 to 1985 as revealed by two national surveys. *Journal of Marriage and the Family* 48(August): 465-479.

Straus, M.A., and S. Lauer
    1993   Corporal Punishment and Crime in Ethnic Group Context. Paper presented at the 1992 meeting of the American Society of Criminology, Durham, NH.

Straus, M.A., and C. Yodanis
    1994   Paths from Corporal Punishment to Physical Abuse in a Nationally Representative Sample of American Parents. Chapter 6 in Murray A. Straus, ed., *Beating the Devil Out of Them: Corporal Punishment by Parents and Its Effects on Children*. Boston: Lexington/Macmillan. (forthcoming)

Suomi, S.J.
    1978   Maternal behavior by socially incompetent monkeys: Neglect and abuse of offspring. *Journal of Pediatric Psychology* 3(1):28-34.

Suomi, S.J., and C. Ripp
    1983   A history of motherless mother monkey mothering at the University of Wisconsin Primate Laboratory. Pp. 49-78 in M. Reite and N.G. Caine, eds., *Child Abuse: The Nonhuman Primate Data*. New York: Alan R. Liss, Inc.

Tharp, R.G.
    1991   Cultural diversity and the treatment of children. *Journal of Consulting and Clinical Psychology* 59(6):799-812.

Trickett, P.K., J.L. Aber, V. Carlson, and D. Cicchetti
    1991   The relationship of socioeconomic status to the etiology and developmental sequelae of physical child abuse. *Developmental Psychology* 27(1):148-158.

Trickett, P.K., and L. Kuczynski
    1986   Children's misbehaviors and parental discipline strategies in abusive and nonabusive families. *Developmental Psychology* 22:115-123.

Trickett, P.K., and E.J. Susman
    1988   Parental perceptions of child-rearing practices in physically abusive and nonabusive families. *Developmental Psychology* 24:270-276.

Tuteur, W., and J. Glotzer
    1966   Further observations on murdering mothers. *Journal of Forensic Studies* 11:373-383.

Twentyman, C.T., and R.C. Plotkin
    1982   Unrealistic expectations of parents who maltreat their children: An educational deficit that pertains to child development. *Journal of Clinical Psychology* 38(3):497-503.

U.S. Senate Committee on Governmental Affairs, Subcommittee on Investigations
    1986   Child Pornography and Pedophilia. Report, October 9. Washington, DC: U.S. Government Printing Office.

Wahler, R.G., and J.E. Dumas
    1986   "A chip off the old block": Some interpersonal characteristics of coercive children across generations. Pp. 49-86 in P. Strain, M. Guralnick, and H. Walkee, eds., *Children's Social Behavior: Development, Assessment, and Modification.* New York: Academic Press.

Weiger, W.A., and D.M. Bear
    1988   An approach to the neurology of aggression. *Journal of Psychiatric Research* 244:160-166.

Weiss, B., K.A. Dodge, J.E. Bates, and G.S. Petit
    1992   Some consequences of early harsh discipline: Child aggression and a maladaptive social information processing style. *Child Development* 63(6):1321-1335.

Weller, S.C., A.K. Romney, and D.P. Orr
    1987   The myth of a subculture of corporal punishment. *Human Organization* 16(1):39-47.

West, D.J., C. Roy., and F.L. Nichols
    1978   *Understanding Sexual Attacks.* London: Heinemann.

Whipple, E.E., and C. Webster-Stratton
    1991   The role of parental stress in physically abusive families. *Child Abuse and Neglect* 15:279-291.

Widom, C.S.
    1989   Does violence beget violence? A critical examination of the literature. *Psychological Bulletin* 106(1):3-28.
    1991   The role of placement experiences in mediating the criminal consequences of early childhood victimization. *American Journal of Orthopsychiatry* 61(2):195-209.
    1992   Child Abuse and Alcohol Use. Prepared for the working group on alcohol-related violence: Fostering interdisciplinary perspectives, convened by the National Institute on Alcohol Abuse and Alcoholism (NIAAA), Washington, DC (May).

Wolfe, D.A.
    1985   Child-abusive parents: An empirical review and analysis. *Psychological Bulletin* 97(3)(May):462-482.
    1991   *Preventing Physical and Emotional Abuse of Children.* New York: Guilford Press.

Wolock, I.
    1982   Community characteristics and staff judgments in child abuse and neglect cases. *Social Work Research and Abstracts* 18(2) Summer:9-15.

Wolock, I., and B. Horowitz
    1979   Child maltreatment and material deprivation among AFDC-recipient families. *Social Service Review* 53(June):175-194.
    1984   Child maltreatment as a social problem: The neglect of neglect. *American Journal of Orthopsychiatry* 54(4)(October):530-543.

Wyatt, G.E.
    1985   The sexual abuse of Afro-American and white American women in childhood. *Child Abuse and Neglect* 9:507-519.

Wyatt, G.E., and M. Newcomb
  1990   Internal and external mediators of women's sexual abuse in childhood. *Journal of Consulting and Clinical Psychology* 58(6):758-767.
Wyatt, G.E., M. Newcombe, M. Riederlee, and C. Notgrass
  in press *The Effects of Child Sexual Abuse and Psychological Functioning.* Newbury Park, CA: Sage Publications.
Young, L.
  1964   *Wednesday's Children: A Study of Child Neglect and Abuse.* New York: McGraw-Hill.
Zeanah, C.H., and P.D. Zeanah
  1989   Intergenerational transmission of maltreatment. *Psychiatry* 52:177-196.
Zigler, E., and N.W. Hall
  1989   Physical child abuse in America: Past, present, and future. In D. Cicchetti and V. Carlson, eds., *Child Maltreatment Theory and Research on the Causes and Consequences on Child Abuse and Neglect.* New York: Cambridge University Press.
Zuravin, S.J.
  1987   The ecology of child maltreatment: Identifying and characterizing high-risk neighborhoods. *Child Welfare League of America* 66(6)(November-December):497-506.
  1988   Fertility patterns: Their relationship to child physical abuse and child neglect. *Journal of Marriage and the Family* 50:983-993.

5

Prevention

In the field of child maltreatment, the goals of preventive interventions are to reduce risk factors associated with child abuse and neglect, to improve the outcomes of individuals or families exposed to such risk factors, and to enhance compensatory or protective factors that could mitigate or buffer the child from the effects of victimization.

OVERVIEW

Building on the discussion in Chapter 4, the panel reviewed research on child maltreatment prevention within a framework that considers individual and family behaviors within a broader context, including the consideration of community, society, and developmental factors. This ecological, developmental model emphasizes the importance of interactive processes in the development of behaviors that lead to child abuse and neglect. In the past, the literature has been dominated by an orientation that emphasizes perceived weaknesses or problem behaviors that require correction and ignores protective factors that may influence outcomes. In recent years, some researchers have begun to examine variables that foster healthy relationships or reduce risk for child maltreatment (Cicchetti and Rizley, 1981; Rosenberg, 1987). The developmental perspective of the panel encourages consideration of significant research areas from the field of child development, such as attachment, autonomy and social relationships, peer competency, parental styles, and so forth, in the evaluation of preventive efforts for child maltreatment. The interaction between risk and protective factors is the approach that the panel believes holds much promise for future prevention research.

The panel examined evidence of what appear to be promising prevention programs, such as home visitation, parental education, and child sexual abuse prevention curriculums. We also examined research on interventions not designed specifically for child maltreatment prevention but that may reduce such behavior by improving the welfare of families that are characterized by multiple problems or by reducing the use of violence in general. The research is organized by the system that is targeted—the individual, the family, the exosystem, or the macrosystem—as outlined in earlier chapters. The framework adopted by the panel in our review of these programs highlights the areas of strength and weakness in current knowledge about prevention strategies. Table 5.1 summarizes the broad range of major prevention programs by developmental period identified in 1988. Many of these interventions are discussed in this chapter. The availability of such programs, in terms of their accessibility by diverse populations, is not certain.

As noted in Chapter 4, a variety of interactive models has been proposed in recent years to describe different systems that influence the causes and consequences of child maltreatment. The interactive models seem particularly useful to guide prevention efforts because they suggest that intervention should take place on every level of the system and they offer a range of interventions that are sensitive to diverse cultural values affecting family life and parental practices. This approach assumes that the transactions between these levels of risk—for example, living in an at-risk neighborhood and in a family at high stress—are major influences on the occurrence of maltreatment rather than the presence of single risk factors. Therefore, the reduction of multiple vulnerabilities *and* the development of compensatory behaviors are emerging goals of child maltreatment prevention.

Although many advocates of the prevention of child abuse and neglect have encouraged the need for a continuum of services (Helfer, 1982), research on maltreatment prevention efforts has generally focused on a single type of maltreatment (physical or sexual abuse, neglect, or emotional maltreatment); a single intervention (such as family preservation programs or maternal-child health programs); or a single risk factor (poverty, alcohol, or harsh parenting). The approach of the panel in preparing a research agenda for the prevention of child maltreatment seeks to encourage the development of interactive research analyses by focusing on the processes by which multiple risk factors coexist in the family system and the family environment.

Our approach differs from that of the traditional public health model for prevention, which considers primary, secondary, and tertiary levels of pre-

TABLE 5.1 Types of Child Abuse and Neglect Prevention Programs

Type of Program	Perinatal		Toddler and Preschool Years	Elementary School Years	Junior and Senior High School Years
	Before Birth	Infancy			
PROGRAMS CURRENTLY AVAILABLE					
Home visitor					
Professional who visits	X	X	X		
Lay visitors	X	X	X		
Extended postpartum contact and rooming-in		X			
Central-location parent education and counseling	X	X	X		
"Total push" programs, which involve services (e.g., home visitor, parental education)	X	X	X		
Respite nursery or day care		X	X		
Child-targeted sex abuse prevention programs			X	X	X
Latch-key demonstration and education for children in self-care after school				X	
Programs for pregnant and parenting teenagers					X
Telephone hotlines or "warm lines" for parents and children		X	X	X	X
Media campaigns		X	X	X	X

TABLE 5.1 (continued)

Type of Program	Perinatal		Toddler and Preschool Years	Elementary School Years	Junior and Senior High School Years
	Before Birth	Infancy			
PROGRAMS NOT AVAILABLE (NA) OR INSUFFICIENTLY AVAILABLE (IA)					
Father or stepfather-targeted abuse prevention	NA	NA	NA	NA	NA
Pedophile or perpetrator-targeted sex abuse prevention			IA	IA	IA
Education and counseling for parents of older children				IA	NA
After-school day care for school-age children; i.e., so-called latchkey child care				IA	

SOURCE: Mueller and Higgins (1988:32).

vention. Although the public health model might be useful in the child maltreatment prevention field, we have not adopted it for the following reasons. First, although most child maltreatment prevention programs (with the exception of child sexual abuse programs) fall into the category of secondary prevention, the programs vary significantly by the type of maltreatment and interactional processes that are the focus of the program, the context of the prevention effort, the nature of the risk assessment process, and the developmental stage of the child. Second, adapting the public health model to child maltreatment research is difficult because many prevention programs are hybrids in terms of this framework. For example, treatment interventions often represent tertiary prevention programs for families that have been reported to child welfare authorities, but such interventions may also offer counseling for the child to mitigate the damaging consequences of maltreatment and to prevent maladaptive behaviors that could influence future parenting styles. Such interventions thus serve as a source of secondary intervention for the child who may become a future parent.

In this chapter, we will review research on prevention programs highlighting theoretical frameworks (where they exist) that guide the development of such programs, illustrating programs that have been evaluated in the professional literature, reviewing the state of current knowledge about the role of prevention in child maltreatment research, and identifying gaps as well as promising opportunities in constructing a research agenda for this area. This review focuses on promising prevention strategies that incorporate multiple factors that are believed to be most likely to be successful in reducing child maltreatment.

Most preventive interventions focus on one particular system within the panel's framework of analysis, as outlined in Chapter 4. Examples include programs designed to improve the parental skillls and cognitive knowledge of high risk mothers (individual system); interventions designed to establish good interactions between parents and children, particularly infants (family microsystem); curriculum-based efforts that seek to develop skills for parenting, conflict resolution, and sexual abuse prevention in school-age populations, ranging from elementary to college students (exosystem); and legislative efforts or public campaigns designed to reform child welfare programs or the use of violence in the media and children's programming (macrosystem). Programs for sexual offenders (discussed in Chapter 7), including incarceration and various forms of treatment services, seek to prevent the reoccurrence of abusive behaviors, but systematic evaluations of these programs are rare. Although various advocacy organizations have urged that systemic change become part of the child maltreatment prevention movement, research on system-based factors has been limited.

Risk Factors and Preventive Interventions

Risk factors are elements that predispose an individual to a dysfunction, although being at risk does not mean that the dysfunction is inevitable. Risk factors can be environmental or individual (including biological) or reflect an interaction between the individual and the environment. Many prevention efforts seek to modify particular risk factors in order to reduce an individual's vulnerability to the disorder (Felner et al., 1991).

As noted in Chapter 4, the etiology of child maltreatment is not yet well understood, but the existing state of knowledge about risk and protective factors can guide the development of future prevention research (Cicchetti et al., 1988; Kazdin, 1989; Willis et al., 1992). Examinations of single risk factors thought to play significant roles in pathways to child maltreatment (such as poverty, substance abuse, and childhood history of abuse) need to move toward studies of the interactions of multiple factors in a situational and developmental context. The transition from single causes to multiple interactions complicates the design of prevention research, and many prevention programs are characterized by an absence of theory demonstrating the etiological factors that the program seeks to change.

To be effective, prevention research needs to establish a clear link between a reduction in selected risk factors and an ultimate decrease in abuse. Until recently, the primary or even sole focus in designing preventive interventions was the identification and modification of problematic or damaging parental practices associated with child maltreatment, such as excessive physical discipline, failure to provide children with basic necessities and care, and mismatches between a parent's expectations and a child's ability (Daro, 1992).

As noted by Daro (1992), this singular focus on parental roles was altered with the recognition of the prevalence of sexual abuse in the late 1970s. Research on victims of sexual abuse suggested that risk factors with respect to perpetrator characteristics, victim characteristics, and sociodemographic variables are far more heterogeneous than physical abuse or neglect victims (Melton, 1992). As a result, prevention advocates had limited information for formulating effective prevention strategies targeted to potential perpetrators or communities in response to sexual abuse.

In the area of sexual abuse, prevention advocates focused on ways to strengthen potential victims to reduce the occurrence of child sexual abuse (Finkelhor, 1984). These efforts, generally identified as part of child assault prevention—or child safety education—provide classroom-based instruction for children of all ages on how to protect themselves from sexual assault and ways to deal with the experience of actual or potential abuse. The primary focus of the school-based programs is to strengthen a child's ability to resist assault, although these programs often include information sessions for parents and school personnel.

The child assault prevention approach has been supplemented in recent years by an emphasis on violence prevention programs, designed to equip students to develop nonviolent methods of conflict resolution in peer relations. Although the generalizability of these programs to the field of child maltreatment has not been systematically assessed, they are included in this review because such programs represent a promising direction for future research. This belief is based on the following assumptions: maltreating families are often characterized by a syndrome of multiple problems (including violence), the use of violence against children may be linked to other types of violent behavior, and efforts to reduce the use of violence in resolving individual conflicts may lead to a reduction of child maltreatment.

Summary

Most studies of prevention of risks for maltreatment have sought to isolate the relative significance of risk factors within the family, including poverty, social isolation, age and education of the mother, unrealistic parental expectations, and prior history of child maltreatment. In designing preventive interventions, researchers have given very little attention to interactions among multiple variables in the determination of risk status for subsequent child maltreatment. Efforts to target a single risk factor are not likely to be as effective in preventing maltreatment as programs based on an ecological developmental model, particularly one focused directly on the family.

THE FAMILY MICROSYSTEM

We begin with a review of parenting education programs because they represent the bulk of existing prevention efforts. The panel believes that exciting research developments exist at other levels of the framework used in this analysis, which convey new insights into the value of a multiple-level approach. These are discussed later in the chapter.

Parental practices in families with young children are a major focus of research on prevention strategies for child maltreatment. Young children spend most of their time in familial settings—even with the increase in maternal employment and the use of child care services, families still provide the bulk of child care (Baydar and Brooks-Gunn, 1991; Hayes et al., 1990). For most abuse and neglect, or the punitive or rejecting parental behavior associated with abuse and neglect, cases of young children are less likely to come to the attention of service providers than are cases of older children and youth, since infants and preschoolers are not in any universal societal institution such as the school system. In the early years, the only time that virtually all children came into contact with a service organization is at birth. Although the majority of children in the United States receive immunizations within the first year of life, not all children have repeated contact with a regular health care provider.

From a prevention perspective, targeting young children and families is critical. The transition to parenthood is a period in which marital conflict, depression, and social isolation can occur, in addition to the inevitable realignment of roles inside and outside the home (Belsky, 1991; Cowan and Cowan, 1988; Deutsch et al., 1988; Egeland and Erickson, 1991; Entwhisle and Doering, 1981; Ruble et al., 1990). Parents may be particularly responsive to interventions during this life transition, given their experience of simultaneous changes, their often limited knowledge about parenting, and their desire to be effective parents. Not surprisingly, then, the majority of primary prevention programs for child abuse and neglect focus on this transition, beginning either prenatally or just after the child's birth and continuing through part or all of the first year of life or even through the second and third years.

Pathways to Parental Practices

Prevention strategies have built on individual, familial, and community-level risk and protective factors that contribute directly to both parental practices and to child well-being. This research foundation has provided the basis for identifying families that are at risk for parental practices associated with child abuse and neglect. Generally, groups have been targeted for prevention efforts by either individual or familial risk factors. In some cases, communities (or hospitals) with a high incidence of families with biological or other individual risk factors are chosen as the site of a prevention effort, with further targeting of at-risk individuals within these already high-risk communities. Increasingly, communities are becoming the target of early intervention programs, as the importance of offering comprehensive, coordinated services is recognized (Schorr, 1988).

The dimensions of prevention services focusing on families with young children vary by delivery setting (home, school, community center, clinic), primary target (family, parent, child), timing of onset (prenatal, infant, toddler, school-age, adolescent), intensity (amount of programming per week), scope and length of program, uniformity of services to client, number of services offered, training of service provider, and curriculum content. While many prevention programs focusing on parental practices have been developed and implemented over the past decades, only a handful have been evaluated in the scientific literature, often measuring outcomes such as the acquisition of cognitive or behavioral skills and observational studies of parent-child interactions. Very few parenting programs have been evaluated in terms of their effects on child maltreatment.

Incidents of child maltreatment may be difficult to identify in the aftermath of preventive interventions (unless such incidents are reported to government authorities). Therefore, improvements in intermediate or surrogate measures are often viewed as indicators of reduced risk status. But here again, uncertainty remains as to whether such measures are correct proxies for child abuse and whether a parent's improved knowledge of childrearing skills is a sufficient measure of effectiveness given the multiple pathways that may result in child maltreatment.

While many child maltreatment prevention programs have the reduction of abuse and neglect as a goal, most programs focus on intermediate or surrogate outcomes, such as parenting behavior, childrearing attitudes, maternal mental health, maternal problem-solving and use of health and social services, subsequent fertility, maternal employment, job training, and school completion (Benasich et al., 1992; Clewell et al., 1989; Olds, 1990). As research reviewed in Chapter 4 indicates, certain types of parenting styles or indicators of maternal well-being are associated with abuse and neglect, suggesting that home visiting and center-based programs with a parental focus can help prevent child abuse and neglect. Indeed, almost all programs aimed at enhancing child competence employ parent-oriented strategies.[1]

As we discuss in Chapter 4 and Chapter 6, we still know very little about pathways for the development of maltreating behaviors in parents, and the sequelae of physical and sexual abuse, parental rejection, parental emotional unavailability, and parental neglect are poorly understood. Important developmental challenges that occur in early childhood have been a focus for prevention because of the recognition of parents' (or more generally, the caregiver's) role in facilitating child well-being. Models of risk and vulnerability as well as family systems and ecological models speak to various factors that promote or restrain development (Bronfenbrenner, 1989; Garmezy and Rutter, 1983; Hinde and Stevensen-Hinde, 1988; Reiss, 1981; Werner and Smith, 1982).

Prevention Programs for Families with Young Children

Four major types of prevention strategies have been developed for families with young children (defined as the prenatal period through age 8) who are at risk of significant social or health problems: (1) comprehensive programs, often including home visitor services that vary widely in both scope and content, (2) center-based programs that include a family support component, parent information services, and early childhood education services, (3) community-based organizations, including voluntary and grass roots services, and (4) hospital-based interventions. Most of these programs have focused on multiple risk factors, and the evaluations of program outcomes focus primarily on child health measures. Only a few have been evaluated in terms of their impact on child maltreatment.

Comprehensive Home Visitation Programs

The majority of home visiting models or short-term, neonatal nursery-based interventions have been developed for children at biological risk of a host of poor outcomes, but they were not developed specifically for child abuse and neglect (Bennett, 1987; Brooks-Gunn, 1990). Home visiting programs initially focused almost exclusively on low-birthweight and preterm children, providing services only in the home environment. A notable exception is the Infant Health and Development Program, which combined home visiting and center-based programming for low-birthweight, premature infants and toddlers and their parents (Brooks-Gunn et al., 1992; Infant Health and Development, 1990; Ramey et al., 1992). Programs for children exposed to drugs in utero are being initiated across the country, but the majority of prior prevention programs in the field of substance abuse have not been guided by empirical data (Kumpfer, 1989).

Home visiting programs designed to provide universal services for all new mothers were popular earlier in this century and continue in many European countries. In the United States, a resurgence of interest in home visitation occurred in the last decade, and the audience for such programs has expanded from children solely at biological risk (from low-birthweight or pre-term births) to children who are at risk because of poverty or child maltreatment. Approaches based on a variety of models that have been initiated and evaluated in the last 10 years include a parent education model (Dunst et al., 1989), a public health model (Olds et al., 1986a,b, 1988), a social support model (Barnard et al., 1988), a mental health model (Greenspan et al., 1987), a parenting education and problem-solving model (Wasik, 1984), and an interactional attachment model (Egeland and Erickson, 1991, in press). Overlaps among these models exist (for example, the public health model includes social support and parenting as program components).

Olds (1990) has reviewed a number of home-based programs. Generally, home visitation programs start during a woman's pregnancy and continue through the first or second years of her child's life (a few begin postnatally). Many home visitors come to the mother's home weekly, others less than once or twice a month. Almost all programs focus on the mother, rather than on other caregivers such as the father or the grandmother.

Programs are likely to focus on environmentally at-risk parents: those who are poor, are young, are single, and have low education. These factors often co-occur in families, making it unlikely that programs have been offered only to one group of poor mothers (the one exception are programs specifically targeting teenage mothers) (Clewell et al., 1989; Klerman, 1991). In a few instances, at-risk communities are being targeted, as in the Hawaii Healthy Start initiative (Fuddy, 1992).

The training and experience of home visitors vary across programs—the public health models use public health nurses, whereas other models employ social workers, early childhood educators, and, in some cases, paraprofessionals.

Home visitors often expand the participant's knowledge about available services and the participant's ability to obtain these services. Home visitors also refer their families for social, educational, welfare, and health services, but such referrals are often not documented even though they may make a large impact on families. For example, Olds (1986a,b) reports that mothers who received home visiting completed more education than those in a control group. Brooks-Gunn and colleagues (in press, b) report that mothers with more educational experience who received home visiting were more likely to receive Medicaid-reimbursed health insurance and Aid to Families With Dependent Children than similarly educated mothers who did not receive home visiting services (presumably these mothers were eligible for these service but were unaware of their eligibility).

The most scientifically rigorous program evaluation of a comprehensive prevention program documented in the literature is the Prenatal/Early Infancy Project conducted by Olds and associates (1980, 1982, 1984, 1986a,b, 1990, 1992). One significant feature of this secondary prevention program is the use of nurse home visitation services for expectant mothers and their families in Elmira, a rural section of upstate New York. Elmira County was part of the standard metropolitan statistical area rated the worst in the United States in 1980 in terms of economic conditions (Boyer and Savageau, 1981), and it had the highest rates of reported and verified case of child abuse and neglect in New York State from the early 1970s through the mid-1980s (Olds, 1992). Of 400 women registered for the study, 90 percent were white, and all of the major findings reported by Olds apply only to this group (Olds, 1992). The Prenatal/Early Infancy Project is characterized by the use of professionally trained nurses as home visitors as well as a rigorous evaluation methodology that includes random assignment of subjects to four treatment groups.[2] The project evaluated prenatal, birth, and postnatal outcome variables, including length of gestation, infant birthweight, quality of maternal interactions with the child, disciplinary behaviors, child maltreatment reports, and postnatal emergency room visits. The major finding of the project was that nurse home visitation services significantly reduced the number of subsequent child maltreatment reports, compared with the control population. The reduction was especially significant among families judged to be at high risk for child maltreatment. The program is now being tested in an urban center in Memphis, Tennessee, with a sample of 1,100 low-income black families to study the generalizability of the findings (Olds, 1992).

The relatively small sample sizes in these studies generally do not provide enough statistical power to assess differences in child abuse and neglect among treatments (Olds, 1990). Although few home visitation programs report actual rates of child abuse and neglect (see review by Olds, 1990), evaluations have assessed risk factors for child maltreatment such as unstable relationships, social isolation, maternal education, personal adjustment and mental health of parents, limited childrearing skills, lack of knowledge about child development, unrealistic expectations and attributions, the quality of the relationship between parent and child, and harsh or punitive parenting.

One frequently cited study compared reported (state-verified) cases of child abuse and neglect over the first two years of the child's life for a subgroup of the Elmira Project mother—those who were poor, unmarried teenagers—with a comparable control group (Olds et al., 1986a,b): the rate was 19 percent in the control group and 4 percent in the nurse visitation group. Two other smaller programs conducted over a decade ago in Denver, Colorado, and Greensboro, North Carolina, also reported on verified cases of child abuse and neglect and found no treatment effects (Gray et al., 1979; Seigel et al., 1980), although they did not divide their sample into subgroups, as did Olds and his colleagues. However, in the Denver program, like the Elmira Prenatal Early Infancy Project, mothers in the home visitation group had more visits to the hospital for serious injuries (a possible marker for abuse and neglect). In the Elmira project, parental practices, as observed in the homes, were less punitive and restrictive in the young mothers who had received the home visitation services. Similar (but modest) effects were seen the Greensboro program.

In his review of 12 well-designed randomized trials of home visiting, Olds (1990) suggests that the most successful programs could be characterized as follows: first, they were designed on comprehensive models, including a focus on maternal, social, behavioral, and psychological factors; second, the schedule included frequent visits and the visitor engaged in positive interactions with the mother, which are believed to have facilitated a relationship between the family and home visitor; and third, the programs targeted at-risk families. He concluded that social support during the prenatal months by itself will not alter birthweight outcomes, and that prenatal visits, by themselves, will not alter maternal and child well-being if not followed by postnatal visits. However, few trials (the Elmira project is the exception) have included different treatments or different home visiting patterns (i.e., pregnancy, post-pregnancy, neither, both) in order to test these premises directly.

Another recent home visitation program that has received significant attention is the Healthy Start program sponsored by the Maternal and Child Health Branch of the Hawaii State Department of Health. The Hawaii program seeks to target families at the time of birth that are at high risk for future incidents of child maltreatment and provides intervention to foster healthy child development and family self-sufficiency. Home visitors visit families weekly, based on their level of need, with the schedule of visits lasting about a year, diminishing to monthly and finally four visits per year until the child reaches age five. To date, only limited evaluations have been conducted to examine the effectiveness of the Hawaii Healthy Start program by comparing child maltreatment reports for families enrolled in the program with those of other high-risk or state populations.[3] Initial results suggest that abuse rates are substantially lower among high-risk families served by the program than among high-risk families who do not receive services. Abuse rates among families identified as low risk are also lower than the state average (Fuddy, 1992).

Center-based Programs

In contrast to the home visitation programs discussed above, which directly target families reported for or at risk of child maltreatment, a number of family-oriented programs have been developed to improve the general welfare of children whose families are characterized by multiple problems, including child abuse and neglect. These programs often require that family members (usually the mother) attend special classes or counseling sessions in a center that offers a wide range of resources. Family support programs may be effective in reducing the prevalence of child maltreatment by addressing multiple risk factors associated with abuse and neglect, including disabilities, poverty, family violence, and poor health. However, the comparative effectiveness of general family support programs and center-based programs that target families based on psychosocial factors associated with poverty, child abuse, punitive parenting, and child failure, such as stressful life events, maternal depression, and low social support, has not been evaluated.

Some center-based programs, which usually start in the first or second year of life, have resulted in cognitive and school improvements for children who have severe developmental delays (e.g., cerebral palsy, Down's syndrome) (Meisels and Shonkoff, 1990; Shonkoff and Hauser-Cram, 1987; Shonkoff et al., 1992). Child development centers, which also provide early center-based intervention, reported sustained effects as well (Bridgemen et al., 1981).

A majority of center-based programs for groups at familial environmental risk focus on poor children. A review of the results from 11 separate (primarily preschool) programs indicates that most children in these programs demonstrated the efficacy of early education immediately following the treatment (Lazar et al., 1982), including significant reduction in grade failure in the middle of elementary school (Ramey, 1991; Wasik et al., 1990). The majority of children from disadvantaged families are served by federal initiatives such as the Parent-Child Development Centers (PCDC) and, for older children, Head Start. Some programs target teenage mothers who, in general, are also poor (Chase-Lansdale et al., in press; Clewell et al., 1989; Klerman, 1991). Programs designed for teenage mothers and for poor mothers include large proportions of single mothers, mothers on welfare, and minority families (Chase-Lansdale and Brooks-Gunn, in press; Duncan, 1991; Huston, 1991).

Community-based Programs

A wide range of community-based programs target poor communities, including national or state programs such as Healthy Start, Fair Start, Head Start, Healthy Beginnings, and the Children's Initiative. These forms of community intervention programs seek to improve health care and social services for families at risk of a range of social and health problems (including low birthweight, teenage pregnancy, as well as child abuse and neglect). Such programs avoid the risks of labeling families and can be integrated into ongoing community services (beyond the demonstration stage) if they are seen as benefiting the entire community. Neighborhood or community-level interventions allow for an examination of differential effects of programs for various groups of families or families with a particular pattern of risk factors (see the Elmira Prenatal/Early Infancy Project, targeted toward families at risk of child health problems, and the Infant Health and Development Program, targeted for low birthweight and premature infants and their parents, as examples; Olds et al., 1986a,b, 1988; Brooks-Gunn et al., 1992, in press a,b). But, apart from the Olds studies of the Elmira project, few community intervention programs have examined the impact of their services on child abuse and neglect.

Community-level interventions are often expensive. Most family-oriented community programs have sought to minimize costs and maximize benefits by targeting poor neighborhoods, in which the majority of parents have at least one known familial risk factor (i.e., poor, single, on welfare, teenage mother, substance abuse).

Several community programs that have followed preschool children report significant effects persisting into the high school years. Reduction in juvenile delinquency and increases in high school graduation have been reported (Zigler, 1992). These few, small studies suggest that community programs for young children may have long-term effects on factors associated with educational and job success and, by inference, spillover effects on the poverty status of the next generation (Brooks-Gunn et al., 1992).

Although few programs have tested the premise that early childhood interventions may have a differential impact and may be particularly effective for the most at-risk families, two studies have supported this finding. The Infant Health and Development Program found that the intervention was most effective for mothers with low compared with high educational attainment; this was true for both African-American and white families (Brooks-Gunn et al., 1992). An analysis of Head Start attendees in three sites nationwide suggests larger effects for African-American than for white families (Lee et al., 1988). This finding may be associated with the fact that poor African-American families are much more likely to live in poor neighborhoods, to be comprised of a single parent, to have been poor longer, and to be more poor than poor white families (Liaw and Brooks-Gunn, in press).

While benefits clearly accrue to poor children, what about the mothers? And do such benefits lead to a reduction in the frequency or severity of child maltreatment? Not all center-based programs for young children report their effects on maternal or familial outcomes, or their effect on reported cases of child abuse and neglect, even though all pay lip service to the relevance of their programs for families. In a recent review of 12 center-based programs begun in the first three years of life for poor families, 7 of the 12 looked at maternal employment as an outcome, and 6 found increased employment for mothers in the intervention group. Of the 12 programs, 5 have reports on parent-child interaction via observation. All but one found that parents in the intervention group had better interaction skills (i.e, positive and supportive interaction, less criticism) than mothers in the control group. The home environments of mothers in such early intervention programs also provided more stimulating learning experiences in all of the studies that looked at the home (Benasich et al., 1992). Mothers also scored higher in warmth and acceptance as a function of early intervention in these studies.

For all three maternal outcome measures just reviewed, similar findings are reported in the one center-based program for children at biological risk—the Infant Health and Development Program (Spiker et al., in press; Bradley et al., in press). Whether these maternal effects are sustained into the elementary school years is not known (Woodhead, 1988; Zigler, 1992). Also, these programs do not report on child maltreatment—a major limitation.

Another group of community-based organizations includes the grassroots volunteer groups such as La Leche League, midwifery programs, and local Visiting Nurse Associations. These programs, often have been in existence longer than the more comprehensive community maternal-child services discussed above, and they appear to play useful roles in decreasing infant mortality and morbidity. Grassroots organizations may exercise some role in preventing child abuse and neglect as well, since they routinely work with high-risk or stressed families, but the scientific literature regarding their operation and outcomes is too limited at present to allow for systematic evaluations regarding their impact on child maltreatment.

In the past decade, a number of community-based interventions have been developed to address the problem of domestic violence (Ohlin and Tonry, 1989; Stark and Flitcraft, 1991). These programs include a range of services, including law enforcement and judicial programs designed to protect women who are victims of physical or sexual assaults by their husbands, as well as battered women's shelters that offer housing, financial, and counseling services to victims of domestic violence and their children. Domestic violence treatment programs may offer some promise in preventing child maltreatment as well. However, the scientific literature regarding the impacts of domestic violence treatment programs on the children who witness spousal assaults, or who may be subject to violence themselves, is too limited at this stage to provide a basis for inferences by the panel.

Hospital-based Interventions

Many hospital centers, clinics, and health professional groups have sought to provide opportunities for parent-child interactions in the neonatal period, recognizing that the quality of parent-infant attachment and bonding in the immediate postpartum period has significant implications for child development (Egeland and Erickson, 1991). Examples include the policy of encouraging mothers to room-in with newborns and the using educational videos for both mothers and fathers at major hospital centers (Holden et al., 1992). The objectives of these services are to heighten parental awareness of the significance and implications of neonatal cues and to identify and correct faulty parental expectations and perceptions of infant behaviors.

Early proponents of hospital mother/child rooming-in policies investigated its effects on subsequent child maltreatment. In two separate studies, O'Connor et al. (1980 and 1982) randomly assigned first-time mothers to rooming-in and no rooming-in conditions to evaluate the impact of this arrangement on subsequent rates of child maltreatment. The 1980 study showed some positive effect of rooming in by the time the child was 17 months in the families that received rooming in, but the 1982 study was more equivocal since prenatal assessments of the risk status of the mother for child maltreatment affected rooming-in assignments (Hollis et al., 1992). Studies by Gray (1983) also examined child maltreatment outcomes with respect to groups that differed in the amounts and timing of maternal-child contact in the neonatal period. Initial evaluations, based on self-reports, suggested no significant differences across the four participating groups, although high rates of subject attrition may have biased the outcome evaluation (Holden et al., 1992).

In addition to early and extended contact strategies, researchers have acknowledged the need to emphasize the capabilities and limitations of newborns for parents, enhance parent-child interactions, and thus address factors that may lead to child maltreatment. A large number of investigations have indicated that programs that encourage parents to practice eliciting responses from their newborns have positive effects on parent-child interactions several weeks to several months postnatally (Holden et al., 1992). However, the effectiveness of this intervention does not depend solely on the cognitive information or demonstrations; motivational factors are particularly significant (Belsky, 1985). Although quite promising, no investigation to date has evaluated the effects of newborn demonstration projects on subsequent rates of child maltreatment (Holden et al., 1992).

Drotar (1992) notes that medical intervention that identifies and corrects physical and nutritional deprivation in infants and young children is not sufficient to prevent the chronic psychological and physical deficits associated with child neglect. A crucial element in successful prevention programs is the development of active and persistent contacts between the caseworker and the parent, emphasizing the parent's role and ability to improve their child's condition, to create a sense of optimism regarding the child's future, to negotiate directly areas of conflict or confusion regarding the standards of adequate care that should be implemented by the parent, to maintain support and advocacy for the parent, and to develop a social system that can maintain the parent once the intervention effort is completed.

Summary

Almost all early intervention programs target the parent (Benasich et al., 1992; Clarke-Stewart and Fein, 1983). Strategies include helping the parent, usually the mother, improve her interactions and teaching skills with her child, providing the mother with problem-solving skills, raising the mother's self-esteem and emotional functioning, and increasing maternal knowledge about child development. Promising design features for parent enhancement efforts with diverse populations include supporting parents in their childrearing responsibilities prior to or as close to the birth of the first child as possible, linking parental enhancement services to a child's specific developmental level, providing opportunities for parents to model the interactions or discipline methods promoted through the interventions, recognizing cultural differences in family and parental styles, and providing referrals for social supports and needed assistance to ensure the safety of the child beyond the immediate intervention period (Daro, 1992).

Although some well-designed, randomized control, clinical trials exist, many early intervention services lack a theoretical framework and their mission is not always well defined (for example, are home visitation programs "rescue missions" or "crisis management services" for troubled families, or are they efforts to change parental attitudes and behavior?). While some interventions demonstrate that knowledge about child development can be transferred to parents in a relatively brief period of time (i.e., 6 to 12 weeks), a time commitment of six to twelve months or more is often needed to change attitudes and strengthen parenting and personnel skills (Daro, 1992). Short-term, low-intensity programs (such as hospital-based neonatal interventions) are not sufficient, by themselves, to alter long-term parent-child relationships to reduce the incidence of child maltreatment. Prevention programs need to focus directly on families most at risk for maltreatment, to accommodate families with differing needs and experiences, and to adapt to changing family situations.

THE EXOSYSTEM

In the panel's framework of analysis, the third level of prevention programs includes interventions within the various state, institutional, school, workplace, and other community systems that influence family functioning. The large majority of existing programs in the exosystem focus on prevention of physical and sexual abuse.

Child maltreatment prevention programs are usually found in the schools: they are primarily child sexual abuse prevention programs designed for children in elementary and high schools. In addition to major efforts in child sexual abuse prevention, two other efforts were reviewed by the panel that may have implications for the prevention of child abuse and neglect. These are the violence prevention programs in the schools designed to educate children, primarily adolescents, about conflict resolution skills, and community-based antipoverty programs, some of which involve vocational or educational assistance. Although such programs may be important in helping improve the welfare of many families, they have not been systematically evaluated in terms of their outcomes for child abuse and neglect.

The Role of the States and Child Abuse
Prevention Challenge Grants

Recognizing the costs of the consequences of child abuse and neglect, the Congress established a program for Child Abuse Prevention Challenge Grants as part of the Comprehensive Crime Control Act of 1984 (P.L. 98-473). The purpose of the legislation was to provide incentives and a source of funding for the states that would be dedicated to preventing child abuse and neglect as well as treating its consequences (General Accounting Office, 1991).

The Challenge Grants Program, funded at $5 million per year, is the only federal funding program dedicated solely to prevention of child abuse and neglect. Additional sources of federal funds can be used to support prevention activities (such as block grants to states included in title XX (Social Services) and title IV-B (Child Welfare Services) of the Social Security Act, but these programs do not require reports from the states on how the funds were spent (General Accounting Office, 1991). States also often draw on other funding sources from a broad range of programs, including day care, teenage parenting, parent education, family counseling, and respite care, in supporting their applications for Challenge Grant funds, but many of these applications are often disallowed after scrutiny by federal officials. As a result, records of the scope and nature of federal and state prevention program efforts in the area of child maltreatment are limited.

The Challenge Grants were designed to assist the states in developing trust funds to endow state programs specifically for the purpose of prevention. Four categories of prevention activities were defined in the program legislation: (1) education and public information seminars, (2) education for professionals, (3) dissemination of information to the public, and (4) development of community prevention programs. According to the General Accounting Office (1991), the states have reported spending 70 percent of their challenge grant funds on the last category alone.

Although community prevention activities constitute the major area of programmatic efforts within the states, no research evaluations have been conducted to study the outcomes of the program activity.

School-Based Sexual Abuse Prevention Programs

Current preventive interventions rest on several core assumptions that influence many programs and materials designed to help children prevent or escape sexual abuse: many children do not know what sexual abuse is, that sexual touch need not be tolerated, that adults want to know about children who experience sexual touches by older persons, and that disclosure of sexual abuse will help stop it (Conte and Fogarty, 1990; Kolko, 1988; Tharinger et al., 1988). Most prevention materials also incorporate several key concepts outlined by Conte et al. (1986): children own their own bodies and can control access to their bodies; the touch continuum recognizes that there are different kinds of touches (e.g., safe and unsafe); secrets about touching can and should be told; and children have a range of supportive individuals whom they can tell about touching problems. Some programs encourage children to trust their own feelings so that when a situation feels uncomfortable or strange they should "go and tell." Others encourage and teach children how to say "no."

Sexual abuse prevention programs have a wide variation in the range of materials presented, the length of the program, the vocabulary that describes the concepts, the location of the program (home or school), the format of presentation (e.g., video, instruction by adult trainers, printed matter), the degree to which the child interacts with the material (e.g., reads a book or role plays the skills), and the occupation of the trainer (Reppucci and Herman, 1991). Programs generally consist of short presentations, although some curricula involve more than 30 short sessions (Committee for Children, 1983).

The tendency to avoid explicit discussions of sexual behavior in the schools has emphasized protective, rather than sexual, themes in the curricula (Finkelhor, 1986), stressing concepts such as good and bad touches and discussions of bullies or relatives who forcefully try to kiss a child (Reppucci and Herman, 1991). The development of sexual abuse prevention programs for children under the age of 10 has been controversial because of criticisms about the appropriateness of teaching young children concepts and actions for understanding and repelling sexual abuse, the absence of consideration of children's developmental capacities in the design and implementation of such programs, the fairness of focusing prevention programs exclusively on potential victims rather than perpetrators, and uncertainties about long-term or unanticipated consequences of such programs on sexual and intimate behaviors (Conte, 1992; Leventhal, 1987; Melton, 1992; Reppucci and Herman, 1991).

Many programs have tried to involve parents, often with disappointing results (Berrick, 1988). Parent programs are rarely evaluated (Miller-Perrin and Wurtele, 1988; Reppucci and Haugaard, 1989). For example, in one study, only 39 of 116 parents whose children were participating in prevention programs attended the parent education meetings (Berrick, 1988). Furthermore, participating parents are likely to be better informed and more likely to discuss sexual behavior and sexual abuse issues with their children anyway (Porch and Petretic-Jackson, 1986).

Evaluations of several different programs using a variety of training formats have been conducted extensively (Binder and McNiel, 1987; Conte et al., 1985; Downer, 1984; Garbarino, 1987; Wolfe et al., 1986; Wurtele et al., 1987, 1989). Typical of these results, Kenning et al. (1987), evaluating the effectiveness of Child Assault Prevention (CAP), found a significant difference in posttest scores for first and second graders on a 25-item knowledge questionnaire.

Few programs examine intimate or long-term types of sexual abuse, molestation by parents, or the concept that some "bad" touches can be sexually arousing (Reppucci and Herman, 1991). Curricula that employ concrete concepts and an interactive learning experience, including rehearsal and modeling, appear to be most effective, such as the studies conducted by Kraizer and her colleagues that use role-playing techniques focused on stranger abductions (Fryer et al., 1987a,b; Kraizer et al., 1989). Although some sexual abuse prevention programs seek to expose abuse, the effectiveness of the program in achieving this goal needs to be more systematically assessed, since current data do not support this desired program effect.

Some studies have examined the issue of negative effects or unanticipated consequences of sexual abuse prevention programs on sexual behaviors and intimacy. Although there is no evidence of adverse long-term effects from such programs, some investigators have documented postprogram anxiety among a small proportion of children (usually 5 to 10 percent of participants) in the form of nightmares, upset stomachs, or similar symptoms (Daro, 1988; Gilbert et al., 1988; Kleemeier and Webb, 1986; Swan et al., 1985; Wurtele, 1988; Wurtele et al., 1989). Empirical data do not currently support fears that prevention programs will have negative consequences for most children, such as increasing anxiety or creating behavioral problems. One comprehensive multisite study of the impact of sexual abuse prevention programs on preschool children was prepared by the Berkeley Family Welfare Research Group (Daro, 1988; Daro et al., 1987; Gilbert, 1988). The Berkeley evaluation reviewed seven representative curricula for preschool children[4] and questioned the developmental readiness of preschoolers to understand the fundamental concepts conveyed in these programs.

Although sexual abuse prevention education programs have generally achieved the goals of teaching prevention knowledge and skill acquisition, it is not clear that these gains will be retained over time or would be useful to a child in an assault situation, especially if the offender was a relative or trusted adult.

Less is known about the efficacy of child sexual abuse prevention programs compared with prevention efforts (such as parental enhancement programs) directed primarily at the physical abuse and neglect of children. There is more disagreement in the child safety field about the key concepts and approaches that should guide the development and implementations of child sexual abuse prevention programs. At this juncture, it seems critical for child sexual assault prevention programs to create more formal and extensive parent and teacher training components. Efforts should be expanded to include extended after-school programs and more in-depth discussion opportunities for certain high-risk groups (e.g., former victims, teenage parents) (Daro, 1992).

Improvements in child sexual abuse prevention programs need to be considered in terms of developing curricula with a more balanced developmental perspective, identifying what skills will make a child less susceptible to sexual abuse in a variety of situations at different age levels, providing opportunities for children to rehearse prevention strategies, offering feedback on a child's performance to facilitate a child's depiction of their involvement in abusive as well as unpleasant interactions, and developing longer programs that can be integrated into regular school curricula and practices (Daro, 1992). Skills learned by a child that are appropriate for stranger abduction situations may not be transferable to assaults involving trusted adult figures (Conte, 1989). The use of role playing and in vivo assessment situations is a promising new technique in the formation of effective prevention programs, but such approaches raise important ethical issues that need to be considered carefully before exposing children to them (see discussion in Chapter 9).

Other Community-based Prevention Programs

Preventive interventions focused on various aspects of community life have been proposed as part of an interactive systems approach to reducing child maltreatment. Potential intervention sites are included in the following discussion, although the panel notes that many such approaches have not been evaluated in the professional literature and their impact on child maltreatment remains uncertain.

Antipoverty and Vocational Training Programs

As noted in Chapter 4, poverty has consistently been associated with child maltreatment, particularly child neglect. Programs designed to improve the income of poor families, especially those headed by a single parent, could become a major source of prevention of child neglect. At a time when higher education has become a mandatory requirement for well-paying jobs, programs designed to increase the career options of young parents through educational and vocational training efforts are commonly viewed as part of the preventive spectrum for child maltreatment (Chase-Lansdale and Brooks-Gunn, in press; Huston, 1991).

But antipoverty or vocational training programs are often not sufficient to deal directly with the complex set of psychological, social, and biological factors that increase risk for child neglect. This behavior may be only one expression of other inadequacies in the parent's life, many of which become apparent early in adolescence (Polansky et al., 1972a, 1981, 1992). Others have argued that child neglect behaviors are responses to the experience of poverty, for which the parent is only partially responsible (Pelton, 1989). Furthermore, the change and unpredictability associated with the lifestyles of neglectful families often affect their involvement in programs that require a commitment to a consistent schedule of meetings.

As a result, some "two generation" programs have sought to incorporate multiple dimensions of vocation training and parent-child interactions. The distinctive features of the two-generation model includes the goals of: (1) self-sufficiency services designed to improve the parent's education level, vocational skills, and employment status and (2) child development services that may include preventive health care, parent education, day care, and early childhood education. One such program is New Chance, a multisite research and demonstration program designed to improve the life prospects and parental skills of young welfare mothers. These programs, and others created as part of the Family Support Act of 1988 (P.L. 100-485), are designed to deal with many of the risk factors associated with child abuse: job training, education, parenting, health, and child development. New Chance is located at 16 different program sites across the country. At each site, the services and activities include building human capital, enhancing personal development, enhancing child development, and case management and counseling.

Educator and Child Care Staff Training

Day care providers, teachers, principals, and others who have ongoing and long-term contact with children are in a position to identify suspected victims of maltreatment and report them to child protective services. Such interventions can be a source of reduced incidence for the recurrence of child maltreatment and may prevent incidents when the offenders become aware that they can be reported for abusive or neglectful actions. Day care providers, educators, and other youth service personnel require training in the identification of child abuse and neglect, guidance in reporting suspected cases, and methods for supporting maltreatment victims and their families, including referrals to relevant treatment services and peer support groups for victims (Abrahams et al., 1992).

Sensationalized reports of child abuse in school or youth service organizations (such as the Boy Scouts) and day care centers (such as the McMartin case) have stimulated legislative and media efforts to improve the background screening and oversight of employees and volunteers who come into contact with children (Finkelhor et al., 1988). Such efforts have been criticized, however, because administrative oversight is extremely expensive and time-consuming and imposes a significant bureaucratic burden on organizations characterized by high staff turnovers and volunteer members. The benefits to be achieved, in terms of a reduction in child maltreatment, may be quite small given the low rates of reported incidence of child maltreatment that occur within educational or institutional settings.

A much greater opportunity exists in the area of educator programs that can improve the processes by which teachers, school administrators, and school health officials can recognize, report, and monitor reports of child maltreatment (Tower, 1992). Such interventions have the opportunity to strengthen the prevention of child maltreatment within the population of children who attend public or private schools. One recent national survey that assessed teacher knowledge, attitudes, and beliefs about child abuse revealed shortcomings in the training and support of teachers with respect to child abuse reporting and prevention (Abrahams et al., 1992). Only 57 percent of the teachers surveyed indicated that their school had written procedures for identifying and reporting suspected child abuse cases; the nature of existing school policies was unclear. Teachers usually report abuse cases to other school personnel, such as the principal, social worker, or nurse, and not directly to child protection agencies. The low percentage of these suspected cases that are eventually reported to child protection agencies may be a cause for special concern (Abrahams et al., 1992).

Violence Prevention in the Schools

Increases in school and community violence, especially in the inner city (Goldstein, 1992) have led many to believe that schools are an ideal location for violence prevention programs (Feindler et al., in press). School-based interventions have several advantages, including accessibility to a broad youth population, mandated attendance, ease in scheduling, and cost effectiveness (Hammond and Yung, 1991).

Despite the interest in violence prevention efforts, most school-based programs have not been evaluated. This review will focus on violence prevention programs that have been evaluated for effectiveness of their goals, recognizing that these programs were not designed to deal specifically with child abuse prevention, but rather the prevention of violence in general or in social or peer relationships. A few promising comprehensive programs, incorporating both school and family settings, are described here because interventions that target multiple levels of systems may be most likely to affect change in the area of child maltreatment.

The London Secondary School Intervention Project on Violence in Intimate Relationships (Jaffe et al., in press) is a violence prevention program designed for use with adolescents. The goals of this program are to challenge stereotypes about wife abuse and violence as a way to resolve conflict, raising awareness and therefore preventing abusive behavior. The program was implemented in several schools in the form of day or half-day workshops focused on topics related to family violence, often including a video or theatrical presentation. Presentations were followed by classroom discussions, intended to help students process the information and develop school-based plans for preventing violence. The evaluation of this program (Jaffe et al., 1990) consisted of a 48-item questionnaire on wife assault, sex roles, dating violence, and behavior in violence-related situations. Pre- and postintervention questionnaires were administered one week before the intervention, one week after the intervention, and in some cases, also six weeks after the intervention. The short-term evaluations suggested significant change in a prosocial direction on some questions, but boys also showed some significant change in the undesired direction regarding excuses for date rape. From one week to six weeks postintervention there was significant change in the undesired direction on six of the questions. The authors suggest that the backlash effect may be from boys who were already involved in abusive relationships.

One popular behavioral change program is Positive Adolescents Choices Training, or PACT, a culturally sensitive program designed for use with African-American middle school students ages 12-15 (Hammond and Yung, 1991). Participants were selected by teachers because of behavior problems, social skills deficits, or a history of being a victim of violence. The goal of PACT was to train the participants in the behavioral components of conflict resolution skills using videotapes and role-playing scenarios in 37-38 sessions, led by two African-American facilitators with 10-12 students in each group. The evaluation of this program was carried out by teachers and blind observers on a small sample of 14 students in treatment and 13 students in the control group. Overall, 75 percent of the intervention group showed improvement on the relevant skills, but only 43 percent of the control group showed skill improvement. School records also suggested less involvement in violent incidents in school by the intervention group than the control group.

These two programs are examples of promising interventions in the area of violence prevention that may have implications for child maltreatment, although they were not designed with the prevention of child maltreatment as a specific objective. In addition to the school-based programs discussed above, several organizations have designed comprehensive multisystem approaches to address the interaction of family and school factors that foster violence. One example of a comprehensive program is the Seattle Project, which focuses on multiple risk factors in the family and school context in an effort to prevent drug abuse and delinquency (Hawkins et al., 1992). A second example of a comprehensive program is the FAST Track program (Bierman et al., in press). This program, which has not yet been evaluated, was designed to help children who show disruptive behavior and poor peer relations both at school and at home. The intervention goals of these multisystem programs are to encourage collaboration among parents, children, and the school to reduce aggressive behavior. This type of multifaceted intervention may have a more pervasive effect on violence in the lives of children than purely school-based programs.

Summary. The relationship between the use of violence in peer relations and the use of violence against children in family situations is not well
understood. Since many families who are reported for child maltreatment
are characterized by other forms of violence (including spouse abuse and
involvement in criminal assaults), interrupting the cycle of violence in one
area of life may have spillover effects on others, but this assumption lacks
empirical evidence. It is also possible that intervening in other areas of
family dysfunction, such as substance abuse, may help prevent child maltreatment (especially maltreatment that is drug-related), although little research has been conducted to test this hypothesis.

Given the increasing number of youth involved in violence, surprisingly few well-designed, rigorously evaluated, and effective prevention
programs exist, and the association between violence prevention programs
and child maltreatment is largely unknown. The lack of consistent positive results in the evaluation of school-based violence prevention programs may be due to the relatively narrow scope of the interventions. It
may not be possible to intervene in school with a child and expect changes
in beliefs, attitudes, and behaviors that may be perpetuated by family and
community. School is not the only relevant context for violence, and
intervening in one context while leaving others untouched may not be
optimally effective.

Although school-based violence prevention programs are a promising
development, no firm conclusions can be drawn at this time regarding their
effectiveness or generalizability for the prevention of child abuse. These
programs do not report on the generalizability of the violence prevention to
other contexts or over time, and it is not known if participants will be less
likely to be perpetrators of family violence. It is the panel's view that
school-based programs will not serve as effective deterrents of physical or
sexual violence toward children, peers, and adults, unless they incorporate
family and community components such as those described by the ecological developmental model presented in this report.

Clergy and Religious Institutions

Religious institutions are often viewed as an underused resource in
preventing and detecting child maltreatment and its effects, but efforts to
address child abuse and neglect in religious institutions have not been assessed. Religious institutions have access to enormous numbers of children
and families and the means to deliver messages about child maltreatment
(Bush, 1991).

Some leaders in the religious community, emphasizing that religious
institutions have a mandate to address moral issues and to care for children,
have taken action in the area of child protection. A nonprofit organization,

Covenant to Care, has been established to link representatives of religious institutions with social workers, to sponsor public education forums, and assist pastors, rabbis, and temple leaders in developing sermons on the topic of child maltreatment (Bush, 1991). The experience of religious institutions in handling increasing numbers of disclosures of abuse that may involve their own members also has not been documented systematically.

Media Roles

The media exercised a significant role in setting an initial political agenda for child abuse and neglect when "The Battered Child" article by Henry Kempe and his colleagues (1962), published in a professional journal, was highly publicized in the popular press. Five years later, every state had passed child abuse reporting laws (Nelson, 1984). The U.S. Advisory Board on Child Abuse and Neglect (1990) has stressed the continued impact of media involvement in child maltreatment issues and the importance of including the media in "a concerted community response" to child abuse.

Media representatives can become important participants in public education about prevention in child abuse and neglect. Survey data from the National Committee for Prevention of Child Abuse involving various forms of print and broadcast media suggest that public awareness of child maltreatment has increased dramatically over the past decade.

Media efforts to prevent child maltreatment may benefit from lessons derived from the role of the media in addressing public health issues. For example, expanded media efforts in child abuse and neglect could adapt the methods used to change human behavior and social expectations (and ultimately alcohol-related traffic fatalities) in the national media campaign to promote the concept of the "designated driver" (Winsten, 1992). Research is needed to evaluate the effectiveness of various types of social marketing and advertising campaigns directed toward the prevention of child maltreatment. For example, quasi-experimental field designs and time series analyses, using matched controls, could be developed to identify the differential effects of programs using print or broadcast media for selected community campaigns.

But the limitations of public awareness or educational campaigns also deserve consideration. Such approaches may be effective with subpopulations who are part of the target audience and who are motivated to change health or social behaviors, and who are willing to seek assistance in making such changes. For groups who have low literacy skills or who are socially isolated from media or educational services, however, public awareness campaigns may have little value unless they are specifically targeted to such subpopulations.

Bystander's Responses

Although child abuse and neglect commonly occurs in the privacy of the home, incidents of child maltreatment occasionally appear in public places such as stores and playgrounds. Witnesses who may be disturbed by cases in which adults punish children too severely usually hesitate to intervene (Oldenburg, 1992). In one random survey, only 17 percent of observers acted to stop someone from hitting a child (National Committee for Prevention of Child Abuse, 1990). Factors that affect the willingness of bystanders to intervene on behalf of children who are inappropriately disciplined by parents or caretakers have not been well studied although uncertainty about appropriate forms of response has been suggested as a significant factor. The vague distinction between acceptable discipline and abuse also may discourage intervention. Social psychology literature on bystander behavior, which seeks to identify situational and individual factors that promote altruistic or prosocial intervention in public, may be useful in future studies of cases of child maltreatment (Davis, 1991; Korbin, 1993).

Summary

Prevention efforts in the exosystem show promise, especially in the design of multisystem approaches that can build on family-school-community approaches. The community mental health approach, and examples of media and community-based interventions designed to reduce smoking and heart disease, represent much promise, but such efforts are only beginning to be developed and evaluated in the area of child maltreatment. Well-designed program evaluations that consider interactive effects of various types of individual, family, and community-based intervention are crucial for developing a knowledge base to guide future efforts. For example, we often do not know if current interventions produce long-term changes in knowledge, skills, and behavior. We also do not know if prevention programs in selected areas of physical or sexual violence involving peers or adults can be generalized to incidents involving child maltreatment by trusted adult figures. Gaining such knowledge will require studies that follow cohorts of sample populations over time, to identify the strength of various program components and the requirements of special populations, such as children who have already experienced abusive behaviors, in designing effective prevention programs.

THE MACROSYSTEM

As noted in Chapter 4, the macrosystem consists of fundamental values and cultural norms that affect public, private, and institutional behaviors.

In selected areas of public health interventions, cultural values are an important element in changing behavior that fosters adverse consequences. Examples that illustrate this point include the rapid change in American values on issues such as smoking, diet, and exercise. As a result, prevention programs increasingly focus on ways to foster social perceptions and cultural changes that would foster the well-being of children. One such approach is encouraging the use of "time outs" to reduce the use of spanking and other forms of physical punishment in child discipline behaviors.

Several areas in the macrosystem have relevance for research on the prevention of child maltreatment. Although these issues are relatively untested in intervention strategies or research evaluations, the panel includes them here because of our belief that they warrant attention in a research agenda for the future.

Corporal Punishment

No research data have suggested that corporal punishment promotes child well-being. Despite the suggestion by several scholars that corporal punishment may be a major risk factor for physical abuse, the idea that spanking puts a parent at risk of going too far and engaging in physical abuse is not mentioned in publications issued by the National Center on Child Abuse and Neglect (the major federal agency). One content analysis by Straus and Yodanis (1994) of 120 books on child abuse found that only 12 percent included an unambiguous recommendation that corporal punishment should not be used.

Reliance on corporal punishment by American parents has been identified by some researchers as an important risk factor for physical abuse (Gelles and Straus, 1988; Gil, 1970; Kadushin and Martin, 1981; Straus and Kaufman Kantor, 1994; Straus and Yodanis, 1994; Zigler and Hall, 1989). But corporal punishment is usually not dealt with in programs to prevent physical abuse, possibly a result of the absence of experimental evidence showing that reduction of corporal punishment reduces the risk of physical abuse as well as the existence of cultural norms in American society that support the use of corporal punishment (Greven, 1991).

The U.S. Advisory Board on Child Abuse and Neglect (1991) has recommended that the use of corporal punishment should be eliminated in all activities and facilities which receive federal financial support. However, corporal punishment is almost universally regarded by the general public as legally and morally correct and "sometimes necessary" (Straus and Kaufman Kantor, 1994). It is almost a counterintuitive reversal of thinking about parental practices for parents to conclude that corporal punishment should *not* be practiced. Consequently, unless an explicit "no hitting of children" element is included in prevention programs (including parent education, pediatric and educator guidelines, media public service announcements, and entertainment programming), parents will continue to use corporal punishment. Research is needed on whether the inclusion of a no-hitting element in such programs reduces physical abuse.

Use of Criminal Sanctions

The use of criminal sanctions is an important aspect of prevention of child abuse because of the popular belief that strict legal standards and punitive measures will reduce the incidence of child maltreatment. In the area of sexual abuse, some offenders are so incapable of change that they must be incapacitated by incarceration. Nevertheless, the use of criminal penalties to deter offenders and the development of judicial and administrative procedures to remove children from abusing parents may be counterproductive in many cases, particularly in situations involving parental offenders and mild to moderate forms of child abuse or neglect. We currently lack evidence that criminal penalties deter child abuse or neglect, and reliance on criminal penalties offers few resources to improve the abilities of parents in dealing with their children.

In considering the effectiveness of criminal sanctions in the area of child maltreatment, it is important to recognize the multiproblem character of abusive and neglectful families. Many of these families are already involved with the legal system because of other behaviors, including substance abuse, juvenile delinquency, and other crimes. Assessment of the impact of criminal sanctions solely in the area of child maltreatment is quite challenging, since the perpetrators may be removed from the home in a variety of other ways involving the court system.

CONCLUSIONS

Despite its limitations, the current base of evaluative research offers preliminary guidelines for shaping programs and systems. The panel's primary conclusion from this review is that comprehensive and intensive programs that incorporate a theoretical framework, identifying critical pathways to child maltreatment, offer the greatest potential for future programmatic efforts. Many community-based intervention programs have demonstrated some impact on knowledge and attitudes, but their impact on abusive behavior toward children remains uncertain. While such programs may offer many advantages, little evidence currently exists that such interventions directly reduce child maltreatment.

New theoretical models that incorporate ecological and developmental perspectives have complicated the development of prevention research, but these models hold much promise, for they suggest multiple opportunities for prevention. Prevention research needs to be guided by rigorous evaluation that can provide knowledge about the importance of different combinations of risk and protective factors, the developmental pathways of various forms of maltreatment, and the importance of replacing or supplementing risk behaviors with compensatory skills. As our knowledge of the etiology of child maltreatment improves, prevention interventions can adapt new theoretical frameworks that will highlight promising interactions and theoretical insights.

Evaluations of home visitation programs, school-based programs for the prevention of sexual abuse and violence, and community-based child maltreatment prevention programs are quite limited. The majority of these evaluations are not controlled experiments, many are compromised by serious methodological problems, and many promising preventive interventions do not systematically examine program outcomes for child maltreatment (Azar, 1988; Daro, 1992; Howing et al., 1989). Children and families who are most at risk for child maltreatment may not participate in prevention interventions, and those who do may not be sufficiently motivated to change or will have difficulty in implementing skills such as "anger management" techniques in their social context, especially if they live in neighborhoods characterized as violent. To this end, a greater understanding is needed regarding how high-risk individuals and families view formal support systems and how members of both formal and informal systems can best work together to provide a consistent and comprehensive network of prevention services for communities at risk of multiple problems, including child maltreatment. Expanded research also is needed on those high-risk individuals and families who successfully engage in prevention programs. More descriptive information is needed to determine the staff characteristics, outreach efforts, and service delivery methods most successful in reaching families at high risk for maltreatment. Once these factors are identified, their impacts on client retention and client outcomes need to be formally tested through well-designed program evaluations.

RESEARCH RECOMMENDATIONS

Research on child maltreatment prevention programs should be based on knowledge of the processes by which specific risk and protective factors lead to child maltreatment. As noted in Chapter 4, we do not yet know if the etiologies of the various forms of child maltreatment are similar or different. In the face of uncertainty, a diverse range of approaches to prevention research should be encouraged to explore promising initiatives.

Recommendation 5-1: Research on home visiting programs focused on the prenatal, postnatal, and toddler periods has great potential for

enhancing family functioning and parental skills and reducing the prevalence of child maltreatment.

The panel recommends that home visiting programs continue to be developed provided that they incorporate appropriate evaluation components. Such evaluations should include rigorous scientific measurements, appropriate measures of child abuse and neglect, and clarification of the theoretical assumptions that shaped the home visitation efforts. We currently lack knowledge about what programs work, for whom they work, and whether they influence child abuse and neglect directly (via a reduction in child abuse and neglect) or indirectly (via changes in parental skills and parental characteristics such as depression, problem solving, fertility, or employment). Both short-term and long-term benefits of programs need to be evaluated. Either a randomized clinical trial or an effective pretest/posttest design must be used. Budgets for home visiting programs must be adequate to carry out such evaluations. Individuals with expertise in evaluation must be included in the program team. The panel makes the same recommendations for other early intervention service programs.

The panel recommends that research on multiple models of home visiting and other early intervention services be funded, since no single model of home visiting has yet been shown to be the most effective. Similarly, no single time period, length of programming, or intensity of program has been identified as the most effective (although the literature suggests that the prenatal and postnatal periods are central, few programs have started home visiting service later; other research suggests that home visiting has to occur somewhat regularly to be effective). The panel recommends that home visiting programs consider varying the time of onset and length of such programs. Programs could offer two or more different sets of service and evaluate the effectiveness of programs of varying lengths, following the scientific practices established in clinical trials.

Other types of prevention programs often find that positive results are best maintained by offering either long-term, continuous services or, after a program ends, a short-term refresher or booster. Such an approach should be considered for home visiting programs.

Home visiting programs typically offer a number of services. Little is known about the mix of services that are necessary to enhance parenting and reduce child abuse and neglect (although the current findings suggest that comprehensive services are most effective). Programs need to be initiated that vary on the type and number of services included; the efforts must be evaluated. Several approaches might be adopted, including direct comparisons of different arms of clinical trials, or from analyses of what program services individual families are actually receiving.

Even when effective, home visiting programs often are unable to give much insight as to how the program was implemented or why the program was effective. The panel recommends that evaluations of home visiting programs include descriptions of what goes on in visits, curriculum with clearly identified objectives (the completion of which may be observed by the home visitor), and direct observation of home visitors in action.

Most home visiting programs have generally not been large enough to determine for whom the intervention is effective. Studies with sufficiently large and diverse samples to allow for subgroup analyses are strongly recommended. Of particular concern are mothers with a history of maltreatment of siblings, mothers of varying ages, and mothers with specific health habits (smoking, alcohol use, etc.).

Home visiting programs should also strive to involve immediate and extended family members who may have caretaking responsibilities for the child, including fathers, stepfathers, boyfriends, grandparents, and other relatives.

Finally, evaluations of home visiting programs should examine results that link short-term outcomes for child maltreatment with other measures, such as maladaptive parenting.

Recommendation 5-2: Research on child sexual abuse prevention needs to incorporate knowledge about appropriate risk factors as well as the relationship between cognitive and behavioral skills, particularly in situations involving known or trusted adults. Sexual abuse prevention research also needs to integrate knowledge of factors that support or impede disclosure of abuse in the natural setting, including factors that influence adult recognition of sexual abuse or situations at risk for child abuse.

With a few notable exceptions, research on prevention of sexual abuse has been rare. Very little is known about the psychometric properties (e.g., validity, stability, reliability) of most measures employed in research on prevention. Key research questions include the following:

• To what extent do children's responses about the prevention of sexual abuse correspond to what they actually would do in the natural environment?

• What level of cognitive performance on prevention measures is associated with meaningful changes in the ability of children to modify their own abuse?

• Are there significant differences between children who have been abused and those at risk for abuse on their performance on prevention measures?

The natural histories of children who have participated in sexual abuse prevention programs also deserve attention. No records exist to determine the exact number or characteristics of children who have been exposed to sexual abuse prevention programs in the elementary schools, yet these children are in a unique position to inform us about preventive interventions. For example, some children may have been able to use prevention knowledge and skills to successfully prevent, avoid, or escape abuse; other children may have been unsuccessful in their efforts; some children may have been abused in situations or in ways that make prevention impossible; and many children may have reactions to or ideas about preventive intervention that could improve the delivery of these programs. The field has generally ignored the criticisms, support, and ideas of children who are actual consumers of child abuse prevention programs, although a recent national survey of more than 1,400 children (age 10 through 16) conducted by Finkelhor may provide new insights about the experiences of children who participate in victimization prevention programs (Finkelhor, 1993).

The tension in many prevention programs over the objectives of encouraging children to disclose abuse or helping children prevent future abuse has not been completely resolved. Although a set of clinical ideas (e.g., coercion, secrecy, manipulation) is thought to explain children's failures to disclose abuse, little systematic study has been undertaken to examine the victimization and disclosure processes. Children may disclose ongoing abuse for a variety of reasons—they grown increasingly fearful, they see the offender beginning to groom a younger sibling, someone asks them about abuse—but the disclosure process is poorly understood. Research on the disclosure process in the natural environment of the child and evaluations of programs to increase disclosures of abuse might improve the development of new prevention and disclosure programs.

The role of parents and other adults in the prevention of sexual abuse has also been a matter of current debate. Critics have suggested that existing programs place too great a burden on children for the prevention of their own abuse, and that more effort should be directed toward learning how parents and other adults can become effective in preventing sexual abuse of children. Others in the prevention movement are suspicious of parents and have sought to introduce prevention programs in schools and elsewhere without prior parent permission. Few data exist to inform these concerns.

Although parents with their own abuse histories may be less likely to recognize child abuse incidents or situations, no data has confirmed a parent's abuse history as a child risk factor for sexual abuse. Factors such as the relationship between the adult and offender, the level of stress, attributional style, and a host of other factors may influence the ability of adults to identify and respond protectively to children around sexual abuse. Yet even when adults are well informed, it is not clear how much sexual abuse can be prevented by adult actions (e.g., how much sexual abuse takes place out of sight of protective adults, what factors prevent disclosure to adults).

The identification of risk factors for sexual abuse is obviously useful in targeting prevention efforts toward those children in greatest need. Much of the research on risk factors for sexual abuse has been carried out with either clinical samples of sexually abused children or with college student samples, both of which have provided insufficient effort to determine whether certain factors (e.g., psychological characteristics of a child, social-environmental variables) increase a child's risk for sexual abuse. For example, clinical reports suggest that offenders do not abuse all children with whom they come in contact. Some children are selected over others, but it is not clear on what basis some children are selected and others are not. It is not currently known whether selection factors involve characteristics of the child, the offender, the environment in which the child is found, or other currently unknown factors. Research identifying such factors and the interplay among them may have clear implications for prevention interventions.

Recommendation 5-3: Research evaluations are needed to identify the extent to which community-based prevention and intervention programs (such as school-based violence or domestic violence prevention programs, Head Start, etc.) focused on families at risk of multiple problems may affect the likelihood of child maltreatment. Research is also needed on these programs to identify methodological elements (such as designs that successfully engage the participation of at-risk communities) that could be incorporated into child maltreatment prevention programs.

If exposure to a greater number of risk factors increases the risk for violence and child abuse, then community-based prevention and intervention programs need to target multiple childhood risk factors in both the family and school domain as well as within the broader social context of the child (e.g., peers, neighborhood, etc.). School-based programs are often limited because the child returns to the environment that contains many of the risk factors associated with violent behavior. Prevention and intervention programs targeted toward one or a few risk factors are not likely to have an impact on violent behavior and child abuse. Our recommendation is that prevention and intervention programs need to be comprehensive and intensive.

In addition to recommending comprehensive and intensive programs that address multiple risk factors associated with violence and abuse, we recommend research evaluations of long-term interventions that involve home-school collaborations, supplemented by booster sessions at developmentally appropriate points in time.

Recommendation 5-4: Evaluations of school-based programs designed to prevent violence and to improve parental skills are needed to identify the subpopulations most likely to benefit from such interventions and to examine the impact of school-based programs on the abusive behaviors of young parents.

Such evaluations should give particular consideration to the specific characteristics of participants who participate in school-based programs, including gender as well as social and cultural characteristics. School-based programs need to be designed for specific characteristics, risk factors, and the social context of the participants in order to determine who most benefits from selected programs. Major prevention programs need to include a long-term follow-up as part of their evaluation. The evaluations of the school-based violence prevention programs described in this chapter were short term and basically assessed whether the intended skills and knowledge were acquired by the participant. None of the program evaluations included long-term assessments of outcomes.

Specifically, we recommend that:

(a) Evaluations of programs examine the characteristics of individuals who benefit from the programs. Most programs are evaluated by comparing the overall mean of the treatment and control groups. We recommend that the range of outcomes within the treatment group be examined in relation to specific characteristics of the participant. Thus, in addition to asking "Does the program work?," we suggest that investigators ask "For whom does the program work and under what circumstances?"

(b) Programs need to be designed to take into account salient characteristics (e.g., gender) and risk factors of the participants. Perhaps the most important characteristic is the child's developmental level. Few of the programs we reviewed seem to take into account the participants' developmental level. For example, prevention programs for adolescents would need to be different from programs for preteens. Adolescence is a period marked by a number of developmental issues, such as greater autonomy and shifting allegiance toward peers, emerging sexuality, and forming intimate relationships with members of the opposite sex, which need to be considered in developing prevention and intervention programs. The assumption of most existing programs seems to be that they are appropriate for all individuals—which does not seem to be the case.

Whenever possible, the development of prevention and intervention programs should be guided by theory (and appropriate models) and replicated in different schools. Recognizing the current limitations of our understanding of the etiology of complex phenomena like child abuse, program developers should describe the processes that they believe lead to child abuse and neglect. One challenge facing prevention researchers is deciding which combinations of risk and protective factors, and which combinations of interactive systems, have the greatest potential to both influence outcomes and be effectively modified through intervention.

Recommendation 5-5: Research should be conducted on values and attitudes within the general public that contribute to, or could help discourage, child maltreatment. The role of the media in reinforcing or questioning cultural norms in areas important to child maltreatment, such as corporal punishment, deserves particular attention.

Important lessons can be learned from the role of the media in fostering healthy or unhealthy behaviors involving the use of alcohol, smoking, drug use, and condoms or safe sex practices. Research is needed that can identify significant pathways in addressing key factors and behaviors that affect child maltreatment, such as parental styles, the use of corporal punishment, alternatives to the use of violence in conflict resolution, and young children's relationships with strangers and abusive caretakers. Rather than focusing solely on the sensational aspects of abusive cases, the media can play an important role in raising questions about the values that should be fostered in family relationships and the protection of children.

Research is needed on whether specific advice to avoid corporal punishment and specific discussion of alternatives contribute to the effectiveness of prevention programs (see Appendix B, Supplemental Views). This includes home visitation programs, early childhood intervention programs, and violence prevention programs for schoolchildren. In connection with the latter, it should be noted that schoolchildren are much more likely to be victims of violence, such as slapping and hitting with objects, by parents than by peers. If school-based programs can teach children to voluntarily use time out to avoid violence, research is needed on whether the same can be done for parents.

There is also a need for empirical research to determine the degrees to which criminal sanctions deter child abuse and the degree to which removal of children protects them from abuse, especially in cases of mild to moderate maltreatment. Research involving case-control designs, which investigate the effect on families and children of mediation versus the use of criminal sanctions in cases of spouse abuse (Sherman, 1992) shows that field experiments can be done within an ethically acceptable framework. Since the relative effectiveness of punitive compared with helping approaches could be different for physical abuse, sexual abuse, and neglect, each of these types of abuse may be analyzed distinctly.

NOTES

1. Sustained effects of early intervention programs are partly, but not primarily, due to alterations in cognitive functioning; for example, differences in intelligence and verbal ability test scores between children who did or did not receive early intervention services tend to dissipate by the middle of elementary school (Lazar et al., 1982; Brooks-Gunn, 1990; Zigler, 1992). Later reductions in school failure and juvenile delinquency are hypothesized to be based on changes in parental commitment to and encouragement of their young children as well as familial functioning more generally (Zigler, 1992), as Bronfenbrenner predicted almost 15 years ago (1979).

2. The four treatment groups are: (1) a control group that did not receive services but participated in the collection of evaluation data; (2) a minimal intervention group that received transportation assistance to attend medical appointments; (3) a group that received extensive nurse home visitors prenatally and transportation services; and (4) a group that received extensive nurse home visitors both prenatally and postnatally as well as transportation assistance. The nurses provided parent education, made efforts to enhance family and other informal social supports, and initiated linkages with professional helpers in the community (Olds et al., 1986a).

3. The National Center on Child Abuse and Neglect awarded a major evaluation study for the Hawaii Healthy Start program to the National Committee for Prevention of Child Abuse in late 1993. The evaluation is expected to be completed in 1994.

4. These curricula included Child Assault Prevention, Children's Self-Help, Talking About Touching, Touch Safety, Child Abuse Prevention Intervention and Education, the Youth Safety Awareness Project, and SAFE—Stop Abuse Through Family Education.

REFERENCES

Abrahams, N., K. Casey, and D. Daro
   1992   Teachers' knowledge, attitudes, and beliefs about child abuse and its prevention. *Child Abuse and Neglect* 16:229-238.
Azar, S.T.
   1988   Methodological considerations in treatment outcomes research in child maltreatment. Pp. 288-298 in G.T. Hotaling, D. Finkelhor, J.T. Kirkpatrick, and M.A. Straus, eds., *Coping with Family Violence: Research and Policy Perspectives.* Newbury Park, CA: Sage Publications.
Barnard, K.E., C.L. Booth, S.K. Mitchell, and R. Telzrow
   1988   Newborn nursing models: A test of early intervention to high-risk infants and families. Pp. 63-81 in E. Hibbs, ed., *Children and Families: Studies in Prevention and Intervention.* Madison, CT: International Universities Press.
Baydar, N., and J. Brooks-Gunn
   1991   Effects of maternal employment and child-care arrangements on preschoolers' cognitive and behavioral outcomes: Evidence from the children of the National Longitudinal Survey of Youth. *Developmental Psychology* 27(6):932-945.
Belsky, J.
   1985   The determinants of parenting: A process model. *Child Development* 55(1)(February):83-96.
   1991   Psychological maltreatment: Definitional limitations and unstated assumptions. *Development and Psychopathology* 3:31-36.
Benasich, A.A., J. Brooks-Gunn, and B.C. Clewell
   1992   How do mothers benefit from early intervention programs? *Journal of Applied Developmental Psychology* 13:311-362.

Bennett, F.C.
   1987   The effectiveness of early intervention for infants at increased biological risk. Pp. 79-112 in M.J. Guralnick and F.C. Bennett, eds., *The Effectiveness of Early Intervention for At-Risk and Handicapped Children.* New York: Academic Press.
Berrick, J.D.
   1988   Parental involvement in child abuse prevention training: What do they learn? *Child Abuse and Neglect* 12:543-553.
Bierman, K., J. Coie, K. Dodge, M. Greenberg, J. Lochman, and R. McMahon
   in press A developmental and clinical model for the prevention of conduct disorders: The FAST Track program. *Development and Psychopathology.*
Binder, R.L., and D.E. McNiel
   1987   Evaluation of a school-based sexual abuse prevention program: Cognitive and emotional effects. *Child Abuse and Neglect* 11(4):497-506.
Boyer, R., and D. Savageau
   1981   *Places Rated Almanac.* Pp. 336-337. New York: Rand McNally.
Bradley, R.H., P.H. Casey, P. Barrett, B. Caldwell, and L. Whiteside
   in press Enhancing the home environment of low birthweight premature infants. In R.T. Grors and D. Spiker, eds., *The Infant Health and Development Program.* Palo Alto, CA: Stanford University Press.
Bridgeman, B., J.B. Blumenthal, and S.R. Andrews
   1981   *Parent Child Development Center: Final Evaluation Report.* Office of Human Development Services. April. Washington, DC: Department of Health and Human Services.
Bronfenbrenner, U.
   1979   Six theories of child development: Revised formulations and current issues. *Annals of Child Development* 6. Greenwich, CT: JAI Press, Inc.
Brooks-Gunn, J.
   1990   Promoting health development in young children: What educational interventions work? Pp. 125-145 in D.E. Rodgers and E. Ginzberg, eds., *Improving the Life Chances of Children at Risk.* Boulder, CO: Westview Press. (An abbreviated version appeared as Brooks-Gunn, J. 1990. Enhancing the development of young children. *Current Opinion in Pediatrics* 2(5):873-877.)
Brooks-Gunn, J., R.T. Gross, H.C. Kramer, D. Spiker, and S. Shapiro
   1992   Enhancing the cognitive outcomes of low-birth-weight, premature infants: For whom is this intervention most effective? *Pediatrics* 89(8):1209-1215.
Brooks-Gunn, J., M. McCormick, S. Shapiro, A.A. Benasich, and G. Black
   in press-a Effects of early education intervention on maternal employment, public assistance, and health insurance. *American Journal of Public Health.*
Brooks-Gunn, J., P.K. Klebanov, F. Liaw, and D. Spiker
   in press-b Enhancing the development of low-birth-weight, premature infants: Changes in cognition and behavior over the first three years. *Child Development.*
Bush, B.J.
   1991   The Role of the Religious Community in Addressing a National Disaster. Testimony before the U.S. Advisory Board on Child Abuse and Neglect, September 14, Denver, CO.
Chase-Lansdale, P.L., and J. Brooks-Gunn, eds.
   in press *Escape from Poverty: What Makes a Difference for Poor Children.* New York: Cambridge University Press.
Chase-Lansdale, P.L., J. Brooks-Gunn, and E. Zamsky
   in press Young multigenerational families in poverty: Quality of mothering and grandmothering. *Child Development.*

Cicchetti, D., and R. Rizley
1981   Developmental perspectives on the etiology, intergenerational transmission, and sequelae of child maltreatment. *New Directions for Child Development* 11:31-55.

Cicchetti, D., S. Toth, and M. Bush
1988   Developmental psychopathology and incompetence in childhood: Suggestions for intervention. In B.B. Lahey and A.E. Kazdin, eds., *Advances in Clinical Child Psychology Vol. 11.* New York: Plenum Press.

Clarke-Stewart, K.A., and G.G. Fein
1983   Early childhood programs. Pp. 918-999 in P.H. Mussen, ed., *Handbook of Child Psychology*, 4th Edition, Vol. 4. New York: John Wiley and Sons.

Clewell, B.C., J. Brooks-Gunn, and A.A. Benasich
1989   Evaluating child-related outcomes of teenage parenting programs. *Family Relations* 38:201-209.

Committee for Children
1983   Talking about touching: A personal safety curriculum. Seattle, WA: Committee for Children.

Conte, J.R.
1992   School-Based Sexual Abuse Prevention Programs. Position paper prepared for the National Research Council's Panel on Research on Child Abuse and Neglect.

Conte, J.R., and L.A. Fogarty
1990   Sexual abuse prevention progams for children. *Education and Urban Society* 22(3):270-284.

Conte, J.R., C. Rosen, L. Saperstein, and R. Shermack
1985   An evaluation of a program to prevent the sexual victimization of young children. *Child Abuse and Neglect* 9(3):319-328.

Conte, J.R., C. Rosen, and L. Saperstein
1986   An analysis of programs to prevent the sexual victimization of children. *Journal of Primary Prevention* 6(3):141-155.

Conte, J.R., S. Wolfe, and T. Smith
1989   What sexual offenders tell us about prevention strategies. *Child Abuse and Neglect* 13(2):293-301.

Cowan, P.A., and C.P. Cowan
1988   Changes in marriage during the transition to parenthood: Must we blame the baby? In G.Y. Michaels and W.A. Goldberg, eds., *The Transition to Parenthood: Current Theory and Research.* New York: Cambridge University Press.

Daro, D.
1988   Prevention Programs: What Do Children Learn? Unpublished manuscript, School of Social Welfare, University of California, Berkeley.
1992   Risk Factors as They Relate to Prevention. Position paper prepared for the National Research Council's Panel on Research on Child Abuse and Neglect.

Daro, D., J. Duerr, and N. LeProhn
1987   Child Assault Prevention Instruction: What Works with Preschoolers. Paper presented at the Third National Family Violence Research Conference, University of New Hampshire, Durham.

Davis, P.W.
1991   Stranger intervention into child punishment in public places. *Social Problems* 38(2):227-246.

Deutsch, F.M., P.N. Ruble, A. Fleming, J. Brooks-Gunn, and C. Stangor
1988   Information-seeking and self-definition during the transition to motherhood. *Journal of Personality and Social Psychology* 55(3):420-431.

Downer, A., ed.
1984 *Prevention of Child Sexual Abuse: A Trainer's Manual.* Seattle, WA: Seattle Institute for Child Advocacy.

Drotar, D.
1992 Prevention of neglect and nonorganic failure to thrive. Chapter in D.J. Willis, E.W. Holden, and M. Rosenberg, eds., *Prevention of Child Maltreatment.* New York: John Wiley and Sons.

Duncan, G.J.
1991 The economic environment of childhood. In A. Huston, ed. *Children in Poverty: Child Development and Public Policy.* Cambridge: Cambridge University Press.

Dunst, C.J., S.W. Snyder, and M. Mankinen
1989 Efficacy of early intervention. Pp. 259-294 in M.C. Wang, M.C. Reynolds, and H.J. Walberg, eds., *Handbook of Special Education: Research and Practice: Vol. 3. Low Incidence Conditions.* Oxford, England: Pergamon Press.

Egeland, B., and M.F. Erickson
1991 Rising above the past: Strategies for helping new mothers break the cycle of abuse and neglect. *Zero to Three* 11(2):29-35.

in press Attachment theory and findings: Implications for prevention and intervention. In S. Kramer and H. Parens, eds., *Prevention in Mental Health: Now, Tomorrow, Ever?.* Northvale, NJ: Jason Aronson, Inc.

Entwhistle, D.R., and S. Doering
1981 *The First Birth: A Family Turning Point.* Baltimore: Johns Hopkins Press.

Feindler, E., R. Hammond, and J. Becker
1992 Prevention and Clinical Interventions for Youth Perpetrators and Victims of Violence. Unpublished manuscript.

Felner, R.D., M.M. Silverman, and R. Adix
1991 Prevention of substance abuse and related disorders in childhood and adolescence: A developmentally based, comprehensive ecological approach. *Family and Community Health* 14(3):12-22.

Finkelhor, D.
1984 *Child Sexual Abuse: New Theory and Research.* New York: Free Press.
1986 Prevention: A review of programs and research. Pp. 224-254 in D. Finkelhor with S. Araji, L. Brown, A. Browne, S. Peters, and G. Wyatt. *A Sourcebook on Child Sexual Abuse.* Beverly Hills, CA: Sage.
1993 Victimization Prevention Programs: A National Survey of Children's Exposure and Reactions. Paper presented to the American Professional Society on the Abuse of Children, San Diego, California. January.

Finkelhor, D., Williams, L.M., with N. Burns
1988 *Nursery Crimes.* Newbury Park, CA: Sage Publications.

Fryer, G.E., S.K. Kraizer, and I. Miyoshui
1987a Measuring actual reduction of risk to child abuse: A new approach. *Child Abuse and Neglect* 11:173-179.
1987b Measuring children's retention of skills to resist stranger abduction: Use of the simulation technique. *Child Abuse and Neglect* 11:181-185.

Fuddy, L.
1992 Hawaii's Healthy Start's Success Shared at the Ninth International Congress on Child Abuse and Neglect. Unpublished paper.

Garbarino, J.
1987 Children's response to a sexual abuse prevention program: A study of the *Spiderman* comic. *Child Abuse and Neglect* 11:143-148.

Garmezy, N., and M. Rutter
1983   *Stress, Coping and Development in Children.* New York: McGraw-Hill.
Gelles, R.J., and M.A. Straus
1988   *Intimate Violence.* New York: Simon and Schuster.
General Accounting Office
1991   *Child Abuse Prevention: Status of the Challenge Grant Program.* May. GAO:HRD91-95. Washington, DC.
Gil, D.G.
1970   *Violence Against Children: Physical Child Abuse in the United States.* Cambridge, MA: Harvard University Press.
Gilbert, N.
1988   Child Sexual Abuse Prevention: Evaluation of Educational Materials for Preschool Programs. Unpublished manuscript, Family Welfare Research Group, School of Social Welfare, University of California, Berkeley.
Goldstein, A.
1992   School Violence: Its Community Context and Potential Solutions. Testimony presented May 4 to the Subcommittee on Elementary, Secondary, and Vocational Education, Committee on Education and Labor, U.S. House of Representatives.
Gray, J., C. Cutler, J. Dean, and C. Kempe
1979   Prediction and prevention of child abuse and neglect. *Journal of Social Issues* 35:127-139.
Gray, E.B.
1983   Final report: Collaborative research of community and minority group action to prevent child abuse and neglect. *Vol. I: Perinatal Interventions.* Chicago: National Committee for Prevention of Child Abuse.
Greenspan, S.I., Weider, A. Leiberman, R. Nover, R. Lourie, and M. Robinson., eds.
1987   *Clinical Infant Reports: No. 3: Infants in Multirisk Families: Case Studies in Preventive Intervention.* New York: International Universities Press.
Greven, P.
1991   *The Child: The Religious Roots of Punishment and the Psychological Impact of Physical Abuse.* New York: Alfred Knopf.
Hammond, W.R., and B. Yung
1991   Preventing violence in at-risk African American youth. *Journal of Health Care for the Poor and Underserved* 2(3):359-373.
Hawkins, J.D., R. Catalano, D. Morrison, J. O'Donnell, R. Abbott, and L.E. Day
1992   In J. McCord and R. Tremblay, eds., *The Prevention of Antisocial Behavior in Children.* New York: Guilford.
Hayes, C.D., J.L. Palmer, and M.E. Zaslow, eds.
1990   *Who Cares for America's Children? Child Care Policy for the 1990s.* National Research Council. Washington, DC: National Academy Press.
Helfer, R.
1982   A review of the literature on the prevention of child abuse and neglect. *Child Abuse and Neglect* 6(3):251-261.
Hinde, R., and J. Stevenson-Hinde
1988   *Relationships Within Families: Mutual Influences.* Oxford: Clarendon Press.
Holden, E.W., D.J. Willis, and M.M. Corcoran
1992   Preventing child maltreatment during the prenatal/perinatal period. Chapter in D.J. Willis, E.W. Holden, and M. Rosenberg, eds., *Prevention of Child Maltreatment.* New York: John Wiley.
Howing, P.T., J.S. Woderski, D.P. Kurtz, and J.M. Gaudin
1989   Methodological issues in child maltreatment research. *Social Work Research and Abstracts* 25(3):3-7.

Huston, A.C.
1991   *Children in Poverty: Child Development and Public Policy.* Cambridge: Cambridge University Press.
Infant Health and Development Program Staff
1990   Enhancing the outcomes of low birth-weight, premature infants: A multisite randomized trial. *Journal of the American Medical Association* 263(22):3035-3042.
Jaffe, P., M. Suderman, and D. Reitzel
in press Primary prevention of wife assault: The development of school-based programs. *Journal of Family Violence.*
Jaffe, P., M. Suderman, D. Reitzel, and S. Killip
1990   Evaluation of a Secondary School Primary Prevention Programme on Violence in Intimate Relationships. Unpublished manuscript. London, Ontario, University of Western Ontario.
Kadushin, A., and J.A. Martin
1981   *Child Abuse: An Interactional Event.* New York: Columbia University Press.
Kazdin, A.E.
1989   Developmental psychopathology: Current research, issues, and directions. *American Psychologist* 44(2):180-187.
Kempe, C.H., F.N. Silverman, B. Steele, W. Droegemueller, and H.R. Silver
1962   The battered child syndrome. *Journal of the American Medical Association* 181(1):17-24.
Kenning, M.K.
1987   Child assault prevention: program evaluation. Unpublished dissertation. U. South Dakota. *Dissertation Abstracts International* 47(8-B)3527. 134 pages.
Kleemeier, C., and C. Webb
1986   Evaluation of a School-Based Prevention Program. Paper presented at the meeting of the American Psychological Association, Washington, DC.
Klerman, L.V.
1991   The association between adolescent parenting and childhood poverty. In A.C. Huston, ed., *Children in Poverty: Child Development and Public Policy.* Cambridge: Cambridge University Press.
Kolko, D.J.
1988   Educational programs to promote awareness and prevention of child sexual victimization: A review and methodological critique. *Clinical Psychology Review* 8(2):195-209.
Korbin, J.E.
1993   Sociocultural Factors in Child Maltreatment. Background paper prepared for the U.S. Advisory Board on Child Abuse and Neglect.
Kraizer, S., S.S. Witte, and G.F. Fryer, Jr.
1989   Child sexual abuse prevention programs: What makes them effective in protecting children? *Children Today* (September/October):23-27.
Kumpfer, K.L.
1989   Children, Adolescents and Substance Abuse: Review of Prevention Strategies. Paper presented to the American Academy of Child and Adolescent Psychiatry Institute on Substance Abuse, New York. October 13.
Lazar, I., R. Darlington, H. Murray, J. Royce, and A. Snipper
1982   Lasting effects of early educations: A report from the Consortium for Longitudinal Studies. *Monographs of the Society for Research in Child Development* 47(203, Serial No. 195).
Lee, V., J. Brooks-Gunn, and E. Schnur
1988   Does Head Start "close the gap?" A comparison of children attending Head Start, no preschool, and other preschool programs. *Child Development* 61:495-507.

Leventhal, J.M.
   1987   Programs to prevent sexual abuse: What outcomes should be measured? *Child Abuse and Neglect* 11:169-171.
Liaw, F.R., and J. Brooks-Gunn
   in press Patterns of low birth weight: Children's cognitive development and their determinants. *Developmental Psychology.*
Meisels, S.J., and J.P. Shonkoff, eds.
   1990   *Handbook of Early Childhood Intervention.* Cambridge: Cambridge University Press.
Melton, G.
   1992   The improbability of prevention of sexual abuse. In D. Willis, E. Holden, and M. Rosenberg, eds., *Prevention of Child Maltreatment.* New York: John Wiley.
Miller-Perrin, C., and S. Wurtele
   1988   The child sexual abuse prevention movement: A critical analysis of primary and secondary approaches. *Clinical Psychology Review* 8:313-329.
Mueller, D.P., and P.S. Higgins
   1988   *Funders' Guide Manual: A Guide to Prevention Programs in Human Services, Focus on Children and Adolescents.* First Edition. April. St. Paul, MN: Amherst H. Wilder Foundation.
National Committee for the Prevention of Child Abuse and Neglect
   1990   *Public Attitudes and Action Regarding Child Abuse and Its Prevention, 1990.* Chicago: The National Committee for Prevention of Child Abuse.
Nelson, B.
   1984   *Making an Issue of Child Abuse: Political Agenda Setting for Social Problems.* Chicago: University of Chicago Press.
O'Connor, S., P.M. Vietze, K.B., Sherrod, H.M., Sandler, and W.A. Altemeier
   1980   Reduced incidence of parenting inadequacy following rooming-in. *Pediatrics* 66:176-182.
O'Connor, S., P.M. Vietze, K.B. Sherrod, H.M. Sandler, S. Gerrity, and W.A. Altemeier
   1982   Mother-infant interaction and child development after rooming-in: Comparison of high-risk and low-risk mothers. *Prevention in Human Services* 1:25-43.
Ohlin, L., and M. Tonry
   1989   *Family Violence.* Chicago: The University of Chicago Press.
Oldenburg, D.
   1992   When abuse goes public. *The Washington Post*, Tuesday, October 6:B5.
Olds, D.L.
   1980   Improving formal services for mothers and children. Chapter in J. Garbarino and S.H. Stocking, eds., *Protecting Children from Abuse and Neglect: Developing and Maintaining Effective Support Systems for Families.* San Francisco: Joseey-Bass.
   1982   The prenatal/early infancy project: An ecological approach to prevention of developmental disabilities. Chapter in J. Belsky, ed., *In the Beginning.* New York: Columbia University Press.
   1984   Case studies of factors interfering with nurse home visitors' promotion of positive care-giving methods in high risk families. *Early Childhood Development and Care* 16:149-166.
   1990   Can home visitation improve the health of women and children at risk? Pp. 79-103 in D.L. Rogers and E. Ginzberg, eds., *Improving the Life Chances of Children at Risk.* Boulder, CO: Westview Press.
   1992   What Do We Know About Home-Visitation as a Means of Preventing Child Abuse and Neglect? Testimony prepared for the House Select Committee on Children and Families: Keeping kids safe—Exploring public/private partnerships to prevent abuse and strengthen families. April 2.

Olds, D.L., and H. Kitzman
1990   Can home visitation improve the health of women and children at environmental risk? *Pediatrics* 86(1)(July):108-116.
Olds, D.L., C.R. Henderson, R. Chamberlin, and R. Tatelbaum
1986a   Preventing child abuse and neglect: A randomized trial of nurse home visitation. *Pediatrics* 78:65-78.
Olds, D.L., C.R. Henderson, R. Tatelbaum, and R. Chamberlin
1986b   Improving the delivery of prenatal care and outcomes of pregnancy: A random-ized trial of nurse home visitation. *Pediatrics* 77:16-28.
1988   Improving the life-course development of socially disadvantaged mothers: A ran-domized trial of nurse home visitation. *American Journal of Public Health* 78:1436-1445.
Pelton, L.H.
1989   *For Reasons of Poverty.* New York: Praeger.
Polansky, N.A., R. Borgman, and C. DeSaix
1972a   *Roots of Futility.* San Francisco: Jossey-Bass.
Polansky, N.A., C. DeSaix, and S. Sharlin
1972b   *Child Neglect: Understanding and Reaching the Parent.* New York: Child Welfare League of America.
Polansky, N.A., M.A. Chalmers, E. Bullenweiser, and D.P. Williams
1981   *Damaged Parents: An Anatomy of Child Neglect.* Chicago: University of Chi-cago Press.
Polansky, N.A., J.M. Gaudin, and A.C. Kilpatrick
1992   Family radicals. *Children and Youth Services Review* 14:19-26.
Porch, T.L., and P.A. Petretic-Jackson
1986   Child Sexual Assault Prevention: Evaluation Parent Education Workshops. Paper presented at the 94th annual convention of the American Psychological Associa-tion, Washington, DC. August.
Ramey, C.T.
1991   Chapter in Huston, ed., *Children in Poverty.* Cambridge, MA: Cambridge Uni-versity Press.
Ramey, C.T., D.B. Bryant, B.H. Wasik, J.J. Sparling, K.H. Fendt, and L.M. LaVange
1992   The infant health and development program for low birth weight, premature in-fants: Program elements, family participation, and child intelligence. *Pediatrics* 89(3):454-465.
Reiss, D.
1981   *The Family's Construction of Reality.* Cambridge, MA: Harvard University Press.
Reppucci, N.D., and J.J. Haugaard
1989   Prevention of child sexual abuse: Myth or reality. *American Psychologist* 44:266-275.
Reppucci, N.D., and J. Herman
1991   Sexuality education and child sexual abuse prevention programs in the schools. In G. Grant, ed., *Review of Research in Education.* Washington, DC.: American Educational Research Association.
Rosenberg, M.S.
1987   New directions for research on the psychological maltreatment of children. *American Psychologist* 42:166-171.
Ruble, D.N., J. Brooks-Gunn, A. Flemmin, G. Fitzmaurice, C. Stangor, and F. Deutsch
1990   Coming of age in the era of AIDS: Sexual and contraceptive decisions. *Milbank Quarterly* 68:59-84.
Schorr, L.
1988   *Within Our Reach: Breaking the Cycle of Disadvantage.* New York: Anchor.

Seigel, E., K. Bauman, E. Schaefer, M. Saunders, and D. Ingram
1980   Hospital and home support during infancy: Impact on maternal attachment, child abuse and neglect, and health care utilization. *Pediatrics* 66:183-190.
Sherman, L.W.
1992   *Policing Domestic Violence* New York: The Free Press.
Shonkoff, J.P., P. Hauser-Cram, M. Wyngaarden Kraus, and C. Cristofk Upshur
1992   Development of Infants with Disabilities and Their Families. *Monograph of the Society for Research in Child Development* 57(6).
Shonkoff, J.P., and P. Hauser-Cram
1987   Early intervention for disabled infants and their families: A quantitative analysis. *Pediatrics* 80:650-658.
Spiker, D., J. Ferguson, J. Brooks-Gunn
in press Enhancing maternal interactive behavior and child social competence in low birth weight, premature infants: Results from the Infant Health and Development Program. *Child Development.*
Stark, E., and A.H. Flitcraft
1991   Spouse abuse. Chapter in Rosenberg, M.L., and M.A. Fenley, eds. *Violence in America.* New York: Oxford University Press.
Straus, M.A., and G.K. Kaufman Kantor
1994   Physical Punishment by Parents: A Risk Factor in the Epidemiology of Depression, Suicide, Alcohol Abuse, Child Abuse, and Wife Beating. *Adolescence* (forthcoming).
Straus, M.A., and C. Yodanis
1994   Paths from corporal punishment to physical abuse in a nationally representative sample of American parents. Chapter 6 in Murray A. Straus, ed., *Beating the Devil Out of Them: Corporal Punishment by Parents and Its Effects on Children.* Boston: Lexington/Macmillan. (forthcoming).
Swan, H.L., A.N. Press, and S.L. Briggs
1985   Child sexual abuse prevention: Does it work? *Child Welfare* 64:667-674.
Tharinger, D.J., J.J. Krivacska, M. Laye-McDonough, and L. Jamison
1988   Prevention of child sexual abuse: An analysis of issues, educational programs, and research findings. *School Psychology Review* 17(4):614-634.
Tower, C.C.
1992   The role of educators in the protections and treatment of child abuse and neglect. National Center on Child Abuse and Neglect. DHHS Publication (ACF) 92-30172. Washington, D.C.: U.S. Department of Health and Human Services.
U.S. Advisory Board on Child Abuse and Neglect
1990   *Child Abuse and Neglect: Critical First Steps in Response to a National Emergency.* August. Washington, DC: U.S. Department of Health and Human Services.
1991   *Creating Caring Communities.* September. Washington, DC: U.S. Department of Health and Human Services.
Wasik, B.H.
1984   *Coping with Parenting Through Effective Problem Solving: A Handbook for Professionals.* Chapel Hill: Frank Porter Graham Child Development Center.
Wasik, B.H., C.T. Ramey, D.M. Byant, and J.J. Sparling
1990   A longitudinal study of two early intervention strategies: Project Care. *Child Development* 61:1682-1696.
Werner, E.E., and R.S. Smith
1982   *Vulnerable but Not Invincible: A Longitudinal Study of Resilient Children and Youth.* New York: McGraw Hill.

Willis, D.J., E.W. Holden, and M. Rosenberg
1992   *Prevention of Child Maltreatment.* New York: John Wiley and Sons.
Winsten, J.A.
1992   Lessons from the Designated Driver Campaign. Paper prepared for presentation at the Automobile Club of Southern California's DUI Symposium, Ontario, CA. November 17.
Wolfe, D.A., T. MacPherson, R. Blount, and V.V. Wolfe
1986   Evaluation of a brief intervention for educating school children in awareness of physical and sexual abuse. *Child Abuse and Neglect* 10(1):85-92.
Woodhead, M.
1988   When psychology informs public policy. *American Psychologist* 43(6):443-454.
Wurtele, S.K.
1988   Harmful Effects of Sexual Abuse Prevention Programs? Results and Implications. Paper presented at the meeting of the American Psychology Association, Atlanta. August.
Wurtele, S.K., S.R. Marrs, and C.L. Miller-Perrin
1987   Practice makes perfect? The role of participant modeling in sexual abuse prevention programs. *Journal of Consulting and Clinical Psychology* 55(4):599-602.
Wurtele, S.K., L.C. Kast, C.L. Miller-Perrin and P.A. Kondrik
1989   Comparison of programs for teaching personal safety skills to preschoolers. *Journal of Consulting and Clinical Psychology* 57:505-511.
Zigler, E.F.
1992   Early childhood intervention: A promising preventative for juvenile delinquency. *American Psychologist* 47:997-1006.
Zigler, E., and N.W. Hall
1989   Physical child abuse in America: Past, present, and future. In D. Cicchetti and V. Carlson, eds., *Child Maltreatment: Theory and Research on the Causes and Consequences on Child Abuse and Neglect.* New York: Cambridge University Press.

6

Consequences of
Child Abuse and Neglect

The consequences of maltreatment can be devastating. For over 30 years, clinicians have described the effects of child abuse and neglect on the physical, psychological, cognitive, and behavioral development of children. Physical consequences range from minor injuries to severe brain damage and even death. Psychological consequences range from chronic low self-esteem to severe dissociative states. The cognitive effects of abuse range from attentional problems and learning disorders to severe organic brain syndromes. Behaviorally, the consequences of abuse range from poor peer relations all the way to extraordinarily violent behaviors. Thus, the consequences of abuse and neglect affect the victims themselves and the society in which they live.

Many complexities challenge our understanding of factors and relationships that exacerbate or mitigate the consequences of abusive experiences. The majority of children who are abused do not show signs of extreme disturbance. Research has suggested a relationship between child maltreatment and a variety of short- and long-term consequences, but considerable uncertainty and debate remain about the effects of child victimization on children, adolescents, and adults. The relationship between the causes and consequences of child maltreatment is particularly problematic, since some factors (such as low intelligence in the child) may help stimulate abusive behavior by the parent or caretaker, but low intelligence can also be a consequence of abusive experiences in early childhood.

The scientific study of child maltreatment and its consequences is in its infancy. Until recently, research on the consequences of physical and sexual child abuse and neglect has been based primarily on retrospective studies of adolescents or adults that are subject to clinical bias and inaccurate recall (Aber and Cicchetti, 1984). Research on the consequences of abuse is also challenged by the hidden nature of much abuse and because these experiences may not come to anyone's attention until years after they occur. Maltreatment often occurs in the presence of multiple problems within a family or social environment, including poverty, violence, substance abuse, and unemployment. Distinguishing consequences that are associated directly with the experience of child maltreatment itself rather than other social disorders is a daunting task for the research investigator.

Research on the consequences of child maltreatment is also uneven and, as a result, we do not yet understand the consequences on children of particular types or multiple forms of abuse. In recent years, much attention has been focused on the consequences of child sexual abuse, especially the adolescent and adult sexual behavior of the victim. Less attention has been given to the short- and long-term consequences of child neglect and physical abuse. Only recently has public awareness expanded to include recognition of the psychological consequences that stem from even the most subtle forms of emotional maltreatment. Some experts now contend that the psychological or emotional components of abuse and neglect are the factor most responsible for the destructive consequences of all types of maltreatment (Brassard et al., 1987; Erickson and Egeland, in press; Newberger, 1973).

Nor do we yet know the importance of the particular timing, intensity, and context of abuse on the outcome. Factors such as the age and developmental status of the child may influence the outcomes of maltreatment experiences. Effects that appear at only one life stage, whether immediately following the maltreatment or later, are often different from those that persist throughout life. What may appear to be adaptive or functional at one point in development (avoiding an abusive parent or desensitizing oneself against feelings) may later compromise the person's ability to draw on and respond to personal relationships in an adaptive and flexible way. Given the wide variations reported in the research literature, certain intrinsic strengths and vulnerabilities within a child and the child's environment may affect the extent to which abuse will have adverse consequences. Disordered patterns of adaptation may lie dormant, only to appear during times of stress or in conjunction with particular circumstances (Sroufe and Rutter, 1984).

Little research has focused on gender differences in the consequences of child abuse and neglect. Early clinical reports of violence primarily describe violent male adolescents, although Widom's (1991b) delinquency analysis had higher rates of arrests for violence of abused and neglected females, a pattern not evident for males. Studies of sexual promiscuity and teenage pregnancy have primarily included females who were sexually abused. Few studies have found consistent differences in the reaction of boys and girls to molestation, although one popular report found boys to have more externalizing and girls to have more internalizing symptoms (Friedrich et al., 1988). The lack of attention to gender differences may result from the small number of male victims of sexual abuse in most studies and lower rates of reporting of childhood sexual abuse in males.

This chapter is organized in a developmental framework. It begins with a description of what is known about the childhood consequences of child maltreatment, followed by a discussion of what is known about the consequences of abuse and neglect in adolescence and adulthood. A discussion of labeling effects, considering the issues of stigma, bias, and discriminatory treatment, is followed by an examination of a number of potential protective factors. The chapter concludes with recommendations for research.

CHILDHOOD

Medical and Physiological Consequences

Physical abuse in infants and young children can lead to brain dysfunction (Dykes, 1986) and sometimes death. Most fatality victims of abuse and neglect are under age 5.[1]   In 1991, an estimated 1,383 children died from abuse or neglect; 64 percent of these deaths were attributed to abuse and 36 percent to neglect (McCurdy and Daro, 1992). However, the number of child deaths caused by abuse and neglect may actually be much higher, since cause of death is often misclassified in child fatality reports (McClain et al., 1993; Robinson and Stevens, 1992).

A child does not need to be struck on the head to sustain brain injuries. Dykes (1986) has indicated that infants who are shaken vigorously by the extremities or shoulders may sustain intracranial and intraocular bleeding with no sign of external head trauma. Thus early neglectful and physically abusive practices have devastating consequences for their small victims.

Neglect cases may occur at any point of a child's development but are often associated with early childhood, when they are more likely to be discovered by health professionals, educators, and child welfare workers. One form of child neglect is associated with *nonorganic failure to thrive* infants. The absence of physical growth in these infants can be measured by objective scales of weight and height (Drotar, 1992). Neglect is usually suspected when such infants demonstrate significant weight gain following hospital admission or child removal from the family. Deprivational dwarfism, a medical term applied to children of small stature whose physical growth is impaired by the absence of nutritional requirements, is another type of child neglect associated with some young children. Even after diagnosis and treatment, the psychological consequences of emotional neglect persist. Polansky et al. (1981) found that young adolescents who in their infancy were diagnosed as failure to thrive were defiant and hostile. Drotar (1992) notes that factors that trigger nonorganic failure to thrive and child neglect should be separated from factors that maintain these behaviors. In early periods of neglectful behavior, the child may exhibit stressful behaviors in the forms of feeding problems, irritability, or deficits in social responsiveness that place increased demands on the parent's caretaking duties (Powell and Low, 1983; Powell et al., 1987). In some cases, nutritional deprivation, combined with increased maternal detachment, sets into motion a "vicious cycle of cumulative psychological risk" (Drotar, 1992:121). Eventually, the parent may begin to perceive the child as quiet, sickly, or not very competent, perceptions that may not be shared by others who observe the child (Ayoub and Milner, 1985; Kotelchuck, 1982). In the absence of growth indicators of nonorganic failure to thrive or deprivational dwarfism, clinical diagnosis of child neglect is quite difficult. Oates (1984a,b; 1992) has described some nonspecific behavioral characteristics of nonorganic failure to thrive infants, which include lack of smiling, an expressionless face, gaze aversion, self-stimulating behavior, intolerance of changes in routine, low activity level, and flexed hips.

Abuse and neglect may result in serious health problems that can adversely affect children's development and result in irremediable lasting consequences. Early studies of physically abused children documented significant neuromotor handicaps, including central nervous system damage, physical defects, growth and mental retardation, and serious speech problems (Elmer and Gregg, 1967; Green et al., 1974; Martin et al., 1974; Morse et al., 1970). Physically abused children have been found to have more mild neurologic signs, serious physical injuries, and skin markings and scars than their nonabused peers (Kolko et al., 1990). Children who have been sexually abused, and some children who have been physically neglected, have shown heightened sexuality and signs of genital manipulation. A particularly serious biological consequence of child and adolescent sexual abuse is the risk of sexually transmitted diseases, including human immunodeficiency virus, gonorrhea, and syphilis.

Cognitive and Intellectual Consequences

Cognitive and language deficits in abused children have been noted clinically (Augoustinos, 1987; Azar et al., 1988; Fantuzzo, 1990; Kolko, 1992). Abused and neglected children with no evidence of neurological impairment have also shown delayed intellectual development, particularly in the area of verbal intelligence (Augoustinos, 1987). Some studies have found lowered intellectual functioning and reduced cognitive functioning in abused children (Hoffman-Plotkin and Twentyman, 1984; Perry et al., 1983). However, others have not found differences in intellectual and cognitive functioning, language skills, or verbal ability (Alessandri, 1991; Allen and Oliver, 1982; Elmer, 1977; Lynch and Roberts, 1982).

Problematic school performance (e.g., low grades, poor standardized test scores, and frequent retention in grade) is a fairly consistent finding in studies of physically abused and neglected children (Eckenrode et al., 1991; Salzinger et al., 1984; Wolfe and Mosk, 1983), with neglected children appearing the most adversely affected. The findings for sexually abused children are inconsistent.

Dodge and colleagues (1990) found that physically harmed 4-year-old children showed deviant patterns of processing social information, related to aggressive behavior, at age 5. Physically harmed children (relative to nonphysically harmed children) were significantly less attentive to social cues, more inclined to attribute hostile intent, and less able to manage personal problems. They explain possible cognitive deficits in abused and neglected children by suggesting that physical abuse affects the development of social-information-processing patterns, which in turn lead to chronic aggressive behavior. The experience of severe physical harm is associated with the "acquisition of a set of biased and deficient patterns of processing social provocation information" (p. 1679).

Differences in findings on the cognitive and intellectual consequences of childhood maltreatment may be related to the failure to control for important variables, such as socioeconomic status, and the lack of statistical power of small sample sizes.[2] Other possible explanations for the inconsistencies in this literature are the tendency of earlier studies to aggregate different types of maltreatment (which may mask different consequences associated with specific forms of child maltreatment) or the inclusion of children who had neurological dysfunction to begin with (which can dramatically influence cognitive and intellectual performance). More recent studies have excluded children with obvious neurological impairments. Yet maltreatment, especially early maltreatment, can cause injury to the central nervous system that results in future cognitive impairments (Lewis and Shanok, 1977).

Psychosocial Consequences

Some studies suggest that certain signs of severe neglect (such as when a child experiences dehydration, diarrhea, or malnutrition without receiving appropriate care) may lead to developmental delays, attention deficits, poorer social skills, and less emotional stability. Consequences of physical child abuse have included deficiencies in the development of stable attachments to an adult caretaker in infants and very young children (Cicchetti, 1989; Cicchetti and Barnett, 1991; Crittenden and Ainsworth, 1989). Poorly attached children are at risk for diminished self-esteem and thus view themselves more negatively than nonmaltreated children. In several studies, school-age victims of physical abuse showed lower self-esteem on self-report (Allen and Tarnowski, 1989; Kinard, 1982; Oates et al., 1985) and parent-report measures (Kaufman and Cicchetti, 1989), but other studies found no differences (e.g., Stovall and Craig, 1990).

The consequences of neglectful behavior can be especially severe and powerful in early stages of child development. Drotar (1992) notes that maternal detachment and lack of availability may harm the development of bonding and attachment between a child and parent, affecting the neglected child's expectations of adult availability, affect, problem solving, social relationships, and the ability to cope with new or stressful situations (Aber and Allen, 1987; Main et al., 1985). One study by Rohner (1986) has presented impressive cross-cultural evidence of the negative consequences of parental neglect and rejection on children's self-esteem and emotional stability.

In a prospective study of the qualitative range of caregiving in a high-risk sample, Egeland and Sroufe (1981a) identified a group of mothers who were psychologically unavailable to their infants. These mothers were detached and unresponsive to their children's bids for care and attention. Children from this group were compared with physically abused, neglected, verbally rejected, and control groups from the same high-risk sample. Using multiple measures across different situations and outcome measures designed to assess the salient developmental issues of each age, the results indicated that children in all maltreatment groups functioned poorly (Erickson et al., 1989). Over time their functioning deteriorated. There were many similarities in terms of the pattern of development between the maltreatment groups, but there were also a number of interesting differences.

Nearly all the children in this study whose mothers were psychologically unavailable were anxiously attached at 18 months of age, with the majority of these classified as anxious avoidant (86 percent). These children were observed with their mothers in a problem-solving situation at 24 months and a teaching task at 42 months and were found to be angry, noncomplacent, lacking in persistence, and displaying little positive affect. One of the most dramatic findings for these children was the nearly 40 point decline in performance on the Bayley Scales of Infant Development between 9 and 24 months. In the preschool classroom, these children presented varied and serious behavior problems.

Studies have reported evidence of other psychosocial problems in young children. Higher incidence of suicide attempts and self-mutilation have been reported in clinical samples (Green, 1978). Comparison studies with nonphysically abused children indicate heightened levels of depression, hopelessness, and lower self-esteem in physically abused children (Allen and Tarnowski, 1989; Kazdin et al., 1985). Greater emotional difficulties in older physically abused children have also been identified (Kinard, 1980, 1982). In a more recent investigation involving prepubescent (ages 7 to 12) maltreated children, Kaufman (1991) found a disproportionate number of the maltreated children who met the diagnostic criteria for one of the major affective disorders.[3]

Linkages between parental behaviors that have emotionally or psychologically destructive consequences on children have not been clearly established. While verbally or symbolically abusive acts designed to terrorize or intimidate a child (such as constant belittling or the destruction of a favorite object or pet) are associated with severe long-term consequences (Vissing et al., 1991), the processes by which children interpret aggressive or neglectful actions are poorly understood. The failure to provide age-appropriate care (such as parental availability and nurturance), cognitive stimulation, or achievement expectations also can have profound psychological impact, especially when such omissions occur during critical child and adolescent developmental periods.

Although causal linkages between parental behaviors and the consequences on the child's development have been assumed, pathways that govern or mediate such linkages have not been well documented (Knudsen, 1992).

Inappropriate sexual behavior, such as frequent and overt self-stimulation, inappropriate sexual overtures toward other children and adults, and play and fantasy with sexual content, are commonly cited as symptoms of sexual abuse in studies that compare sexually abused with nonabused or nonclinical children (Kendall-Tackett et al., 1993). Across six studies of sexually abused preschoolers (those most likely to manifest such symptoms), approximately 35 percent of the abused children showed such behaviors. Sexual abuse has also sometimes been associated with the onset of sexual activity in middle childhood. Reported rates vary widely because of differences in samples, measurement instruments, and definitions of the outcome behavior. The lowest estimates (of 7 percent) were based on a large study that included many well-functioning and older children.

While sexualization seems relatively specific to sexual abuse, inappropriate sexual behavior has been noted in nonsexually abused children. Deblinger et al. (1989) compared the reports of inappropriate sexual behaviors across sexually abused, physically abused, and nonabused psychiatrically hospitalized children matched for age, sex, and socioeconomic status. They found that approximately the same percentage of sexually inappropriate behavior in physically abused (17 percent) as in sexually abused children (18 percent). However, early sexual abuse may occur and not be documented until much later in life (Stein and Lewis, 1992). In a recent review of studies reporting quantitative findings about the impact of sexual abuse of minors, Kendall-Tackett et al. (1993) found that sexually abused children were often more symptomatic than their nonabused counterparts in terms of fear, nightmares, general post-traumatic stress disorder, withdrawn behavior, neurotic mental illness, cruelty, delinquency, sexually inappropriate behavior, regressive behavior, running away, general problem behaviors, and self-injurious behavior. Estimates of sexually abused children diagnosed as meeting the DSM-III-R criteria for post-traumatic stress disorder range from 21 percent (Deblinger et al., 1989) to 48 percent (McLeer et al., 1988).[4]

Sexually abused children, particularly those abused by a family member, may show high levels of dissociation, a process that produces a disturbance in the normally integrative functions of memory and identity (Trickett and Putnam, in press). Many abused children are able to self-hypnotize themselves, space out, and dissociate themselves from abusive experiences (Kluft, 1985). In some clinical studies, severely abused children appear to be impervious to pain, less empathetic than their nonabused peers, and less able than other children to put their own suffering into words (Barahal et al., 1981, Straker and Jacobson, 1981).

Behavioral Consequences

Physical aggression and antisocial behavior are among the most consistently documented childhood outcomes of physical child abuse. Most studies document physical aggression and antisocial behavior using parent or staff ratings (Aber et al., 1990; Hoffman-Plotkin and Twentyman, 1984; Perry et al., 1983; Salzinger et al., 1984); other measures, such as child stories (Dean et al., 1986); or observational measures across a wide variety of situations, including summer camps and day care settings (Alessandri, 1991; Bousha and Twentyman, 1984; Howes and Eldredge, 1985; Howes and Espinosa, 1985; Kaufman and Cicchetti, 1989; Main and George, 1985; Trickett and Kuczynski, 1986; Walker et al., 1989). Some studies indicate that physically abused children show higher levels of aggression than other maltreated children (Hoffman-Plotkin and Twentyman, 1984; Kaufman and Cicchetti, 1989) although other studies indicate that neglected children may be more dysfunctional (Rohrbeck and Twentyman, 1986).

A prospective study comparing preschool children who were classified as physically harmed with those who were unharmed (Dodge et al., 1990) found that children with a history of physical harm were rated six months later as more aggressive by teachers and peers. These differences were not accounted for by the child's demographic or family background. Evidence from other longitudinal studies indicates continued problems of aggression and anger (Egeland and Sroufe, 1981b) and the development of conduct disorder (Rogeness et al., 1986). Children who experienced severe violence were reported (by their parents) in the National Family Violence Survey to have higher rates of conduct problems and rule violating behaviors than those who did not experience severe violence (Straus and Gelles, 1990; Hotaling et al., 1990).

Maltreated children may also be less competent in their social interactions with peers (Straus and Gelles, 1990; Howes and Espinosa, 1985). For some physically abused children, this may manifest in withdrawal or avoidance (Kaufman and Cicchetti, 1989), or fear, anger, and aggression (Main and George, 1985).

Effects of Witnessing Domestic Violence

Not much is known about the psychosocial status of siblings of abused children. Several studies suggest that the child's experience of witnessing violence toward siblings or parents may be as harmful as the experience of victimization itself (Rosenbaum and O'Leary, 1981). Some studies have suggested that children who see violence in their homes may view such behavior as an appropriate means of resolving conflict and also see violence as an integral part of a close relationship (Groves et al., 1993; Jaffe et al., 1988; Straus, 1992). However, research on the effects of a child's witnessing family violence is contradictory and characterized by methodological flaws. In many studies of the effects of observing family violence, for example, the child subjects are often themselves the victims of physical child abuse.

A few studies in the area of physical aggression and violence suggest that siblings of aggressive children exhibit high rates of aggressive/oppositional behavior (Patterson et al., 1989; Patterson, 1982). These findings have been confirmed in observational studies showing that aggressive and hostile behavior is exhibited by various members of families of aggressive children.

Related evidence examining the role of interparental conflict suggests witnessing verbal hostility and physical violence between parents is associated with significantly higher levels of child internalizing and externalizing behavior on parent rating scales, and lower levels of child competence based on direct interviews (Fantuzzo et al., 1991) compared with witnessing verbal hostility alone. The impact of observing parental conflict and violence has been demonstrated on various clinical measures of child functioning (see Fantuzzo and Lindquist, 1986; Jaffe et al., 1990, 1991; Widom, 1989c; Wolfe and Jaffe, 1991). Studies have generally not examined whether the results are due to exposure to parental violence, the effects of confounding variables such as child rejection, limited caretaking skills, and parental involvement, or other forms of family conflict associated with a dysfunctional home environment.

ADOLESCENCE

Research on the developmental consequences of child abuse and neglect is still relatively new. Studies of the consequences of child abuse and neglect that appear in adolescence have generally not differentiated between consequences that are derived from earlier childhood experiences with maltreatment and consequences that are unique to adolescent experiences with abuse and neglect.

Delinquency

An extensive body of work has examined the relationship between childhood victimization and later delinquency (for reviews, see Gray et al, 1986; Garbarino and Plantz, 1986; Widom, 1989c, 1991b). Although the majority of abused children do not become delinquent, and the majority of delinquents are not abused as children, this research indicates that abused and neglected children are at increased risk for juvenile delinquency. Prospective studies estimate the incidence of delinquency in adolescents who have been abused or neglected as children to be about 20 to 30 percent (Widom, 1989c). Retrospective studies, in which delinquents were asked about their early backgrounds, estimated rates from approximately 8 to 26 percent (Widom, 1989c). What is not known is whether specific, or combined, institutional responses to incidents of abuse (such as arrest of the perpetrator, foster care, and the provision of mental health services) influence the probability of delinquent behavior by abused or neglected children.

In one study, childhood abuse or neglect significantly increased a child's risk for an arrest during adolescence by more than 50 percent (26 versus 17 percent) (Widom, 1989b).[5] Abused and neglected children began their official criminal activity approximately one year earlier than the control subjects (16.5 versus 17.3 years) and had approximately twice the number of arrests. Early childhood victimization was associated with increased risk of arrest as a juvenile (prior to age 18) compared with controls. When considering delinquency, degrees of aggression must be taken into account. Some clinical studies indicate that violent delinquents are more likely to have suffered severe abuse than nonviolent delinquents (Lewis and Shanok, 1977; Lewis et al., 1979, 1982).

An epidemiological study of medical hospital records of delinquent and nondelinquent adolescents matched for age, sex, race, and socioeconomic status found that the delinquent sample had significantly more accidents, injuries, and illnesses than the nondelinquents (Shanok and Lewis, 1981;

Lewis et al., 1985). Of note, white delinquents experienced far greater numbers of adverse medical events than white nondelinquents, although the medical histories of black delinquents were only slightly more adverse than their black nondelinquent counterparts.

Violence

Almost 30 years ago, Curtis (1963) suggested that abused and neglected children would "become tomorrow's murderers and perpetrators of other crimes of violence, if they survive" (p. 386). Subsequently, a number of small-scale clinical reports described prior abuse in the family backgrounds of adolescents who attempted or succeeded in killing their parents (Easson and Steinhilber, 1961; King, 1975; Sendi and Blomgren, 1975). Since then, larger and more systematic studies have explored the relationship between child abuse, neglect, and violent behavior in delinquents (Alfaro, 1981; Geller and Ford-Somma, 1984; Gutierres and Reich, 1981; Hartstone and Hansen, 1984; Kratcoski, 1982).

These studies, which differ in design, scope, and quality, reveal contradictory findings. Some studies provide strong support for the cycle of violence (Geller and Ford-Somma, 1984; Lewis et al., 1979, 1985; Straus et al., 1980; Vissing et al., 1991). In a clinical study of 97 incarcerated male delinquents (Lewis et al., 1979), neuropsychiatric vulnerabilities and histories of abuse and family violence distinguished the more violent subjects from their less violent delinquent counterparts.[6] When these 97 delinquents were followed into young adulthood, the abused delinquents who also were most impaired neuropsychiatrically were found to have committed the greatest numbers of crimes as adults (Lewis et al., 1989).

Other studies have not found significant differences between abused and nonabused delinquents (Kratcoski, 1982). In one study, abused delinquents were less likely to engage in later aggressive crimes (Gutierres and Reich, 1981). Fagan et al. (1983) found low incidences of both child abuse and parental violence among violent juvenile offenders. In most studies, the majority of abused children did not become delinquents or violent offenders.

Widom (1989b) did not find that abused and neglected children had significantly higher rates of arrest as juveniles for violent crimes than controls (4 versus 3 percent) although abused or neglected females appeared to be at increased risk of arrest for violent crimes during adolescence (Widom, 1991b).

Inconsistencies in studies of the relationship between early childhood maltreatment and subsequent violent behaviors may be attributed to various factors, including study designs, reliance on reports of maltreatment, and the use of arrests for violence as the only measure of violent behavior.

Becoming a Runaway

In national surveys in which runaways were asked about their early childhood histories, most runaways do not report having been sexually or physically abused prior to their leaving home. However, abusive experiences in the home may increase the chances of an adolescent's becoming a runaway. Pagelow (1984) noted that "many runaway children are not running toward something, but rather are running away from something—a home life in which they were subject to abuse, particularly sexual abuse" (p. 49). Only a handful of studies have attempted to describe the extent to which adolescents who run away report experiences with abuse. In two studies, sexual abuse victims were found to have run away from home more often during adolescence than clinical controls (Herman, 1981; Meiselman, 1978). In the 1988 National Survey of Missing, Abducted, Runaway, and Thrownaway Children in America, approximately 3 percent of the runaways reported having been sexually abused and 1 percent physically harmed (Finkelhor et al., 1990). In contrast, in a runaway shelter in Ohio, 75 percent of the youths reported having experienced physical maltreatment (McCord, 1983). One prospective study traced official criminal histories for a large sample of abused and neglected children and matched controls and found direct support for a relationship between early childhood victimization and adolescent running away (Widom, 1991b).[7]

The results of these studies suggest that there may be a link between childhood victimization and running away. The hypothesized linkage between maltreatment experiences and running away warrants further examination, since it may shed light on at least one pathway to problem behaviors and on possible intervention points. In the case of children who run away, delinquent behavior during adolescence may represent an adaptive response to the immediate situation of an abusive home, although such a response may be dangerous and ultimately harmful to the child. For these children, one might speculate that the long-term consequences may be different for abused children who do not manifest this type of acting out during adolescence. At the same time, the effects of early abusive experiences may be manifest in ways not related to delinquency or running away, but may lie in more subtle manifestations of emotional damage such as low self-esteem, depression, withdrawal, or, in the extreme, suicide.

Intimacy, Sexual Problems, and Teenage Pregnancy

Briere (1992a,b) has suggested that abuse-related symptomatology can wax and wane across the life span (Friedrich and Reams, 1987). This variability may reflect developmental issues. For example, intimacy and sexual problems may first appear in adolescence when the individual confronts these issues. Other effects, such as revictimization or substance abuse, may also occur in young adulthood.[8]

Many clinicians and researchers have described a relationship between childhood sexual abuse and sexually promiscuous or dysfunctional behavior (e.g., sexual offenses, prostitution) in adolescence (Allen, 1980; Becker et al., 1986; Burgess et al., 1987; Courtois, 1979; DeYoung, 1982; Fehrenbach et al., 1986; Finkelhor, 1979; Finkelhor et al., 1989; Groth, 1979; Greenwald, 1970; Herman and Hirschman, 1977; James and Meyerding, 1977; Seghorn et al., 1987; Silbert and Pines, 1981; Wyatt, 1988). However, the methodological weaknesses of these studies do not provide empirical support for a causal relationship between sexual abuse, sexual dysfunction, and promiscuity. Indeed, in a review of research on the impact of child sexual abuse, Browne and Finkelhor (1986:66) cautioned that "although clinical literature suggests that sexual abuse during childhood plays a role in the development of other problems ranging from anorexia nervosa to prostitution, empirical evidence about its actual effects is sparse."

Female victims of child sexual abuse are often thought to be at increased risk of becoming pregnant as teenagers, an important outcome of child sexual abuse because of the theoretical link between early parenting and inadequate childrearing practices. In a review of this literature, Bohigan (1989) concluded that existing research had not yet clearly established a relationship between child sexual abuse and adolescent pregnancy, but that abusive mothers do have more children at younger ages (Zuravin, 1988).[9] One difficulty in interpreting this literature is that a teenager's pregnancy may result from a variety of factors, including forced sexual intercourse, promiscuity, and inadequate contraceptive protection following a history of sexual abuse (Gershenson et al., 1989).

Although victims of childhood abuse may be increasingly vulnerable to sexual promiscuity and at increased risk for teenage pregnancy, solid empirical evidence does not yet exist. Research is needed to clarify and extend our knowledge about possible causal relationships between different forms of childhood victimization and adolescent pregnancy, taking into account relevant demographic variables and confounding factors such as socioeconomic status (Brooks-Gunn and Furstenberg, 1989; Chase-Landale et al., 1991).

Alcohol Problems

Recent research has called attention to alcohol problems that may be a consequence of child maltreatment. Researchers have hypothesized that for abused and neglected children, alcohol use may serve a number of possible functions: (1) to provide psychological escape from an abusive and aversive environment; (2) to serve as a form of self-medication in which the child tries to gain control over his or her negative life experiences; (3) to act as a form of self-enhancement to improve the child's self-esteem (Miller et al., 1989); or (4) to reduce feelings of isolation and loneliness (for a review, see Ireland and Widom, in press). Similar to escaping from an abusive home environment by running away, alcohol use may serve as a coping strategy adopted by abused and neglected children.

Despite the hypothesized association, evidence supporting this relationship is sketchy. Relatively few studies have examined alcohol problems in adolescents who were abused or neglected in childhood, and even fewer have looked at these connections in nonclinical samples. One study found that physical abuse was significantly related to alcohol use in a cohort of high-risk youth prior to the initial interview, but not during the follow-up period about one year later (Dembo et al., 1990).

In addition, parental alcohol problems may be antecedent to child maltreatment and may have an important role in influencing the parent's maltreating behavior. Since most child abuse is committed by biological parents, familial factors may contribute to a relationship between childhood victimization and a child's subsequent risk for alcohol problems. Children of parents with alcohol problems are generally at increased risk for the development of alcohol problems (Goodwin et al., 1973, 1977; Russell et al., 1985; Schuckit, 1986). If parents with alcohol problems are more likely to abuse or neglect their children, then multiple reasons might support hypotheses that their offspring will be at increased risk for the development of alcohol problems. Research is needed to disentangle the effects of an abusive or neglectful home environment on alcoholism from family history of alcoholism, multiple problems commonly facing abusive families, and other predispositions for alcohol problems.

Illicit Drug Use or Abuse

Illicit drug use or abuse in adolescence has sometimes been viewed as a form of psychological escape or as a form of self-medication to control negative sensations (Cavaiola and Schiff, 1989; Harrison et al., 1989a,b; Singer et al., 1989). Illicit drug use may also result from a need for self-enhancement and improved self-esteem (Dembo et al., 1987, 1989). Drugs may be used to reduce feelings of isolation and loneliness, by providing the adolescent with a peer group, as he or she becomes part of the drug culture (Singer et al., 1989).

In contrast to the sparse literature on adolescent alcohol problems and childhood victimization, several studies suggest a relationship between childhood victimization and adolescent substance abuse, although the results of this research are sometimes inconsistent (Benward and Densen-Gerber, 1975; Cavaiola and Schiff, 1989; Dembo et al., 1987, 1989; Gomes-Schwartz et al., 1985; Harrison et al., 1989; Lindberg and Distad, 1985a; Runtz and

Briere, 1986; Sansonnet-Hayden et al., 1987; Singer et al., 1989). One study by Harrison et al. (1989b) of adolescent males in a chemical dependency treatment program found that male victims of sexual abuse used a wider variety of drugs than nonvictims and used more drugs to self-medicate but did not report an earlier onset of drug use. In contrast, Goldston et al. (1989) found that drug abuse was more common among a control group of girls than sexually abused girls. A study of 444 adolescent girls admitted to chemical dependency treatment programs found that sexually abused girls did not differ in the overall prevalence or frequency of substance use from nonvictims, although the victims were more likely to report regular use of particular drugs and to report an earlier age of onset of drug use (Harrison et al., 1989a). These findings of earlier onset of substance use by female sexual abuse victims support the self-medication hypothesis, rather than motivations associated with peer pressure. Sex differences in the use of illicit drugs may be related to differences in socialization experiences, to age-related patterns of drug use, or to actual gender differences in age of onset of drug behavior (Colten and Marsh, 1984).

Most studies of the association between illicit drug use and childhood victimization have focused on sexually abused children in clinical settings or in detention facilities. With some exceptions, these studies are cross-sectional designs, include information about childhood abuse experiences based on retrospective self-reports, and do not utilize control groups. These methodological limitations suggest that a causal connection between childhood victimization and adolescent substance use or abuse has not been established.

Self-Destructive Behavior, Depression, and Suicide Attempts

Several writers have suggested that severe childhood maltreatment also is related to later self-destructive behavior (Gutierres and Reich, 1981), withdrawal (George and Main, 1979; Kagan, 1977; Martin and Beezley, 1977), and depression (Allen and Tarnowski, 1989; Kazdin et al., 1985). Although this body of work is not extensive, some abused and neglected children appear to engage in self-abusive and self-destructive behavior in adolescence. Lindberg and Distad's (1985a) small study of 27 adolescents with incest histories found that one-third had attempted suicide. Sansonnet-Hayden et al. (1987) found that depressive symptoms and schizoid/psychotic symptoms (hallucinations) significantly differentiated adolescent inpatients with a history of sexual abuse from those with no history of sexual abuse, although it was not clear whether these behaviors came before or after the abusive experiences. Prospective and longitudinal research appears warranted to assess the extent to which this self-destructive and negative life trajectory characterizes abused and neglected children.

Summary

Victims of child abuse and neglect are at increased risk for delinquency and running away. However, existing research indicates that the majority of childhood victims do not manifest these behaviors. Significantly less is known about connections between childhood victimization and other problem behaviors, such as teenage pregnancy, alcohol and illicit drug use and abuse, self-destructive behavior, and suicide. Alcohol and illicit drug use are both illegal for teenagers, creating a natural confounding of alcohol or substance use with delinquency. For example, alcoholics often attempt other destructive behaviors, including suicide attempts (Schuckit, 1986). Diagnoses of alcoholism are complicated by the presence of antisocial personality disorder, which in turn, may include components of criminal behavior and sexual promiscuity. Engaging in any one of these behaviors, then, might increase the likelihood of involvement in other at-risk behaviors.

A variety of adolescent problems may be related to early childhood victimization. Current knowledge about these outcomes is still uncertain. Research is needed to document the increased risk, scope, and magnitude of adolescent problem behaviors among maltreated children compared with children and adolescents in control groups.

ADULTHOOD

Our knowledge of the long-term consequences of childhood maltreatment into adulthood is extremely limited, with sparse information on intellectual and academic outcomes and medical and physiological sequelae. Some research has addressed parenting behaviors (particularly the intergenerational effects of abuse), but the vast majority of existing research has focused on psychosocial outcomes and, in particular, psychopathology.

Intergenerational Cycles of Abuse

A popular belief in both the scholarly and popular literature is that adults who were abused as children are more likely to abuse their own children. As noted in Chapter 4, Kaufman and Zigler (1987) estimated the rate of intergenerational transmission of abuse to be 30 percent (with a 5 percent margin of error). This means that about one-third of the individuals who were abused or neglected as children will abuse their own children and that two-thirds will not. "Being maltreated as a child puts one at risk for becoming abusive but the path between these two points is far from direct or inevitable" (Kaufman and Zigler, 1987:190).

Kalmuss (1984) used data from the National Family Violence Survey to explore the relationship between family aggression and severe marital aggression in the next generation. She found that children who observed hitting between their parents were more likely to be involved in severe marital aggression than children who were hit as teenagers. However, the probability of marital aggression increased dramatically when respondents had experienced both types of family aggression.

Studies addressing sexual maladjustment and/or problems in intimate relationships among adults with a history of sexual abuse show little consistency. Studies that find no differences in marital and sexual adjustment often use college student samples, which may reflect less severe abuse or less severe consequences (Trickett, 1992).

Recent studies have indicated that women with histories of sexual abuse before age 18 (especially incest survivors) are more likely to be poor contraceptors, to have multiple sexual partners, and to have short-term intimate relationships than women with no abuse histories. They were also at increased risk for unintended and terminated pregnancies and for sexually transmitted diseases (Wyatt et al., in press).

Long-term Consequences of Child Maltreatment

Over the last decade, there has been a dramatic recent increase in the number of clinical and research reports retrospectively linking childhood sexual abuse to specific forms of adult psychopathology. In adults, short- and long-term psychosocial problems have been noted (Gil, 1988): (1) cognitive distortions, such as guilt, shame, and self-blame (Gold, 1986; Jehu et al., 1984/85); (2) mood disturbance, such as anxiety or depression (Peters, 1984, 1988; Stein et al., 1988); (3) posttraumatic stress (Craine et al., 1988; Lindberg and Distad, 1985b; Wyatt et al., 1992); (4) interpersonal problems, such as isolation, fear of intimacy, and revictimization (Briere and Zaidi, 1989; Harter et al., 1988); (5) self-injurious behavior (suicide attempts or self-mutilation (DeWilde et al., 1992; Walsh and Rosen, 1988); (6) substance abuse (Ladwig and Anderson, 1989; Root, 1989); (7) borderline personality disorder (Stone, 1990); (8) somatization and somatoform disorders, particularly chronic pelvic pain (Loewenstein, 1990; Greenwald, 1990); (9) eating disorders (Demitrack et al., 1990, 1991); (10) some forms of chronic psychosis (Beck and van der Kolk, 1987; Bryer et al., 1987); and (11) multiple personality disorder (Putnam, 1989; Ross et al., 1989).

These studies' reliance on retrospective self-reported information to determine a history of childhood victimization can be problematic (Briere, 1992a; Widom, 1988; Wolfe and Mosk, 1983). Recollection of a history of childhood victimization can be influenced by what Cicchetti and Rizley (1981:40) called "the influence of contemporary adaptation on recall." The passage of time may also work against accurate or complete recall of childhood traumas. One example of the potential impact of time on recollection of childhood victimization may be found in Russell's (1984) research, in which she found that older women reported less sexual abuse than younger women. Although one might conclude from this that the incidence of sexual abuse had increased over the years, other possible explanations are that the passage of time leads to forgetfulness about these experiences or that older women may simply be more embarrassed about revealing this information. Memories of abusive experiences change during one's lifetime, and thus retrospective studies cannot guarantee the validity of information about childhood victimization. Briere (1992a) suggests that future studies might include additional variables relevant to report bias, such as social desirability, tendency toward repression, and attitudes toward abuse disclosure.

Several recent studies, producing inconsistent results, have examined the sequelae of physical child abuse. At present, these have focused primarily on interpersonal aggression (McCord, 1983; Pollock et al., 1990; Widom, 1989a).

An even smaller number of studies have examined problems associated with psychological maltreatment (Briere and Runtz, 1988a; Garbarino et al., 1986; Brassard et al., 1987; Vissing et al., 1991). With few exceptions (McCord, 1983; Widom, 1989b), there is virtually no information about the adult status of neglected children.

Furthermore, childhood victimization often occurs in the context of multiproblem homes, in which child abuse and/or neglect may be only one of the family's problems. Other family variables, such as poverty, unemployment, parental alcoholism or drug problems, and other factors that affect social and family functioning, need to be disentangled from the specific effects of childhood abuse or neglect. Control groups matched on socioeconomic status and other relevant variables become necessary and vital components of this research, in order to determine the effect of childhood victimization on later behavior, in the context of family and demographic characteristics. This is particularly true of consequences such as aggression, delinquency and other problem behaviors (Widom, 1989c) that are correlated with demographic characteristics. For example, in one 8-year follow-up study of incarcerated delinquent boys (Lewis et al., 1989), almost all were known to the criminal justice system as adults. The constellation of violent abusive upbringing and neuropsychiatric and cognitive vulnerabilities was associated with adult violent crime. Beitchman et al., (1991) recently concluded that the child sexual abuse literature "has been vague in separating effects directly attributable to sexual abuse from effects that may be due to preexisting psychopathology in the child, family dysfunction, or to the stress associated with disclosure" (p. 538).

Few studies have assessed the long-term consequences on the development of abused and neglected children, beyond adolescence and into adulthood.   Research is needed on the long-term physical, psychological, and social consequences of child maltreatment to address the methodological deficiencies currently associated with retrospective studies.

ISSUES OF STIGMA, BIAS, AND DISCRIMINATION

Problem behaviors may result from the chain of events occurring subsequent to the victimization rather than the victimization experience per se. For example, a child's removal from family members following maltreatment and foster care placement can be associated with deleterious effects (Bohman and Sigvardsson, 1980; Bryce and Ehlert, 1977; Canning, 1974; Frank, 1980; Littner, 1974).

Furthermore, racial and ethnic minority children can encounter discrimination against their race, color, language, life and family styles, and religious and cultural beliefs that affect their self-esteem and exacerbate the initial and lasting effects of both types of victimization (Wyatt, 1990).

The observed relationship between early childhood victimization and later problem behaviors may also be affected by practices of the juvenile justice system that disproportionately label and adjudicate maltreatment victims as juvenile offenders because of survey bias (Smith et al., 1980). In reviewing the literature on the relationship between child maltreatment and delinquency, Garbarino and Plantz (1986) suggested that behavioral responses to maltreatment may ultimately lead to delinquency as a consequence of maltreatment. For example, a child who becomes estranged from his or her parents or from prosocial peers may develop friendships with antisocial friends. In turn, this association with delinquent friends leads to the adoption of a highly visible delinquent lifestyle.

INTERACTION OF RISK AND PROTECTIVE FACTORS

Abused and neglected children appear to be at risk of a variety of negative outcomes, yet many studies show that not all abused and neglected children grow up to become dysfunctional adults. For example, a number of studies of sexual abuse victims have found a surprising proportion of them to be asymptomatic (Caffaro-Rouget et al., 1989; Conte and Schuerman, 1987; Kendall-Tackett et al., 1993: Mannarino and Cohen, 1986; Tong et al., 1987). Similar findings have been reported for the intergenerational transmission of abuse from abused child to abusive parent (Kaufman and Zigler, 1987) and the transmission of violence from abused child to perpetrator of violence (Widom, 1989b,c).

Garmezy (1981) has called attention to the role of protective factors described as dispositional attributes, environmental conditions, and positive events that can mitigate the effects of early negative experiences. Various demographic, background, and clinical variables that may influence the consequences of childhood maltreatment include the child's sex (Dean et al., 1986; Mangold and Koski, 1990; Walker et al., 1989), and family socioeconomic status (Margolin, 1990; Vondra et al., 1990; Walker et al., 1989). The level of marital and family violence (Cappell and Heiner, 1990; Trickett and Kuczynski, 1986) also deserves attention as a protective factor, one that may have a number of interactive effects on the consequences of child maltreatment.

Intelligence

Although high intelligence (including good cognitive abilities, social competence, and creativity) and good scholastic attainment may exert a protective effect in the context of an abusive environment, the role of intelligence as a mediator between childhood victimization and later problem behaviors is poorly understood. Intelligence may play a direct role or it may act as a mediator between childhood victimization and other factors as school performance and problem-solving skills.[10]

Frodi and Smetana (1984) found that controlling for IQ eliminates differences between maltreated and nonmaltreated children in their ability to identify emotional behaviors. Furthermore, high-IQ children have been found to maintain good achievement test performance at both low and high levels of stress, whereas low-IQ children show a drop in performance under high stress (Garmezy et al., 1984). Lower levels of intelligence appear to be related to higher rates of delinquency (Werner, 1983; Werner and Smith, 1982; Wilson and Herrnstein, 1985). However, Moffit, Gabrielli, Mednick, and Schulsinger (1981) found a negative relationship between IQ and delinquency (high IQ—less likelihood of becoming delinquent), while controlling for socioeconomic status.

Temperament

As noted in Chapter 4, conflicting evidence exists as to whether some infants and young children with difficult temperaments elicit abusive behaviors by their parents or caretakers (Petit and Bates, 1989). Although some have found that children with difficult temperaments may be singled out for abuse (Friedrich and Boriskin, 1976; Herrenkohl and Herrenkohl, 1981), other researchers have not found this to be the case (Dodge et al., 1990; Silver et al., 1969). As noted in Chapter 4, child factors are generally viewed as contributory, not causal or predictive factors, in a transactional model because they influence behavior only in the presence of other risk factors (Starr, 1992). Temperament is most likely to interact with early childhood experiences to exacerbate in some cases, or to minimize in other cases, a child's level of risk for the development of later problem behaviors.

Cognitive Appraisal of Events

Research suggests that a person's cognitive appraisal of life events strongly influences individual responses to particular events (Lazarus and Launier, 1978). The same event may be perceived by different individuals as irrelevant, benign, positive, or threatening and harmful. In considering the effects of childhood victimization, the child's cognitive appraisal of events will determine at least in part whether they are experienced as neutral, negative, or harmful. Abuse perceived as parental rejection may have more harmful effects than abuse perceived as arising from the parent's externally imposed frustrations. Research on perceptions of children may contribute to understanding the long-term consequences of abuse (Herzberger et al., 1981).

Research on the extent to which abused and neglected children's cognitive appraisal of events mediates the subsequent development of dysfunctional behaviors has been studied as part of a 14-year longitudinal study of 2,000 families (Zimrin, 1986). In this study, 35 families with abused children were identified, including a small group of abused children (n = 9) who had survived the trauma of their childhood and became well-adjusted adults. Variables that appeared to distinguish the survivors from the other children were: fatalism, self-esteem, cognitive abilities, hope and fantasy, behavior patterns, and external support. Zimrin's interpretation of these results was that the child's cognitive appraisal or perception of their good personal resources, intellectual potential, good self-image, and hope, coupled with relatively sound external resources, enhanced the lives of the survivor children.

In women who were sexually abused as children, Wyatt and Newcomb (1990) found that attributions of self-blame for the abuse were related to the severity of negative outcomes. Self-esteem and internal locus of control were found to mediate depression in a mixed group of maltreated adolescents (Moran and Eckenrode, in press).

Feelings of hopelessness, of loss of control of one's life course, may decrease a person's ability to deal with stressful life events. The acquisition of certain negative attributional styles or maladaptive coping strategies might serve as an important mechanism linking childhood victimization to later dysfunctional behavior. However, different attributional styles and coping strategies may also lead to more positive outcomes. Future research should investigate the extent to which individual perceptive and cognitive styles mediate children's responses to abuse and neglect.

Relationship with a Significant Person

Clinicians and child protection service workers have recognized the importance of significant persons in the lives of abused and neglected children, yet the role of such individuals in protecting victimized children from long-term negative consequences is poorly documented. In the literature on children's responses to the stress of hospital admissions, for example, a supportive relationship with a nurse reduced emotional disturbance during hospitalization (Visintainer and Wolfe, 1975). For individuals with a history of childhood victimization, the experience of having one biological parent, or foster parent, who provided support and love while growing up was associated with better outcomes in adulthood (Egeland and Jacobvitz, 1984; Egeland et al., 1984). Despite the fact that few competent "survivors" are found among longitudinal samples of physically or emotionally neglected children (Farber and Egeland, 1987), competent children were more likely to be those children whose mothers showed some interest in them and were able to respond to them emotionally.

Among sexually abused children, the presence of a supportive, positive relationship with a nonabusive parent or sibling has been considered a positive mediating variable (Conte and Schuerman, 1988). In her review of research on the effects of sexual abuse in childhood, Berliner (1991) noted that the level of impact of child sexual abuse was related to whether the child was believed and supported by his or her nonabusive family members (Everson et al., 1989; Gomes-Schwartz et al., 1990; Morrow and Sorell, 1989). Furthermore, in an examination of the prevalence of depressive disorder among a sample of 56 maltreated children, Kaufman (1991) found that the quality of social support affected the likelihood of abused children's developing depressive disorder.[11]

Developing a relationship with a significant person in one's life sometimes occurs naturally, but children who are severely abused or neglected may experience significant barriers in this area. Research is needed to assess the extent to which the lives of abused and neglected children are characterized by a relationship with a significant person and the extent to which a significant personal relationship mitigates long-term negative consequences.

Placement Experiences and Foster Care

Although placement outside the home may be a potentially protective factor affecting the long-term consequences of abused and neglected children, the role of placement and foster care remains controversial in studies of child maltreatment (Runyan et al., 1982). Methodological problems in the research literature on the impact of placement experiences on abused and neglected children weaken its scientific validity; improved research is needed to be relevant to public policy (Wald et al., 1988; Widom, 1991a). Studies have suggested that under certain conditions foster care placement experiments may protect abused and neglected children. Although some children are injured by foster parents, the rate of reported abuse by foster parents is reported to be lower than that of the general population, and far lower than the rate of re-abuse by abusive parents (Bolton et al., 1981). Some studies suggest that foster care improves on the relatively poor results of parent treatment programs (Cohn and Collignon, 1979; Herrenkohl et al., 1980; Magura, 1981). Studies of adults who grew up in foster homes found no evidence of more problems such as delinquency, criminality, mental illness, and marital failure than in the general population (see Widom, 1991a). Other studies found that children who had been in foster care at least a year were rated by their social workers as being better off (physically and socially) than at the time they entered foster care (Kent, 1976) and that the well-being of the majority of the children had improved in terms of physical development, IQ, and school performance after six months in foster care (Fanshel and Shinn, 1978).

Critics of foster care stress the need to maintain biological family ties, the desire to minimize government interference in family life, the financial cost of placement, and the concern that foster care may actually be worse for children than leaving them in the home (Hubbell, 1981; Wald, 1976; Wald et al., 1988). Examinations of foster care experiences have described the inadequacy, failures, and high costs of the system (Gruber, 1978; Schorr, 1982), the high rate of behavior problems (Bohman and Sigvardsson, 1980; Bryce and Ehlert, 1977; Frank, 1980; Littner, 1974), and school problems (Canning, 1974) among foster children. However, these studies did not compare rates of such behaviors in nonfoster care children or present information about these children prior to their placement.

Out-of-home placements may pose additional risks for the abused or neglected child, and the trauma of separation from one's biological family can also be damaging. Although some out-of-home placements may exacerbate stress in children from abusive and neglectful households, such placements may not always be detrimental. Using a matched historical cohort design with children who had been maltreated, Runyan and Gould (1985) found no support for the idea that foster care is responsible for the subsequent problems of delinquency among victims of maltreatment.

Widom (1991a) also examined the role of placement experiences in relation to delinquency and violence. Abused and neglected children in foster care and other out-of-home residential experiences, who typically come from multiproblem families, are a particularly vulnerable group because they have experienced both a disturbed family situation and separation from their natural parents. In this research, under certain circumstances, out-of-home placements did not necessarily lead to higher risk of arrest for delinquency and violence, especially if the child spent a significant amount of time in the first placement, in which the child would have the opportunity to develop attachments (and thus a stronger sense of self and self-esteem). Children who spent more than 10 years in their first placement had the lowest overall rates of arrests as an adolescent for delinquency and for violence.

In speculating about the effects of foster care on behavioral consequences, the developmental literature on children's responses to other forms of stressful life events should be considered. For example, children's responses to parental divorce (Wallerstein and Kelly, 1980; Wallerstein, 1983) and bereavement (Rutter, 1966) vary by age and level of development. Yarrow and Goodwin (1973) found that a child who moved from a foster home to a permanent adoptive home before the age of 6 months tended to show only transitory distress. By contrast, in somewhat older children (between age 7-12 months), such a change involved more pervasive disturbances. Similarly, according to Rutter (1966), the age period of greatest risk for the stress of hospital admission is between 6 months and 4 years of age. Children below the age of 6-7 months may be relatively immune because they have not yet developed selective attachments and therefore do not experience separation anxiety. Children above the age of 4 years are also less vulnerable, probably because they have the cognitive skills necessary to understand the situation.

Research on the impact of placement decisions is needed to help social workers and therapists identify the different needs of abused and neglected children and their families and to design programs to facilitate a positive outcome. In particular, research is needed on the role of family strengths or weaknesses as well as child characteristics that may influence the success or lack of success of placement experiences. Children who experience multiple placement experiences may require special services, and research is needed to identify particular resources for this subgroup of abused and neglected children.

Summary

Individual characteristics, such as high intelligence, certain kinds of temperament, the cognitive appraisal of victimization experiences, a relationship with a significant person, and some out-of-home placement experiences may serve as buffers for childhood victims. But conflicting or indirect evidence about most of these characteristics and experiences results in a major gap in our knowledge about what factors make a difference in the lives of abused and neglected children. Research is needed to determine the role of protective factors and mediating individual characteristics, particularly how they influence a child's vulnerability for problem behaviors.

RESEARCH RECOMMENDATIONS

Research on the consequences of child abuse and neglect can offer significant insights in the development of interventions. In particular, research on consequences can help improve our understanding of the nature, magnitude, and significance of abusive and neglectful experiences in childhood. Such experiences appear to result in tragic and costly outcomes for children, their families, and society as a whole. Knowing more about the nature of the consequences of child abuse and neglect will help justify preventive interventions. Such knowledge will also help improve treatment programs designed to expand the role of protective factors that may mitigate destructive consequences of maltreatment experiences.

Recommendation 6-1: Research that simultaneously assesses consequences across multiple outcomes for multiple types of maltreatment should be supported.

Research is needed that assesses direct and subtle consequences across a broad range of domains (cognitive and intellectual, medical and physiological, psychosocial, behavioral, and psychiatric). The effects of different and multiple types of child maltreatment in a variety of cultural contexts should also be considered in future research programs. The common practice of treating abused and neglected children together, or eliminating one type of maltreatment from study, may reveal only a partial portrait of childhood victims' risk for later consequences. Existing research has focused on physical and sexual abuse, with relatively little attention to neglect or emotional maltreatment, yet the accumulation of stress associated with chronic neglect may produce consequences for young children similar to those produced through physical abuse. This would seem particularly important given that the number of reported cases of child neglect far surpasses those of physical abuse in national statistics.

In particular, research on emotional maltreatment deserves to be expanded as a significant gateway in understanding its consequences and its role in stimulating other forms of child maltreatment. Emotional maltreatment studies deserve support because they could provide insight into the development of severe forms of behavior disorders and developmental delays in children.

Recommendation 6-2: The consequences of child abuse and neglect should be examined in a longitudinal developmental framework that examines the timing, duration, severity, and nature of effects over the life course in a variety of cultural environments.

One of the most promising developments in the field of child maltreatment studies has been the appearance of longitudinal studies. In the case of child sexual abuse, most follow-up studies have been for approximately 12 to 18 months. While some relationships have extensive correlational support, relatively little is known about the temporal sequencing of outcomes such as low self-esteem or the use of alcohol or illicit drugs. Further research to clarify the directionality of these potential linkages should be encouraged.

It would be especially informative to know how the consequences of abuse differ depending on the developmental stage and cultural environment of the individual. A few studies suggest the promise of an approach that can analyze specific age differences in the expression and nature of outcomes. For example, if victims are assessed as children, the full extent of the consequences may not be manifest. As children grow and develop, new symptoms associated with their abuse may emerge that can be examined in prospective longitudinal studies. Much can be learned from research on the processes by which other forms of parental unavailability and apparent rejection or neglect (resulting from actions such as divorce, death, or chronic injury) have psychological influences on the child.

The identification of specific effects of child maltreatment at certain ages may be an artifact of the existing state of knowledge. At present, there has not yet been sufficient research on the relationship between the age of onset of child abuse and subsequent symptomatology.

Longitudinal studies of the consequences of maltreatment are complicated by a variety of factors in the developmental process. Certain problem behaviors manifest at one age may change as an individual ages. Adults may perceive their victimization as a child differently from earlier points in their lives.

In the absence of longitudinal research, well-designed, cross-sectional retrospective designs may be the most effective, immediate means of identifying the prevalence and effects of maltreatment in adults. Cross-sectional studies conducted with techniques to minimize memory performance error (using anchoring and boundary techniques), can provide retrospective information which can be verified in prospective longitudinal studies.

Recommendation 6-3: Intergenerational studies require support to identify relevant cycles and key factors that affect intergenerational transmission of child maltreatment.

Generational studies of child abuse and neglect are needed to help identify the familial or cultural patterns passed on from generation to generation that society defines as abusive. In addition, future research needs to: (1) emphasize family dynamics that serve as protective factors versus those that exacerbate the effects of abuse; (2) assess and evaluate the parameters of abusive experiences (e.g., frequency, severity, method) and the relationship of the characteristics of abuse experiences with symptom severity; and (3) develop methods and measures for quantifying family processes that may be psychologically harsh or abusive, especially in the area of emotional maltreatment.

Recommendation 6-4: Research needs to consider the co-occurrence of multiple forms of child victimization in the social context of child maltreatment behaviors.

The assessment of consequences for abused and neglected children is complicated by the co-occurrence of other problems (or co-morbidity) in the children and their parents. Certain forms of childhood victimization constitute acute stressors, and child maltreatment often occurs against a background of chronic adversity. The presence or absence of certain characteristics or other adverse events may influence a child's response to childhood victimization, and in some cases the combined effects of two stressors (such as family environment and poor caretaking) may be greater than the sum of the two considered separately. The social context is particularly important, since the effects of abuse or neglect often cannot be separated from other problems confronting families experiencing a variety of problems—poverty, unemployment, stress, alcohol and drug problems, and violence in the community.

Research in the area of childhood victimization has generally not examined interrelationships among problem behaviors and symptoms of dysfunction in other spheres of living. Since childhood victims may be at risk for the development of multiple problem behaviors, an examination of the co-occurrence of problems should provide a fruitful direction for future research.[12]

Research on complicated problem behaviors or multiple-risk environments is especially important at this time to identify whether clusters of problem behaviors or combined risks have common origins. Research is also needed to determine whether certain types of problem behaviors represent discrete behaviors with different etiologies. These contrasting models have different implications for intervention strategies. Researchers who emphasize syndromes believe that reducing problem behaviors depends on identifying and modifying a common underlying trait. However, if specific problem behaviors represent specific etiologies, then a single general intervention strategy might fail to reduce the problems of most individuals.

Recommendation 6-5: Research on the role of protective factors, including gender differences in vulnerability and manifestations of subsequent problem behaviors, needs further examination.

In many different studies of various types of maltreatment, researchers have identified a small but significant group who have few or no problems. These "protected" children should be targeted for future study. What protective factors or interventions occur in the lives of the abused or neglected children that appear to lead to more positive outcomes? Studies are needed with sample sizes and diverse cultures large enough to examine multiple outcomes, while simultaneously adjusting for relevant demographic characteristics.

For example, we have little evidence about similarities or differences in gender responses to experiences of early abuse and neglect. In studies of violence and sexuality, research on the nonsterotypic relationship (violence: female and sexuality:male) may yield important insights. Large-scale studies assessing the consequences of child abuse and neglect for boys and girls are necessary to compare outcomes for different types of maltreatment.

Recommendation 6-6: Research is needed to improve the methodological soundness of child maltreatment studies, to test hypotheses, and to develop relevant theories of the consequences of childhood victimization.

In the short term, research efforts to describe, document, and evaluate relationships suggested by the clinical literature are necessary. However, in the long term, the field must develop and test hypotheses and build theory. For example, researchers might design research to test specific theories of the effects of child abuse (physical and sexual) against effects expected using a generalized stress model.

Studies also need to determine the influence of sample selection criteria on patterns of consequences. The absence of appropriate comparison groups is a severe methodological flaw in many studies of child maltreatment consequences. Furthermore, a major controversy in the field concerns the extent to which researchers study different types of maltreated subjects. Existing research on the short-term effects of child maltreatment is often based on cases that have been reported to child protection services or law enforcement agencies. Researchers need to select samples from nontraditional populations, such as community and pediatric samples, to improve generalizability of their findings and to avoid the biases inherent in the child protective services reporting system.

NOTES

1. In 1991, 79 percent of the children who died were under age 5, and 54 percent were under age 1 (McCurdy and Daro, 1992).

2. A recent study of cognitive abilities found that physically abused children showed lower receptive language scores than nonabused children (Vondra et al., 1990). However,

these children did not differ from children in families with low socioeconomic status. This indicates that the children's cognitive deficits were related to their family backgrounds and living environments, rather than specifically to the abuse experience.

3.   Overall, 18 percent of the sample met the criteria for major depression, and 25 percent met the criteria for dysthymia.

4.   It is not clear whether there is a specific relationship between child sexual abuse and post-traumatic stress disorder because many other children have related symptoms such as fears, nightmares, somatic complaints, autonomic arousal, and guilt feelings (Kendall-Tackett et al., 1993).

5.   In research using a cohorts design study, children who were abused and neglected approximately 20 years ago were followed up through an examination of official criminal records and compared with a matched control group of children with no official record of abuse or neglect (Widom, 1989b).

6.   When a subsample of incarcerated delinquents was compared with a matched sample of nondelinquents, neuropsychiatric vulnerabilities and histories of abuse distinguished the delinquents from the nondelinquents (Lewis and Shanok, 1977). Within the comparison group, neuropsychiatric problems and abuse distinguished the more aggressive nondelinquents from their less aggressive nondelinquent peers.

In Lewis's original study (Lewis et al., 1979), abuse and other family violence were examined separately. Data in the later follow-up study (Lewis et al., 1989) suggested that the two phenomena were almost always present in households of seriously delinquent children. These findings complicate the task of identifying the relative importance of different experiential variables.

7.   Specifically, as adolescents (before age 18), abused and neglected children were significantly more likely to have an arrest as a runaway than controls (5.8 versus 2.4 percent). Interestingly, the percentage of these abused and/or neglected children who had official contact with the system (as in arrests) was still small, and similar to the percentages in the studies of runaways who reported a history of childhood victimization.

8.   Examinations of these potentially stage-specific effects (Kagan, 1977) are difficult in research based on one-shot retrospective reports.

9.   In a review of 29 studies that gathered data on fertility outcomes of maltreating families, Zuravin and Taylor (1987) concluded that neglectful families had more children than abusive families and began bearing children at an earlier age. Zuravin (1988), however, found that "abusive and neglectful mothers compared to control mothers space their first two children closer in years, have their first child at a younger age, and have more live births, more unplanned live births, and more children by different fathers" (p. 988).

10.   The assessment of high intelligence and scholastic achievement should not be limited to the use of standardized measures of IQ, but should include a variety of other measures that comprehensively assess the child's ability to process information and to adapt to the world.

11.   Abused children with more positive supports and fewer conflictual relationships were less likely to be depressed than the other maltreated children in the study. The nondepressed maltreated children were also more likely to report that they felt more cared about by their supports than the depressed children.

12.   For example, the co-occurrence of alcoholism, antisocial personality disorder, and substance use has been noted among male jail detainees (Abram, 1990).

REFERENCES

Aber, J.L., and J.P. Allen
    1987   The effects of maltreatment on young children's socioemotional development: An attachment theory perspective. *Developmental Psychology* 23:406-414.

Aber, J.L., J.P. Allen, V. Carlson, and D. Cicchetti
1990   The effects of maltreatment on development during early childhood: Recent stud-
        ies and their theoretical, clinical and policy implications. Pp. 579-619 in D.
        Cicchetti and V. Carlson (eds.) *Child Maltreatment: Theory and Research on
        Causes and Consequences.* New York: Cambridge University Press.
Aber, J.L., and D. Cicchetti
1984   The socio-emotional development of maltreated children: An empirical and theo-
        retical analysis. Pp. 147-205 in H. Fitzgerald, B. Lester, and M. Yogman (eds.)
        Theory and Research in Behavioral Pediatrics Vol. II. New York: Plenum Press.
Abram, K.
1990   The problem of co-occurring disorders among jail detainees: Antisocial disorder,
        alcoholism, drug abuse, and depression. *Law and Human Behavior* 14:333-345.
Alessandri, S.M.
1991   Play and social behavior in maltreated preschoolers. *Development and Psycopathology*
        3:191-205.
Alfaro, J.D.
1981   Report on the relationship between child abuse and neglect and later socially
        deviant behavior. In R.J. Hunner and Y.E. Walker, eds., *Exploring the Relation-
        ship Between Child Abuse and Delinquency.* Montclair, NJ: Allanheld, Osmun.
Allen, D.M.
1980   Young male prostitutes: A psychosocial study. *Archives of Sexual Behavior* 9:399-
        426.
Allen, D., and K. Tarnowski
1989   Depressive characteristics of physically abused children. *Journal of Abnormal
        Child Psychology* 17:1-11.
Allen, R.E., and J.M. Oliver
1982   The effects of child maltreatment on language development. *Child Abuse and
        Neglect* 6:299-305.
Augoustinos, M.
1987   Developmental effects of child abuse: A number of recent findings. *Child Abuse
        and Neglect* 11:15-27.
Ayoub, C.C., and S.S. Milner
1985   Failure to thrive parental indicators, types, and outcome. *Child Abuse and Neglect*
        9:491-499.
Azar, S.T., K.T. Barnes, and C.T. Twentyman
1988   Developmental outcomes in abused children: Consequences of parental abuse or a
        more general breakdown in caregiver behavior? *Behavior Therapist* 11:27-32.
Barahal, R.M., J. Wareman, and H.P. Martin
1981   The social and cognitive development of abused children. *Journal of Consulting
        and Clinical Psychology* 53:335-343.
Beck, J.C. and B. Van der Kolk
1987   Reports of childhood incest and current behavior of chronically hospitalized psy-
        chotic women. *American Journal of Psychitary* 144(11):1474-1476.
Becker, J.V., M.S. Kaplan, J. Cunningham-Rathner, and R. Kavoussi
1986   Characteristics of adolescent incest sexual perpetrators: Preliminary findings. *Journal
        of Family Violence* 1(1):85-97.
Beitchman, J.H., K.J. Zucker, J.E. Hood, G.A. DaCosta, and D. Ackman
1991   A review of the short-term effects of childhood sexual abuse. *Child Abuse and
        Neglect* 15:537-556.
Benward, J., and J. Densen-Gerber
1975   Incest as a causative factor in antisocial behavior. *Contemporary Drug Problems*
        4:323-340.

Berliner, L.
1991   Effects of sexual abuse on children. *Violence Update* 1(10)(June):1,8,10-11.
Bohigan, G.M.
1989   Recognition of Childhood Sexual Abuse as a Factor in Adolescent Health Issues. Informational report of the Council on Scientific Affairs, American Medical Association, April.
Bohman, M., and S. Sigvardsson
1980   Negative social heritage. *Adoption and Fostering* 3:25-34.
Bolton, F.G., R.H. Lanier, and D.S. Gia
1981   For better or worse? Foster parents and foster children in an officially reported child maltreatment population. *Children and Youth Services Review* 3:37-53.
Bousha, D.M., and C.T. Twentyman
1984   Mother-child interactional style in abuse, neglect, and control groups: Naturalistic observations in the home. *Journal of Abnormal Psychology* 93:106-114.
Brassard, M.R., R. Germain, and S.N. Hart
1987   *Psychological Maltreatment of Children and Youth.* Elmsford, NY: Pergamon Press.
Briere, J.
1992a   Methodological issues in the study of sexual abuse effects. *Journal of Consulting and Clinical Psychology* 60(2):196-203.
1992b   *Child Abuse Trauma: Theory and Treatment of the Lasting Effects.* Interpersonal Violence: The Practice Series. Newbury Park, CA: Sage Publications.
Briere, J., and M. Runtz
1988a   Multivariate correlates of childhood psychological and physical maltreatment among university women. *Child Abuse and Neglect* 12:331.
1988b   Post sexual abuse trauma. Pp. 85-99 in G.E. Wyatt and G.J. Powell, eds. *Lasting Effects of Child Sexual Abuse.* Newbury Park, CA: Sage.
Briere, J., and L.Y. Zaidi
1989   Sexual abuse histories and sequelae in female psychiatric emergency room patients. *American Journal of Psychiatry* 146:1602-1606.
Brooks-Gunn, J., and F.F. Furstenberg, Jr.
1989   Adolescent sexual behavior. *American Psychologist* 44(2):249-257.
Browne, A., and D. Finkelhor
1986   The impact of child sexual abuse: A review of the research. *Psychological Bulletin* 99(1):66-77.
Bryce, M.E., and R.C. Ehlert
1977   144 foster children. *Child Welfare* 53:582-587.
Bryer, J.B., B.A. Nelson, J.B. Miller, and P.A. Krol
1987   Childhood sexual and physical abuse as factors in adult psychiatric illness. *American Journal of Psychiatry* 144:1426-1430.
Burgess, A., C. Hartman., and A. McCormack
1987   Abused to abuser: Antecedents of socially deviant behaviors. *American Journal of Orthopsychiatry* 144:1431-1436.
Caffaro-Rouget, A., R.A. Lang, and V. vanSanten
1989   The impact of child sexual abuse. *Annals of Sex Research* 2:29-47.
Canning, R.
1974   School experiences of foster children. *Child Welfare* 53(9):582-587.
Cappell, C., and R. Heiner
1990   The intergenerational transmission of family aggression. *Journal of Family Violence* 5(2):135-152.

Cavaiola, A.A. and M. Schiff
1988   Behavioral sequelae of physical and/or sexual abuse in adolescents. *Child Abuse and Neglect* 12:181-188.

Chase-Lansdale, P.L., J. Brooks-Gunn, and R.L. Paikoff
1991   Research and programs for adolescent mothers: Missing links and future promises. *Family Relations* 40(4):396-404.

Cicchetti, D.
1989   How research on child maltreatment has informed the study of child development: Perspectives from developmental psychopathology. Pp. 377-431 in D. Cicchetti and V. Carlson, eds., *Child Maltreatment: Theory and Research on the Causes and Consequences of Child Abuse and Neglect.* New York: Cambridge University Press.

Cicchetti, D., and D. Barnett
1991   Toward the development of a scientific nosology of child maltreatment. Pp. 346-377 in D. Cicchetti and W. Grove, eds., *Thinking Clearly About Psychology: Essays in Honor of Paul E. Meehl.* Minneapolis: University of Minnesota Press.

Cicchetti, D., and R. Rizley
1981   Developmental perspectives on the etiology, intergenerational transmission, and sequelae of child maltreatment. *New Directions for Child Development* 11:31-55.

Cohn, A.H., and F.C. Collignon
1979   *NCHSR Research Report Series. Vols. I and II: Evaluation of Child Abuse and Neglect Demonstration Projects, 1974-1977.* DHEW Publication number PHS 79-3217.1

Colten, M.E., and J. Marsh
1984   A sex-roles perspective on drug and alcohol use by women. Pp. 219-248 in Widom, C.S., ed., *Sex Roles and Psychopathology.* New York: Plenum.

Conte, J.R., and J.R. Schuerman
1987   Factors associated with an increased impact of child sexual abuse. *Child Abuse and Neglect* 11:201-211.
1988   The effects of sexual abuse on children: A multidimensional view. *Journal of Interpersonal Violence* 2(4):380-390.

Courtois, C.A.
1979   The incest experience and its aftermath. *Victimology* 4:337-347.

Craine, L.S., C.H. Henson, J.A. Colliver, and D.G. MacLean
1988   Prevalance of a history of sexual abuse among female psychiatric patients in a state hospital system. *Hospital and Community Psychiatry* 39:300-304.

Crittenden, P.M., and M.D.S. Ainsworth
1989   Child maltreatment and attachment theory. Pp. 432-463 in D. Cicchetti and V. Carlson, eds., *Child Maltreatment: Theory and Research on the Causes and Consequences of Child Abuse and Neglect.* New York: Cambridge University Press.

Curtis, G.C.
1963   Violence breeds violence—perhaps? *American Journal of Psychiatry* 120(October):386-387.

Dean, A.L., M.M. Malik, W. Richards, and S.A. Stringer
1986   Effects of parental maltreatment on children's conceptions of interpersonal relationships. *Developmental Psychology* 22:617-626.

Deblinger, E., S.V. McLeer, M.S. Atkins, D.L. Ralphe, and E. Foa
1989   Post-traumatic stress in sexually abused, physically abused, and nonabused children. *Child Abuse and Neglect* 13:313-408.

Dembo, R., L. LaVoie, J. Schmeider, and M. Washburn
1987   The nature and correlates of psychological/emotional functioning among a sample of detained youths. *Criminal Justice and Behavior* 14:311-334.

Dembo, R., L. Williams, L. LaVoie, E. Berry, A. Gatreu, E. Wish. J. Schmeider, and M. Washburn
1989   Physical abuse, sexual victimization, and illicit drug use: Replication of a structural analysis among a new sample of high-risk youths. *The International Journal of Addictions* 24:121-138.

Dembo, R., L. Williams, L. LaVoie, A. Getreu, E. Berry, L. Genung, J. Schmeidler, E.D. Wish, and J. Kern
1990   A longitudinal study of the relationship among alcohol use, marijuana/hashish use, cocaine use, and emotional/psychological functioning problems in a cohort of high-risk youths. *The International Journal of the Addictions* 25:1341-1382.

Demitrack, M.A., F.W. Putnam, T.D. Brewerton, H.A. Brandt, and P.W. Gold
1990   Relation of clinical variables to dissociative phenomenon in eating disorders. *American Journal of Psychiatry* 147(9):1184-1188.
1991   Comment. *American Journal of Psychiatry* 148(9):1274-1275.

DeWilde, E.J., I.C. Kienhorst, R.F. Diekstra, and W.H. Wolters
1992   The relationship between adolescent suicidal behavior and life events in childhood and adolescence. *American Journal of Psychiatry* 149(1):45-51.

DeYoung, M.
1982   *The Sexual Victimization of Children.* Jefferson, NC: McFarland Press.

Dodge, K.A., J.E. Bates, and G.S. Pettit
1990   Mechanisms in the cycle of violence. *Science* 250 (December 21):1678-1683.

Drotar, D.
1992   Prevention of neglect and nonorganic failure to thrive. Pp. 115-149 in D.J. Willis, E.W. Holden, and M. Rosenberg, eds., *Prevention of Child Maltreatment: Developmental and Ecological Perspectives.* New York: John Wiley.

Dykes, L.
1986   The whiplash shaken infant syndrome: What has been learned? *Child Abuse and Neglect* 10:211-221.

Easson, W.M., and R.N. Steinhilber
1961   Murderous aggression by children and adolescents. *Archives of General Psychiatry* 4:47-55.

Eckenrode, J., M. Laird, and J. Doris
1991   Maltreatment and Social Adjustment of School Children. National Center on Child Abuse and Neglect. Grant 90CA1305. U.S. Department of Health and Human Services, Washington, DC.

Egeland, B., and D. Jacobvitz
1984   Intergenerational Continuity of Parental Abuse: Causes and Consequences. Paper presented at the Conference on Biosocial Perspectives on Abuse and Neglect. Maine.

Egeland, B., D. Jacobvitz, and L.A. Sroufe
1984   Breaking the cycle of abuse. *Child Development* 59:1080-1088.

Egeland, B., and L.A. Sroufe
1981a   Attachment and early maltreatment. *Child Development* 52:44-52.
1981b   Developmental sequelae of maltreatment in infancy. *New Directions for Child Development* 11:77-92.

Elmer, E.
1977   A follow-up study of traumatized children. *Pediatrics* 59:273-279.

Elmer, E., and G. Gregg
1967   Developmental characteristics of abused children. *Pediatrics* 40(4)(October):596-602.

Erickson, M.F., and B. Egeland
in press The quiet assault: A portrait of child neglect. In *Handbook of Child Maltreatment.*
Erickson, M.F., B. Egeland, and R. Pianta
1989 The effects of maltreatment on the development of young children. Pp. 647-684 in D. Cicchetti and V. Carlson, eds., *Child Maltreatment: Theory and Research on the Causes and Consequences of Child Abuse and Neglect.* New York: Cambridge University Press.
Everson, M.D., W.M. Hunter, D.K. Runyon, G.A. Edelsohn, and M.L. Coulter
1989 Maternal support following disclosure of incest. *American Journal of Orthopsychiatry* 59:197-207.
Fagan, J., K. Hansen, and M. Jang
1983 Profiles of chronically violent delinquents: Empirical test of an integrated theory. Pp. 91-119 in J. Kleugel, ed., *Evaluating Juvenile Justice.* Beverly Hills, CA: Sage.
Fanshel, D., and E.B. Shinn
1978 *Children in Foster Care: A Longitudinal Investigation.* New York: Columbia University Press.
Fantuzzo, J.W.
1990 Behavioral treatment of the victims of child abuse and neglect. *Behavior Modification* 14:316-339.
Fantuzzo, J.W., and C.U. Lindquist
1986 The effects of observing conjugal violence on children: A review and analysis of research methodology. *Journal of Family Violence* 4(1):77-94.
Fantuzzo, J.W., L.M. DePaola, L. Lambert, T. Martino, G. Anderson, and S. Sutton
1991 Effects of interparental violence on the psychological adjustment and competencies of young children. *Journal of Consulting and Clinical Psychology* 59:258-265.
Farber, E.A., and B. Egeland
1987 Invulnerability among abused and neglected children. Pp. 253-288 in E.J. Anthony and B. Cohler, eds., *The Invulnerable Child.* New York: Guilford Press.
Fehrenbach, P.A., W. Smith, C. Monastersky, and R.W. Deisher
1986 Adolescent sexual offenders: Offender and offense characteristics. *American Journal of Orthopsychiatry* 56(2)(April):225-233.
Finkelhor, D.
1979 *Sexually Victimized Children.* New York: Free Press.
1990 Early and long-term effects of child sexual abuse: An update. *Professional Psychology: Research and Practice* 21(5):325-330.
Finkelhor, D., G. Hotaling, I.A. Lewis, and C. Smith
1989 Sexual abuse and its relationship to later sexual satisfaction, marital status, religion, and attitudes. *Journal of Interpersonal Violence* 4(4)(December):379-399.
Finkelhor, D., G. Hotaling, and A. Sedlak.
1990 *Missing, Abducted, Runaway, and Thrownaway Children in America. First Report: Numbers and Characteristics, National Incidence Studies, Executive Summary.* May. Washington, D.C.: U.S. Department of Justice.
Frank, G.L.
1980 Treatment needs of children in foster care. *American Journal of Orthopsychiatry* 50:256-263.
Friedrich, W.N., and J.A. Boriskin
1976 The role of the child in abuse: A review of the literature. *American Journal of Orthopsychiatry* 46(4)(October):580-590.

Friedrich, W.M., and R.A. Reams
    1987   Course of psychological symptoms in sexually abused young children. *Psycho-
            therapy* 24:160-170.
Friedrich, W.N., R.L. Beilke, and A.J. Urquiza
    1988   Behavior problems in young sexually abused boys. *Journal of Interpersonal Vio-
            lence* 3(1):21-28.
Frodi, A., and J. Smetana
    1984   Abused, neglected, and nonmaltreated preschoolers' ability to discriminate emo-
            tions in others: The effects of IQ. *Child Abuse and Neglect* 8:459-465.
Garbarino, J., E. Guttman, and J.W. Seeley
    1986   What is psychological maltreatment? Pp. 1-21 in J. Garbarino, E. Guttman, and J.
            Seeley, eds., *The Psychologically Battered Child*. San Francisco: Jossey-Bass.
Garbarino, J., and M.C. Plantz
    1986   Child abuse and juvenile delinquency: what are the links? Pp. 27-39 in J. Garbarino,
            C.J. Schellenback, J.M. Sebes, eds. *Troubled Youth, Troubled Families: Under-
            standing Families At-Risk for Adolescent Maltreatment*. New York: Aldine Pub-
            lishing Co.
Garmezy, N.
    1981   Children under stress: Perspectives on antecedents and correlates of vulnerability
            and resistance to psychopathology. In A.I. Rabin, J. Arnoff, A.M. Barclay, and
            R.A. Zucker, eds., *Further Explorations in Personality*. New York: John Wiley.
Garmezy, N., A. Masten, and A. Tellegen
    1984   The study of stress and comptence in children. A building block for developmen-
            tal psychopathology. *Child Development* 55:97-111.
Geller, M., and L. Ford-Somma
    1984   Violent Homes, Violent Children. A Study of Violence in the Families of Juvenile
            Offenders. February. New Jersey State Department of Corrections, Trenton, Divi-
            sion of Juvenile Services. Prepared for the National Center on Child Abuse and
            Neglect. Washington, DC.
George, C., and M. Main
    1979   Social interactions of young abused children: Approach, avoidance, and aggession.
            Child Development 35:306-318.
Gershenson, H.P., J.S. Musick, H.S. Ruch-Ross, V. Magee, K.K. Rubino, and D. Rosenberg
    1989   The prevalence of coercive sexual experience among teenage mothers. *Journal of
            Interpersonal Violence* 4:204-219.
Gil, E.
    1988   *Treatment of Adult Survivors of Childhood Abuse*. Walnut Creek, CA: Launch
            Press.
Gold, E.R.
    1986   Long-term effects of sexual victimization in childhood: An attributional approach.
            Journal of Consulting and Clinical Psychology 54:471-475.
Goldston, D.B., D.C. Turnquist, and J.F. Knutson
    1989   Presenting symptoms of sexually abused girls receiving psychiatric services. *Jour-
            nal of Abnormal Psychology* 98:314-317.
Gomes-Schwartz, B., J.M. Horowitz, and M. Sauzier
    1985   Severity of emotional distress among sexually abused preschool, school-age, and
            adolescent children. *Hospital and Community Psychiatry* 28:238-243.
Gomes-Schwartz, B., J.M. Horowitz, and A. Cardarelli
    1990   *Child Sexual Abuse: The Initial Effects*. Newbury Park, CA: Sage.

Goodwin, D.W., F. Schulsinger, L. Hermansen, S.B. Guze, and G. Winokur
1973   Alcohol problems in adoptees raised apart from alcoholic biological parents. *Archives of General Psychiatry* 28:238-243.
Goodwin, D.W., F. Schulsinger, J. Knop, S. Mednick, and S.B. Guze
1977   Alcoholism and depression in adopted daughters of alcoholics. *Archives of General Psychiatry* 34:751-755.
Gray, E., J. Garbarino, and M. Planz
1986   *Child Abuse: Prelude to Delinquency.* Findings of a research conference conducted by the National Committee for the Prevention of Child Abuse, April 7-10, 1984. Washington, DC: U.S. Department of Justice, Office of Juvenile Justice and Delinquency Prevention.
Green, A.H.
1978   Psychopathology of abused children. *Journal of the American Academy of Child Psychiatry* 17:92-103.
Green, A.H., R.W. Gaines, and A. Sandgrund
1974   Child abuse: Pathological syndrome of family interaction. *American Journal of Psychiatry* 131(8):882-886.
Greenwald, E., H. Leitenberg, S. Cado, and M.J. Tarran
1990   Childhood sexual abuse: Long-term effects on psychological and sexual functioning in a nonclinical and nonstudent sample of adult women. *Child Abuse and Neglect* 14:503-513.
Greenwald, H.
1970   *The Elegant Prostitute.* New York: Ballantine.
Groth, A.
1979   Sexual trauma in the life histories of sex offenders. *Victimology* 4:6-10.
Groves, B.M., B. Zuckerman, S. Marans, and D.J. Cohen
1993   Silent victims: Children who witness violence. *Journal of the American Medical Association* 269(2):262-264.
Gruber, A.R.
1978   *Children in Foster Care.* New York: Human Sciences Press.
Gutierres, S., and J.A. Reich
1981   A developmental perspective on runaway behavior: Its relationship to child abuse. *Child Welfare* 60:89-94.
Harrison, P.A., N.G. Hoffman, and G.E. Edwall
1989a   Differential drug use patterns among abused adolescent girls in treatment for chemical dependency. *The International Journal of the Addictions* 24:499-514.
1989b   Sexual abuse correlates: Similarities between male and female adolescents in chemical dependency treatment. *Journal of Adolescent Research* 4:385-399.
Harter, S., P.C. Alexander, and R.A. Neimeyer
1988   Long-term effects of incestuous child abuse in college women: Social adjustment, social cognition, and family charateristics. *Journal of Consulting and Clinical Psychology* 56:5-8.
Hartstone, E., and K. Hansen
1984   The violent juvenile offender: An empirical portrait. Pp. 82-112 in R. Mathias, P. DeMuro, and R.S. Allison, eds., *Violent Juvenile Offenders: An Anthology.* San Francisco: National Council on Delinquency and Crime.
Herman, J.
1981   *Father-Daughter Incest.* Cambridge, MA: Harvard University Press.
Herman, J., and L. Hirschman
1977   Father-daughter incest. *Signs: Journal of Women in Culture and Society* 2(Summer):735-756.

Herrenkohl, R., and E. Herrenkohl
  1981   Some antecedents and developmental consequences of child maltreatment. Pp. 57-
          76 in R. Rizley and D. Cicchetti, eds., *New Directions for Child Development,
          Developmental Perspectives on Child Maltreatment* 11. San Francisco: Jossey-
          Bass.
Herrenkohl, R.C., E.C. Herrenkohl, M. Seech, and B. Egolf
  1980   The repetition of child abuse: How frequently does it occur? *Child Abuse and
          Neglect* 3:67-72.
Herzberger, S.D., D.A. Potts, and M. Dillon
  1981   Perceptions of abused and non-abused children toward their parents. *Journal of
          Consulting and Clinical Psychology* 49:81-90.
Hoffman-Plotkin, D., and C. Twentyman
  1984   A multimodal assessment of behavioral and cognitive deficits in abused and ne-
          glected preschoolers. *Child Development* 55:794-802.
Hotaling, G.T., M.A. Straus, and A.J. Lincoln
  1990   Intrafamily violence and crime and violence outside the family. Chapter 25 in
          M.S. Straus and R.J. Gelles, eds., *Physical Violence in American Families: Risk
          Factors and Adaptations to Violence in 8145 Families.* New Brunswick, NJ:
          Transaction Publishers.
Howes, C., and R. Eldridge
  1985   Responses of abused, neglected, and nonmaltreated children to the behaviors of
          their peers. *Journal of Applied Developmental Psychology* 6:261-270.
Howes, C., and M.P. Espinosa
  1985   The consequences of child abuse for the formation of relationships with peers.
          Child Abuse and Neglect 9:397-404.
Hubbell, R.
  1981   *Foster Care and Families: Conflicting Values and Policies.* Philadelphia: Temple
          University Press.
Ireland, T.O., and C.S. Widom
  in press Childhood victimization and risk for alcohol and drug arrests. *International Jour-
          nal of the Addictions.*
Jaffe, P., S.K. Wilson, and D. Wolfe.
  1988   Specific assessment and intervention strategies for children exposed to wife batter-
          ing: Preliminary empirical investigation. *Canadian Journal of Community Mental
          Health* 7:157-163.
Jaffe, P.G., D.J. Hurley, and D. Wolfe
  1990   Children's observations of violence: Critical issues in child development and
          intervention planning. *Canadian Journal of Psychiatry* 35(6):466-470.
Jaffe, P.G., D.A. Wolfe, and S.K. Wilson
  1991   *Children of Battered Women.* Newbury Park, CA: Sage Publications.
James, J., and J. Meyerding
  1977   Early sexual experience and prostitution. *American Journal of Psychiatry* 134:1382-
          1385.
Jehu, D., M. Gazan, and C. Klassen
  1984   Common therapeutic targets among women who were sexually abused in child-
          hood. *Journal of Social Work and Human Sexuality* 3:25-45.
Kagan, J.
  1977   The child in the family. *Daedalus: Journal of the American Academy of Arts and
          Sciences* 106:33-56.

Kalmuss, D.
  1984   The intergenerational transmission of marital aggression. *Journal of Marriage and the Family* 46(February):11-19.
Kaufman, J.
  1991   Depressive disorders in maltreated children. *Journal of the American Academy of Child and Adolescent Psychiatry* 30:257-265.
Kaufman, J., and E. Zigler
  1987   Do abused children become abusive parents? *American Journal of Orthopsychiatry* 57:186-192.
Kaufman, J., and D. Cicchetti
  1989   The effects of maltreatment on school-aged children's socioemotional development: Assessments in a day camp setting. *Developmental Psychology* 15:516-524.
Kazdin, A., J. Moser, D. Colbus, and R. Bell
  1985   Depressive symptoms among physically abused and psychiatrically disturbed children. *Journal of Abnormal Psychology* 94:298-307.
Kendall-Tackett, K.A., L. Williams, and D. Finkelhor
  1993   The impact of sexual abuse on children: A review and synthesis of recent empirical studies. *Psychological Bulletin* 113(1):164-180.
Kent, J.T.
  1976   A follow-up study of abused children. *Journal of Pediatric Psychology* 1:25-31.
Kinard, E.M.
  1980   Emotional development in physically abused children. *American Journal of Orthopsychiatry* 50:686-696.
  1982   Experiencing child abuse: Effects on emotional adjustment. *American Journal of Orthopsychiatry* 52:82-91.
King, C.H.
  1975   The ego and the integration of violence in homocidal youth. *American Journal of Orthopsychiatry* 45:134-135.
Kluft, R.P., ed.
  1985   *Childhood Antecedents of Multiple Personality.* Washington, DC: American Psychiatric Press.
Knudsen, D.
  1992   *Child Maltreatment: Emerging Perspectives.* Dix Hills, NY: General Hall, Inc.
Kolko, D.
  1992   Characteristics of child victims of physical violence: Research findings and clinical implications. *Journal of Interpersonal Violence* 7(2):244-276.
Kolko, D., J. Moser, and S. Weldy
  1990   Medical/health histories and physical evaluation of physically and sexually abused child psychiatric patients: A controlled study. *Journal of Family Violence* 5(4):249-266.
Kotelchuck. M.
  1982   Child abuse and neglect: Prediction and misclassification. Pp. 67-104 in R.H. Starr, ed. *Child Abuse Prediction: Policy Implications.* Cambridge, MA: Ballinger.
Kratcoski, P.C.
  1982   Child abuse and violence against the family. *Child Welfare* 61:435-444.
Ladwig, G.B., and M.D. Anderson
  1989   Substance abuse in women: Relationship between chemical dependency of women and past reports of physical and/or sexual abuse. *International Journal of the Addictions* 24(8):739-754.

Lazarus, R.S., and R. Launier
  1978   Stress-related transactions between person and environment. In L.A. Pervin and
          M. Lewis, eds., *Perspectives in Interactional Psychology.* New York: Plenum.
Lewis, D.O., and S.S. Shanok
  1977   Medical histories of delinquent and nondelinquent children: An epidemiological
          study. *American Journal of Psychiatry* 134:1020-1025.
Lewis, D.O., S.S. Shanok, J.H. Pincus,, and G.H. Glaser
  1979   Violent juvenile delinquents: Psychiatric, neurological, psychological, and abuse
          factors. *Journal of the American Academy of Child Psychiatry* 18:1161-1167.
Lewis, D.O., J. Pincus, S. Shanok, and G. Glaser
  1982   Psychomotor epilepsy and violence in a group of incarcerated adolescent boys.
          American Journal of Psychiatry 139:882-887.
Lewis, D.O., M. Feldman, and A. Barrengos
  1985   Race, health, and delinquency. *Journal of the American Academy of Child Psy-
          chiatry* 24(2):161-165.
Lewis, D.O., R. Lovely, C., Yeager, and D. Della Famina
  1989   Toward a theory of the genesis of violence: A follow-up study of delinquents.
          Journal of the American Academy of Child and Adolescent Psychiatry 28:431-436.
Lindberg, F.H., and L.J. Distad
  1985a   Survival responses to incest: Adolescents in crisis. *Child Abuse and Neglect*
          9:193-212.
  1985b   Post-traumatic stress disorder in women who experienced childhood incest. *Child
          Abuse and Neglect* 9:329-334.
Littner, N.
  1974   *Some Traumatic Effects of Separation and Placement.* New York: Child Welfare
          League of America.
Loewenstein, R.J.
  1990   Somatoform disorders in victims of incest and child abuse. Pp. 75-111 in Kluft,
          R.P., ed., *Incest-Related Syndromes of Adult Psychopathology.* Washington, DC:
          American Psychiatric Press.
Lynch, M.A., and J. Roberts
  1982   *Consequences of Child Abuse.* New York: Academic Press.
Magura, S.
  1981   Are services to prevent foster care effective? *Child and Youth Services Review*
          3:193-212.
Main, M., and C. George
  1985   Response of abused and disadvantaged toddlers to distress in agitates: A study in
          the daycare setting. *Developmental Psychology* 21:407-412.
Main, M., N. Kaplan, and J. Cassidy
  1985   Security in infancy, childhood, and adulthood: A move to the level of representa-
          tion. Pp. 66-104 in I. Bretherton and E. Waters, eds., *Growing Pains In Attach-
          ment Theory and Research.* Monographs for Society of Research in Child Devel-
          opment. Chicago: University of Chicago Press.
Mangold, W.D., and P.R. Koski
  1990   Gender comparisons in the relationship between parental and sibling violence and
          nonfamily violence. *Journal of Family Violence* 5(3):225-235.
Mannarino, A.P., and J.A. Cohen
  1986   A clinical-demographic study of sexually abused children. *Child Abuse and Ne-
          glect* 10(1):17-23.
Margolin. L.
  1990   Fatal child neglect. *Child Welfare* 119(4):309-339.

Martin, H.P., and P. Beezley
   1977   Behavioral observations of abused children. *Developmental Medicine and Child Neurology* 19:373-387.
Martin, H.P., P. Beezley, E.F. Conway, and C.H. Kempe
   1974   The development of abused children. *Advances in Pediatrics* 21:25-73.
McClain, P.W., J.J. Sacks, R.G. Froehlke, and B.G. Ewigman
   1993   Estimates of fatal child abuse and neglect, United States, 1979 through 1988. *Pediatrics* 91(2):338-343.
McCord, J.
   1983   A forty year perspective on effects of child abuse and neglect. *Child Abuse and Neglect* 7:265-270.
McCurdy, K., and D. Daro
   1992   Current Trends in Child Abuse Reporting and Fatalities: The Results of the 1991 State Survey. August 31. Presented at the Ninth International Congress on Child Abuse and Neglect. Chicago, IL.
McLeer, S.V., E. Deblinger, M.S. Atkins, E.B. Foa, and D.L. Ralphe
   1988   Post-traumatic stress disorder in sexually abused children: A prospective study. *Journal of the American Academy of Child and Adolescent Psychiatry* 27(5):650-654.
Meiselman, K.
   1978   *Incest: A Psychological Study of Causes and Effects with Treatment Recommendations.* San Francisco: Jossey-Bass.
Miller, B.A., W.R. Downs, and D.M. Gondoli
   1989   Delinquency, childhood violence, and the development of alcoholism in women. *Crime and Delinquency* 35:94-108.
Moffit, T.E., W.F. Gabrielli, S.A. Mednick, and F. Schulsinger
   1981   Socioeconomic status, IQ, and delinquency. *Journal of Abnormal Psychology* 90:152-156.
Moran, P.B., and J. Eckenrode
   in press Protective personality characteristics among adolescent victims of maltreatment. *Child Abuse and Neglect.*
Morrow, K.B., and G.T. Sorell
   1989   Factors affecting self-esteem, depression, and negative behaviors in sexually abused female adolescents. *Journal of Marriage and the Family* 51:677-786.
Morse, C.W., O.J. Sahler, and S.B. Friedman
   1970   A 3-year follow-up study of abused and neglect children. *American Journal of Diseases of Children* 120:439-446.
National Center on Child Abuse and Neglect
   1988   *Study Findings: Study of National Incidence and Prevalence of Child Abuse and Neglect.* Washington, DC: U.S. Department of Health and Human Services. [NIS 2].
Newberger, E.H.
   1973   The myth of the battered child syndrome. In R.H. Bourne and E.H. Newberger, eds., *Critical Perspectives on Child Abuse.* Lexington, MA: Lexington Books.
Oates, R.K.
   1984a   Similarities and differences between nonorganic failure to thrive and deprivation dwarfism. *Child Abuse and Neglect* 8:439-445.
   1984b   Non-organic failure to thrive. *Australian Paediatrics Journal* 20:95-100.
   1992   Research on failure to thrive. Paper presented to the National Symposium on Child Victimzation. Washington, DC.

Oates, R.K., D. Forrest, and A. Peacock
  1985   Self-esteem of abused children. *Child Abuse and Neglect* 9:159-163.
Pagelow, M.D.
  1984   *Family Violence.* New York: Praeger.
Patterson, G.
  1982   *Coercive family processes.* Eugene, OR: Castalia Publishing Company.
Patterson, G.R., B.D. DeBaryshe, and E. Ramsey
  1989   A developmental perspective on antisocial behavior. *American Psychologist* 44:329-335.
Perry, M.A., L.D. Doran, and E.A. Wells
  1983   Developmental and behavioral characterisitcs of the physically abused child. *Journal of Clinical Child Psychology* 12:320-324.
Peters, S.D.
  1984   The Relationship Between Childhood Sexual Victimization and Adult Depression Among Afro-American and White Women. Unpublished doctoral dissertation, University of California, Los Angeles.
  1988   Child sexual abuse and later psychological problems. In G.E. Wyatt and G.J. Powell, eds., *Lasting Effects of Child Sexual Abuse.* Newbury Park, CA: Sage Publications.
Petit, G.S., and J.E. Bates
  1989   Family interaction patterns and children's behavior problems from infancy to 4 years. *Developmental Psychology* 25(3):413-420.
Polansky, N.A., M.A. Chalmers, E. Buttenwieser, and D.P. Williams
  1981   *Damaged Parents: An Anatomy of Child Neglect.* Chicago: University of Chicago Press.
Pollock, E.E., J. Briere, L. Schneider, J. Knop, S.A. Mednick, and D.W. Goodwin
  1990   Childhood antecedents of antisocial behavior: Parental alcoholism and physical abusiveness. *American Journal of Psychiatry* 147:1290-1293.
Powell, G.F., and J.L. Low
  1983   Behavior in non-organic failure to thrive. *Journal of Developmental and Behavioral Pediatrics* 4:26-33.
Powell, G.F., J.L. Low, and M.A. Spears
  1987   Behavior as a diagnostic aid in failure to thrive. *Journal of Developmental and Behavior Pediatrics* 8:18-24.
Putnam, F.W.
  1989   *Diagnosis and treatment of multiple personality disorder.* New York: Guilford Press.
Robinson, D.H., and G.M. Stevens
  1992   Child Abuse and Neglect Fatalities: Federal and State Issues and Responses. Congressional Research Service Report for The United States Congress. April 16.
Rogeness, G., S. Amrung, C. Macedo, W. Harris, and C. Fisher
  1986   Psychopathology in abused and neglected children. *Journal of the American Academy of Child Psychiatry* 25:659-665.
Rohner, R.P.
  1986   *The Warmth Dimension: Foundations of Parental-Acceptance-Rejection Theory.* Beverly Hills, CA: Sage.
Rohrbeck, C., and C. Twentyman
  1986   Multimodal assessment of impulsiveness in abusing, neglecting, and nonmaltreating mothers and their preschool children. *Journal of Consulting and Clinical Psychology* 54:231-236.

Root, M.P.
1989   Treatment failures: The role of sexual victimization in women's addictive behavior. *American Journal of Orthopsychiatry* 59(4):542-549.

Rosenbaum, A., and K.D. O'Leary
1981   Children: The unintended victims of marital violence. *American Journal of Orthopsychiatry* 51:692-699.

Ross, C.A., G.R. Norton, and K. Wozney
1989   Multiple personality disorder: An analysis of 236 cases. *Canadian Journal of Psychiatry* 34(5):413-418.

Runtz, M., and J. Briere
1986   Adolescent acting out and childhood history of sexual abuse. *Journal of Interpersonal Violence* 1:326-334.

Runyan, D.K., and C.L. Gould
1985   Foster care for child maltreatment: Impact on delinquent behavior. *Pediatrics* 75(3):562-568.

Runyan, D.K., C.L. Gould, D.C. Trost, and F.A. Loda
1982   Determinants of foster care placement for the maltreated child. *Child Abuse and Neglect* 6:343-350.

Russell, M., C. Henderson, and S.B. Blume
1985   *Children of Alcoholics: A Review of the Literature.* New York: Children of Alcoholics Foundation.

Russell, D.E.H.
1984   The prevalence and seriousness of incestuous abuse: Stepfather vs. biological fathers. *Child Abuse and Neglect* 8:15-22.

Rutter, M.
1966   *Children of Sick Parents: An Environmental and Psychiatric Study.* Institute of Psychiatry Maudsley Monographs No. 16. London: Oxford University Press.

Salzinger, S., S. Kaplan, D. Pelcovitz, C. Samit, and R. Krieger
1984   Parent and teacher assessment of children's behavior in child maltreating families. *Journal of the Amercian Academy of Child Psychiatry* 23:458-464.

Sansonnet-Hayden, H., H. Haley, K. Marriage, and S. Fine
1987   Sexual abuse and psychopathology in hospitalized adolescents. *Journal of the American Academy of Child and Adolescent Psychiatry* 26:753-757.

Schorr, E.L.
1982   The foster care system and health status of foster children. *Pediatrics* 69:521-528.

Schuckit, M.A.
1986   Alcohol and alcoholism. Pp. 2106-2111 in Petersdorf, R.E., Adams, R.D. Brunwald, E. Isselbacker, K.J. Martin, and J.D. Wilson, eds. *Harrison's Principles of Internal Medicine.* New York: McGraw Hill International.

Seghorn, T., R. Prentky, and R. Boucher
1987   Childhood sexual abuse in the lives of sexually aggressive offenders. *Journal of American Academy of Child and Adolescent Psychiatry* 26:262-267.

Sendi, I.B., and P.G. Blomgren
1975   A comparative study of predictive criteria in the predisposition of homicidal adolescents. *American Journal of Psyhciatry* 132:423-427.

Shanok, S.S., and D.O. Lewis
1981   Medical histories of abused delinquents. *Child Psychiatry and Human Development* 11:222-231.

Silbert, M.H., and A.M. Pines
1984   Early sexual exploitation as an influence in prostitution. *Social Work* 28:285-289.

Silver, L.B., C.C. Dublin, and R.S. Lourie
    1969   Does violence breed violence? Contributions from a study of the child abuse
            syndrome. *American Journal of Psychiatry* 126(September):404-407.
Singer, M.I., M.K. Petchers, and D. Hussey
    1989   The relationship between sexual abuse and substance abuse among psychiatrically
            hospitalized adolecsents. *Child Abuse and Neglect* 13:319-325.
Smith, C.P., D.J. Berkman, and W.M. Fraser
    1980   *A Preliminary National Assessment of Child Abuse and Neglect and the Juvenile
            Justice System: The Shadows of Distress.* Washington, DC: Office of Juvenile
            Justice and Delinquency Prevention.
Sroufe, L.A., and M. Rutter
    1984   The domain of developmental psychopathology. *Child Development* 55:1184-1199.
Starr, R.H., Jr., ed.
    1992   Physical abuse of children. In V.B. Van Hasselt et al., eds., *The Handbook of
            Family Violence.* New York: Plenum Press.
Stein, A., and D.O. Lewis
    1992   Discovering physical abuse: Insights from a follow-up study of delinquents. *Child
            Abuse and Neglect* 16:523-531.
Stein, J.A., J.M. Golding, J.M. Siegel, M.A. Burnam, and S.B. Sorenson
    1988   Long-term psychological sequelae of child sexual abuse. The Los Angeles Epidemiologic
            Catchment Area Study. In G. Wyatt and G. Powell, eds., *Lasting Effects of Child
            Sexual Abuse.* Newbury Park, CA: Sage.
Stone, M.H.
    1990   Incest in the borderline patient. Pp. 183-204 in R.P. Kluft, ed., *Incest-Related
            Syndromes of Adult Psychopathology.* Washington, DC: American Psychiatric
            Press.
Stovall, G., and R.J. Craig
    1990   Mental representations of physically and sexually abused latency-aged females.
            Child Abuse and Neglect 14:233-242.
Straker, G., and R.S. Jacobson
    1981   Aggression, emotional maladjustment, and empathy in the abused child. *Develop-
            mental Psychology* 17:762-765.
Straus, M.A.
    1992   Children as witnesses to marital violence: A risk factor for life-long problems
            among a nationally representative sample of American men and women. Pp. 98-
            104 in D.F. Schwartz, ed., *Children and Violence: Report of the 23rd Ross Roundtable
            on Critical Approaches to Common Pediatric Problems.* Columbus, OH: Ross
            Laboratories.
Straus, M.A., and R.J. Gelles, eds.
    1990   *Physical Violence in American Families: Risk Factors and Adaptations to Vio-
            lence in 8145 Families.* New Brunswick, NJ: Transaction Publishers.
Straus, M.A., R.J. Gelles, and S.K. Steinmetz
    1980   *Behind Closed Doors: Violence in the American Family.* New York: Doubleday/
            Anchor.
Tong, L., K. Oates, and M. McDowell
    1987   Personality development following sexual abuse. *Child Abuse and Neglect* 11:371-
            383.
Trickett, P.K.
    1992   The Developmental Impact of Different Types of Child Abuse and Neglect. Back-
            ground paper prepared for the National Research Council Panel on Research on
            Child Abuse and Neglect.

Trickett, P.K., and L. Kuczynski
1986   Children's misbehaviors and parental discipline strategies in abusive and non-abusive families. *Developmental Psychology* 22:115-123.

Trickett, P.K., and F.W. Putnam
in press The impact of child sexual abuse on females: Toward a developmental, psycho-biological integration. *Psychological Science*

Visintainer, M.A., and J.A. Wolfe
1975   Psychological preparation for surgical pediatric patients: The effects on children's and parents' stress responses and adjustment. *Pediatrics* 56:187-202.

Vissing, Y.M., M.A. Straus, R.J. Gelles, and J.W. Harrop
1991   Verbal aggression by parents and psychosocial problems by children. *Child Abuse and Neglect* 15:223-238.

Vondra, J., D. Barnett, and D. Cicchetti
1990   Self-concept, motivation, and competence among preschoolers from maltreating and comparison families. *Child Abuse and Neglect* 14:525-540.

Wald, M.S.
1976   State intervention on behalf of neglected children: Standards for removal of children from their homes, monitoring the status of children in foster care, and termination of parental rights. *Stanford Law Review* 28:625-706.

Wald, M.S, J.M. Carlsmith, and P.H. Liederman
1988   *Protecting Abused and Neglected Children.* Stanford, CA: Stanford University Press.

Walker, E., G. Downey, and A. Bergman
1989   The effects of parental psychopathology and maltreatment on child behavior: A test of the diathesis-stress model. *Child Development* 60:15-24.

Wallerstein, J.S.
1983   Children of divorce: The psychological tasks of the child. *American Journal of Orthopsychiatry* 53(2):230-243.

Wallerstein, J.S., and J.B. Kelly
1980   *Surviving the Breakup: How Children and Parents Cope with Divorce.* New York: Basic Books.

Walsh, B.W., and P. Rosen
1988   *Self-Mutilation: Theory, Research, and Treatment.* New York: Guilford.

Werner, E.E.
1983   Vulnerability and Resilency Among Children at Risk for Delinquency. Paper presented at the annual meeting of the American Society of Criminology, Denver, CO.

Werner, E.E., and R.S. Smith
1982   *Vulnerable but Invincible: A Longitudinal Study of Resilient Children and Youth.* New York: McGraw-Hill.

Widom, C.S.
1988   Sampling biases and implications for child abuse research. *American Orthopsychiatric Association* 58(2):260-270.
1989a   The cycle of violence. *Science* 244:160-166
1989b   Child abuse, neglect, and violent criminal behavior. *Criminology* 27(2):251-271.
1989c   Does violence beget violence? A critical examination of the literature. *Psychological Bulletin* 106(1):3-28.
1991a   The role of placement experiences in mediating the criminal consequences of early childhood victimization. *American Journal of Orthopsychiatry* 61(2):195-209.
1991b   Childhood victimization and adolescent problem behaviors. In M.E. Lamb and R. Ketterlinus, eds., *Adolescent Problem Behaviors.* New York: Lawrence Erlbaum Press.

Wilson, J.Q., and R.J. Herrnstein
  1985   *Crime and Human Nature*. New York: Simon Schuster.
Wolfe, D.A., and P.G. Jaffe
  1991   Child abuse and family violence as determinants of child psychopathology. *Canadian Journal of Behavioral Science* 23(3):282-299.
Wolfe, D.A., and M.D. Moske
  1983   Behavioral comparisons of children from abusive and distressed families. *Journal of Consulting and Clinical Psychology* 51:702-708.
Wolfe, J.A., and M.A. Visintainer
  1979   Pre-hospital psychological preparation for tonsillectomy patients: Effects on children's and parents adjustment. *Pediatrics* 64(5):646-655.
Wyatt, G.E.
  1988.   The relationship between child sexual abuse and adolescent sexual functioning in Afro-American and white American women. *Annals of the New York Academy of Sciences* 528:111-122.
  1990   Sexual abuse of ethnic minority children: Identifying dimensions of victimization. *Professional Psychology* 21:338-343.
Wyatt, G.E., and M. Newcomb
  1990   Internal and external mediators of women's sexual abuse in childhood. *Journal of Consulting and Clinical Psychology* 58(6):758-767.
Wyatt, G.E., D. Guthrie, and C.M. Notgrass
  1992   Differential effects of women's sexual abuse and subsequent sexual revictimization. *Journal of Consulting and Clinical Psychology* 60(2):167-173.
Wyatt, G.E., M. Newcomb, and M. Reederle, and C. Notgrass
  in press *The Effects of Child Sexual Abuse on Women's Sexual and Psychological Functioning*. Newbury Park, CA: Sage Publications.
Yarrow, M.R., and M.S. Goodwin
  1973   The immediate impact of separation: Reactions of infants to a change in mother figures. In L.J. Stone, H.T. Smith, and L.B. Murphy, eds., *The Competent Infant: Research and Commentary*. New York: Basic Books.
Zimrin, H.
  1986   A profile of survival. *Child Abuse and Neglect* 10:339-349.
Zuravin, S.
  1988   Fertility patterns: Their relationship to child physical abuse and child neglect. *Journal of Marriage and Family* 50:983-993.
Zuravin S., and R. Taylor
  1987   Family Planning Behaviors and Child Care Adequacy. Final report submitted to the U.S Department of Health and Human Services, Office of Population Affairs (Grant FPR 0000028-01-0).

7

Interventions and Treatment

Examples of intervention in child maltreatment include the investigation of child abuse reports by state child protection agencies, clinical treatment of physical and psychological injuries, family counseling, self-help services, the provision of goods and services such as homemaker or respite care, legal action against the perpetrator, and removal of the child or the offender from the home. This chapter reviews interventions that occur after suspected child maltreatment has been reported to child protection agencies. These treatment interventions are viewed by some as a form of tertiary prevention, for they are often designed not only to remedy whatever harm may have occurred, but also to prevent future occurrences of child maltreatment and to minimize the negative consequences of child maltreatment experiences for children and their families.

Some observers believe that the concept of treatment, in the field of child maltreatment studies, should be restricted to interventions that are therapeutic in nature, thus distinguishing such programs from social and legal efforts to investigate or prosecute reports of child abuse and neglect. However, the panel believes that therapeutic programs should be viewed within a broader social context that includes interventions by social and legal agencies. Access to therapeutic care is often determined by social service or law enforcement personnel, and the availability of medical or psychological services is significantly uneven in different social sectors. As a result, only a small percentage of victims have access to the services that they need (McCurdy and Daro, 1993). Thus, in the panel's view, "treatment" should include the processes by which child maltreatment reports are assessed, investigated, and substantiated.

In this review, treatment approaches are categorized by the systems and developmental levels for which they are designed. Many studies of interventions for victims of child maltreatment distinguish between different types of abuse, particularly sexual abuse. However, victims of child physical abuse, sexual abuse, neglect, and emotional maltreatment often experience similar psychological effects (e.g., fearfulness, aggression, low self-esteem, and depression) (Erickson and Egeland, 1987; Conte and Berliner, 1988). In addition, although treatment programs may be targeted to victims of a specific form of maltreatment, populations served by these programs may include victims of multiple forms of abuse. For example, increased awareness of emotional or psychological maltreatment has suggested that this form of child abuse may be an underlying factor in all forms of child victimization, although few treatment programs focus on it directly.[1]

Historical, empirical, organizational, and social factors complicate an understanding and analysis of intervention systems for child maltreatment. Multiple agencies have responsibility for determining policies that guide interventions in child abuse and neglect and coordinating human and financial resources to fulfill these objectives. Research that describes or evaluates the methods and mechanisms used to identify or confirm cases of child maltreatment; to assess the severity of child and family dysfunction, personal and social resources, and family strengths; and to match clients to appropriate treatments is minimal.

Although project evaluations that assess the benefits and limitations of treatment evaluations are often required by federal and state sponsors, problematic methodological issues characterize research in this area. Such issues include the following: the research generally does not include controlled experiments, has limited sample size, uses questionable measures to assess performance, and common assessment strategies have not been used across different interventions, making it difficult to know what works for whom. These issues need to be addressed to improve the use of research evaluations in the development of services and programs,

Furthermore, it is difficult to isolate factors specifically associated with child abuse and neglect in programs that often include families with multiple problems. Research on service delivery and accessibility is complicated by ethical, legal, and logistical problems. Researchers in this area have limited resources to collect compatible data, and the results of project evaluations are rarely published in the professional literature. In addition, clinicians who provide treatment services in child abuse and neglect cases may lack time, resources, and skills to develop systematic research evaluations.

Despite these limitations, a few significant outcome evaluations of treatment interventions do exist in the research literature on child maltreatment. In 1987, Cohn and Daro reviewed four major studies of multiple site program evaluations funded by the federal government since 1974.[2] These four studies, collectively, represented over $4 million invested in child maltreatment research over a 10-year period, involving 89 different demonstration treatment programs for which the government spent about $40 million and collected data on 3,253 families experiencing abuse and neglect problems (Cohn and Daro, 1987). Although these studies demonstrated how to provide direct services to both adults and children, documented improved client outcomes in individual and family functioning, and indicated reduced propensities for sexual abuse in families, the analysis of these studies provided significant cause for concern, concluding that treatment efforts in general were "not very successful" (p. 440):

> Child abuse and neglect continue despite early, thoughtful, and often costly intervention. Treatment programs have been relatively ineffective in initially halting abusive and neglectful behavior or in reducing the future likelihood of maltreatment in the most severe cases of physical abuse, chronic neglect, and emotional maltreatment. One-third or more of the parents served by these intensive demonstration efforts maltreated their children while in treatment, and over one-half of the families served continued to be judged by staff as likely to mistreat their children following termination.

Given this pessimistic assessment of the benefits that have been obtained through federally funded treatment interventions, much effort has been directed toward programs that will improve the treatment of victims or eliminate the potential for child abuse and neglect behavior.[3]

In this chapter, the panel reviews the strengths and weaknesses of different types of interventions, identifying gaps in knowledge and highlighting areas in which research can lead to the development of improved programs. This review is not comprehensive, but it is intended to reflect the general state of research in this area. The interventions discussed here include those commonly classified as treatment (such as family counseling or self-help services) for both the victim and the perpetrator, the administrative and legal processing of reported child abuse cases, the assessment of families, and foster care placement. In keeping with a process-oriented approach, the panel has included discussions of child protective services, law enforcement, and medical responses to reports of child maltreatment because of their potential to exacerbate or diminish the negative consequences of child maltreatment and influence the provision and effectiveness of treatment.

It should be noted, however, that this review is selective. The fragmentary nature of research on the intervention process and the absence of research reviews and controlled studies inhibited the panel's ability to evaluate the strengths and limitations of this field of work. Furthermore, we did not have sufficient time to evaluate the full spectrum of case handling and legal procedures associated with reports of child maltreatment. We have thus focused our attention on those areas in which important theoretical and data collection efforts have been achieved in identifying future research priorities for studies of the intervention processes. A broad range of topics germane to the study of child maltreatment, such as the recidivism records of child molesters, the reliability of child witness testimony, and the relationship of child maltreatment reports to child custody disputes, are not addressed here because the panel did not have a sufficient scientific research record on which to evaluate the quality of the reported findings.

TREATMENT EFFORTS AT THE INDIVIDUAL LEVEL

Treatment of Child Victims

As discussed in Chapter 6, the form of a child's response to maltreatment may be influenced by their age and developmental level. The panel has incorporated a developmental perspective into this review of treatment programs for individuals in order to assess the efficacy of treatment both in reducing the negative effects of maltreatment at different developmental stages and also in improving the victim's functioning during such critical developmental milestones as attachment, peer competency, and parenting styles.

Despite the large literature on the detrimental effects of child maltreatment that Chapter 6 outlines, the majority of treatment programs do not provide services directed at the psychosocial problems of the abused child. Children's involvement in treatment programs has generally occurred in the context of family-based services in which they have received direct programmatic attention[4] (Kolko, in press). The multiple therapeutic components of such programs make it difficult to determine the specific contribution of child treatment to outcomes.

Some treatment studies have examined the benefits of day or residential treatment/care programs for very young children, many of which use play or art therapy techniques (Azar and Wolfe, 1989). Studies of physically maltreated youngsters who have participated in specialized day care or residential programs have generally included diverse therapeutic activities for children as well as other parent or family-based services (e.g., counseling, homemaker and family and individual therapy and support groups) (Culp et al., 1987a,b, 1991; Elmer, 1977; Parish et al., 1985; Sankey et al., 1985).

Therapeutic day care can address problems with attachment, self-concept, emotional behavior problems, and physical problems in abused and neglected children (Daro, 1988). In a recent study of physically abused children, therapeutic day care resulted in significant pre- and post-test gains (compared with controls) in all tested developmental areas, including fine and gross motor skills, cognitive development, social and emotional functioning, and language development (Culp et al., 1987a,b).

A series of studies focused on samples of preschool physically abused children have found limited improvements in social behavior and peer relations. Although sample sizes were small, these studies are notable for their use of objective and repeated measures, experimental designs, and clearly described intervention procedures (Fantuzzo et al., 1987, 1988).

Case studies and clinical anecdotes offer glimpses of psychodynamic, insight-oriented and behavioral methods employed in individual and group treatments of sexually abused children (Becker et al., 1982; Gagliano, 1987; Gilbert, 1988; Van Leeven, 1988). Clinical literature on the treatment of child sexual abuse tends to emphasize the importance of expression and exploration of feelings, alteration of attributions of responsibility, and reduction of fear and anxiety (Berliner and Wheeler, 1987). To the panel's knowledge there are minimal outcome data on the comparative effectiveness of group and individual treatments for sexually abused children. Treatment interventions for child victims of abuse and neglect draw extensively from approaches for treating other childhood and adolescent problems with similar symptom profiles (Bonner and Walker, 1991). Empirical evaluations of programs that address child or adolescent problems in the areas of depression (Kolko et al., 1988; Lewinsohn et al., 1990), anxiety (Kendall et al., 1992), aggression or antisocial behavior (Kazdin, 1989; Kazdin et al., 1987; Pepler and Rubin, 1991), and social or peer disturbances (Kolko et al., 1990) have reported positive outcomes.[5] Replication of this work to determine the effectiveness of these treatment approaches with victims of child abuse and neglect would be extremely helpful.

Empirical evidence indicating a sustained reduction in the sequelae of abuse over time is not available from programs that directly and consistently involve abused or neglected children. Experimental designs and standardized outcome assessments, including adequate follow-ups, have rarely been used to evaluate interventions designed for maltreated children (Bonner and Walker, 1991; Browne and Finkelhor, 1986; Wheeler and Berliner, 1988). Five experimental treatment outcome investigations were funded in 1990 by the National Center for Child Abuse and Neglect to examine individual and group interventions for sexually and physically abused children in clinical settings, but the results of these studies are not yet known. With few exceptions, detailed descriptions of treatment protocols that would facilitate replication are not available.

Therapeutic interventions for child victims of maltreatment are limited in part because the psychological effects of abuse have not been well formulated in terms of theoretical constructs that can provide a basis for intervention (Wheeler and Berliner, 1988). Treatment approaches also rarely address the cumulative impact of victimization on children who may have additional experiences of racial or ethnic discrimination.

Treatment of Adult Survivors

The treatment of adult survivors of childhood sexual victimization is a newly emerging field; the first programs appeared in the late 1970s (Forward and Buck, 1978; Giaretto, 1976; Herman and Hirshman, 1977; Meiselman, 1978). Adult survivors are seen in various health centers (for somatic complaints, depression, or anxiety) and clinics for weight reduction, sexually transmitted diseases, and family planning. In contrast, few, if any, treatment programs or studies are available for adult survivors of physical or emotional abuse or child neglect.

Research on the treatment of adult survivors is submerged in the literature on adult psychological disorders such as addiction, eating disorders, borderline personality disorders, and sexual dysfunction (Alpert, 1991). It is difficult to isolate information specifically about the treatment of adult victims of child abuse from other adult patients because many adult survivors of child abuse do not identify themselves as such. However, a small but growing literature is beginning to address the treatment of adults abused as children. Most research focuses on female survivors of sexual abuse, particularly incest, but studies of the treatment of male victims of sexual abuse are expanding (Vander May, 1988).

Although a variety of individual and group approaches have been used in the treatment of adult survivors (including self-support techniques, building affect-regulation skills, cognitive interventions, exploration of desensitization of trauma, and emotional processing) (Briere, 1992), studies of the efficacy of these treatments are minimal. Most empirical research involves consumer evaluations of therapy (Jehu, 1988), changes in measures of mood disturbance (Alexander and Follette, 1987; Jehu, 1988; Roth and Newman, 1991; Roth et al., 1988), social adjustment and interpersonal problems (Alexander and Follette, 1987; Jehu, 1988), self-esteem (Alexander and Follete, 1987; Herman and Schatzow, 1984), sexual dysfunction (Jehu, 1988), guilt and assertiveness (Cole, 1985; Herman and Schatzow, 1984; Tsai and Wagner, 1978), and psychological well-being and overall sexual functioning (Wyatt et al., in press).

Studies have examined predictors associated with positive treatment outcomes in adult survivors. Factors considered in these studies include the existence of a support system (Goodman and Nowack-Schibelli, 1985; Herman and Schatzow, 1984), motivation and expectations (Herman and Schatzow, 1984), education, experience of "lesser" sexual abuse (Follette et al., 1991), and involvement in individual therapy while attending group therapy (Follette et al., 1991; Goodman and Nowack-Scibelli, 1985).

To the panel's knowledge, only one controlled outcome study of the treatment of adult survivors has been conducted (Alexander et al., 1987, 1991; Follette et al., 1991). This study used a randomized design to demonstrate that group therapy was significantly effective relative to a waiting-list control condition for adult survivors of incest and that treatment gains were maintained at a six-month follow-up. Differential benefits of different types of group therapy were also identified, with the more structured format providing more anxiety relief and the less structured interpersonal groups providing more opportunities for interpersonal learning and improved social adjustment (Alexander et al., 1991).

Future research on the treatment of adult survivors should pay particular attention to operationally defining moderating and mediating variables, clearly describing treatment methods, employing a broad range of outcome measures, using control or comparison groups, and administering follow-up assessments (Alpert, 1991). A developmental approach also needs to be integrated in such research, as the value of particular forms of therapy may vary at different stages of recovery (Alpert, 1991).

Treatment for Adult Sex Offenders

The treatment of child molesters is a controversial issue. Treatment programs are frequently offered to adult and adolescent offenders as part of plea bargaining negotiations in criminal prosecutions. The traditional assumption has been that children and society are better protected by offender treatment than by traditional prosecution and incarceration if the treatment service is effective (Finkelhor et al., 1988). However, there is currently considerable debate about whether child molesters can be effectively treated.

The most common approaches to treating child molesters are comprehensive treatment programs aimed at simultaneously treating multiple aspects of deviant sexual behavior. These programs usually incorporate educational approaches, behavior therapy, and relapse prevention (Prentky, 1990). Group therapy, widely used in the treatment of pedophiles, allows patients with similar problems to share experiences, confront their behaviors, and understand motivations that govern sexual acts against children (Langevin, 1983). Its primary purpose is to identify and confront cognitive distortions, rationalizations, excuses for offending, and behaviors that signal potential reoffending (Salter, 1988). However, the lack of controlled studies, the difficulties of comparisons between studies using different and sometimes contradictory techniques, and the lack of replication complicate assessment of the value of group therapy in treating child molesters (Crawford, 1981).

Relapse prevention, which includes a variety of techniques including stress management training, cognitive restructuring, and victimization therapy (Prentky, 1990), is also a frequent component of offender treatment programs. First developed in the treatment of addictive behaviors, such as substance abuse, relapse prevention was adapted for use with sex offenders to reduce the risk of re-offending (Marques, 1988; Laws, 1989; Pithers, 1990).

Although many different approaches to the treatment of sexual offenders have been tried (including group therapy, family systems treatment, chemical interventions, and relapse prevention), scientific data indicating sustained reductions in recidivism are not available (Becker, 1991). Most studies follow offenders only for one year after treatment, and it is not known if treatments are effective in eliminating molestation behavior beyond that period.

Adolescent Sex Offenders

Until recently, adolescent sexual offenders have been neglected in clinical and research literature, and empirically tested models to explain why adolescents commit sexual crimes or develop deviant sexual interest patterns are minimal (Becker, 1991). The components and goals of treatment for adolescent sex offenders are similar to those involved in the treatment of adult sex offenders. In general, the treatment of adolescent sex offenders focuses more on family contexts and less on behavioral and chemical techniques such as aversive conditioning and chemical interventions (Knopp et al., 1986). Preliminary outcome data on the treatment of juvenile sex offenders show positive outcomes (Kavoussi et al., 1987). However, the National Adolescent Perpetrator Network (established in 1983) has called attention to the lack of substantive research in the field and the lack of consensus regarding basic principles of treatment (National Adolescent Perpetrator Network, 1988). Studies that employ standardized measures of treatment outcomes and long-term follow-ups on homogeneous samples are likely to be revealing about the effectiveness of treatment for this population (Kavoussi et al., 1987).

Self-Help Services for Abusive Adults

Self-help support and treatment programs are based on the premise that individuals can benefit from learning about the victimization experiences of others. These programs have attracted popular support in a wide range of health services, including the treatment of alcoholism, weight loss, and rape counseling programs, and they have also been applied in the treatment of both physically and sexually abusive adults. Parents Anonymous, a self-help group for physically abusive parents that started in the early 1970s, currently provides free, confidential group services to approximately 30,000 families each year in 1,200 chapters across the United States. A self-help component has also been integrated into treatment programs for intrafamilial sexual abuse (Giaretto, 1982). Parents United had 135 active chapters in the United States and Canada in 1988, which included self-help groups for the incest offender, the nonoffending spouse, children, and adults molested as children. Other groups similar to Parents Anonymous and Parents United are continually being formed.

Few empirical studies with reliable outcome measures have been used to evaluate the effectiveness of individual self-help programs or to identify the characteristics of individuals who are most likely to benefit from such efforts. A comparison study of self-help groups conducted by Berkeley Planning Associates found that self-help groups and lay therapists were reliable predictors for reduced recidivism (Cohn, 1979). One evaluation of Parents Anonymous, conducted by Behavior Associates, found that physical abuse stopped after one month of attendance and verbal abuse showed a significant decrease after two months of attendance (Ehresman, 1988).

MICROSYSTEM APPROACHES: FAMILY-ORIENTED INTERVENTIONS

Most treatment interventions for physical abuse, child neglect, and emotional abuse seek to change parents or the home environment. Only recently have treatment services begun to incorporate empirical findings that build on ecological, developmental models of child maltreatment and examine the interactions of family members, abusive parents' perceptions of their children, behavioral characteristics that may restrict parenting abilities, and emotional reactions to stressful childrearing situations (Wolfe, 1992:9). Contemporary parent training programs focus on improving cognitive-behavioral skills and usually adapt behavioral methods designed originally to assist non-abusive families with behaviorally disturbed children (Wolfe, 1992:10). Family systems treatments target the psychodynamic interplay in relationships in families. Intensive home-based services and family preservation services directly correspond to ecological, developmental theories of maltreatment and provide services directed at the overall needs of abusive families.

A lack of consensus still exists regarding the effectiveness of a wide range of treatment services for maltreating families (Azar and Wolfe, 1989; Isaacs, 1982). Outcome studies have indicated positive behavioral and attitudinal changes as a result of family or parent treatment, but few studies have examined the effects of such interventions on subsequent reports of child abuse and neglect beyond one year. Definitive conclusions about the generalizability of the findings from studies of family-oriented programs in reducing subsequent maltreatment are difficult to develop because the participants in these programs often present varied types of parental dysfunction.

Research in this area is dominated by single-case studies. Group studies that have been used are often characterized by a lack of random assignment to treatment conditions, small sample sizes, and inappropriate comparison groups (Kaufman, 1991).

Parental Enhancement

Most parental enhancement programs focus on training abusive parents in child management (e.g., effective discipline), childrearing (e.g., infant stimulation), and self-control skills (e.g., anger control). Programs for neglectful parents typically focus on areas such as nutrition, homemaking, and child care. Parental enhancement programs may help some families who experience child management problems when a sexually abusive father is removed from the home. In these cases, child management skills help develop positive child-parent interaction in sexually abusive families.

The efficacy of parent-training approaches for physically abusive parents has been supported by various single-case studies, one study using repeated measures, and group design studies (Azar and Twentyman, 1984; Crimmins et al., 1984; Gilbert, 1976; Jeffrey, 1976; Reid et al., 1981; Szykula and Fleischman, 1985; Wolfe et al., 1981a,b, 1982). Studies of multiple approaches and diverse populations have provided consistent evidence that parents can acquire behavioral skills and use them in interactions with their children, at least in clinical settings (Golub et al., 1987). Some evidence suggests that training has reduced parental distress or symptomatology and, in some instances, improved child functioning (Wolfe et al., 1988) and reduced the likelihood of child placement (Szykula and Fleischman, 1985). Efforts to expand the scope of parental enhancement programs have fostered attention to parents' cognitive-attributional and affective repertoires (see Azar and Siegel, 1990). Therapeutic directions highlight the need to incorporate diverse skills and to evaluate the effectiveness of individual approaches (see Azar and Wolfe, 1989).

Project 12-Ways is an intervention program for high-risk abusive and neglectful parents based on an ecobehavioral approach—that is, an approach that includes attention to environmental as well as individual and family factors. Following an in-depth assessment, parents participate in customized programs including the use of groups, behavioral methods, and parental aides to offer specialized services including parent-child relations, home safety, nutrition and health maintenance, assertiveness training, job placement and vocational skills training, stress reduction training, alcoholism treatment, and financial planning (Lutzker, 1984). Positive findings from single-subject case reports, reports of clients attaining treatment goals in the majority of cases, and lower recidivism rates for program clients compared with controls for a five-year period of program evaluation support this approach to family treatment (Lutzker, 1984; Luztker and Rice, 1987). However, no comparison data were collected, and client assignment to Project 12-Ways was not random. Evidence also suggests that treatment gains are not maintained when compared with a comparison group (Wesch and Lutzker, 1991).

At present, few definitive studies demonstrate the efficacy of parent training in reducing re-abuse. Evaluations of the clinical impact of intervention on subsequent re-abuse (recidivism) rates and child and family functioning are needed (Kolko, in press). The severity of family dysfunction evident in some cases of abuse or neglect may also limit the applicability of parent-training methods.

Family Systems Treatment

Family systems treatment, commonly used in the treatment of intrafamilal sexual abuse, seeks to change the psychosocial interactions among family members. Clinical descriptions of family therapy combined with individual and group therapy suggest its potential usefulness for families who are highly dysfunctional, although controlled evaluations of family therapy in child sexual abuse have not been conducted (Alexander, 1990; Bentovim and Van Elburg, 1987; Giaretto, 1976, 1978; Ribordy, 1990; Sgroi, 1982; Walker et al., 1988). Some programs have indicated a recidivism rate as low as 3 percent (Anderson and Shafer, 1979).

Home-Based Services and Family Preservation Services

Home-based services and family preservation services address the overall needs of families, include both children and parents, and focus directly on contextual factors, such as poverty, single parenthood, and marital discord, that increase stress, weaken families, and elicit aggressive behavior (Kolko, in press). These programs target functional relationships among diverse individual, family, and systemic problems by combining traditional social work with various therapeutic counselling approaches.

The use of home-based services has been advocated in response to the multiple problems found among abusive and neglectful families, difficulties in providing services in a traditional format, and interests in reducing the number of children placed in foster care. The breadth of potential family dysfunction has encouraged hands-on approaches that address risk factors at multiple levels of the family system, such as financial problems, disruption, social isolation, and behavioral deviance (Frankel, 1988).

Applications of the home-based approach in child maltreatment have become increasingly popular in recent years. Studies of *home-based services* have found that a multisystemic approach using multiple treatment modalities resulted in greater improvements in parent-child relationships and child behavior problems than simple parent training in child management skills (Brunk et al., 1987; Nichol et al., 1988). However, the generalizabilty of these findings is limited by methodological problems, including the absence of clear targets for certain conditions (Nichol et al., 1988), follow-up information (Brunk et al., 1987; Nichol et al., 1988), and minimal treatment conditions (Brunk et al., 1987).

Home-based approaches have demonstrated particular effectiveness with neglectful families (Daro, 1988). The crisis conditions of some neglectful families, including poverty at the time of the report of neglect, have sometimes been described as the most recent manifestation of a deeply troubled history of the offending parent (Polansky et al., 1975, 1981). Treatment of neglectful behavior sometimes requires not only resolution of the immediate stressful conditions, but also intensive, long (perhaps more than 12 months), and often expensive interventions to alter the parent's fundamental concepts of self, relationships with others, and beliefs about one's ability to affect the circumstances of life.

Family preservation programs are designed to prevent the placement of children outside the home while ensuring their safety. Family preservation services are often characterized by their intensity (20-30 hours per week), short duration (often 6 weeks), and their flexibility in providing a range of therapeutic and support services tailored to the needs of families in crisis. Family preservation programs are often designed to address multiple goals, including the protection of children, strengthening family bonds, providing stability in crisis situations, increasing family skills and competencies, fostering family use of formal and informal helping resources, and preventing unnecessary out-of-home placement of children (Tracy et al., 1991).

The Homebuilders program (Kinney et al., 1977), established in the State of Washington in the 1970s, is the most widely disseminated and replicated family preservation program (Kammerman and Kahn, 1989; Meyers, 1991; Smith, 1991). The Homebuilders model is notable for its individualized interventions, program intensity, flexible schedule, small caseloads, goal orientation, time limited services, and program evaluation efforts (Whittaker et al., 1990). Individual programs vary by such factors as method of operation (drawing on public agency staff or private contracts), level of training, availability of staff, and availability of funds to purchase goods or services for families (Kammerman and Kahn, 1989). The majority of children remain at home following service termination or at follow-up.[6]

Most of the evaluative research on family preservation programs reports success on a limited number of measures, such as preventing the placement of children and short-term improvement in family functioning (Bath and Haapala, 1993). However, the effectiveness of family preservation services remains unclear because most evaluative studies have suffered from methodological problems such as small samples, little reliability with respect to validity of measures, and nonexperimental designs (Kinney et al., 1977; Paschal and Schwahn, 1986; Rossi, 1992; Wells and Beigel, 1991). Research on family preservation services is also complicated by variations in definitions of outcome, the target population, and the quality of services (Wells and Biegel, 1991).[7]

Recent empirical studies have rigorously examined multiple outcomes of treatment and used experimental and quasi-experimental designs (Feldman, 1991; Mitchell et al, 1988; Nelson, 1990, 1991; Pecora et al., 1991; Schwartz et al., 1991; Yuan and Struckman-Johnson, 1991; Yuan et al., 1991). These studies have revealed equivocal findings about the effectiveness of family preservation programs, including high placement avoidance rates in control groups (Feldman, 1991; Mitchell et al., 1988; Yuan et al., 1991), little difference at follow-up between control and treatment conditions (Mitchell et al., 1988; Yuan et al., 1990), and the fading of treatment effects over time (Feldman, 1991).

In a recent review of family preservation research, Rossi (1991) observes that "one of the major problems with existing evaluations is that they treat children and their families as if their problems were all the same (p. 61, cited in Bath and Haapala, 1993). It is likely that mixing clients of different ages, problem types, referral sources, and service domains has weakened the findings of studies. One recent study evaluated outcomes of family preservation services in different subpopulations of a relatively large sample within one service domain. Significant differences were found between families experiencing different types of maltreatment: fewer physically abused children were placed than those in the neglect and combined groups (Bath and Haapala, 1993).

Despite equivocal evidence of long-term effectiveness, family preservation services are currently believed to be a cost-effective alternative to the institutionalization or foster care placements for many children. If a child is not placed in foster care as a result of successful family-based services, the projected state savings in foster placement and administrative costs alone are estimated to be $27,000 (Daro, 1988).[8] Child welfare and social service agencies are often legislatively required to provide permanent homes or use the least restrictive settings for children and encourage the use of family preservation programs.

Family Income and Supplemental Benefits

The relationship of poverty to child maltreatment, specifically child neglect, is thought to be significant (see Chapter 4). Several government programs designed to alleviate or mitigate the effects of poverty on children are often part of a comprehensive set of services for low-income, maltreating families. Such programs include Social Security supplemental income programs, Aid to Families with Dependent Children (AFDC), Women with Infants and Children food supplement program (WIC), Head Start, rent-subsidy programs, and school lunch programs, among others.

Gil (1970) has stated that almost 60 percent of families reported for incidents of abuse and neglect received aid from public assistance agencies during or prior to the study year. However, while national and local child welfare programs designed to improve the well-being of all poor families may provide food, shelter, and other necessary resources, for children in households characterized by neglect or abuse, the relationship between income support, material assistance, and the subsequent reduction of maltreatment has not been systematically addressed.

COMMUNITY EXOSYSTEM INTERVENTIONS

Family-oriented interventions often exist within a context of a broad range of diverse services provided by community agencies. Medical personnel diagnose and treat physical conditions associated with child maltreatment. Child protection services personnel investigate suspected cases of child maltreatment, select and refer families for treatment services, and decide whether to allow a child to remain in the home. Child welfare services authorities provide financial and social services to families who may be in distress. Courts of law and law enforcement personnel intervene when questions are raised about the safety of the child or the community. Understanding these responses to child maltreatment is important in understanding the experiences of children and families following reports of maltreatment. Yet little is known about the efficacy of these community-based interventions.

A few treatment programs have been developed at the community level to provide services to families, such as counseling and educational services for the parents, supervised day care, and specialized referrals for community services, including mental health care, housing, and substance addiction treatment (Zuravin and Taylor, 1987). Although such neighborhood-focused programs may assist children who are victims of abuse or neglect, program evaluations usually do not consider outcomes in terms of maltreatment subpopulations.

Medical Treatment of Child Abuse

Health professionals in private practice, community health clinics, and hospitals are often the first point of contact for abused children and their families when serious physical injuries are sustained. Medical examinations of abused children enable physicians to identify physical conditions requiring medical treatment (including sexually transmitted disease and pregnancy), collect forensic evidence, document abuse histories, and refer abusive families to other services. Psychosocial examinations can document the nature, severity, and chronicity of behaviors exhibited by the abused child. Nurses and hospital social workers also play an influential role in managing or detecting child abuse cases in medical settings.

Health professionals are required by law to report cases of suspected abuse to child protection agencies, but the use of discretion in such reports is common. The 1988 National Incidence Survey suggested that only two-thirds of suspected cases are reported by health professionals (NCCAN, 1988).

Little is known about treatments recommended for abused children in medical settings, and even less is known about specific treatment outcomes. Studies suggest, however, that many health professionals may not be sufficiently trained to detect or validate signs of abuse or to deal with the physical, psychological, and legal aspects of evaluating maltreated children, particularly sexually abused children.[9] For example, one study showed that many pediatricians were not able to label correctly a diagram of the female genitalia (Ladson et al., 1987).

Examinations of suspected abuse, specifically sexual abuse, sometimes have been described as "revictimizing" children. Sexual examinations sometimes frighten many children and can involve sensations similar to those experienced during victimization. The psychological effects of medical examinations following sexual assault (e.g., the use of the colposcope, which provides light and magnification and allows photographic recording of genital examinations) have not been clarified. The reliability of diagnostic conclusions in physical examinations for sexual abuse has been questioned and is currently the subject of study.

Medical examinations of sexually abused children often include testing for sexually transmitted diseases. Sexual abuse is a potential mode of transmission of infection by the human immunodeficiency virus (HIV) in children, although the incidence of HIV transmission through child sexual abuse is unknown. One recent study attempted to estimate the number of children infected with HIV as a result of pediatric sexual abuse in the United States and Canada (Gellert et al., 1993). This study concluded that sexual abuse resulted in HIV infection in 52 percent of home settings when both biological parents were present and a coinfection rate of HIV and other sexually transmitted diseases of 33 percent (Gellert et al., 1993). Selective testing guidelines have been developed for HIV infection based on normative practice among child abuse assessment experts (Gellert et al., 1990), but policies regarding selective testing of sexually abused children have not yet been clarified.

Child Protective Services

Child protective service officials are obligated to respond to cases of suspected child maltreatment. They evaluate the validity of complaints, perform risk assessments of families, monitor cases, and develop and implement family service plans.

Child protection agencies receive and screen initial reports of child abuse and neglect from educators, health personnel, police, members of the public (e.g., neighbors, family friends), relatives (including siblings and parents), and others to determine whether investigation is required. Limited resources often prevent child protection agencies from responding to increasing numbers of reports (see Chapter 3) within the 24 or 48 hours mandated by state child welfare legislation (Child Welfare League of America, 1986). In most locales the system is understaffed, many caseworkers are poorly trained, and high turnover rates are common.[10] In New York City in 1991, for example, 77 percent of the workers who investigate child abuse reports resigned, were laid off, or transferred to jobs in other agencies (Dugger, 1992).

Less than half of the reported cases of child abuse and neglect are substantiated (Knudsen, 1988; NCCAN, 1988).[11] When a report is substantiated, an agency official selects and refers families to specific treatment services, monitors the treatment process, and decides whether the child can safely remain in the home during treatment. However, one national survey has indicated that more than one-third of confirmed cases of child maltreatment received no therapeutic or supportive services (McCurdy and Daro, 1993).

The processes that determine child protective services responses to maltreated children and their families have not attracted much research attention, although such influences have a profound influence on the treatment process. Evaluations of CPS operations are complicated by the emergency situation in which many investigations occur, as well as variations in definitions of child maltreatment, and the absence of clear objectives, procedures, or standards of evaluation. However, a few studies have made an initial effort to document and characterize the various stages of the CPS process and their effects on children and families (Crittenden, 1992).

Intake and Assessment

Recent efforts to examine risk assessment factors have been initiated (American Public Welfare Association, 1989; NCCAN, 1991, 1992; Tatara,

1989, 1990), but the factors that influence the treatment of specific cases still need further clarification. There has been little systematic study of factors that influence classification or misclassification of reports. The decision to investigate reports of child maltreatment can be influenced by ambiguous definitions, time restrictions, descriptions of the alleged maltreatment, its presumed seriousness, and even which worker takes the call (Knudsen, 1988)—all of which may have important consequences for certain types of clients and for specific categories of maltreatment. For example, middle-class families are less likely to be defined as dangerous and in need of intervention than lower-class families (Knudsen, 1988). Complaints against ex-spouses known to be involved in custody disputes are likely to be viewed as less dangerous for a child than battering reports made by medical personnel (Knudsen, 1988).

Investigation and Substantiation

Factors that influence the methods used to investigate allegations of maltreatment are poorly understood. State agencies often lack consistent criteria to help workers to make informed judgments in their investigations of reported or suspected child maltreatment. Factors that appear to be correlated with the substantiation of a report include the beliefs or assumptions of child protective services workers, the age of an alleged victim, and reports of multiple or recent incidents (Thoennes and Tjaden, 1990). However, empirical data do not confirm a causal relationship for any single factor, and data describing the life course of cases over time are not available.

Case Management and Referrals

Research on the nature and effectiveness of referral decisions involving maltreating families is difficult, and we know little about the operation of the referral system and follow-up services; the character of cases that are likely to receive services; the nature, intensity, and length of the services provided; and outcomes resulting from intervention services for different types of child maltreatment. Many factors can affect referral decisions, including availability of services, costs to clients and sponsors, ease of access, client attitudes, perceived need, and organizational relations (Knudsen, 1988). Recent clinical reports of child abuse cases suggest that many cases are closed immediately after services have been initiated and, in some instances, even prior to actual service delivery.[12]

The confidential nature of reports and investigations, the lack of systematic record-keeping and compatible data, and political sensitivity inhibit the observation and analysis of decisions made by child protective services workers (Knudsen, 1988). Improvements in knowledge about factors that foster or inhibit service referrals may increase the potential for flexible responses and tailoring of interventions for individual families. Some methods that bear empirical evaluation have been proposed to enhance this outcome, including the use of multiple informants, semistructured interview measures, interdisciplinary evaluation teams, and statistically derived assessment profiles that could translate into service plans (Baglow, 1990).

Child Welfare Services

Foster Care

The number of children placed in foster care during the past decade has increased dramatically. In 1990, the U.S. House of Representatives Select Committee on Children, Youth, and Families (1990) estimated that nearly 500,000 children were in out-of-home placements and that by 1995 the population of children in out-of-home care may be more than 840,000 children. The decision to allow a maltreated child to remain with family members or relatives during treatment is a critical and controversial aspect of the case management process. Children can be removed from the home for a variety of reasons, including physical illness or incapacity of the child's caregiver, mental illness of the parent (often the mother), child personality or emotional problems, severe neglect or abuse, criminal involvement of the parent, or family problems, such as substance abuse, and homelessness (Aber, 1980; Jenkins and Sauber, 1966; Runyan and Gould, 1985; Runyan et al., 1982; Weinberger and Smith, 1970; Widom, 1991). In some cases temporary foster care (sometimes called "respite care") is provided to protect the child and to provide a period for family members to improve the conditions that resulted in the child's removal from the home. Some children placed in foster care, particularly in urban areas, reside with relatives who subsequently receive foster care support payments, a procedure known as "kinship care." A child's permanent removal from the home and legal termination of parental rights may be sought by child welfare officials when family or parental characteristics associated with abusive or neglectful behavior show no signs of improvement. Foster care is often viewed as a temporary solution to an emergency situation and the average length of time in foster care has been decreasing in recent years: the median amount of time in foster care remains 1.5 years (Pelton, 1989). However, five years has been shown as the average length of time spent by children in foster care in some cities (Fanshel, 1981; Wiltse and Gambrill, 1973). One study of 772 foster children in San Francisco suggested that two-thirds of the children were expected to remain in foster care until their maturity (Wiltse and Gambrill, 1973). In addition to the length of placement, research has indicated that the majority of children who remain in foster care for at least six months experience two or more placements (Knitzer and Allen, 1978; Tatara, 1989). Proponents of foster care point to the potential for serious physical harm that can occur when abused and neglected children remain in a dangerous environment, and the psychological and developmental risks to the child that can occur from uncertain living arrangements. Critics argue that family preservation is an important cultural value, children should not be removed unnecessarily from their homes, the costs of placing a child in foster care are significant, and foster care placement may have detrimental consequences,[13] including the potential for abuse while in foster care as well as developmental effects (particularly if young children experience multiple placements). Furthermore, the supply of foster care homes has become increasingly limited, especially in large cities (Kammerman and Kahn, 1989). As a result, community resistance to the forced removal of a child from the home remains high.

Current governmental policies seek to reduce the numbers of children requiring foster care or adoptive placement, to reduce the time lag between temporary and permanent placement of young children, and to reduce multiple placements for children. Although public policy decisions regarding the use of foster care must ultimately reflect value judgments within the community, the lack of solid empirical evidence about the nature of placement experiences and selection criteria hinders decision making in this area (Wald, 1976; Wald et al., 1988).

Criteria Regarding Out-of-Home Placement Decisions

Research on the placement of physically abused and neglected children has yielded diverse and contradictory findings, influenced by differences in methodology and in the variables selected for study (Hunter et al., 1990). Many foster care studies do not distinguish between maltreated and nonmaltreated children, although one recent study indicated that approximately 50 percent of the 199,000 children who entered foster care in 1988 were abused or neglected (Tatara, 1989, 1992).[14] Children placed in foster care represent a highly heterogeneous population, characterized by different types of severity of maltreatment and family demographics (Aber, 1980). Placement decisions are often influenced by measures of parental functioning or cooperation (Boehm 1962, 1967), availability of maternal support (Hunter et al., 1990; Phillips et al., 1971), maternal health and caregiver cooperation (Meddin, 1984), the presence or absence of other relatives (Widom, 1991), and in sexual abuse cases, the initial history or statement (Jaudes and Morris, 1990).

Research has shown that placement decisions for abused and neglected children are affected by judgments about selected characteristics of families and the children (Aber, 1980; Runyan et al., 1982; Widom, 1991). Two studies have suggested that poor families, in particular, are more likely to have a child removed, even after controlling for the nature of the abuse (Katz et al., 1986; Ross and Katz, 1983).

Treatment for Children in Foster Care

Although children in foster care are known to be at high risk for severe emotional, behavioral, and physical difficulties, comprehensive physical and mental health services are not available for children in foster care (Goerge and Kranz, 1988; Schuerman et al., 1990). Two different studies found that children in foster care were generally underreferred for clinical services (Hochstadt and Harwicke, 1985; Meddin and Hansen, 1985).

Research on services provided to children in foster or kinship care is difficult. Information about children in foster care is often dispersed among biological parents, foster parents, relatives, and caseworkers, and cooperation among agencies providing services is frequently hampered by issues of confidentiality, rigid funding and eligibility requirements, budgetary restrictions, and the specialized nature of professional services that tend to focus on isolated problems (National Commission on Children, 1991). Therapists who provide treatment to children in foster care are often influenced by financial and contractual considerations, interagency relations and history, and the effects of decisions on future referrals (Molin, 1988).

Legal Intervention in Child Maltreatment

A small proportion of child maltreatment cases that are substantiated by child protection agencies can become involved with juvenile courts, family courts, and criminal courts, but no cohesive policy exists to guide the justice system's response to child abuse and neglect cases (Smith et al., 1980). Juvenile courts handle dependency proceedings, including adoption and foster care placements, when evidence exists that a parent is unable to protect and properly care for a child. Child maltreatment cases may be relevant to family courts when one parent seeks action against the other and evidence of abuse (usually sexual abuse) is considered in visitation or family custody decisions. Criminal courts handle charges against adults who have severely harmed or molested a child and can mandate that child abusers receive treatment.

Areas of convergence and conflict between the goals of service providers and the legal system in the treatment of child abuse and neglect have been documented, yet much uncertainty remains. Research on criminal prosecution of child abusers suggests that many abusers, sexual molesters in particular, are not deterred by incarceration or threats of retribution (Tjaden and Thoennes, 1992). In some cases, the prosecution of an offender can be an impediment to treatment. For example, a parent's willingness to comply with treatment may be diminished if he or she believes that statements made during therapy will be used to incriminate them or terminate their parental rights (Davidson et al., 1981). Psychological problems that underlie maltreatment are usually not resolved by criminal sanctions because courts and prisons often lack resources to provide adequate treatment to offenders. An unsuccessful prosecution can also reduce the effectiveness of voluntary or court-ordered treatment, encourage noncompliance, and subject the child to further maltreatment (DeFrancis and Lucht, 1974).

Legal interventions in child maltreatment are complicated by many factors, such as the absence of physical evidence, difficulties in obtaining consistent and reliable testimony from children, emotional trauma that might be incurred in forcing a child victim to testify against a parent or other adult who may have harmed him or her, and inconclusive scientific evidence regarding the effectiveness of treatment in halting abusive and neglectful behavior.[15] Almost nothing is known about the quality of court experiences for children or adults who are affected by physical abuse, neglect, or emotional maltreatment. However, even though relatively low numbers of sexually abused children involve court proceedings (Goodman et al., 1989; Martin and Hamilton, 1989),[16] the legal treatment of child sexual abuse cases has attracted significant research attention (Goodman et al., 1989; Runyan et al., 1988). For example, the Department of Justice has sponsored numerous studies on the experience of the criminal and juvenile justice systems in handling child maltreatment cases, the effects of participation in the justice system on children, and the validity of children's statements and behaviors as indicators of abuse (Whitcomb, 1992).[17] Researchers have also examined the effects of preparing a child for the experience of testifying, and methods to support the child through the legal system experience (King et al., 1988). However, systematic evaluations of the largest victim support programs (Court Appointed Special Advocates and the Guardian ad litem programs[18]) have not been conducted. The impact of *guardian ad litems* and volunteer Court Appointed Special Advocates on the outcome of court cases and on the children they represent is not known.

The role of the courts in ordering particular forms of treatment to prevent child abuse and neglect, such as the use of Norplant (an implantable contraceptive) for women who have histories of being reported for child maltreatment (Feringa, Iden, and Rosenfield, 1992; Scott, 1992); the use of castration for male sexual offenders; or the placement of newborns in foster care if the mother tests positively for illegal drugs is particularly controversial, given the absence of research evidence supporting these actions as effective treatment or prevention programs.

SOCIAL/MACROSYSTEM INTERVENTIONS

Social and cultural values have influenced the development of interventions in child maltreatment in both professional and public institutions. In many situations, these values are complementary and reinforcing, but conflicts can arise. National policies, professional services, and institutional programs may sometimes be governed by different priorities that reveal inconsistent policies and fundamental value conflicts.

The principal values that strongly influence the current American social context for responding to reported or suspected child maltreatment include child safety and family preservation. The rights of individual privacy, confidentiality, and other liberties that are often constitutionally guaranteed also influence both the provision of social and professional interventions as well as evaluations of their effectiveness.

The conditions under which child, parental, or community rights should supersede all other rights and obligations, and the criteria that should be considered in balancing long-term dangers against immediate threats, are unclear. The safety of the child is usually a paramount interest, but minimal risks to the child may be tolerated to help families remain intact. Various anecdotal reports have illustrated cases in which children were not adequately protected because an offender remained in a caretaking role for the child during treatment or delays in court proceedings. For some children, foster care or removal of the offender from the home is the only way to protect the child from imminent harm, even though the out-of-home placement may result in further psychological or social damage and long-term costs to society. Research defining the best interests of the child is becoming a significant issue in determining the outcomes of assignment of visitation and custodial rights in court decisions.

CONCLUSIONS

Medical, psychological, social, and legal interventions in child maltreatment cases are based on assumptions that such interventions can reduce the negative physical, behavioral, and psychological consequences of child abuse and neglect, foster attitudes and behaviors that improve the quality of parent-child interactions and limit or eradicate recurrences of maltreatment. Interventions have been developed in response to public, professional, legal, and budgetary pressures that often have competing and sometimes contradictory policies and objectives. Some intervention services focus on protecting the child or protecting the community; others focus on providing individual treatment for the child, the offender, or both; others emphasize developing family coping strategies and improving skills in parent-child interactions. Assumptions about the severity of selected risk factors, the adequacy of caretaking behaviors, the impact of abuse, and the steps necessary to prevent abuse or neglect from recurring may vary given the goals and context of the intervention.

Little is known about the character and effects of existing interventions in treating different forms of child maltreatment. No comprehensive inventory of treatment interventions currently exists, and we lack basic descriptive and evaluative information regarding key factors that influence the delivery and outcomes of treatment for victims and offenders at different developmental stages and in different environmental contexts. A coherent base of research information on the effectiveness of treatment is not available at this time to guide the decisions of case workers, probation officers, health professionals, family counselors, and judges.

Investigations of child maltreatment reports often influence the development and availability of other professional services, including medical examinations, counseling, evaluation of risk factors, and substantiation of complaints. Research on various federal, state, and private agency involvement in treatment interventions has not been systematically organized, and information that describes how these groups interact is not readily available.

Although the panel acknowledges the challenges of performing research in this area, future study designs require particular sensitivity to the need for adequate sample sizes, well-characterized and designed samples, and validated and comparable measures. Specific causal relationships between services and outcomes have not been determined through experimental research designs with random assignment of subjects to treatment and control or comparison groups. In contrast, there have been successful applications of randomized clinical trials for other social problems, such as school-age pregnancy (Klerman and Horwitz, 1992) as well as randomized programs involving the response of law enforcement agencies to domestic violence reports (Sherman, 1992). Some researchers have suggested reforms in the data collection processes in clinical and legal decision making in child maltreatment cases so that service plans can be used for research purposes as well (Aber, 1980).

RESEARCH RECOMMENDATIONS

Recommendation 7-1: Research on the operation of the child protection system, including an evaluation of the sequential stages by which

children receive treatment following reports of maltreatment, is a priority need. The factors that influence different aspects of case handling
decisions, factors that improve the delivery of case services, and alternatives to existing arrangements for providing services to children and
families in distress need to be described and evaluated.

A research framework that provides standardized classifications and
descriptions of child maltreatment investigations, adjudications, and referral
decisions should be developed to analyze the operation of the child protection system. This classification system should be employed in a national
study designed to facilitate data collection and to clarify the types of agencies involved in the system, the forms of maltreatment that stimulate treatment referrals, the range of interventions available for selected forms of
maltreatment, the costs of investigating and responding to reports of child
maltreatment, and the outcomes of case reports. Analysis is needed of the
interaction among different agencies involved in intervention and treatment
and the degree to which decisions made by one agency affect outcomes in
others.

Recommendation 7-2: Controlled group outcome studies are needed
to develop criteria to assess the effects of treatment interventions for
maltreated children. Adequate measures need to be developed to assess
outcomes of treatment for victims of abuse and neglect, and methods by
which developmental, social, and cultural variations in abuse symptomatology
can be integrated into treatment goals and assessment instruments need
to clarified. The criteria that promote recovery and treatment modalities appropriate for children depending on their sex, age, social class,
cultural background, and type of abuse need to be identified.

Research on the impact of abuse on children of different ages and in
different contexts needs to be integrated into effective treatment strategies.[19] All treatment programs should include some assessment of important outcomes for the child and other family members. In assessing treatment outcomes, consideration needs to be given to the child's developmental
stage, cognitive abilities, and gender. The types of therapies (e.g., individual, group, family) and therapeutic techniques, including goals, intensity, and duration that are effective for groups of victims (e.g., young children, school-age children, adolescents), need to be identified. The criteria
selected for treatment outcome studies are particularly important because
they shape the emphasis of the intervention. The treatment of children with
developmental disabilities, past histories of abuse, and factors associated
with maintenance of treatment effects (e.g., concomitant therapy for parents), require special attention because they can all influence treatment outcomes.

The gap between research information on critical factors and conditions under which treatment is provided also needs to be bridged by identifying individual, social, cultural, and contextual variables that affect the use and outcome of treatment interventions. In implementing this recommendation, closer integration of diverse research and practice traditions needs to be developed to improve the quality of treatment interventions in response to child maltreatment.

Recommendation 7-3: Well-designed outcome evaluations are needed to assess whether intensive family preservation services reduce child maltreatment and foster the well-being of children in the long term.

In addition to examining the role of family preservation programs in preventing foster care and other out-of-home child placement decisions, evaluations of family preservation services need to consider the effects of such programs in encouraging positive parent and child interactions and other factors that affect child and family well-being. Evaluations should examine the methods by which families acquire skills that foster positive family interactions and the factors that reduce crises that lead to the need for services. Such evaluations should also measure the impact of family preservation programs on parent and child functioning, psychological health, and long-term consequences for the child and family that are associated with participation in the program. Comparing families in family preservation services with those in alternative services or those who receive no services could test the efficacy of various models of intensive family preservation services as well as the effect of key service components, such as the intensity and duration of services on outcomes.

The costs of family preservation services, including all services received by families during counseling and after termination, need to be determined. Such research will provide data on the costs of treating families and would furnish a baseline from which to compare the effectiveness of different approaches.

Recommendation 7-4: Studies of foster care that examine the conditions and circumstances under which foster care appears to be beneficial or detrimental to the child are urgently needed.

Special consideration should be given to factors that might be related to outcomes, such as characteristics of the process by which the child was removed from the original home, characteristics of the foster family, and characteristics of the child (including age at placement or adoption). Evaluations of regional studies of children placed in foster care as a result of child maltreatment should be conducted to develop a comprehensive physical and mental health needs assessment for this special population. The proposed evaluations should draw on the study of abuse effects to develop a physical and mental health profile that can be used in planning treatment interventions for these children.

Recommendation 7-5: Large-scale evaluation studies of treatments for perpetrators of sexual and physical abuse and neglect (familial as well as extrafamilial), with lengthy follow-up periods and control groups of untreated or less intensively treated offenders, need to be designed to compare different treatment modalities. Because of their relatively low costs, evaluations of self-help and support programs may be particularly beneficial. Early intervention through the treatment of adolescent offenders also deserves special consideration at this time.

A large-scale evaluation to test comparative studies of self-help, support, and other therapeutic techniques should be conducted to describe ways in which such peer- and professional-led groups maintain a healthy or unhealthy change-oriented approach. The length of service and scope of participation in programs warrants research attention. Evaluations should examine factors that promote change in abusive behavior and psychological processes associated with abusive behavior (e.g., attitudes), and should identify participant and organizational characteristics associated with differential effectiveness.

Recommendation 7-6: Effective interventions for neglectful families need to be identified. Large-scale evaluation studies of child neglect should be developed to determine types of interventions that can mitigate chronic neglectful behaviors among offending parents and improve outcomes for children victimized by neglect.

Information should be sought about the historical, social, and psychological characteristics of neglectful parents in order to identify key variables that may become the focus of treatment interventions. Strategies for recruiting and retaining neglectful families in treatment programs need to be developed and could benefit from comparative studies of strategies used in modifying other behaviors that are resistant to change, such as drug addiction. Future efforts should explore the relative merits of long-term impacts of infant stimulation programs and other intensive services for neglected children and examine the relative contributions of intervention methods for different factors associated with neglect, such as lack of parental involvement or investment, lack of resources, a misunderstanding of the child's needs, social isolation, and maternal depression.

NOTES

1. An excellent review of research on emotional maltreatment is included in a special issue of *Development and Psychopathology*, Vol. 3(1), 1991.

2. Study I: Berkeley Planning Associates' evaluation of the 11 joint OCD/SRS demonstration programs in child abuse and neglect conducted between 1974 and 1977 with a client impact sample of over 1,600 families; Study II: Abt Associates' evaluation of 20 demonstration and innovative treatment projects funded by the National Center on Child Abuse and Neglect between 1977 and 1981 with a client impact sample of 488 families; Study III: E.H. White's evaluation of 29 service improvement grants funded by the National Center on Child Abuse and Neglect between 1978 and 1981 with a client impact of 165 families; Study IV: Berkeley Planning Associates' evaluation of 19 clinical demonstration projects funded by the National Center on Child Abuse and Neglect between 1978 and 1982 with a client impact of 1,000 families.

3. The National Center on Child Abuse and Neglect offered nine demonstration grants ($200,000/grant) to investigate this area in 1990, but the results of these studies have not yet been published.

4. Studies that include school-age children primarily as participants in parent training or multisystemic programs are described later in this chapter under family treatments.

5. A critical component of these programs was supplemental parent training (Kazdin et al., 1987; Kazdin, 1989).

6. In the Homebuilders model, 90 percent of 134 children remained in the home during the 16-month follow-up (Kinney et al., 1977).

7. Although researchers generally agree that prevention of external placement is an appropriate indicator of programmatic success, the use of this measure alone poses several problems: (1) it is difficult to compare placement rates over time and across communities because not all children who enter family preservation programs would have been placed; (2) placements are affected by factors that are external to success or failure in treatment, such as the availability of after-care services or institutional placements in a community; (3) improvements in the quality of parent-child relationships are not a documented outcome (Daro, 1988; Wells and Biegel, 1991).

8. This figure assumes that the child would be in foster care a total of 8 years, the average length of stay for the Maryland caseload, and that the family-based services would be provided for a total of 15 months, with intensive intervention during the initial 3 months (Daro, 1988).

9. Current training in child abuse focuses predominantly on physical abuse and typically covers only identification and reporting (Alexander, 1990).

10. In New York City, for example, although workers have an average of 19.5 cases, some workers have up to 30. In most states, caseworkers are required to have only a college degree; only in New Mexico and North Dakota are degrees in social work required (Dugger, 1992).

11. Some researchers have indicated that the substantiated/unsubstantiated dichotomy is overly simplistic and inappropriate for capturing the complexity of the child protection system decision-making process (Giovannoni, 1989).

Since the 1970s the nation has witnessed a steady decline in the percentage of child maltreatment reports that are substantiated as well as an increase in the total number of reports. Although the rising percentage of unsubstantiated reports does not necessarily reflect an ineffective or inefficient reporting system, it increases pressure on resources and emphasizes the need to reexamine present reporting laws and investigatory systems (Eckenrode et al., 1988).

12. The decision to close cases may be in response to the administrative problem of increased caseloads, but one effect of this practice is to remove potentially useful social service agency pressure and monitoring that can motivate parents to participate in treatment. Some

evidence suggests that institutional or legal pressures enhance treatment outcomes (Wolfe, 1985).

13. See Chapter 6 for a fuller discussion of the consequences of foster care.

14. It is possible that the proportion may be even higher, since several of the other categories, such as child abandonment), could reasonably be considered as stemming from child maltreatment.

15. Since the 1970s, state legislatures have passed laws to facilitate prosecution of child maltreatment cases. The rules governing the admissibility of evidence have been broadened by the Supreme Court. The types of out-of-court or hearsay statements that can be admitted into court proceedings have been expanded, and several states allow videotaped versions of children's testimony or shielding a child witness from the defendant during their testimony (Reppucci and Aber, 1992). The latter two innovations continue to be controversial because they restrict the defendants' Sixth Amendment right to confront witnesses in criminal trials. Empirical studies have not yet documented the impact of these techniques (Reppucci and Aber, 1992).

16. According to 52 law enforcement agencies responding to a Police Foundation survey, only 39 percent of child sexual abuse cases result in arrest; 42 percent of these cases are not prosecuted because they lack sufficient evidence to meet criminal standards of proof beyond a reasonable doubt or involve children viewed as too young to be credible witnesses (Martin and Hamilton, 1989). In the majority of sexual abuse cases that are prosecuted, children do not actually testify in criminal court. In one study of sexual abuse cases referred for prosecution, approximately 8 percent of child victims testified (Goodman et al., 1989).

17. Negative consequences of testifying in sexual abuse cases appear to be specifically associated with multiple testimonies, the harshness of direct and cross-examination experiences, age, lack of corroborative evidence, and lengthy delays in the criminal prosecution process (Goodman et al., 1989; Runyan et al., 1988). Intimidating atmospheres and fear of the separation from a loved one also have particularly negative effects on children (Goodman et al., 1989). Researchers have not attempted to identify the percentage of children traumatized by testifying, the risk factors for experiencing trauma, or the types of abuse that cause the most trauma to testify about (Reppucci and Aber, 1992).

Assessing the validity of behaviors and statements of suspected victims of child abuse in the absence of definitive physical evidence poses many challenges. The accuracy and reliability of a child's allegations are affected by factors such as the consistency of the account, vocabulary appropriate to the child's developmental level, lack of motivation to fabricate the account, appropriate affect, spontaneity, and consistency with corroborative evidence (Perry and Wrightsman, 1991). Most of research in this area has focused on sexual abuse victims. Young children's interactions with anatomical dolls is one type of behavior commonly evaluated in assessing suspected victims of child sexual abuse. Although anatomical dolls often help children describe what has happened to them and are often used in the assessment of young children, conflicting evidence exists about behavioral differences between the behavior of sexually abused and nonabused children with anatomical dolls (Kendall-Tackett, 1992; Realmuto and Wescoe, 1992).

18. Victim witness programs are available in more than 7,000 communities across the United States (Whitcomb, 1992). Approximately 13,000 trained volunteers serve as Court Appointed Special Advocates in dependency hearings and advise judges and prosecutors about victims' needs and request specific intervention. *Guardian ad litems* are attorneys appointed by juvenile courts to represent a child's best interests, accompany the child to court proceedings, and obtain necessary social, medical, and mental health services.

19. Existing measures developed to address psychological and other aspects of human functioning are not necessarily associated with abuse impacts (particularly sexual abuse impacts). Researchers may require new assessment instruments that are sensitive to abuse-related symptomatology with reasonable psychometric characteristics in order to evaluate outcomes of intervention studies (Briere, 1992; Elliott and Briere, 1991).

REFERENCES

Aber, J.L.
1980   The involuntary child placement decision: Solomon's dilemma revisited. In G. Gerber, C. Ross, and E. Zigler, eds., *Child Abuse: An Agenda for Action*. New York: Oxford University Press.

Alexander, P.C.
1990   Interventions in incestuous families. Pp. 324-344 in S.W. Henggeler and C.M. Borduin, eds., *Family Therapy and Beyond: A Multisystemic Approach to Treating the Behavior Problems of Children and Adolescents*. Pacific Grove, CA: Brooks/Cole.

Alexander, P.C., and V.M. Follette
1987   Personal constructs in the group treatment of incest. Pp. 211-229 in R.A. Neimeyer and G.J. Neimeyer, eds., *Personal Construct Therapy Casebook*. New York: Springer.

Alexander, P.C., R.A. Neimeyer, V.M. Follette, and M.K. Moore
1989   A comparison of group treatments of women sexually abused as children. *Journal of Consulting and Clinical Psychology* 57(4):479-483.

Alexander, P.C., R.A. Neimeyer, and V.M. Follette
1991   Group therapy for women sexually abused as children: A controlled study and investigation of individual differences. *Journal of Interpersonal Violence* 26(2):218-231.

Alexander, R.C.
1990   Education of the physician in child abuse. *Pediatric Clinics of North America* 37(4):971-987.

Alpert, J.A.
1991   Treatment of Adults Who Were Abused as Children. Background paper for the Child Abuse Treatment Working Group of the American Psychological Association.

American Public Welfare Association
1989   National Conference on CPS Risk Assessment from Research to Practice. Designing the Future of Child Protective Services: Summary of Highlights. Burlington, VT, May 9-10, 1989. American Public Welfare Association, Washington, DC.

Anderson, L., and G. Shafer
1979   The character-disordered family: A community treatment model for family. *American Journal of Orthopsychiatry* 49(July):436-445.

Azar, S.T., and B.R. Siegel
1990   Behavioral treatment of child abuse: A developmental perspective. *Behavior Modification* 14:279-300.

Azar, S.T., and C.T. Twentyman
1984   An Evaluation of the Effectiveness of Behavioral versus Insight-Oriented Group Treatments with Maltreating Mothers. Paper presented at the annual meeting of the Association for Advancement of Behavior Therapy. Philadelphia, PA.

Azar, S.T., and D.A. Wolfe
1989   Child abuse and neglect. Pp. 451-493 in E.J. Mash and R.A. Barkely, eds., *Treatment of Childhood Disorders*. New York: Guilford.

Bath, H.I., and D.A. Haapala
1993   Intensive family preservation services with abused and neglected children: An examination of group differences. *Child Abuse and Neglect* 17(2):213-225.

Baglow, L.J.
1990   A multidimensional model for treatment of child abuse: A framework for cooperation. *Child Abuse and Neglect* 14:387-395.

Becker, J.
    1991   Treatment Methods for Perpetrators of Child Sexual Abuse. Background paper
            prepared for the Child Abuse Treatment Working Group of the American Psycho-
            logical Association.
Becker, J.V., L.J. Skinner, and G.G. Abel
    1982   Treatment of a four-year-old victim of incest. *American Journal of Family Therapy*
            10:41-46.
Bentovim, A., and A. Van Elburg
    1987   Child sexual abuse: Children and families referred to a treatment project and the
            effects of intervention. *British Medical Journal* 295(6611):1453-1457.
Berliner, L., and J.R. Wheeler
    1987   Treating the effects of sexual abuse on children. *Journal of Interpersonal Vio-
            lence* 2:415-434.
Boehm, B.
    1962   An assessment of family adequacy in protective cases. *Child Welfare* 41:10-16.
    1967   Protective services for neglected children in social work practice. *Proceedings of
            the National Conference on Social Welfare*. New York: Columbia University
            Press.
Bonner, B.L., and C.E. Walker
    1991   Treatment of Abused and Neglected Children. Background paper prepared for the
            Child Abuse Treatment Working Group of the American Psychological Associa-
            tion.
Briere, J.
    1992   *Child Abuse Trauma: Theory and Treatment of the Lasting Effects of Interper-
            sonal Violence: The Practice Series*. Newbury Park, CA: Sage Publications.
Browne, A., and D. Finkelhor
    1986   Initial and long-term effects: A review of the research. Pp. 143-179 in D. Finkelhor,
            ed., *A Sourcebook on Child Sexual Abuse*. Beverly Hills, CA: Sage.
Brunk, M., S.W. Henggeler, and J.P. Whelan
    1987   Comparison of multisystemic therapy and parent training in the brief treatment of
            child abuse and neglect. *Journal of Consulting and Clinical Psychology* 55:171-
            178.
Child Welfare League of America
    1986   *Too Young to Run: The Status of Child Abuse in America*. New York: Child
            Welfare League of America.
Cohn, A.
    1979   Effective treatment of child abuse and neglect. *Social Work* 24(6)(November):513-
            519.
Cohn, A.H., and D. Daro
    1987   Is treatment too late: What ten years of evaluative research tell us. *Child Abuse
            and Neglect* 11:433-442.
Cole, C.
    1985   Group design for adult female survivors of childhood incest. *Women Therapy*
            4(3):71-82.
Conte, J.R., and L. Berliner
    1988   The impact of sexual abuse on children: Empirical findings. Pp. 72-93 in L.E.A.
            Walker, ed., *Handbook on Sexual Abuse of Children: Assessment and Treatment
            Issues*. New York: Springer Publishing Company.
Crawford, D.A.
    1981   Treatment approaches with pedophiles. Pp. 181-217 in M. Cook and K. Howells,
            eds., *Adult Sexual Interest in Children*. New York: Academic Press.

Crimmins, D.B., A.S. Bradlyn, J.S. St. Lawrence, and J.A. Kelly
1984   A training technique for improving the parent-child interaction skills of an abu-
        sive-neglectful mother. *Child Abuse and Neglect* 8:533-539.
Crittenden, P.M.
1992   The social ecology of treatment: Case study of a service system for maltreated
        children. *American Journal of Orthopsychiatry* 62(1):22-34.
Culp, R.E., M.T. Richardson, and J.S. Heide
1987a   Differential developmental progress of maltreated children in day treatment. *So-
        cial Work* 376:497-499.
1987b   Maltreated children's developmental scores: Treatment versus nontreatment. *Child
        Abuse and Neglect* 11:29-34.
Culp, R.E., V. Little, D. Letts, and H. Lawrence
1991   Maltreated children's self-concept: Effects of a comprehensive treatment pro-
        gram. *American Journal of Orthopsychiatry* 61(1):114-121.
Daro, D.
1988   *Confronting Child Abuse: Research for Effective Program Design.* New York:
        Free Press.
Davidson, H.A., R.M. Horowitz, T.B. Marvell, and O.W. Ketchum
1981   *Child Abuse and Neglect Litigation: A Manual for Judges.* March. Washington,
        DC: National Legal Resource Center for Child Advocacy and Protection, Ameri-
        can Bar Association.
DeFrancis, V., and C.L. Lucht
1974   Child abuse legislation in the 1970s. Denver, CO: American Humane Association.
Dugger, C.W.
1992   Shortage of trained caseworkers imperils young victims of abuse. *The New York
        Times.* December 28.
Eckenrode, J., J. Munsch, J. Powers, and J. Doris
1988   The nature and substantiation of official sexual abuse reports. *Child Abuse and
        Neglect* 12:311-319.
Ehresman, L.W.
1988   Two decades of effective child abuse prevention and treatment: Beating the odds.
        Missing and Abused (Fall).
Elliott, D., and J. Briere
1991   Studying the long-term effects of sexual abuse: The trauma symptom checklist
        (TSC) scales. Pp. 57-74 in A.W. Burgess, ed., *Rape and Sexual Assault III: A
        Research Handbook.* New York: Garland Publishing.
Elmer, E.
1977   *Fragile Families, Troubled Children.* Pittsburgh: University of Pittsburgh Press.
Erickson, M.F., and B. Egeland
1987   A developmental view of the psychological consequences of maltreatment. *School
        Psychology Review* 16(2):156-168.
Fanshel, D.
1981   Decision-making under uncertainty: Foster care for abused and neglected chil-
        dren? *American Journal of Public Health* 71:685-686.
Fantuzzo, J.W., A. Stovall, D. Schatel, C. Goins, and R. Hall
1987   The effects of peer social initiations on the social behavior of withdrawn mal-
        treated preschool children. *Journal of Behavior Therapy and Experimental Psy-
        chiatry* 4:357-363.
Fantuzzo, J.W., L. Jurecie, A. Stovall, A.D. Hightower, and C. Goins
1988   Effects of adult and peer social initiations on the social behavior of withdrawn,
        maltreated preschool children. *Journal of Consulting and Clinical Psychology*
        56:258-265.

Feldman, L.H.
    1991   Evaluating the impact of intensive family preservation services in New Jersey.
            Pp. 47-71 in K. Wells and D.E. Biegel, eds., *Family Preservation Services: Re-
            search and Evaluation.* Newbury Park, CA: Sage Publications.
Feringa, B., S. Iden, and A. Rosenfield
    1992   Norplant: Potential for coercion. Pp. 53-64 in S. Samuels and M. D. Smith, eds.,
            Norplant and Poor Women. Menlo Park, CA: Henry J. Kaiser Family Founda-
            tion.
Finkelhor, D., G.T. Hotaling, and K. Yllö
    1988   *Stopping Family Violence: Research Priorities for the Coming Decade.* Newbury
            Park, CA: Sage Publications.
Follette, V.M., P.C. Alexander, and W.C. Follete
    1991   Individual predictors of outcome in group treatment for incest survivors. *Journal
            of Consulting and Clinical Psychology* 59(1):150-155.
Forward, S., and C. Buck
    1978   *Betrayal of Innocence: Incest and its Devastation.* Los Angeles: JP Tarcher.
Frankel, H.
    1988   Family-centered home-based services in child protection: A review of the re-
            search. *Social Service Review* 61:137-157.
Gagliano, C.
    1987   Group treatment for sexually abused girls. *The Journal of Contemporary Social
            Work* (February):102-108.
Gellert, G.A., M.J. Durfee, and C.D. Berkowtiz
    1990   Developing guidelines for HIV antibody testing among pediatric victims of sexual
            abuse. *Child Abuse and Neglect* 14:9-17.
Gellert, G.A., M.J. Durfee, C.D. Berkowitz, K.V. Higgins, and V.C. Tubiolo
    1993   Situational and sociodemographic characteristics of children infected with human
            immunodeficiency virus from pediatric sexual abuse. *Pediatrics* 91(1):39-44.
Giaretto, H.
    1976   The treatment of father-daughter incest: A psychosocial approach. *Children To-
            day* 34:2-5.
    1978   Humanistic treatment of father-daughter incest. *Journal of Humanistic Psychol-
            ogy* 18(Fall):59-76.
    1982   A comprehensive child sexual abuse treatment program. *Child Abuse and Neglect*
            6:263-278.
Gil, D.G.
    1970   *Violence Against Children: Physical Child Abuse in the United States.* Cam-
            bridge, MA: Harvard University Press.
Gilbert, C.
    1988   Sexual abuse and group therapy. *Journal of Psychosocial Nursing* 26:19-23.
Gilbert, M.T.
    1976   Behavioral approach to the treatment of child abuse. *Nursing Times* 72:140-143.
Giovannoni, J.M.
    1989   Substantiated and unsubstantiated reports of child maltreatment. *Children and
            Youth Services Review* 11:299-318.
Goerge, R.M., and R. Kranz
    1988   Appendix A. *Data Requirements for Planning Child and Adolescent Mental Health
            Services in Illinois.* Chapin Hall Center for Children at the University of Chicago.
Golub, J.S., M. Espinosa, L. Damon, and J. Card
    1987   A video-tape parent education program for abusive parents. *Child Abuse and
            Neglect* 11:255-265.

Goodman, B., and D. Nowak-Scibelli
1985   Group treatment for women incestuously abused as children. *International Journal of Group Psychotherapy* 35:531-544.
Goodman, G.S., B.L. Bottoms, B.B. Herscovici, and P. Shaver
1989   Determinants of the child victim's perceived credibility. Pp. 1-22 in S.J. Ceci, D.F. Ross, and M.P. Toglia, eds., *Perspectives on Children's Testimony*. New York: Springer Verlag.
Herman, J., and L. Hirshman
1977   Father-daughter incest. *Signs* 2:1-22.
Herman, J., and E. Schatzow
1984   Time-limited group therapy for women with a history of incest. *International Journal of Group Psychotherapy* 34:605-616.
Hochstadt, N.T., and N.J. Harwicke
1985   How effective is the multidisciplinary approach? A follow-up study. *Child Abuse and Neglect* 9:369-372.
Hunter, W.M., M. Coulter, D. Runyan, and M. Everson
1990   Determinants of placement for sexually abused children. *Child Abuse and Neglect* 14:407-417.
Isaacs, C.D.
1982   Treatment of child abuse: A review of the behavioral interventions. *Journal of Applied Behavior Analysis* 15:273-294.
Jaudes, P.K., and M. Morris
1990   Child sexual abuse: Who goes home? *Child Abuse and Neglect* 14:61-68.
Jeffery, M.
1976   Practical ways to change parent-child interaction in families of children at risk. In R.E. Helfer and C.H. Kempe, eds., *Child Abuse and Neglect*. Cambridge, MA: Ballinger Publishing Co.
Jehu, D.
1988   *Beyond Sexual Abuse: Therapy with Women Who Were Victims in Childhood*. Chicester: Wiley.
Jenkins, S., and M. Sauber
1966   *Paths to Child Placement (Family Situations Prior to Foster Care)*. New York: The Community Council of Greater New York.
Kammerman, S.B., and A.J. Kahn
1989   *Social Services for Children, Youth and Families in the U.S.* June. New York: The Annie E. Casey Foundation.
Katz, M., R.L. Hampton, E.H. Newberger, R.T. Bowies, and J.C. Snyder
1986   Returning children home: Clinical decision making in cases of child abuse and neglect. *American Journal of Orthopsychiatry* 56(2)(April):253-262.
Kaufman, K.L.
1991   Individual and Group Treatment of Offending and Non-offending Parents/Caregiver: Physical Abuse, Psychological Maltreatment, and Neglect. Paper for the American Psychological Association, Child Abuse Treatment Working Group.
Kavoussi, R.J., M.S. Kaplan, and J.V. Becker
1987   Psychiatric diagnoses in adolescent sex offenders. *American Academy of Child and Adolescent Psychiatry* 27(2):241-243.
Kazdin, A.E.
1989   Developmental psychopathology: Current research, issues, and directions. *American Psychologist* 44(2):180-187.
Kazdin, A.E., K. Esveldt-Dawson, N. French, and A. Unis
1987   Problem-solving skills training and relationship therapy in the treatment of antisocial child behavior. *Journal of Consulting and Clinical Psychology* 55(1):76-85.

Kendall, P.C., T.E. Chansky, M. Kane, R. Kim, E. Kortlander, K Ronan, F. Sessa, and L.
     Siqueland
1992   Anxiety Disorders in Youth: Cognitive-Behavioral Interventions. New York: Pergamon
       Press.
Kendall-Tackett, K.A.
1992   Use of anatomical dolls by Boston-area professionals. Child Abuse and Neglect
       16(3):423-428.
King, N.M.P., W.M. Hunter, and D.K. Runyan
1988   Going to court: The experience of child victims of intrafamilial sexual abuse.
       Journal of Health Politics, Policy, and Law 13(Winter):1-17.
Kinney, J., B. Madsen, T. Fleming, and D. Haapala
1977   Homebuilders: Keeping families together. Journal of Consulting and Clinical
       Psychology 4(4):667-673.
Klerman, L.V., and S. Horwitz
1992   Adolescent pregnancy and parenting: The role of service programs. Chapter in
       S.M. Coupey, L.V. Klerman, eds., Adolescent Medicine: State of the Arts Re-
       views. Philadelphia: Hanley Bethus.
Knitzer, J., and M.L. Allen
1978   Children without homes: An examination of public responsibility to children in
       out-of-home care. Washington, DC: Children's Defense Fund.
Knopp, F.H., J. Rosenberg, and W. Stevenson
1986   Report on nationwide survey of juvenile and adult sex offender treatment pro-
       grams and providers. New York: Safer Society Press.
Knudsen, D.D.
1988   Child Protective Services. New York: Charles C Thomas.
Kolko, D.
in press Child physical abuse. In J. Briere et al., eds., Handbook of Child Maltreatment.
       Chicago: Association for the Prevention of Sexual Abuse of Children.
Kolko, D.J., J.T. Moser, and S.R. Weldy
1988   Behavioral/emotional indicators of child sexual abuse among child psychiatric in
       patients: A comparison with physical abuse. Child Abuse and Neglect 12:529-541.
1990   Medical/health histories and physical evaluation of physically and sexually abused
       child psychiatric patients: A controlled study. Journal of Family Violence 5(4):249-
       266.
Ladson, S., C.F. Johnson, and R.E. Doty
1987   Do physicians recognize sexual abuse? American Journal of Diseases of Children
       141:411-415.
Langevin, R.
1983   Sexual Strands: Understanding and Treating Sexual Anomalies in Men. Hillsdale,
       NJ: Lawrence Erlbaum Press.
Laws, D.R., ed.
1989   Relapse Prevention with Sex Offenders. New York: Guilford Press.
Lewinsohn, P.M., G.N. Clarke, H. Hops, and J. Andrews
1990   Cognitive-behavioral group treatment of depression in adolescents. Behavior Therapy
       21:385-401.
Lutzker, J.R.
1984   Project 12-ways. Treating child abuse and neglect from an ecobehavioral perspec-
       tive. Pp. 260-295 in R.F. Dangel and R.A. Polster, eds., Parent Training: Foun-
       dations to Research and Practice. New York: Guilford Press.
Lutzker, J., and J.M. Rice
1987   Project 12-Ways: Measuring outcome of a large in-home service for treatment and
       prevention of child abuse and neglect. Child Abuse and Neglect 8:519-524.

Marques, J.K.
1988 The sex offender treatment evaluation project: California's new outcome study. Pp. 235-243 in R.A. Prentky and V. Quinsey, eds., *Human Sexual Aggression: Current Perspectives*. New York: New York Academy of Sciences.

Martin, S.E., and E.E. Hamilton
1989 Law Enforcement Handling of Child Abuse Cases: Policies, Procedures, and Issues. Paper presented at the American Society of Criminology, Chicago.

McCurdy, K., and D. Daro
1993 Current trends in child abuse reporting and fatalities: The results of the 1992 annual fifty state survey. Working paper 808. April. Chicago, IL: National Committee for Prevention of Child Abuse.

Meddin, B.J.
1984 Criteria for placement decisions in protective services. *Child Welfare* 63:367-373.

Meddin, B.J., and I. Hansen
1985 The services provided during a child abuse and/or neglect case investigation and the barriers that exist to service provision. *Child Abuse and Neglect* 9:175-182.

Meiselman, K.
1978 *Incest: A Psychological Study of Causes and Effects with Treatment Recommendations*. San Francisco, CA: Jossey-Bass.

Meyers, J.
1991 Family Preservation Services: President's message and guest editorial. *The Child, Youth, and Family Services Quarterly* 14(3):1.

Mitchell, C., P. Tovar, and J. Knitzer
1988 *Evaluating the Bronx Homebuilders Program: The First Thirty Families*. New York: Bank Street College of Education, Division of Research Demonstration and Policy.

Molin, R.
1988 Treatment of children in foster care: Issues of collaboration. *Child Abuse and Neglect* 12:241-250.

National Adolescent Perpetrator Network
1988 Preliminary report from the National Task Force on Juvenile Sexual Offending. *Juvenile and Family Court Journal* 39(2):1-67.

National Center on Child Abuse and Neglect
1988 *Study Findings: Study of National Incidence and Prevalence of Child Abuse and Neglect*. Washington, DC: U.S. Department of Health and Human Services. [NIS-2].
1991 Conference Proceedings: Symposium on Risk Assessment in Child Protective Services. December. Washington, DC: U.S. Department of Health and Human Services.
1992 New Directions in Child and Family Research: Shaping Head Start in the 90s. Conference Proceedings. Washington, DC: Department of Health and Human Services.

National Commission on Children
1991 *Beyond Rhetoric: A New American Agenda for Children and Families*. Washington, DC: U.S. Government Printing Office.

Nelson, K.
1990 How do we know that family-based services are effective? *The Prevention Report* 1-3. University of Iowa, National Resource Center on Family Based Services.
1991 Populations and outcomes in five family preservation programs. Pp. 72-91 in K. Wells and D.E. Biegel, eds., *Family Preservation Services: Research and Evaluation*. Newbury Park, CA: Sage Publications.

Nichol, A.R., J. Smith, B. Kay, D. Hall, J. Barlow, and B. Williams
   1988   A focused casework approach to the treatment of child abuse: A controlled com-
            parison. *Journal of Child Psychology and Psychiatry* 29:703-711.
Parish, R.A., P.A. Myers, A. Brandner, and K. Templin
   1985   Developmental milestones in abused children, and their improvement with a fam-
            ily-oriented approach to the treatment of child abuse. *Child Abuse and Neglect*
            9:245-250.
Paschal, J., and L. Schwahn
   1986   Intensive crisis counseling in Florida. *Children Today* 15(6)(November/Decem-
            ber):12-16.
Pecora, P.J., M.W. Fraser, and D.A. Haapala
   1991   Client outcomes and issues for program design. In K. Wells and D.E. Biegel, eds.,
            Family Preservation Services: Research and Evaluation. Newbury Park, CA:
            Sage Publications.
Pelton, L.H.
   1989   *For Reasons of Poverty: A Critical Analysis of the Public Child Welfare System in
            the United States.* New York: Praeger.
Pepler, D.J., and K.H. Rubin
   1991   *The Development and Treatment of Childhood Aggression.* Hillsdale, NJ: Lawrence
            Erlbaum Press.
Perry, N.W., and L.S. Wrightman
   1991   *The Child Witness: Legal Issues and Dilemmas.* Newbury Park, CA: Sage
            Publications.
Phillips, M.H., A.W. Shyne, E.A. Sherman, and B.L. Haring
   1971   *Factors Associated with Placement Decisions in Child Welfare.* New York: Child
            Welfare League of America.
Pithers, W.D.
   1990   Relapse prevention with sexual aggressors: A method for maintaining therapeutic
            gain and enhancing external supervision. Pp. 343-361 in W. Marshall, M. Laws,
            and I. Barbaree, eds., *Handbook of Sexual Assault: Issues, Theories and Treat-
            ment of the Offender.* New York: Plenum.
Polansky, N.A., C. Hally, and N.F. Polansky
   1975   *Profile of Neglect.* Washington, DC: Public Services Administration, U.S. De-
            partment of Health, Education, and Welfare.
Polansky, N.A., M.A. Chalmers, E. Buttenwieser, and D.P. Williams
   1981   *Damaged Parents: An Anatomy of Child Neglect.* Chicago: University of Chi-
            cago Press.
Prentky, R.A.
   1990   Sexual Violence. A review prepared for the Panel on the Understanding and
            Control of Violent Behavior, National Research Council.
Realmuto, G.M., and S. Wescoe
   1992   Agreement among professionals about a child's sexual abuse status: Interviews
            with sexually anatomically correct dolls as indicators of abuse. *Child Abuse and
            Neglect* 16:719-725.
Reid, J.B., P.S. Taplin, and R. Lorber
   1981   A social interactional approach to the treatment of abusive families. In R. Stuart,
            ed., *Violent Behavior: Social Learning Approaches to Prediction, Management,
            and Treatment.* New York: Brunner/Mazel.
Reppucci, N.D., and M.S. Aber
   1992   Chapter 11: Child Maltreatment Prevention and the Legal System. Pp. 249-266 in
            D.J. Willis et al., eds., *Prevention of Child Maltreatment.* New York: John Wiley.

Ribordy, S.C.
1990   Treating intrafamilial child sexual abuse from a systemic perspective. *Journal of Psychotherapy and the Family* 6:71-87.

Ross, C., and M. Katz
1983   Decision-making in a child protection agency. Unpublished manuscript, Yale University, New Haven.

Rossi, P.H.
1992   Assessing family preservation programs. *Children and Youth Services Review* 14:75-95.

Roth, S., and E. Newman
1991   The process of coping with sexual trauma. *Journal of Traumatic Stress* 4(2):279-297.

Roth, S., E. Dye, and L. Lebowitz
1988   Group therapy for sexual-assault victims. *Psychotherapy* 25(1):82-93.

Runyan, D.K., and C.L. Gould
1985   Foster care for child maltreatment: Impact on delinquent behavior. *Pediatrics* 75:562-568.

Runyan, D.K., C.L. Gould, D.C. Trost, and F.A. Loda
1982   Determinants of foster care placement for the maltreated child. *Child Abuse and Neglect* 6:343-350.

Runyan, D.K., M.D. Everson, G.A. Edelsohn, W.M Hunter, and M.L. Coulter
1988   Impact of legal intervention on sexually abused children. *The Journal of Pediatrics* (October):647-653.

Salter, A.
1988   Chapter 9: Offender treatment. Pp. 111-130 in *Treating Child Sex Offenders and Victims: A Practical Guide*. Newbury Park, CA: Sage Publications.

Sankey, C.C., E. Elmer, A.D. Halenchko, and P. Schulberg
1985   The development of abused and high-risk infants in different treatment modalities: Residential versus in-home care. *Child Abuse and Neglect* 9:237-243.

Schuerman, J.R., et al.
1990   *Study of Non-placement Service Provision in DCFS: A Report to the Illinois Department of Children and Family Services*. Chapin Hall Center for Children at the University of Chicago.

Schwartz, I.M., P. AuClaire, and L.J. Harris
1991   Family preservation services as an alternative to the out-of-home placement of adolescents: The Hennepin County experience. In K. Wells and D.E. Biegel, eds., *Family Preservation Services: Research and Evaluation*. Newbury Park, CA: Sage Publications.

Scott, J.R.
1992   Norplant and women of color. P. 39-52 in S. Samuels and M. D. Smith, eds., *Norplant and Poor Women*. Menlo Park, CA: Henry J. Kaiser Family Foundation.

Sgroi, S.
1982   *Handbook of Clinical Intervention on Child Sexual Abuse*. Lexington, MA: D.C. Heath.

Sherman, L.W.
1992   *Policing Domestic Violence*. New York: The Free Press.

Smith, C.P., D.J. Berkman, and W.M. Fraser
1980   *Reports of the National Juvenile Justice Assessment Centers: A Preliminary National Assessment of Child Abuse and Neglect and the Juvenile Justice System: The Shadows of Distress*. April. Washington, D.C.: U.S. Department of Justice.

290 UNDERSTANDING CHILD ABUSE AND NEGLECT

Smith, S.L.
    1991   Family preservation services: State legislative initiatives. Denver, CO: National Conference of State Legislatures.
Szykula, S.A., and M.J. Fleischman
    1985   Reducing out-of-home placements of abused children: Two controlled field studies. *Child Abuse and Neglect* 9(2):277-283.
Tatara, T.
    1989   Characteristics of children in foster care. *Division of Child, Youth, and Family Services Newsletter* (American Psychological Association) 12(3):16-17.
    1990   *Fourth National Roundtable on CPS Risk Assessment Summary of Highlights.* Washington, DC: American Public Welfare Association.
    1992   Characteristics of Children in Substitute and Adoptive Care: A Statistical Summary of the VCIS National Child Welfare Data Base. Based on FY 82 through FY 88 Data. March.
Thoennes, N., and P.G. Tjaden
    1990   The extent, nature, and validity of sexual abuse allegations in custody/visitations disputes. *Child Abuse and Neglect* 14(2):151-163.
Tjaden, P.G., and N. Theonnes
    1992   Predictors of legal intervention in child maltreatment cases. *Child Abuse and Neglect* 16:807-821.
Tracy, E.M., D.A. Haapala, and P.J. Pecora, eds.
    1991   *Intensive Family Preservation Services: An Instructional Sourcebook.* Cleveland, OH: Case Western Reserve University.
Tsai, M.M., and N.N. Wagner
    1978   Therapy groups for women sexually molested as children. *Archives of Sexual Behavior* 7:417-427.
U.S. House of Representatives, Select Committee on Children, Youth, and Families
    1990   *No Place to Call Home: Discarded Children in America.* January 12. Washington, DC: U.S. Government Printing Office.
Van Leeven, V.
    1988   Resistances in the treatment of a sexually molested six year old girl. *International Review of Psychological Annals* 15:149-156.
Vander May, B.J.
    1988   The sexual victimization of male children: A review of previous research. *Child Abuse and Neglect* 12:61-72.
Wald, M.S.
    1976   State intervention on behalf of neglected children: Standards for removal of children from their homes, monitoring the status of children in foster care, and termination of parental rights. *Stanford Law Review* 28:625-706.
Wald, M.S., J.M. Carlsmith, and P.H. Leiderman
    1988   *Protecting Abused and Neglected Children.* Stanford, CA: Stanford University Press.
Walker, C.E., B.L. Bonner, and K.L. Kaufman
    1988   *The Physically and Sexually Abused Child: Evaluation and Treatment.* New York: Pergamon.
Weinberger, P., and P. Smith
    1970   The disposition of child neglect cases referred by caseworkers to a juvenile court. In A. Kadushin, ed., *Child Welfare Services: A Sourcebook.* London: Macmillian.
Wells, K., and D.E. Biegel
    1991   Conclusion. Pp. 241-250 in K. Wells and D.E. Biegel, eds., *Family Preservation Services: Research and Evaluation.* Newbury Park, CA: Sage Publications.

Wesch, D., and J.R. Luztker
1991   A comprehensive 5-year plan for evaluating Project 12-Ways: An ecobehavioral approach for treating and preventing child abuse and neglect. *Journal of Family Violence* 6:17-35.

Wheeler, J.R., and L. Berliner
1988   Treating the effects of sexual abuse on children. Pp. 227-247 in G.E. Wyatt and G.J. Powell, eds., *Lasting Effects of Child Sexual Abuse.* Newbury Park, CA: Sage Publications.

Whitcomb, D.
1992   *When the Victim is a Child.* Second Edition. March. Washington, DC: U.S. Department of Justice. Office of Justice Programs. National Institute of Justice.

Whittaker, J., J. Kinney, E.M. Tracy, and C. Booth, eds.
1990   *Reaching High-Risk Families: Intensive Family Preservation in Human Services.* New York: Aldine.

Widom, C.S.
1991   The role of placement experiences in mediating the criminal consequences of early childhood victimization. *American Journal of Orthopsychiatry* 61(2):195-209.

Wiltse, K.T., and E.D. Gambrill
1973   Decision-making processes in foster care. Unpublished paper, School of Social Welfare, University of California, Berkeley.

Wolfe, D.A.
1985   Child-abusive parents: An empirical review and analysis. *Psychological Bulletin* 97(3)(May):462-482.
1992   The role of intervention and treatment services in the prevention of child abuse and neglect. Background paper for the U.S. Advisory Board on Child Abuse and Neglect, U.S. Department of Health and Human Services. July 30.

Wolfe, D.A., and J. Sandler
1981   Training abusive parents in effective child management. *Behavior Modification* 5(3)(July):320-335.

Wolfe, D.A., J. Sandler, and K. Kaufman
1981a   A competency-based parent training program for abusive parents. *Journal of Consulting and Clincal Psychology* 49:633-640.

Wolfe, D.A., K. Kaufman, J. Aragona, and J. Sandler
1981b   *The Child Management Program for Abusive Parents: Procedures for Developing a Child Abuse Intervention Program.* Winter Park, FL: Anna Publishing, Inc.

Wolfe, D.A., J. St. Lawrence, K. Graves, K. Brehony, D. Bradlyn, and J.A. Kelly
1982   Intensive behavioral parent training for a child abusive mother. *Behavior Therapy* 13(4):438-451.

Wolfe, D.A., B. Edwards, I. Manion, and C. Koverola
1988   Early intervention for child abuse and neglect: A preliminary investigation. *Journal of Consulting and Clinical Psychology* 56:40-47.

Wyatt, G.E., M. Newcomb, M. Riederlee, and C. Notgrass
in press *The Effects of Child Sexual Abuse on Women's Sexual and Psychological Functioning.* Newbury Park, CA: Sage Publications.

Yuan, Y.T., and D.L. Struckman-Johnson
1991   Placement outcomes for neglected children with prior placements in family preservation programs. In K. Wells and D.E. Biegel, eds., *Family Preservation Services: Research and Evaluation.* Newbury Park, CA: Sage Publications.

Zuravin, S.J., and R. Taylor
1987   The ecology of child maltreatment: Identifying and characterizing high-risk neighborhoods. *Child Welfare* LXVI(6):497-506.

8

Human Resources, Instrumentation, and Research Infrastructure

Child maltreatment research in the 1990s will require a diverse mix of professional skills and collaborative efforts. The development of human resources, instrumentation, and research infrastructure in this field is complicated by numerous difficulties, including methodological problems in gaining access to relevant data and study populations; the absence of support for problem-oriented research efforts in academic centers; legal and ethical complexities associated with this kind of research; the lack of a shared research paradigm that can integrate interdisciplinary efforts across maltreatment types (physical abuse, sexual abuse, child neglect, and emotional maltreatment); the absence of data and report archives; and funding inconsistencies associated with changing research priorities in the field of child maltreatment studies.

A variety of disciplines and subject areas contributes to studies of child maltreatment, including medicine (especially pediatrics and psychiatry), psychology, social work, criminal justice, law, sociology, public health, nursing, anthropology, demography, education, statistics, and epidemiology. But few systematic efforts have been made to integrate research on child maltreatment with the knowledge that has evolved from recent studies of normal child development, family systems, and adult and child sexual behavior. Very little progress has been made in integrating research on various social pathologies that include marital violence, community violence, substance abuse, poverty, and injuries.

These disciplines and fields of study have concerned themselves primarily with training practitioners who can provide effective treatment and prevention services rather than undertake research. For example, the 1991 report of the Task Force on Social Work Research describes the limited support for research careers within most social work education programs, the lack of systematic arrangements for collaboration between academic and service agencies in practice-relevant research, and an absence of researcher/practitioner positions in service agencies (Task Force on Social Work Research, 1991). Furthermore, academic training for professionals who must work in the area of child maltreatment has not kept pace with the demands for expertise (Gallmeier and Bonner, 1992). Governmental or private support for pre- and postdoctoral education in child maltreatment has been almost nonexistent, except for a brief 3-year program in the late 1980s and a few graduate fellowships administered by the National Center for Child Abuse and Neglect (NCCAN). Most medical researchers are trained during subspecialty fellowships, often by federal clinical or bench research programs. Although a few research universities provide internal fellowship support, no external fellowship training program exists for physicians interested in child abuse. Research fellows who receive training grant awards in areas such as family violence or child development may sometimes focus on child maltreatment issues, but there is little continuity of effort or professional development associated with such opportunistic endeavors.

Consequently, at this juncture, considerable effort is needed to deepen and broaden the human resources, instrumentation, and research infrastructure available for addressing the key research questions. For human resources, we need young research investigators who have been educated in a relevant discipline and who wish to focus their early research studies on selected child maltreatment problems; mature research scientists who wish to contribute their expertise in interdisciplinary child maltreatment research; and specialists in child abuse research who wish to integrate their individual studies into broader collaborative efforts that can explore biological, psychological, legal, social, and cultural aspects of this problem. Efforts are also needed to foster bridges between experienced practitioners and academic scientists who have expertise in theoretical and methodological resources.

This chapter describes existing research programs for child maltreatment studies and current governmental and private support for research on child maltreatment. It concludes with recommendations for priorities for strengthening the human resources, instrumentation, and research infrastructure as part of a multiyear commitment to the development of this field.

THE RESEARCH COMMUNITY

No empirical data are available to describe trends in research personnel working in the child maltreatment area, but several disturbing elements are apparent in examining the resources available to this field. About a dozen child maltreatment research programs exist at various universities, medical centers, and child advocacy organizations, but the depth and quality of these centers and the skills and affiliations of their research staff are generally unknown.[1] No organized effort has been made to prepare a directory of research centers in the field or to describe or calibrate the growth of child maltreatment studies over the past few decades. At least 10 universities organized NCCAN-funded interdisciplinary training programs on child maltreatment studies in the period 1987-1990, but few of these programs remained in operation when federal funding was no longer available (Bolig, 1992).

Several professional societies (including the American Psychological Association, the American Academy of Pediatrics, the American Medical Assoication, and the National Association of Social Workers) have organized task forces or special studies focused on child abuse and neglect, but the level of relevant research expertise within these and other professional organizations is relatively unknown. Practitioners and research scientists have organized specialty societies, such as the American Professional Society on the Abuse of Children and the International Society for the Prevention and Treatment of Child Abuse. These societies sponsor conferences and publications to present research knowledge and interpret findings, but they lack resources to organize research committees or to prepare reports to assess critical trends in the availability of research personnel for child maltreatment studies.

TRAINING ISSUES

Graduate and postdoctorate training in child maltreatment studies was not available until the past decade. In the mid-1980s, despite growing research interest in this field, only one interdisciplinary graduate program in child abuse and neglect had been described in the literature (Duquette and Jones, 1979; Gallmeier and Bonner, 1992). Researchers who are active in the field today received their motivation and training through a variety of circumstances, through personal exposure to child maltreatment cases in medical or social service settings, through personal encouragement from faculty and mentors, and through personal exposure to the crusading efforts of Henry Kempe and other child advocates who shaped social policy in the 1960s. Researchers have been trained in a variety of disciplines, and their research projects are located in a variety of institutional arrangements in the academic sector, including family violence research centers, child development or human behavior research programs, family law research institutes, and social or pediatric medicine departments in medical schools.

Child maltreatment studies do not constitute a separate discipline, but they draw heavily on the traditions and methodology of many social, behavioral, legal, and health disciplines. The field of child maltreatment studies is evolving toward an area of multidisciplinary concentration, characterized by the following: a research literature with key classical texts that are considered essential reading in the training process, a group of experienced researchers who can lead training programs, and a set of essential methods that need to be mastered by researchers in the field. These factors need to be integrated into the training program for new researchers.

The U.S. Advisory Board on Child Abuse and Neglect has identified the necessity of the institutionalization and replication of interdisciplinary training in child maltreatment (1990). Although many universities offer graduate courses in child abuse and neglect, often based in their school of social work, school of education, or school of human ecology or human development, less than half a dozen universities sponsor graduate or postgraduate training programs in this field. Yet the number of Ph.D. and other advanced degrees that involve dissertations on child maltreatment studies has been increasing over the past decade, reflecting a growing emphasis on research in this field and a recognition of the importance of graduate training in professional practice (see Figure 8.1). A total of 403 Ph.D. dissertations on child maltreatment were prepared in the period 1974-1991.[2]

NCCAN funded $150,000 each year during 1988-1991 to each of 10 interdisciplinary graduate training programs that enrolled a total of 418 students from social work, psychology, law, medicine, nursing, education, and other disciplines.[3] These training programs were dispersed geographically and included both public and private institutions. Three programs were based in pediatric departments of medical schools, four were in academic departments of social work and psychology, and three were in specialized university research centers. The majority of the programs were directed by an interdisciplinary faculty as well as drawing on community professionals from law enforcement, child protective services, and the judiciary. The training programs achieved consensus regarding the general body of information necessary for practicing professionals in the field of child maltreatment, although considerable variability existed in the length of the programs, student eligibility requirements, and time requirements for classroom instruction and practical experience (Gallmeier and Bonner, 1992). The largest number of students in the training programs came from social work (n = 114) and psychology (n = 97). Other significant disciplines of the enrolled students included law (n = 56), medicine (n = 36), nursing (n = 29), and education (n = 20) (Gallmeier and Bonner, 1992). Students received stipends ranging from $531 to $7,000 per academic year with an average stipend of $1,959 (Gallmeier and Bonner, 1992).

Follow-up studies with these students by Gallmeier and Bonner (1992) suggested that interdisciplinary training influenced the students' career de-

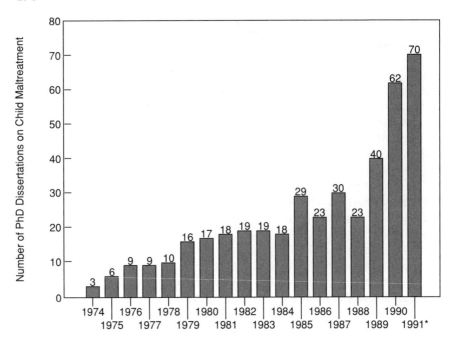

FIGURE 8.1   Ph.D. Dissertations in Child Maltreatment (U.S.)   *Estimate for 1991 is not complete. SOURCE: Bolig, 1992.

velopment, often resulting in specialization in child abuse and neglect. They reported that 61 percent of the participants in these graduate programs are now working in child abuse and neglect positions, 33 percent have been involved in research, and 12 percent have published or made presentations (30 percent) on child abuse and neglect. The reasons for the lack of continuation of funding for graduate training programs are not clear, but one implicit goal of the NCCAN program was the institutionalization of interdisciplinary training in this field, an objective that did not appear to be successful in the short life of these centers.

Analysis of the training programs and other interdisciplinary educational centers indicates that a crucial factor in initiating and maintaining such efforts is the availability of adequate funding (Gallmeier and Bonner, 1992). Extramural funding is particularly important in building and integrating interdisciplinary efforts within schools that are traditionally organized around separate disciplines and often in separate colleges (social work, medicine, and law). An essential element in the design and operation of these centers is the appointment of a full-time faculty member or administrative officer who assumes responsibility for coordinating and directing the program.

INSTRUMENTATION ISSUES

Researchers in the child maltreatment field face complex methodological issues in selecting appropriate instruments and study samples to measure the behavioral, physiological, or attitudinal factors under examination. The absence of support for methodological and instrumental research in child maltreatment studies has impeded scientific progress. Instrumentation research represents a powerful opportunity to move this field beyond theoretical or design problems toward the collection and analysis of empirical data.

In many cases, research instruments may simply not be available. Measures have been developed to assess normal child behavior or other problems in nonabuse samples, but they may not be adequate to assess child maltreatment issues and they may not be standardized on diverse cultural or ethnic populations. Furthermore, available research instruments adapted from other fields may not provide significant information for the practitioner. For example, studies using the Louisville Child Behavior Checklist (a measure of psychopathology in children) find that sexually abused children fall between the means of nonabused children and children in psychiatric care, but this insight provides limited guidance in treatment or clinical care. Finally, difficulties in the use of instruments may result from training—researchers have often come from disciplines that give inadequate attention to the importance of valid and reliable measures and empirical results. For example, in the 1960s and early 1970s the research community, primarily social workers and pediatricians, placed little emphasis on quantitative measurement of social or psychological phenomena. From the mid-1970s to the mid-1980s, sociologists became heavily involved in child maltreatment research, but sociology as a discipline does not emphasize development and use of multi-item measures (Straus and Wauchope, 1992). In recent years, perhaps as a result of the emphasis on parent-child relationships, psychologists have become the predominant investigators of child maltreatment, and they bring to the field a well-developed tradition of test development.

Measures of personality or psychopathology commonly used in child maltreatment studies have high rates of reliability and validity. In contrast, standard instruments are generally not available to measure family characteristics (Straus, 1964; Straus and Brown, 1978). Overall, the use of standard measures of family characteristics and social environmental characteristics seems to be less frequent in child maltreatment research than in family research. This may be because child maltreatment research depends heavily on agency cases for both the sample and data, or it may reflect disciplinary biases in the training of the research community.

As noted in the previous chapters, methodology and instrumentation issues present one of the most significant barriers to the development of child maltreatment research. A number of issues deserve particular attention:

- Uncertainties about the nature and significance of the phenomena to be measured. Current research emphasizes at least three different phenomena (the presence or severity of maltreatment, outcomes or effects, and risk factors) that pose different types of methodological challenges in determining their fundamental characteristics and properties.
- Absence of large sets of empirical data and inconsistencies in the type of data collected. Several different types of data have been used to create measures of the above phenomena, including direct observation in the field or laboratory, structured performance in response to a standardized task, self-report through interview or questionnaire, and coding case records or other qualitative materials. Until the recent creation of the National Data Archive of Child Abuse and Neglect,[4] no central depositories were available to facilitate the secondary analyses of empirical data sets created through retrospective or prospective studies.[5]
- Inconsistencies regarding the reliability or validity of measures used in child maltreatment research. Current instruments differ in the extent to which they have evidence demonstrating such desirable psychometric qualities as reliability and validity.

One analysis of the measurements commonly used in maltreatment studies was generated from a review by Straus (1992) of 617 articles published in the journal *Child Abuse and Neglect* for the period 1979-1989. Although a single journal is inadequate, this is the longest established (since 1978) of the journals specializing in research on intrafamily maltreatment (there are now at least four others), and it is a publication of the International Society for the Prevention of Child Abuse and Neglect. Of 617 articles reviewed, 86 percent did not use an instrument[6] to measure any variable at all. Even though there was an increase in the use of instruments in the second half of this decade, even in the late 1980s, two-thirds used no quantitative measure. Perhaps more important, the instruments invoked are predominantly those that are borrowed from other fields, rather than developed specifically for studies of child maltreatment.

The development and use of standardized measures in child maltreatment research are complicated by an additional set of pragmatic and professional factors, including the lack of budgetary support in research projects for establishing reliability, validity, and normative work for instrumentation; publication policies that discourage discussions of psychometric work that may lengthen the reporting of research results; and research sponsors' preference for substantive rather than methodological interests.

INFORMATION SERVICES

An additional topic that deserves consideration in examining research infrastructure issues is a quantitative and qualitative examination of the scientific literature on child maltreatment. Before 1970, electronic databases recorded only a dozen or so journal articles on this topic per year (Willis et al., 1991). By 1990, the annual record of psychological and behavioral publications alone was over 400 articles per year (Willis et al., 1991). But the research literature on child maltreatment is highly disaggregated—articles appear in dozens of specialty journals in medicine, psychology, social work, criminal justice, law, and other disciplines. As a result, it is difficult to track the development of any particular line of inquiry or to compare research results from separate studies.

Research literature on child maltreatment is also characterized by a large amount of "fugitive" research reports, such as project, evaluation, or workshop reports that do not appear in archived journals or books. The absence of systematic archiving impedes academic researchers who are particularly dependent on the scholarly literature for research materials.

The National Clearinghouse on Child Abuse and Neglect and the National Clearinghouse on Family Violence in Fairfax, Virginia, supported by NCCAN, provide database searches of more than 15,000 documents in the clearinghouse files. The database is available to the public through DIALOG Information Services, Inc. (File 64), which indexes publications, pamphlets, brochures, grants, profiles, and bibliographies designed to disseminate child maltreatment information to professionals and the public. NCCAN also funds the National Information Clearinghouse on Infants with Disabilities and Life-Threatening Conditions in Columbia, South Carolina. Other public and private clearinghouse services include literature that may be relevant to child maltreatment studies, such as the National Clearinghouse on Service Integration operated by the National Center for Children in Poverty at Columbia University in New York and the Resource Center for Substance Abuse Prevention and Disability in Washington, D.C.

In addition, NCCAN supports two national resource centers that provide information assistance and literature on child maltreatment issues: the National Resource Center on Child Abuse and Neglect, located near Denver, Colorado, and the National Resource Center on Child Sexual Abuse in Huntsville, Alabama. The purpose of the NCCAN-supported clearinghouse and national resource centers is to improve the capacity of public and private agencies to respond effectively to child abuse and neglect (NCCAN, 1992).[7]

In 1977 NCCAN published 21 *User Manuals* designed to provide guidance to professionals involved in the child protection system and to enhance the quality of services available for children and families. Recently up-

dated, the manuals provide reviews of information and resources on selected topics, including a guide for child protective services caseworkers;
the role of educators in the prevention and treatment of child abuse and
neglect; preventing and treating child sexual abuse; and protecting children
in substance abusing families. These exemplary documents provide valuable illustrations of the types of synthesis reports that are needed at this
time to link recent research findings to social service.

Other information services are available through clearinghouse programs
established within the National Institute of Justice (NIJ). The National
Criminal Justice Reference Services has a collection of more than 116,000
books, articles, and reports dealing with criminal justice issues. The document database can be searched directly on DIALOG, CD-ROM, or by calls
to the reference service. Associated clearinghouses are the Juvenile Justice
Clearinghouse for the Office of Juvenile Justice and Delinquency Prevention; the Bureau of Justice Statistics Clearinghouse; the Bureau of Justice
Assistance Clearinghouse; and the National Victims Resource Center for
the Office for Victims of Crime.

NIJ has developed a series of exemplary information services, including the "Research in Action" and "Research in Brief" programs of the National Criminal Justice Reference Services and the Issues and Practices in
Criminal Justice series. The "Research in Action" series disseminates re-
prints of feature articles published in the NIJ publication *NIJ Reports*. "Research in Brief" provides easy-to-read summaries of research results and
policy discussions on selected aspects of criminal justice. In addition, the
Office of Juvenile Justice and Delinquency Prevention disseminates summaries of selected research papers. Examples of relevant papers featured in
these services include "Prosecuting Child Sexual Abuse—New Approaches"
by Debra Whitcomb (Research in Action, 1986); "The Cycle of Violence"
by Cathy Spatz Widom (Research in Brief, 1990); "Police and Child Abuse:
New Policies for Expanded Responsibilities" by Susan Martin and Douglas
Besharov (*Issues and Practices in Criminal Justice*, 1991); and "Child Sexual
Abuse Victims and Their Treatment" by Beverly Gomes-Schwartz et al.
(Office of Juvenile Justice and Delinquency Prevention paper, 1988). NIJ
information services provide excellent summaries of current or recently
completed research projects to encourage the dissemination and use of re-
search findings throughout the criminal justice system.

Although some useful resources can be identified, the field of child
maltreatment studies has not successfully developed a comprehensive information service designed to integrate research publications from diverse professional and private sources in an easily accessible format. Except for the
NIJ "Research in Brief" and "Research in Action" programs, which focus
primarily on criminal justice research, to the panel's knowledge no comprehensive database currently exists that reviews on an ongoing basis child

maltreatment research findings from the fields of psychology, social work, medicine, and other relevant disciplines.

FEDERAL FUNDING FOR RESEARCH ON CHILD MALTREATMENT

Federal research support for studies of child maltreatment is divided among 28 separate offices in 5 federal departments: the departments of Health and Human Services, Justice, Education, Defense, and Department of Transportation (NCCAN, 1992).[8] No central repository currently exists to maintain an ongoing index of federally supported research on child maltreatment. The forms of federal research support are diverse, including large research center program support awards, individual research awards, data collection efforts, evaluations of demonstration projects, and individual training grants. With the exception of the National Center for Child Abuse and Neglect, which has a small research program focused explicitly on studies of child maltreatment, most federal agencies support child maltreatment research in the context of other scientific objectives or program responsibilities, such as research on violence, maternal and child health care, and criminal justice. As a result, federally supported research activities that may advance scientific knowledge of the identification, causes, consequences, treatment, and prevention of child abuse and neglect are often difficult to identify because they are embedded within studies that have multiple objectives.

Because of variations in criteria defining child maltreatment research and the absence of a central indexing service, information about the levels and types of federal research support for child maltreatment studies is difficult to obtain. The panel experienced difficulty in documenting the current level of effort of federal research support in this area as well as in estimating the relevance of individual federal research projects to studies of child maltreatment. An initial set of research figures for fiscal 1992 only were provided by the research subcommittee of the Interagency Committee on Child Abuse and Neglect. These figures are summarized in Table 8.1.

A 1990 study for the Federal Interagency Task Force on Child Abuse and Neglect stated that federal agencies reported a total of $8,168,931 in fiscal 1989 for the support of extramural research on "child abuse and neglect, its consequences and services," of which 70 percent ($5,753,061) "was used for research primarily relevant to child abuse and neglect" (Westover, 1990:30). These figures were cited by the U.S. Advisory Board on Child Abuse and Neglect in the draft of their third annual report (U.S. Advisory Board on Child Abuse and Neglect, 1992:43). The Westover report indicated that intramural support for research conducted by agency staff on child abuse and neglect was "at a minimum of $660,000" for fiscal 1989.

TABLE 8.1 Federal Funding for Child Maltreatment Research, Fiscal 1992 ($ millions)

Agency	Research Budget
U.S. Department of Health and Human Services	
Administration for Children, Youth and Families	
National Center for Child Abuse and Neglect	$5.4
Children's Bureau	0.4
Public Health Service	
National Institute of Mental Health	
Violence and Traumatic Stress Branch	3.2
Service Systems Branch	0.6
National Institute of Child Health and Human Development	2.1[a]
National Institute on Alcohol Abuse and Alcoholism	0.1
Centers for Disease Control and Prevention	0.0[b]
Maternal and Child Health	0.2
U.S. Department of Justice	
Office of Juvenile Justice and Delinquency Prevention	1.5
Office of Justice Programs/National Institute of Justice	0.9
U.S. Department of Education	
National Institute on Disability and Rehabilitation Research	0.2
U.S. Department of Defense	
Family Advocacy Programs (Navy, Air Force)	0.2
Total	$14.8

NOTE: As noted in the text, over 28 federal agencies or offices have reported research activities in the field of child maltreatment. Many federal research activities involve isolated studies that include child maltreatment issues as part of larger program efforts focused on issues such as family functioning, child development, and substance abuse. These broadly focused studies are not included in the table.

Research budgets reported were derived from a review of research project summaries that are judged by the federal funding officials to be directly relevant to child maltreatment. Projects that have an indirect relationship to child maltreatment research have not been included in compiling these estimates. The research budgets include both extramural and intramural research, although a large majority of the federal research (over 90 percent in fiscal 1992) is extramural.

[a]NICHD also supported a much larger set of research projects, not focused specifically on child abuse and neglect, but focused on issues which could be considered among the antecedents for child maltreatment. This larger set of research projects totaled $14,877,313 in FY 1992.

[b]In recent fiscal years, CDC has funded about $150,000 per year in child maltreatment research, although no projects were reported for FY 1992.

SOURCE: Forum on Federal Funding, Child Abuse and Neglect Research, FY1992, Interagency Task Force on Child Abuse and Neglect, December 3, 1992.

It is important to note that these figures reflect only research that is "primarily relevant" to child abuse and neglect studies. Additional research efforts indirectly related to child maltreatment are also sponsored by the federal agencies, although the level of investment in these secondary research efforts is not possible to calculate at this time in the absence of consensus about the relevance of studies about parent-child interactions, substance abuse, family violence, and juvenile delinquency to child maltreatment.[9]

For example, the National Institute of Child Health and Human Development reported to the panel that it supported 99 active research projects as of March 30, 1992, "with relevance for child abuse and neglect." The total cost of these projects alone was reported as $14,439,618. But only a few of these projects specifically focus on abused children. Most research supported by the institute concerns the relationship of the mother (caretaker) and infant or child and intervening factors that may damage the development of this relationship and thus may serve as antecedents for or help to explain the role of buffering or protective factors in the prevention of child maltreatment. However, child abuse and neglect is not generally addressed as an outcome measure in studies supported by NICHD.

The relevance of child maltreatment research to the central mission of each federal department appears to be idiosyncratic and uneven. For example, the Department of Defense sponsors research that is directly relevant to child maltreatment issues through its Family Advocacy Program. One such study, developed by the Family Research Laboratory at the University of New Hampshire and sponsored by the U.S. Navy in coordination with NCCAN, is examining a sample of Navy fathers who had committed incest with their daughters matched with a sample of Navy men who were not incest offenders.

Although the U.S. Department of Education sponsors prevention, public awareness and education, and demonstration project activities in areas such as the needs of American Indian children, projects for migrant families, and intervention activities for children of alcoholics, no research is currently being conducted by that department on the process by which educators detect, identify, and report child maltreatment or the relationship between child maltreatment and academic performance.

Adopting a comprehensive, precise view of research on child maltreatment presents certain difficulties of identification, organization, and taxonomy. Efforts to prevent child abuse and neglect and to improve child welfare are found among a wide range of federal programs within the U.S. Department of Health and Human Services, including Head Start, Aid to Families With Dependent Children, the JOBS program, the Child Care and Development Block Grant, Medicaid, Healthy Start, the Maternal and Child Health Block Grant, and the Alcohol, Drug Abuse and Mental Health Block Grant, even though these efforts are not "child abuse" in name and no

systematic effort has been made to evaluate the lessons for child maltreatment learned from them.[10] Various direct services for abused children and
their families, demonstration projects, and educational and information dissemination activities are scattered throughout other federal program efforts,
including the Office of Science and Education Extension Service in the U.S.
Department of Agriculture, the Bureau of Indian Affairs in the Department
of the Interior, and the Interagency Council on the Homeless in the U.S.
Department of Housing and Urban Development.

However, only a few federal programs sponsor intramural or extramural
research on child abuse and neglect. Table 8.2 presents a summary of the
federal agencies that responded to a 1989 survey indicating that they conducted or sponsored data collection efforts or research directly related to
child abuse and neglect. As noted earlier, most of these child maltreatment
research programs are imbedded in more comprehensive research efforts
such as those focused on family violence, injuries, or juvenile justice.

Clearly, not all research on children, families, poverty, and violence is
relevant to studies of child maltreatment. However, the fragmented and
specialized character of the current federal research portfolio for studies on
families, children, and violence can hamper systematic efforts to organize
and build on advances in research. The specialized roles of federal programs that are relevant to studies of child maltreatment continue to inhibit
the development of this field. Research investigators and program officers
in separate agencies are often unaware of previous studies, data, or active
projects related to their research interests. Researchers funded by separate
agencies to conduct studies on aspects of child maltreatment often work
with separate theoretical paradigms, use different sample populations, develop project-specific methodologies, draw on separate research databases,
and present their results in a wide variety of journals and professional meetings. The absence of a central tracking and documentation resource center
and the diffuse organization of the federal research portfolio, as well as the
fragmented bureaucratic and legislative requirements that are associated with
child maltreatment, inhibit the development of a dynamic and interdisciplinary research field.

Recognizing the current inabilities to describe with accuracy all relevant
federal research programs, we present a brief overview of federal research
activities that are significantly related to child maltreatment below.[11]

U.S. Department of Health and Human Services

Administration on Children, Youth, and Families

National Center for Child Abuse and Neglect. NCCAN is the lead
source of funding within the federal government for activities that address

TABLE 8.2   Federal Agencies or Offices Having Research Activities Specific to Child Abuse and Neglect (N = 28)

Agency or Office	Ongoing Data Collection	Research	Primarily Relevant to CA/N
Department of Defense:			
U.S. Air Force	X		BOTH
U.S. Army	X		BOTH
U.S. Navy	X	X	BOTH
Office of Family Policy and Support	X		BOTH
Department of Education:			
National Institute on Disability and Rehabilitation Research, OSERS		X	CA/N
Dept. of Health and Human Services:			
Alcohol, Drug and Mental Health Admin. Antisocial and Violent Behavior Branch, NIMH		X	CA/N
National Institute on Drug Abuse		X	BOTH
Children's Bureau, ACYF, OHDS		X	RELT'D
Center for Environmental Health and Injury Control, CDC, PHS		X	RELT'D
Indian Health Service, PHS	X	X	RELT'D
National Center on Child Abuse and Neglect, ACYF, OHDS	X	X	CA/N (ALL ACTIV)
National Institute of Child Health and Human Development, NIH HRSA, PHS		X	CA/N
Office of Planning, Policy and Legislation, OHDS	X		BOTH
Department of Justice[a]:			
Federal Bureau of Investigation	X	X	RELT'D
Office of Juvenile Justice and Delinquency Prevention		X	RELT'D
Department of Transportation:			
U.S. Coast Guard	X		BOTH
Total agencies or offices	9	11	

[a]Research sponsored by the National Institute of Justice was not reported in the survey.

SOURCE: Westover (1990:28).

child abuse and neglect (NCCAN, 1992). NCCAN allocates federal funds appropriated through several pieces of legislation (primarily the Child Abuse Prevention and Treatment Act, as amended);[12] assists states and communities in activities for child abuse prevention, identification, and treatment; and coordinates federal child maltreatment activities, including a federal interagency task force composed of 31 representatives of 8 federal departments and agencies.

The primary function of NCCAN is not research, but the agency has discretionary funds for research studies. NCCAN research programs on child abuse and neglect are focused primarily on intrafamilial abuse and generally exclude offenders who are not a parent, custodian, guardian, or person responsible for the child.

NCCAN administers four categories of federal funding to support state programs for child abuse and neglect activities, including (1) basic grants for improving child protection services agencies and child maltreatment intervention programs; (2) medical neglect grants to states to enable them to respond to reports of medical neglect, including instances of withholding treatment from disabled infants; (3) Children's Justice Act grants to improve state handling of child abuse cases in order to reduce adverse consequences to the child, particularly in child sexual abuse cases; and (4) challenge grants to encourage the development of trust funds to support child maltreatment prevention activities (NCCAN, 1992). At times, these state grants support individual research projects, but neither NCCAN nor the states maintain a central inventory that tracks current state research projects on child maltreatment or the findings of such projects.

Of particular interest to the panel are aspects of the NCCAN extramural research grants and demonstration awards, discussed below.

(1) *Discretionary Research and Demonstration Projects.* In the 17 years since its formation, NCCAN has funded 181 research grants, totalling $51.6 million. In fiscal 1991, NCCAN funded approximately 16 new discretionary research awards ($6.7 million) and 5 new demonstration projects ($4.6 million).

NCCAN's data collection projects including two National Studies of the Incidence and Prevalence of Child Abuse and Neglect (commonly referred to as the National Incidence Studies or NIS-1 or NIS-2) and a two-year planning grant for the third National Incidence Study. In addition, the National Child Abuse and Neglect Data System (NCANDS), developed by an NCCAN contractor, collects and analyzes information from state child protective service agencies to provide a comprehensive overview of similarities and differences and to encourage greater uniformity and consistency among state reporting data systems (see Chapter 3 for further details about NIS and NCANDS).

(2) *Use of Peer Review and Research Expertise.* NCCAN is required by law to use reviewers who have backgrounds in research on child abuse and neglect. The NCCAN peer review system has been criticized because in the early 1980s some projects were funded out of sequence of the priority scores assigned to them by reviewers.[13] Under its current administrative leadership, NCCAN has taken steps to strengthen its research infrastructure, to improve the peer review quality of its discretionary grants program, and to strengthen third-party evaluations of demonstration awards. However, problems still remain. In contrast to the study section procedures utilized by the National Institute of Mental Health and the peer review process administered by NIJ, NCCAN is governed by the administrative procedures of all research programs of the Administration for Children, Youth, and Families, which have only one annual submission date, with no opportunity for revisions and resubmittals if research priorities should change in the following year. In addition, major demonstration projects funded by NCCAN consistently lack strong evaluation components, a situation that results in the loss of important research data for practitioners and researchers. The following factors that generally discourage the development of an effective research program in child maltreatment within NCCAN have been identified by the panel:

• The absence of a multiyear program plan to guide the development of research fields and the training of young investigators;
• Annual changes in research priorities that guide the solicitations for Request for Proposals (RFPs) and that inhibit opportunities for revisons and resubmissions;
• RFPs that set upper limits at less than the cost of conducting the designated research;
• Limited funds for investigator-initiated research proposals;
• Limited amount of feedback to those who propose research;
• The use of reviewers who lack research experience in the evaluation of research grant proposals; and
• The absence of staff members at NCCAN who have research experience.

(3) *Mandated Studies.* In addition to discretionary research and demonstration projects, NCCAN develops certain studies in response to legislative requirements, often by selection of contractors from nonacademic institutions. Since 1974, Congress has mandated the preparation of eight different reports, including the series of National Incidence Studies and five special studies on the following topics: nonpayment of child support in maltreating families; the maltreatment of handicapped children; child maltreatment in alcohol abusing families; high-risk child abuse and neglect groups; and

guardian ad litem efforts. The results of these mandated studies are often delayed and are rarely published in the peer-reviewed literature.

U.S. Advisory Board on Child Abuse and Neglect. The U.S. Advisory Board on Child Abuse and Neglect, which was legislatively mandated in the 1988 amendments to the Child Abuse Prevention and Treatment Act, has established a task force to address research needs. The board does not sponsor research programs itself, but it has published two annual reports with research policy recommendations and it is preparing a third report examining research infrastructure issues within federal programs on child maltreatment.

Children's Bureau. The Children's Bureau administers formula grants to states under Titles IV-B and IV-E of the Social Security Act for foster care maintenance payments; adoption assistance for children with special needs; and child welfare services to children and their families who are in need of such services.

The need for foster care or child welfare services often may result from incidents of child maltreatment. Child welfare services also seek to assist families in promoting supportive behaviors that will prevent abuse and neglect and reunite families when possible. The Children's Bureau supports child welfare training programs and occasionally supports research and demonstration projects in areas relevant to child maltreatment, such as the prevention of parent-child separation; foster family care; institutional care; licensing; and adoption of special needs children. In fiscal 1992, for example, the Children's Bureau supported projects on the prevention of foster care placement of children at risk for domestic violence; a study on family environment, stress, and cognitive functioning in physical and sexual abuse; and the development of a multistate foster care data archive.

Other ACYF Programs. Activities relevant to child maltreatment research interests are located in various other offices and centers within the Administration for Children, Youth, and Families, including the Family and Youth Services Bureau (which administers programs for youth at risk, including runaway and homeless youth and youth affected by alcohol and drug abuse) and the Head Start Bureau (which funds resource centers and educational materials to promote self-sufficiency and provide opportunities for parents to enhance their skills).

Public Health Service

Several organizational components within the Public Health Service have developed intramural and extramural research projects relevant to child maltreatment.

National Institute of Mental Health. Recently transferred to the National Institutes of Health, the National Institute of Mental Health (NIMH) supports research and training projects in several areas in mental health studies that are relevant to child maltreatment. NIMH sponsors studies of victims of interpersonal violence, including research on risk factors and mental health consequences of childhood victimization experiences; studies on the perpetrators of violence, including research on the causes and management of aggressive and violent behavior in children, adolescents, and adults; and research on legal and mental health issues, including the handling of mentally disordered adults and juvenile offenders in the criminal justice system and mental health issues of family law (NCCAN, 1992).

NIMH research projects on child maltreatment are sponsored in the same manner as other research at the National Institutes of Health, involving the use of research experts in study section reviews of research proposals; active support for investigator-initiated research as well as research that falls within topics designated as priorities within the NIMH program plan; and appropriate feedback to research investigators who are often encouraged to strengthen and resubmit their proposals if funds are not available to support their work upon the initial submission.

Most of the NIMH research is funded through the Branch on Violence and Anti-Social Behavior, which supports studies on victimization and related legal intervention as well as studies on the perpetrators of interpersonal violence. The 1990 survey prepared for the Inter-Agency Task Force on Child Abuse and Neglect (Westover, 1990) estimated that NIMH spends about $1.0 to $1.5 million annually in extramural research on child maltreatment studies. At least one demonstration project (involving the development of an interview protocol for diagnosing or treating child sexual abuse) has been funded through the NIMH Small Business Development program.

In addition, NIMH supports training grant awards for both individual investigators and research institutions. NIMH has supported pre- and postdoctoral studies focused on child maltreatment and currently supports research fellows through institutional training grant awards in the area of family violence, sexual aggression, law and mental health, and spouse abuse, many of whom are working on different aspects of child abuse and neglect. The total amount of training grant awards for fiscal 1991 was about $400,000.

Because of the scientific strength of the NIMH research program and the perceived weaknesses of NCCAN's scientific review process, some critics—including the U.S. Advisory Board on Child Abuse and Neglect—have proposed that the lead agency responsibility for supporting research on child maltreatment should be transferred from NCCAN to NIMH. Others have urged caution in considering such a move, noting that such a transfer could lessen the importance of the situational context of child maltreatment and widen the gap between federally supported research and the social service officials and clinicians who are often a key audience for research findings on child maltreatment.

National Institute of Child Health and Human Development (NICHD). NICHD provides research in a broad range of areas related to child development, parent-child interactions, and family functioning, much of which is relevant to child maltreatment studies. Recent studies supported by NICHD include examination of social influences on child development, pathways to secure attachment, medical complications and parenting, prematurity and maternal depression effects on infants, the psychobiology of stress in failure-to-thrive infants, and domestic violence and evaluation of children's testimony. NICHD provides extensive support for research studies on early child care that have contributed to the etiology of child maltreatment. NICHD also provides support for the research on animal behaviors that are relevant to child maltreatment studies. Yet NICHD is not listed in the 1992 federal guide to funding resources for child abuse and neglect and family violence programs (NCCAN, 1992).

Substance Abuse and Mental Health Services Administration. Following the recent formation of the Substance Abuse and Mental Health Services Administration (SAMHSA), several research institutes previously associated with the Alcohol, Drug Abuse and Mental Health Administration, such as NIMH, the National Institute on Alcohol Abuse and Alcoholism (NIAAA), and the National Institute on Drug Abuse, were transferred to the National Institutes of Health. NIAAA, for example, is currently sponsoring projects on childhood victimization and risk for alcohol problems and a 5-year study to examine the reciprocal effects of alcohol and family violence in the development of alcohol problems in adult women. Other programs within SAMSHA that have research relevance to child maltreatment studies include research sponsored by the Office for Substance Abuse Prevention and the Office for Substance Abuse Treatment.

Centers for Disease Control and Prevention. The broad scope of the Centers for Disease Control and Prevention (CDC), which is to prevent unnecessary mortality and morbidity, encompasses a wide range of activities relevant to child maltreatment. For example, CDC's National Center for Health Statistics analyzes childhood mortality data and trends. CDC's Division of Injury Control, particularly the Intentional Injuries Section, focuses specifically on both accidental and intentional injuries and sponsors research on child abuse, child homicide, and assaults among family members and other intimates. CDC research studies sponsored in fiscal 1992 include analyses of geographic patterns of fatal child abuse and neglect in children less than 5 years of age; estimates of fatal child abuse and neglect in the United States; and the development of a computerized inventory of federally funded research on injury control.

Maternal and Child Health Bureau. The Maternal and Child Health Bureau within the Health Resources and Services Administration sponsors a range of activities to improve the health status of mothers and children. Although the bureau funds a limited number of research studies (most notably, the home visitation research program conducted by David Olds at the University of Rochester), it has supported a broad range of projects addressing issues such as family violence, injury prevention, minority health care, the relationship between teenage pregnancy and child maltreatment, coordinated care for child abuse victims, child prostitution, drug-addicted infants, and the sequelae of child maltreatment.

The bureau has also supported the development of interventions such as the Resource Mothers program that are designed to support new mothers in dealing with the emotional and behavioral stresses that result from the demands of a newborn.

The Indian Health Service. The Indian Health Service seeks to improve the health status of American Indians and Alaskan Natives through a comprehensive set of health care and prevention programs. It supports only a few research projects but has funded a wide range of demonstration efforts in the area of child maltreatment, including adolescent behavior problems, alcoholism and alcohol abuse, childhood injuries and child safety, and child homicide.

Office of Disease Prevention and Health Promotion. The Office of Disease Prevention and Health Promotion has addressed research issues on child maltreatment in the preparation of its report *Health Objectives for the Year 2000.* This report targets specific Public Health Service goals relevant to the reduction of the reported incidence of child maltreatment.

Department of Justice

Office of Juvenile Justice and Delinquency Prevention (OJJDP)

OJJDP is part of the Office of Justice Programs, which provides research support for a wide range of programs and services related to the handling of child maltreatment cases within the law enforcement and judicial system. OJJDP's research program seeks to develop knowledge regarding national trends in juvenile delinquency; develop a statistical and systems program for sharing data collection among juvenile justice agencies; identify developmental pathways to delinquent careers; examine methods for preventing, intervening, and treating delinquency; and analyze practices and trends in the juvenile justice system. It also provides technical training and assistance to various public and private agencies who serve the juvenile justice system. A special area of emphasis is the Missing and Exploited Children's Program ($8.4 million in fiscal 1992), which includes research and demonstration programs focused on data collection, improving the response to missing children incidents, examining the psychological impact of abductions on children and families, and behavioral analysis of child molesters and abductors. In addition, the Juvenile Justice Institute, within the OJJDP, has a research budget in fiscal 1992 of $10.7 million. About $1.5 million of the total OJJDP budget in fiscal 1992 was directly related to child maltreatment studies.

National Institute of Justice

NIJ is a separate branch in the department's Office of Justice Programs. NIJ has a research program designed to improve court processes, including the tracking and handling of child maltreatment cases as well as alternative methods of case disposition. NIJ is sponsoring a comprehensive multisite review of child abuse case processing in the justice system, to be conducted by the American Bar Association's Center on Children and the Law in collaboration with other contractors. It also supports research designed to improve the coordination of criminal and juvenile court actions in child maltreatment cases and the supervision and management of sex offenders, including child molesters. The total research budget of NIJ in fiscal 1992 was $12 million, of which $900,000 was directly related to child maltreatment studies.

Other Federal Departments

Other federal departments and agencies, including the Department of Education (through the National Institute on Disability and Rehabilitation Research), the Department of Defense (through the Family Advocacy Programs in the various armed service branches), and the Department of Transportation (through the Coast Guard's Family Advocacy Program) have small research or data collection programs relevant to child maltreatment studies. A comprehensive inventory of such programs is available in the 1992 *Guide to Funding Resources for Child Abuse and Neglect and Family Violence Programs*, U.S. Department of Health and Human Services (NCCAN, 1992).

STATE ROLES IN RESEARCH ON CHILD MALTREATMENT

No comprehensive inventory of state research programs exists for studies on child maltreatment issues, and it is unlikely that the total amount of research funds available from individual state agencies is significant (i.e., greater than $1 million per year). However, individual scientists reported to the panel that they have received occasional research support from various state agencies, including the maternal and child health departments, family services offices, and the children's trust funds in the states of Hawaii, Illinois, and Minnesota. The decentralized and sporadic nature of state-funded research efforts discourages efforts to build collaborative interdisciplinary research teams focused on complex research topics. For example, when states require evaluation of child maltreatment treatment or other intervention programs, they often have limited funds available for such research. It might be preferable for states to pool resources to develop larger, better funded, and more rigorous evaluation teams.

States are a potential source of support for specific training and data collection programs in areas such as the criminal justice, education, and public health systems that need to be integrated into comprehensive studies of outcomes and consequences of child abuse and neglect. It is useful to think of the state agencies as important partners in building an expanded research base for studies of child maltreatment.

State science programs are expected to assume a larger role in sponsoring research related to domestic health, social, and environmental issues in the decades ahead. The 1992 report of the Carnegie Commission on Science, Technology and Government, for example, concluded that new scientific and technological advisory organizations will be needed to foster better communication between and within the states. These organizations will need to improve the gathering of scientific knowledge, of learning from one another, and of suggesting research priorities in national science and technology forums (Carnegie Commission on Science, Technology and Government, 1992). Studies on child maltreatment should be viewed as an important opportunity for building collaborative state research organizations directed toward long-term improvements in social service programs in areas such as child protection, child welfare, family counseling, and foster care.

PRIVATE FOUNDATIONS

In addition to governmental research funding, at least eight private foundations have selected child abuse and neglect as a priority funding area. These foundations are the Bodman Foundation, the Carnegie Corporation of New York, the Annie E. Casey Foundation, the Foundation for Child Development, the William T. Grant Foundation, the Santa Fe Pacific Foundation, and the Edwin S. Webster Foundation. Despite this interest, the amount of funds provided by private foundations for studies on child maltreatment is quite limited.

Many other foundations support closely related research in fields such as poverty, maternal and child health, and family relationships. For example, at least 15 nongovernmental sources have been identified for research on child psychology and child development, and 13 nongovernmental sources are identified for research on child welfare.[14] However, no comprehensive inventory of appropriate funding sources for child maltreatment research from the private philanthropic community exists.

The nongovernmental sector may be an important source of potential support for dissertation and graduate studies on the relationships among child maltreatment, child development, family welfare, poverty, and parenting practices. It is most important, therefore, to see the private sector as a collaborator in strengthening the research foundation for studies on child maltreatment.

CONCLUSIONS

The infrastructure for child maltreatment research has developed in a haphazard, piecemeal fashion, reflecting the absence of a national plan for providing research, education, and professional support for studies of child abuse and neglect. Governmental roles in this area have been complicated by the absence of sufficient funds to support a robust research program, uncertainties about the most promising research directions to pursue, an emphasis on categorical program efforts in governmental research agencies, tensions between the role of the federal and state governments in sponsoring projects in areas such as child maltreatment, and child and family welfare, and conflicting social values about the proper interventions to develop in response to child maltreatment incidents. Tensions also exist in the allocation of funds between professional and social services for maltreated children and their families and research projects that seem to provide no immediate benefits for these groups.

Given the current status and evolution of child maltreatment studies, it is important to maintain a broad diversity of parallel efforts. Top-down or centralized approaches should be avoided that may discourage or fail to recognize the significance of emerging theoretical paradigms, instrumentation research, and other approaches that seek to extend the boundaries of current knowledge about the causes, scope, and consequences of child abuse and neglect. In particular, attention to cultural and ethnic issues that affect our understanding of childhood needs, child development, and family life require a breadth of effort that currently does not exist in the research community.

While diversity of effort is important to maintain, the panel concludes that better national leadership is needed to organize the research base. Such leadership requires more informed documentation of research efforts so that scientific findings, instrumentation, theory, and data can be better recorded, integrated, and disseminated to researchers and practitioners. There is also a pressing need to connect education and research so that individuals who become caseworkers, family counselors, administrators, legal officials, and future scientists have a richer understanding of the complexities of child maltreatment. Finally, the development of both young and mature scientists needs attention to build a foundation for future explorations of the intricate scientific questions that lie ahead.

RESEARCH RECOMMENDATIONS

Human Resources

Recommendation 8-1: **Better measures are needed to assess the strengths and weaknesses of the available pool of researchers who can contribute to studies of child maltreatment.** A directory of active research investigators, identifying key fields of research interests, should be developed in collaboration with professional societies and child advocacy organizations, whose members have research experience on child abuse and neglect.

Recommendation 8-2: **Governmental agencies and foundations that sponsor research in child maltreatment need to recognize the importance of strengthening research resources in the disciplines that contribute to understanding of child abuse and neglect. In particular, efforts to cross-fertilize research across and within disciplines are necessary at this time.**

Researchers in child maltreatment projects increasingly need to cross disciplinary boundaries, in terms of theories, instrumentation, and constructs, and to integrate relevant literature from multiple disciplines. For example, researchers in the area of physical abuse focus on attachment behaviors, while those who study sexual abuse examine symptoms of behavioral distress. These areas have much in common, but they are difficult to integrate in the current literature because the two forms of abuse are treated as distinct entities. Similarly, research on stress and trauma needs to integrate findings from the psychological literature with more recent physiological findings, such as those that examine the relationship between sexual abuse, stress, and early puberty.

Recommendation 8-3: **The creation of a corps of research-practitioners familiar with studies of child maltreatment, especially in the fields of law, medicine, psychology, social work, sociology, criminal justice, and public health, should be an explicit goal of federal, state, and private agencies that operate programs in areas of child welfare, child protection, maternal and child health, and family violence.**

The purpose of the development of staff positions for research-practitioners is to encourage the development of studies on selected child maltreatment issues as well as to facilitate the integration of relevant research findings into agency services and programs.

Recommendation 8-4: The cultural and ethnic diversity of the corps of research investigators concerned with child maltreatment studies is not broad enough to explore the importance of culture and ethnicity in theories, instrumentation, and other aspects of research on child abuse and neglect. Special efforts are needed at this time to provide educational and research support for researchers from ethnic and cultural minorities to strengthen the diversity of human resources dedicated to this topic.

Training Programs

Recommendation 8-5: The interdisciplinary nature of child maltreatment research requires the development of specialized disciplinary expertise as well as opportunities for collaborative research studies. Postdoctoral training programs designed to deepen a young scientist's interests in research on child abuse and neglect should be given preference at this time over graduate student dissertation support, although both training efforts are desirable in the long-term.

The absence of external fellowship training for health professionals interested in child maltreatment research is particularly appalling, given the broad range of roles that health professionals are expected to play in detecting, identifying, confirming, treating, and preventing child abuse and neglect. In addition, fellowship support is necessary to cultivate interdisciplinary training in such areas as pediatrics, forensics, forensic pathology, infectious diseases, gynecology, sociology, psychiatry, psychology, and criminal justice. Researchers in this field need resources to mentor young trainees and to guide postdoctoral investigators to funding for new research projects.

Recommendation 8-6: Federal agencies should develop mechanisms to provide continuing support, in collaboration with state agencies, for interdisciplinary training programs that can provide graduate and postgraduate education in the examination of child maltreatment issues.

Although most graduate and postgraduate education occurs within academic settings, child maltreatment research relies heavily on clinical and programmatic service needs. Therefore, the panel supports the need for providing research and training opportunities for scientist-practitioners in a variety of settings. Training in program research may sometimes involve field studies based in major national advocacy or direct service agencies.

The panel believes this approach is most appropriate, provided such studies are administered by academic programs.

Recommendation 8-7:   Research agencies should give priority attention to the development and dissemination of research instruments that have been shown to be effective in improving the quality of data collected in child maltreatment studies. Particular attention should be given in the near term to instruments that improve the identification of child maltreatment in order to lessen research dependence on reported cases of child abuse and neglect. Attention should be given to the development of instruments that are sensitive to ethnic and cultural differences and that can improve the quality of etiology and consequences studies in selected subgroups.

NCCAN has recently called attention to inadequacy in measurement by stating that research proposals should use standard and valid instruments whenever possible. This is a much needed step, but it can cause problems if rigidly applied.

For example, a program guideline that requires the use of established instruments would severely curtail the development of new measures. Most new measures are, in fact, developed as part of a substantive research project. Those that survive and become established measures do so because the investigator provided appropriate methodological information (a copy of the full instrument, a description of how it was developed, clear scoring instructions, reliability coefficients, and information on validity whenever possible). This basic type of information is rarely provided, hence the scarcity of established instruments despite the fact that literally thousands of tests and scales have been developed.

Since inadequate measurement can undermine even the best-designed study, the panel concludes that agencies supporting research on child maltreatment (such as NCCAN) and research on measures of psychological or social interest (such as the National Science Foundation) should collaborate to encourage the development of new measures and to validate existing instruments that are used in research on child maltreatment. Although there is a vast array of such instruments, it may be possible to identify variables that should have priority in measure development. One group consists of techniques to measure individual experiences with child maltreatment per se, such as measures of physical, sexual, and psychological abuse and neglect. This approach would relieve the field of its overdependence on agency samples and case records.

Measures of etiologic variables and measures of the effects of child maltreatment are more difficult to deal with because they involve a broader spectrum of psychological and sociological measures. One strategy is to select a few key concepts for measure development, knowing in advance that consensus may be impossible. Agencies funding child maltreatment research can encourage proposals for research to develop and validate measures of these concepts. However, because the need for adequate measures of child, family, and social environmental variables covers such a wide range, agencies funding social science research of all types need to collaborate in their efforts to foster measure development. Without such a commitment, peer review committees tend to focus on substantive issues and are not likely to emphasize the importance of measurement research.

Instruments that can assist in the identification of maltreated children are particularly important because they allow the researcher to move away from relying solely on witness testimony (which may often involve only the victim and the offender). The concurrent validity of available measures with real-world abuse experiences is largely unknown. Instruments also need to integrate cultural factors that can affect responses to questions about physical punishment, family experiences, and so forth.

Research Infrastructure

Recommendation 8-8: Several multidisciplinary centers should be established to encourage the study of child maltreatment and to integrate research in the training of service providers. The purpose of these centers should be to assemble a corps of faculty and practitioners focused on selected aspects of child abuse and neglect, and to provide a critical mass in developing long-term research studies, evaluating major demonstration projects to build on and expand the existing base of empirical knowledge, and building a research-based curriculum for the law, medical, and social service schools.

The proposed centers should have a regional distribution, be associated with major academic centers, have the capacity to educate professionals of various disciplines, and launch major research efforts. Examples of the cancer and diabetes research centers funded by the National Institutes of Health could serve as models, or the Prevention Intervention Research Centers established by NIMH in 1983.

Recommendation 8-9: The level of financial support currently available for research on child maltreatment is poorly documented. The Congress should request that the General Accounting Office conduct a thorough review of all ongoing federally supported research on child abuse and neglect to identify and categorize research programs that are directly or indirectly relevant to this area, particularly if their primary goal is in support of a related objective, such as the reduction of family violence, injuries, infant mortality, and so forth.

Recommendation 8-10: Very small amounts of research funds are available for in-depth, prospective, long-term studies of child maltreatment. The research budgets for the National Center on Child Abuse and Neglect, the National Institute of Mental Health, the National Institute of Child Health and Human Development, the Centers for Disease Control and Prevention, and the Department of Justice as the primary funders of child maltreatment studies, should be reviewed to identify sources of support that might be pooled for longitudinal studies of interest to several agencies.

The role of the federal government in supporting research on child maltreatment should be to develop studies and information that can lead to improvements in the treatment and prevention of child abuse and neglect as well as extending the scientific understanding of the principles and factors that influence this behavior. A formula should be developed among these, and other, federal agencies to ensure that a designated portion of available federal research funding is directed toward collaborative long-term studies. The development of long-term, prospective studies will require greater attention to the need for central archiving systems and technical guides for data collection and storage to facilitate secondary use of large data sets. Agencies that have active research programs focused directly on child maltreatment studies should explore ways in which child maltreatment questions might be integrated into national research surveys and data collection efforts sponsored by other programs within their departments.

Recommendation 8-11: State agencies have an important role in developing and disseminating knowledge about factors that affect the identification, treatment, and prevention of child maltreatment. NCCAN should encourage the development of a state consortium that can serve as a documentation and research support center, allowing the states to collaborate in child maltreatment studies and facilitating the dissemination of significant research findings to state officials and service providers.

The empirical base of knowledge that guides state programs and practices in the area of child maltreatment needs national attention and sustained organization. The states need a consortium device to organize regional and national research seminars, foster collaborative research studies, and disseminate relevant research findings to a wide pool of personnel. An ongoing information service, such as the "Research in Brief" program operated through the Department of Justice, would be an asset to the service providers within the states at this time.

Recommendation 8-12: As best as can be determined, the federal government currently spends about $15 million per year on research directly related to child maltreatment. Recognizing that fiscal pressures and budgetary deficits diminish prospects for significant increases in research budgets generally, special efforts are required to develop new funds for research on child abuse and neglect. In addition, governmental leadership is required to identify and synthesize research from related fields that offers insights into the causes, consequences, treatment, and prevention of child maltreatment.

As a first step in expanding the research portfolio for child maltreatment studies, the panel recommends that the relevant research budgets of NCCAN, NIMH, NICHD, CDC, and DOJ be doubled over the next three years.

The contributing role of child maltreatment needs to be recognized by Congress in developing programs to address a wide range of social problems and family pathologies. Our country currently spends little on building the knowledge and resource base we need to treat and prevent incidents of child abuse and neglect, particularly in light of the enormous human, economic, and social costs associated with cases of violence involving a child. Second, the panel recommends that strong leadership is necessary, within Congress as well as a consortium of government agencies, private foundations, and research scientists, to convene a task force to identify ways in which research areas relevant to child maltreatment (such as substance abuse, family violence, child homicides, juvenile delinquency, and so forth) can be more systematically integrated into the research infrastructure for child abuse and neglect. Since child maltreatment is known to be a significant factor in the development of social disorders such as intentional injury, substance abuse, delinquency, and family violence, research on child abuse and neglect should be an integral part of the funding programs for each of these areas. The goal of the proposed task force should be the development of a formula whereby each agency sponsoring relevant research should be encouraged to allocate 10 percent of its funds to studies on basic and applied research studies on child maltreatment, administered through a consortium effort that would foster long-term studies and encourage the transfer of knowledge among these separate programs.

Recommendation 8-13: Effective incentives and dissemination systems should be developed to convey empirical findings to individuals who are authorized to make social welfare decisions on behalf of children. We need to strengthen the processes by which science is used to inform and advise legislative and judicial decision makers. And we need effective partnerships among scientists, practitioners, clinicians, and governmental officials to encourage the use of sound research results in formulating policies, programs, and services that affect the lives of thousands of children and their families.

NOTES

1. These centers include the Crime Victims Research Center, University of South Carolina Medical Center; the Family Development Center, Boston Children's Hospital; the Family Violence Center, University of Texas at Tyler; the Family Research Laboratory, University of New Hampshire; the Family Violence Research Program, University of Northern Illinois; the Henry Kempe National Center for the Treatment and Prevention of Child Abuse and Neglect, University of Colorado; the Research Center, National Committee on the Prevention of Child Abuse, Chicago; the Ohio Research Center for the Prevention of Child Abuse, Columbus; the Child and Family Research Group, San Diego Children's Hospital; and the Child Abuse Training and Research section, Department of Pediatrics, University of Oklahoma Health Sciences Center.

2. An analysis of schools awarding Ph.D.s with child abuse dissertations indicates that the institutions that have awarded the largest numbers of Ph.D.s with dissertations in this field are professional schools that do not have research-intensive programs. In the period 1974-1991, the leading educators in this area, based on numbers of Ph.D. dissertations, were the California Schools of Professional Psychology (47) and the U.S. International University (8). In the same period of time, dissertations on child abuse were also awarded by the University of Maryland (10), Michigan State University (8), Florida State University (8), Memphis State University (7), the University of California at Berkeley (7), the University of Missouri (7), and the University of Pittsburgh (7). Six other educational institutions awarded 6 Ph.D. dissertations each; 11 institutions awarded 5 such dissertations; and at least 10 institutions awarded 4 or fewer such dissertations.

3. The ten universities were Indiana University, New York University, Ohio State University, Temple University, University of California at Los Angeles, University of California at San Diego, University of Michigan, University of Oklahoma, University of Pittsburgh, and University of South Carolina.

4. The National Data Archive on Child Abuse and Neglect, funded by NCCAN, is located in the Family Life Development Center at Cornell University. As of spring 1992, the archive had 11 data sets, including data from national studies on the incidence of child maltreatment, opinion surveys on the prevalence of childhood sexual abuse, national incidence studies on missing and runaway youth, and relationships between child maltreatment and subsequent criminal behavior or academic and social adjustment.

5. The National Data Archive on Child Abuse and Neglect has developed a guide for the preparation of data sets for analysis and dissemination that seeks to facilitate the sharing of social science research data in this field.

6. An instrument was defined as a measurement that combines the values of three or more "items," observations," or "indicators" to gauge an underlying continuum that can only be partly measured by a single item. Measures used in child maltreatment research generally can be classified within three dimensions: the phenomenon measured, the type of data used, and the reliability and validity of the measure.

7. See NCCAN (1992) for addresses and phone numbers for NCCAN and the national clearinghouse and resource centers.

8. In addition, the National Science Foundation funds a range of methodological studies through its disciplinary research programs in sociology, psychology, and law and social sciences, that are relevant to child maltreatment studies.

9. In addition, three other federal departments (Housing and Urban Development, Interior, and Transportation) provide training or other services or technical assistance in specific areas such as homelessness, Indian affairs, or family support programs.

10. See comments from the Department of Health and Human Services to the General Accounting Office (1992: Appendix IV).

11. A more comprehensive review of all federal programs and activities relevant to child maltreatment is included in the NCCAN report (1992). Much of the detail describing federal programs included in this chapter is derived from this report.

12. P.L. 93-247

13. For an example of recent criticism of the NCCAN research program, see R. Gelles (1979).

14. 1992 Directory of Research Grants.

REFERENCES

Bolig, R.
  1992   Child Abuse and Neglect Research Infastructure. September. Background paper prepared for the National Research Council Panel on Research on Child Abuse and Neglect.
Carnegie Commission on Science, Technology and Government
  1992   *Science, Technology, and the States in America's Third Century.* September. New York: Carnegie Commission.
Duquette, D.N., and C.O. Jones
  1979   Interdisciplinary education of lawyers and social workers as advocates for abused children and their families. *Child Abuse and Neglect* 3(1):137-143.
Gallmeier, T.M., and B.L. Bonner
  1992   University-based interdisciplinary training in child abuse and neglect. *Child Abuse and Neglect* 16:513-521.
Gelles, R.J.
  1979   *Family Violence.* Beverly Hills, CA: Sage Publications.
Gomes-Schwartz, B., J. Horowitz, A.P. Cardarelli
  1988   *Child Sexual Abuse Victims and Their Treatment.* Washington, DC: U.S. Department of Justice, Office of Juvenile Justice and Delinquency Prevention.
Martin, S. and D. Besharov
  1991   Police and Child Abuse: New Policies for Expanded Responsibilities. June. Washington, DC: U.S. Department of Justice, Office of Justice Programs, National Institute of Justice.
National Center for Child Abuse and Neglect
  1992   *A Guide to Funding Resources for Child Abuse and Neglect and Family Violence Programs.* Washington, DC: Administration for Children and Families, U.S. Department of Health and Human Services.
Straus, M.A.
  1964   Measuring families. Chapter 10 in H.T. Christenson, ed., *Handbook of Marriage and the Family.* Chicago: Rand McNally.
  1992   Measurement Instruments in Child Abuse Research. Background paper prepared for the National Research Council Panel on Research on Child Abuse and Neglect.
Straus, M.A. and B. Brown
  1978   *Family Measurement Techniques.* Minneapolis: University of Minnesota Press. Revised edition 1990 (with John Touliatos and Barry Perlmutter).
Straus, M.A. and B. Wauchope
  1992   Measurement instruments. Pp. 1236-1240 in E.F. Borgatta and M.L. Borgatta, eds., *Encyclopedia of Sociology.* New York: Macmillan Publishing Co.
Task Force on Social Work Research
  1991   *Building Social Work Knowledge for Effective Services and Policies.* Washington, DC: Implementation Committee on Social Work Research. November.

U.S. Advisory Board on Child Abuse and Neglect
    1990   *Child Abuse and Neglect: Critical First Steps in Response to a National Emergency.* August. Washington, DC: U.S. Department of Health and Human Services.
    1992   Research Policy and Child Maltreatment: Developing the Scientific Foundation for Effective Protection of Children. First draft report. June 22. U.S. Department of Health and Human Services.
U.S. General Accounting Office
    1992   Child abuse: Prevention programs need greater emphasis. August. Report to the Chairman, Subcommitttee on Oversight of Government Managment, Committee on Governmental Affairs, U.S. Senate. GAO/HRD 92-99.
Westover Consultants
    1990   Inter-agency Task Force on Child Abuse and Neglect. Prepared for the Office of Human Development Services, U.S. Department of Health and Human Services.
Widom, C.S.
    1989   The cycle of violence. *Research in brief.* Washington, D.C.: U.S. Department of Justice.
Willis, D., G. Broyhill, and M. Campbell
    1991   Child abuse: Abstracts of the psychological and behavioral literature, Volume 2, 1986-1990. *PsychInfo.* Washington, DC: American Psychological Association.
Whitcomb, D.
    1986   Prosecuting sexual abuse. *Research in Action.* Washington, DC: U.S. Department of Justice, National Instiute of Justice. Reprinted from NIJ Reports/NSI 197, May.

9

Ethical and Legal Issues in Child Maltreatment Research

Child maltreatment research requires a host of ethical and legal considerations in formulating a research agenda for this field. Although research in this field typically focuses on children who have been identified through case reports of child abuse or neglect, studies on prevention and intervention strategies as well as those on the etiology or consequences of child maltreatment may uncover previously undetected incidents of prior, current, or imminent abuse. The ethical and legal obligations of research investigators to their research subjects[1] can be problematic, especially when research topics involve embarrassing, violent, and illegal actions (Myers, 1992; Sieber, 1992a,b).

The panel reviewed the state of knowledge about ethical issues in child maltreatment research, both to identify gaps in that knowledge base and to highlight areas in which studies are needed to examine basic assumptions and guidelines that influence research behavior and project outcomes. Such studies can help clarify the needs and values of the research community, research subjects, and other parts of society; strengthen the integrity of research on child maltreatment, especially in the development of large data sets; and offer guidance when conflicts develop among competing interests.

Certain key ethical questions deserve explicit attention in the field of child maltreatment studies:

• Is it acceptable to misinform or withhold information about the purpose of a study from prospective subjects in a child maltreatment research project?

- What is the relationship between confidentiality certificates and mandatory reporting requirements?
- What are the limits and obligations of mandated reporting in the context of research activities?
- Should information obtained in a study of children's behavior be disclosed to parents or guardians?

The panel also selected several legal issues for review, although the scope of effort in this area was limited by the composition of the panel and the mandate of the study. As a result, the issue of children's rights in the context of adult relationships is not thoroughly explored in this study, even though this issue can be an integral aspect of research efforts. Comprehensive reviews of legal issues in the field of child maltreatment have recently been published (see, for example, Myers, 1992), but such reviews focus primarily on legal issues associated with the treatment of child abuse cases within administrative agencies and the courts rather than research studies.

The questions noted above are not completely resolved in the following discussion, but the panel has identified areas in which further research may assist in their resolution.

FRAMEWORK OF ANALYSIS

Ethical and legal issues that require consideration in formulating a research agenda for studies of child maltreatment fall within the following three categories:

(1) *The use of human subjects in research.* Research with human subjects involves a well-documented set of ethical and legal issues, associated with many different types of scientific studies and investigations, including experimental, field, and clinical research, surveys, observational studies, and interviews (Levine, 1986; Sieber, 1992b; Stanley and Sieber, 1992).

(2) *The use of children in research.* The particularly vulnerable and dependent status of children places special obligations on research investigators, including greater protections for the child's privacy, confidentiality, and autonomy (Levine, 1991; Melton, 1982, 1983). The developmental status of the child requires special consideration, since differences in the maturity between a preschool child and an adolescent may alter their needs for protection (Thompson, 1992).

(3) *Socially sensitive research.* Scientists involved in child maltreatment studies must confront ethical and legal questions similar to those that arise on other socially sensitive topics that sometimes include criminal activities, such as research on substance abuse behaviors, prostitution, sexual behaviors, and violence.

This discussion identifies significant ethical and legal issues from each of these categories that should be considered in developing a research agenda for child maltreatment studies. Such issues should be raised explicitly now to strengthen this area of empirical study and to inform the development of policies, regulations, and legislation that may affect subject rights and researcher obligations.

The panel anticipates that ethical and legal issues will gain increasing prominence with the growth of research activities on child maltreatment, especially as researchers acquire the ability and resources to conduct long-term prospective studies of nonclinical samples involving large numbers of children and families. Appropriate consideration of such issues can strengthen the integrity of research on child maltreatment. Disregard for these issues can disrupt research investigations and can stimulate additional legislative or bureaucratic requirements that could diminish the scope or creativity of future efforts. Consequently, the panel's research agenda includes topics that can foster greater understanding and possible resolution of difficult ethical or legal issues in child maltreatment research.

ISSUES IN RESEARCH ON HUMAN SUBJECTS

Three fundamental principles have guided the ethical framework for research on human subjects: (1) respect for persons—the obligation to treat individuals as autonomous agents and the need to protect those with diminished autonomy; (2) beneficence—the principle commonly interpreted as "doing no harm" as well as maximizing possible benefits and minimizing possible harm; and (3) justice—the principle of fairness, including a fair sharing of burdens and benefits (Levine, 1986).

In most cases, these principles are mutually reinforcing and potential conflicts can be resolved by appropriate research designs and informed consent procedures (Levine, 1986). But at times, value conflicts and ethical dilemmas can arise. For example, a scientist might be uncertain whether to emphasize the principle of beneficence or respect for persons in determining whether or not to disclose to a parent information revealed by a child, especially if the child is an adolescent.

Research on both victims and offenders in child maltreatment studies is subject to the same federal regulations that govern all human subjects research (45 CFR 46). In addition, federal regulations require additional protections for children involved in research (Subpart D). Some studies of child maltreatment may also be governed by Section 46.407, "Research not otherwise approvable which presents an opportunity to understand, prevent, or alleviate a serious problem affecting the health or welfare of children." Technically, federal regulations apply to federally funded research, although most institutions that receive federal funds apply the same regulations to nonfederally funded studies. In addition to federal regulations, several professional associations (such as the American Psychological Association) have adopted guidelines that apply to human subjects research.

Federal regulations and professional guidelines generally address the following substantive norms: There should be (1) a good research design, (2) competent investigators, (3) a favorable balance of harm and benefit, (4) informed consent, and (5) equitable selection of research subjects.

Federal regulations require that the scientist prepare a protocol that seeks to achieve scientifically valid results. The interest of the scientist in validity affects all phases of the research project, including the development of the research design, recruitment and selection of the project sample, assignment of research subjects to control and experimental groups, choice of research instrumentation, and evaluation of research outcomes. In addition, the research protocol discusses the need for human subjects, associated risks and benefits, and the use of appropriate safeguards for risks associated with the research. The research protocol is reviewed by an appropriately constituted institutional review board to assess the impact of the proposed research on human subjects and to ensure that the safeguards are adequate.

In the research protocol, the research investigator must develop an appropriate informed consent procedure that includes an explanation of potential risks of the research project to each research subject.[2] Parents or authorized guardians (who may be court-appointed) are asked to provide permission for the child's research participation. The assent of the child (who is too young to give legal consent) must also be obtained. Both the child and the parent or guardian have the right to veto participation in the study at any point during the procedure. A waiver of requirements of some aspects of informed consent can be obtained as long as certain limits are observed (Levine, 1986). For example, consent might be waived if the procedure presents no greater burden than mere inconvenience and appropriate safeguards for confidentiality are in place, such as in the use of records without identifiers. Also, a waiver of parental permission may be obtained when parents are not likely to act in the child's best interests.

Research that involves deception or unusual psychological stress often includes provision for a session to debrief or desensitize research subjects following any period of experimental manipulation to ensure that they have not been harmed as a result of the research procedure.

All human subjects research should be voluntary and noncoercive. This condition is particularly important when the research involves persons of dependent status, such as children, prisoners, and the mentally disabled. Special protections for dependent persons have evolved in federal regulations and professional guidelines, and these conditions are particularly relevant to child maltreatment research (Levine, 1991; Stanley and Sieber, 1992).

The National Institutes of Health has established the Office for Protection from Research Risks (OPRR) which provides legal and ethical guidance to research scientists, administrators, and institutional research boards. The office is authorized to suspend research with human subjects that involves violations of Department of Health and Human Services regulations for the protection of human subjects. Where necessary, it can withdraw an institution's departmental assurance of compliance with the regulations.

Each research institution that receives federal funds for human subjects research is required to organize an Institutional Review Board (IRB); the IRB reviews research protocols to determine whether they comply with federal regulations governing human research. Although IRBs are not the primary arbiters of scientific matters, frequently they discuss aspects of research design and procedures, both in terms of their impact on research subjects and on the likelihood of achieving the stated objective. If risks are involved in the research project, IRB members may request modifications in research design features to improve the validity of the study or to provide safeguards for human subjects in the proposed research project. Many funders require evidence of IRB approval prior to a funding decision and some scientific journals require evidence of IRB approval prior to acceptance of research manuscripts.

A properly constituted IRB may have as few as 5 members, drawn from a variety of disciplines and affiliations, including research scientists, administrative officials, health professionals—such as physicians, nurses, and other specialists involved in selected aspects of clinical care—and ethicists. Regulations require that IRBs include at least one nonscientist and a community representative, such as a ministers, social worker, or other individual who provides community services. Child maltreatment research protocols are often reviewed by IRBs that examine numerous other clinical or scientific studies unrelated to issues of child abuse and neglect. Because of the small number of research scientists associated with child maltreatment research, IRB members (or research investigators) who are not familiar with the literature or methodology of studies of child abuse and neglect may call on expert consultants to examine protocols in this area for relevant risks and safeguards.

Child victimization can be controversial or sensational in nature, especially when sexual abuse is involved. The potential legal liability of the research institution should emotional harm occur to children or their families during the course of the research can lead to rigorous requirements on the research investigators to demonstrate the need for the research, the validity of the research design, appropriate selection of research subjects and methodologies, and careful treatment of research data and interpretations including safeguards for privacy and confidentiality.

The wide variation in child maltreatment research projects needs to be considered in reviewing the significance of ethical and legal issues. Some projects involve only limited contact with research subjects, such as reviews of report records. Survey projects may be done in an anonymous fashion or with identifying information provided for follow-up interviews and evaluations. Some projects require more extensive interactions, and possible interventions, with parents and children. Some studies may raise only one or another ethical or legal issue; some may raise all of them. Projects that involve large numbers of research subjects, whose behavior is studied in the home over extensive periods of time, are more likely to contain a wider range of difficult ethical and legal issues than those that involve small study samples requiring only minimal interactions between the investigator and subject in an institutional setting.

ETHICAL ISSUES IN CHILD MALTREATMENT RESEARCH

Many ethical issues arise in the course of human subjects research, some of which have special relevance for studies of child maltreatment. Five issues that deserve special attention include: (1) the recruitment of research subjects; (2) informed consent and deception; (3) assignment of subjects to experimental or control programs; (4) issues of privacy, confidentiality, and autonomy; and (5) debriefing or desensitizing of research subjects following research procedures that involve deception or significant stress.

Recruitment of Subjects

Investigators often have difficulty identifying and recruiting large and representative groups of subjects, especially when investigating controversial or low-base-rate phenomena. Scientists are thus dependent on various institutions and personnel for the assessment and recruitment of appropriate subjects. Potential subjects for child maltreatment research may be referred by family service programs prior to or following a report of child abuse and neglect, or they may be selected from case reports by child protective service or child welfare officials. Since case workers often identify and recruit potential subjects, the nature of the relationships among the scientific investigator, the case worker, and the research subject in child maltreatment studies deserves special consideration.

Researchers generally are familiar with the requirements of voluntarism in human subjects research, but they are often not present when potential subjects are recruited for their project. Many child welfare agencies have a less than ideal clinical relationship with the parents of abused or neglected children (Bradley and Lindsay, 1987). The status of these research subjects, many of whom may be under investigation or involved in legal proceedings, is comparable to that of other "captive populations" in human subjects research. Potential subjects may be told, or may incorrectly believe, that participation in the research will be beneficial to their family or may mitigate severe penalties (such as the removal of their children). As a result, elements of real or perceived coercion may exist in a subject's initial agreement to volunteer for the research.

A second issue to consider in subject recruitment is the offering of monetary payments or desired goods in return for research participation. A modest financial stipend is generally appropriate to cover the inconvenience and transportation costs incurred by a participant in a research study (Bradley and Lindsay, 1987). However, large sums may be coercive, especially for low-income participants (Keith-Spiegel and Koocher, 1985; Koocher and Keith-Spiegel, 1990). The American Psychological Association guidelines for research indicate that subjects must be informed of their right to terminate their participation without forfeiting their honoraria (American Psychological Association, 1987; Bradley and Lindsay, 1987). Instead of monetary stipends, some investigators offer such items as videotapes of the subjects' children, small household appliances, and toys for the children as incentives for participation, a practice that has not been discussed in professional research guidelines.

Informed Consent and Deception

One of the most difficult ethical issues to resolve in child maltreatment studies is the extent to which the true purpose of the research project is disclosed to and discussed with the subject or parent. As noted by Bradley and Lindsay (1987), in all areas of human research scientists must walk a fine line between protection of their subjects and procedures designed to enhance the validity and merit of scientific results. The social stigma and legal consequences of child abuse and neglect, as well as the possible ramifications for individuals and their families, require a careful review of fundamental principles that should guide responsible research practice in this area.

Researchers typically believe that full disclosure of the purpose of a child maltreatment study would limit participation to admitted abusers, a procedure that would severely curtail the strength and scope of their research. Subjects therefore might be told that they are participating in a study of "families or children with problems" or "ways that families punish children who misbehave." One study of research procedures in child maltreatment studies has recommended that researchers be encouraged in their publications to include details about what was told to the subjects regarding the purpose of the study (Bradley and Lindsay, 1987).

Accurate but incomplete descriptions of the purpose of the research study are common, and good clinical judgment is often the primary source of guidance in developing such descriptions. In some cases, prospective subjects may be told that some information is being withheld deliberately (Levine, 1986). The withheld information may involve the purpose of the entire study or the nature of some methods used in the study. Many scientists believe that subjects should never be deliberately deceived about the nature of the study, but the deliberate withholding of information may be necessary to maintain the validity of the study. In cases in which information is deliberately withheld, professional guidelines have urged that disclosure should be given (dehoaxing) at the conclusion of the subject's participation and the subject should be returned to a good state of mind about the experience (desensitizing) (American Psychological Association, 1987; Holmes, 1976a,b; Sieber, 1992b). However, dehoaxing is sometimes harmful, and desensitizing is sometimes impossible.

Deception research has profound implications, since it may carry over into relationships of the subjects with their own family members as well as with clinicians, social workers, law enforcement personnel, and so forth. For example, parents who are presented with photos in which their child appears to be misbehaving (such as destroying a toy or scribbling on a wall) may conclude that their child is "bad" or may feel that prior negative perceptions of their child have been confirmed (Bradley and Lindsay, 1987). Such research practices may be uncommon, but they can affect other areas of deceptive research if inadequate safeguards are in place.

The methods of obtaining consent and parental permission are also important to consider. The process of obtaining consent involves more than the completion of a written form—it requires a discussion, in lay terms, of the purpose of the study and potential risks that may accompany the research. The consent form itself is the legal record documenting that such a discussion has occurred. Studies of college students often rely on written consent forms, but such instruments may be poorly suited to studies of populations that are younger, undereducated, underserved, or have learning disabilities. When subjects have literacy problems, or when English is not their primary language, face-to-face methods with orally presented information about the research can facilitate the consent process.

Similar problems can arise in the course of asking questions in the research process, particularly if written self-report measures are employed. In some cases, the researcher presents the entire procedure in the subjects' native language(s), sometimes assisted by translators. Studies that focus on particular ethnic groups must adapt their instruments to the traditional practices of that group. Appropriate comparative groups should be employed to distinguish maltreatment from cultural practice as well as to identify cultural practices that may contribute to maltreatment.

Some research investigators have developed strategies that use proxies or analogous behaviors to study physical abuse (Bauer and Twentyman, 1985; Frodi and Lamb, 1980; Pruitt and Erickson, 1985; Wolfe et al., 1983). Although such approaches may successfully resolve many ethical problems in experimental design, they present particular responsibilities for the investigator to fully debrief the research subjects.

The issue of mandatory reporting is important to consider in the process of identifying informed consent (see the section on mandatory reporting requirements in Chapter 3). When issues of privacy and confidentiality are discussed in the informed consent procedure, a statement such as the following might be included and explained carefully:[3]

> What is discussed during our session will be kept confidential with two exceptions: I am compelled by law to inform an appropriate other person if I hear and believe that you are in danger of hurting yourself or someone else, or if there is reasonable suspicion that a child, elder, or dependent adult has been abused.

Assignment of Research Subjects

An important ethical issue that arises in many human subject studies is the ethical acceptability of randomly assigning research participants to experimental and control treatment groups. Although random assignment is essential to scientific validity, it may be ethically impermissible if it means that a potentially life-saving or therapeutic intervention is withheld from the research subject. This issue is particularly complex when a given intervention is thought to be sufficiently effective that withholding it may constitute inhumane treatment (Kaufman and Zigler, 1992:279).

Indeed, it may be unethical to select *any* group of abused children for a control sample in which children would not have access to possibly therapeutic services. But modifications of experimental designs can resolve dilemmas between beneficence and requirements for scientific validity (Kaufman and Zigler, 1992:279). Such modifications include treatment partitioning, in which control subjects are randomly assigned to alternative treatment programs; "waiting list" controls, which make use of the often significant time lag in gaining access to a treatment program or after its discontinuance; or selecting control subjects from nearby or comparable communities that do not have access to service programs (Cook and Campbell, 1979; Seitz, 1987).

The National Institutes of Health has issued policy statements for inclusion of minorities and women in research, which should be considered in the development of child maltreatment studies (National Institutes of Health, 1991).

Ethnic and social class representation should also be considered in the assignment of research subjects to experimental and control groups. Race has often been used as a grouping variable but it has less value than characteristics linked more directly to ethnicity and culture. These latter variables often are stronger influences on attitudes and practices that are transmitted intergenerationally. The terms black or Hispanic are more political concepts than terms that accurately reflect the heritage or nationality of groups that vary by culture, national origin, and other factors (Wyatt, 1991). Sociocultural studies of child maltreatment often need to consider the immigration status of research subjects, their generational status, the extent of their acculturation, and household density. A more flexible typology is needed to identify or "unpack" critical group variables that influence behaviors and relationships. Important differences within and between ethnic groups that reflect their sociocultural experience cannot be ignored in their assignments to control or comparison groups in scientific studies.

Privacy, Confidentiality, and Autonomy

Throughout the research project, issues of privacy, confidentiality, and autonomy may arise. Guidelines should be prepared prior to interviews or observational studies regarding the conditions under which a researcher will divulge to parents or guardians details about the child's behavior. Parents may wish to know details about the sexual behavior of their child. Parents may also have attitudes about certain child behaviors (such as thumb-sucking, bedwetting, and masturbation) that differ significantly from those of the research investigator. Parental perceptions of risks and benefits may also differ from those of the researcher. Researchers may be reluctant to disclose information revealed by the child in any case, but particularly when the parent appears to be hostile, punitive, or acting not in the best interests of the child.

The AIDS epidemic has given new force to many of these dilemmas. The growing number of cases of HIV transmission as a result of child sexual abuse, for example, raises special issues of reporting, criminal proceedings, and the possibility of discrimination based on HIV status.

Another issue that affects privacy and confidentiality is data sharing, particularly when large sets of social behavior data collected for one study (such as alcoholism) are subsequently used by other researchers for studies on child maltreatment. The issues of data sharing in the use of public records are sufficiently complex that they are the focus of a separate National Research Council study (Duncan et al., 1993).

Debriefing

As in the area of recruitment of research subjects, research reports of child maltreatment studies rarely describe procedures used at the end of the project; either debriefings do not occur, or they are not considered important enough to warrant discussion in journal articles (Bradley and Lindsay, 1987). Holmes (1976a,b) has provided a useful, though dated, outline of the depth of debriefing required in deceptive research, an approach that has substantial application in the field of maltreatment studies even if deception is not present. Debriefing subjects in a post-project interview may strengthen the research study by identifying misclassified subjects (Adair et al., 1985), increase the sophistication of the research participants, and revise misunderstandings by the subjects regarding the nature of the experiment or negative characteristics of their own or their child's performance (Bradley and Lindsay, 1987).

Post-project discussions and follow-up meetings also provide opportunities for the researcher to convey useful information and insight to parents and children about practices, such as discipline, that might improve their lives.

RESEARCH ON CHILDREN AND FAMILIES

The Importance of Validity

The validity of scientific research takes on special relevance in studies of children and other vulnerable populations, when research results are likely to influence social policy and public perceptions of the problem under study (Sieber, 1992a). Information that scientists disseminate about child victimization is often socially and politically sensitive and can affect both parental and professional behavior as well as public policy. Scientific information, communicated through the popular media, can influence the manner in which abusive parents view abuse, and the ways in which victims view themselves. High-quality research is needed to provide information that has a factual, scientific basis, rather than information based on conjecture or opinion.

Because validity is important but hard to achieve in research on children and families, factors that affect validity are receiving increased attention. These factors include the definitions of child maltreatment, instrumentation and research methods, selection of subject samples, collection of data, interpretation of findings, and safeguards for ensuring privacy, confidentiality, and reliability in the research study.

Child maltreatment research often involves retrospective study of reported cases, an approach that provides a convenient, but often limited, assessment of basic psychological and ecological factors that influence the development of child victimization. In contrast, multivariate longitudinal studies of large populations that include abused as well as nonabused children are presumed to provide more valid and generalizable conclusions, as long as appropriate methods are employed (Weis, 1989; Widom, 1988). Such studies require greater resources, time, and effort not only from investigators and participants but also from institutions and service personnel who are expected to identify, treat, and prevent child abuse and neglect. Large prospective studies also expose greater numbers of children, families, and researchers to risks and uncertainties associated with observations of sensitive family behavior over extensive periods of time.

A related issue of validity is associated with the reliability of child reports and testimony. As noted in previous chapters, the accuracy and veracity of child reports and the validity of psychological measures purporting to reveal incidents of abuse or neglect remain unresolved issues. The issue of the reliability of adult memories of childhood abuse, in particular, remains controversial.

One major methodological problem associated with studies of child abuse and neglect is how to get a sample of young children to talk candidly about abuse and attempted abuse, especially abuse involving sexual behavior (Finkelhor and Strapko, 1992:161). Depending on the children's social context, their level of maturity and quality of interactions with peers and other families, and so forth, many children may not be able to identify certain forms of abusive behavior or to perceive it as such. Adult survivors may not recall incidents of abuse that occurred during their childhood, even if the investigator has obtained records that document such experiences. Children, or their parents, may be unwilling to discuss incidents that are personally embarrassing, violent, or stressful, especially if they believe that they were responsible for these incidents or that discussion of the incidents will cause harm to family members, not change their interactions with the offender, and not prevent future such incidents. Exaggeration, manipulation, and distortion of the circumstances of the abuse experience, especially in retrospective studies, are also possibilities.

Interviews in which researchers or therapists have been viewed as manipulating children into disclosing incidents of abuse that did not actually occur has generated much discussion about the roles and responsibilities of professionals in this field. Such concern has resulted in symposia and articles about the boundaries of appropriate professional behavior in conducting interviews with children about incidents of abuse and neglect, especially in cases in which no report of abuse has been filed.

Many investigators seem to be able to conduct intensive interviews with children about these matters successfully, but several ethical issues require consideration in this research. As identified by Finkelhor and Strapko (1992), these issues include: (1) whether and how to get parental permission to conduct such interviews; (2) how to handle state reporting requirements, especially when research interviews reveal abusive or neglectful practices that do not appear to harm the children and that the children do not wish to disclose; and (3) how to reduce the trauma of the interview itself.

Such issues are particularly important to address and resolve in developing prevention efforts so that unintended consequences may be avoided.

Research evaluations, especially in the area of child sexual abuse, have suggested that some prevention programs (such as the "good touch, bad touch" educational programs) may not diminish child maltreatment, often stimulate greater disclosure of abuse reports among the child participants, and may have unintended long-term consequences on adult sexual behavior (such as distrust of physical or sexual intimacy) that have not been carefully considered in the development of the program (Conte, 1987).

In addition to these ethical issues, legal considerations may affect the validity of child maltreatment research. For example, who is authorized to give permission for a child to participate in a study of child abuse and neglect if the parent is the alleged perpetrator or cooperated with the abusing parent? Do individual parties have a right of access to information disclosed in the course of a research study if the information is pertinent to a case that is in litigation or that may be appealed?

Dissemination of Research Results

Research on child maltreatment receives much public attention because it affects children and adults directly and shapes norms and perceptions that can influence policy directives much more rapidly than research in fields of study more distant from everyday human activity (Sieber, 1992a). Research on human behavior often involves unique subject populations that cannot be replicated. As such it is far more politically and socially sensitive than research in the physical sciences, in which controversial or uncertain research findings can often be tested by replication. Thus, breakthroughs in the physical sciences are far easier to verify, but also far more difficult to discuss or interpret without specialized training. They are more likely to be discussed in the media only when significant scientific generalizations (or exorbitant research costs) have been achieved that are understandable to the public. Public misinterpretation or misunderstanding of physical sciences research findings, even if it occurs, rarely has immediate social consequences.

Problems can arise when misinformation about child abuse and neglect is disseminated to the general public. Such problems are particularly significant when members of the research community are the initial sources of reports of invalid research results on child maltreatment. Unconfirmed or inaccurate research findings may also be publicized by the press against the advice or wishes of the researchers. Such incidents can result in vigorous, often sensational, discussions in media and social policy circles.

RESEARCH ON SOCIALLY SENSITIVE TOPICS

Scientific studies of child maltreatment require extraordinary care and confidentiality in eliciting, safeguarding, and disclosing information from respondents because of the socially sensitive nature of the research subject. Family disciplinary practices, the use of violence between family members, and expressions of anger or rage are difficult to detect, observe, and record. Research on children's sexual development is one of the most unexamined areas in all of social science and is impeded by a variety of social taboos (Finkelhor and Strapko, 1992; Furstenberg et al., 1989; Wyatt et al., in press). Political sensitivities have impeded governmental support for studies of sexual behavior in general and discussions of sexual behavior with children in particular. Ethical ambiguities surround this topic.

Unlike priests, physicians, and lawyers, social scientists are not traditionally entitled to testimonial privilege. Scientists do not have an unrestricted right to determine whether to reveal to a law enforcement officer or a court official the identity of their research subjects or the nature or sources of their information. Field researchers who conduct studies of criminal behavior or socially sensitive behavior may be subject to legal interventions when data are thought to be relevant to cases that are in litigation or are under judicial or legislative review (Myers, 1992). Conflicts between the interests of law enforcement officials and the goals of the research community have resulted in the development of specific legislative exemptions— called certificates of confidentiality—that protect some scientists from subpoenas of their research data.

The certificate of confidentiality is the most effective, yet underutilized, protection against subpoena. Researchers involved in socially sensitive studies also have sometimes relied on anonymous data collection, the use of aliases, transmission of data to colleagues in foreign countries, and statistical strategies as ways of guarding the confidentiality of their data (Sieber, 1992b).

The U.S. Department of Health and Human Services may authorize certificates of confidentiality for research investigators conducting socially sensitive research to protect the identities of their research subjects (Levine, 1986; 42 CFR Part 2a). The certificates provide immunity from subpoena, and are most commonly requested in the conduct of research sponsored by the National Institute of Mental Health, the National Institute of Alcoholism and Alcoholic Abuse, and the National Institue of Drug Abuse, although the research need not be funded by or connected with any federal agency (Sieber, 1992b). Certificates of confidentiality are available on application to the NIH Office for Protection from Research Risk for any funded or unfunded research if there is concern that confidentiality is necessary to achieve the research objectives. Certificates of confidentiality are also available for research funded by the Department of Justice. Legal protections have established that information developed through research supported by the National Institute of Justice, for example, "shall be immune from the legal process" (42 U.S.C. 3789).

Although the federal certificate of confidentiality may preempt state reporting requirements, legal opinions on this matter differ (Sieber, 1992a). Few researchers have obtained certificates of confidentiality (Melton, 1990), and none have tested the relevance of such waivers to the mandatory reporting requirements of state child welfare laws. Hence, the prevailing practice is for researchers to assume that certificates of confidentiality or waivers do *not* preempt state reporting laws, and the informed consent procedure serves as the mechanism by which scientists warn research subjects of their reporting obligations. There appears to be no penalty for the researcher who testifies after obtaining a certificate of confidentiality, but criminal penalties do exist for those who deliberately withhold evidence of suspected child maltreatment.

CONCLUSIONS

Researchers who seek to foster valid and creative research projects must address fundamental ethical issues in the recruitment of research subjects; the process of obtaining informed consent; the assignment of subjects; debriefing, dehoaxing, and desensitizing subjects when deception or stressful research is involved; and in providing referrals for children and family members in distress. The ethical and legal issues in child maltreatment research discussed here have been derived from legal and ethical literature regarding the use of human subjects in research, the use of children as research subjects, and the conduct of research on socially sensitive topics.

If larger prospective, longitudinal studies of child maltreatment are developed, as recommended in this report, the ethical and legal issues discussed in this chapter will acquire greater importance and emphasis. The need to ensure the validity of large cohort studies and to develop rigorous evaluations of interventions that might serve as models for other communities will require increased emphasis on issues of scientific validity, data sharing, conflicts between principles of confidentiality and disclosure, and the need for legal protections. Finally, the nature of professional and legal rights and obligations in areas such as mandated reporting, confidentiality for research subjects, and informed consent require more detailed review and analysis.

RESEARCH RECOMMENDATIONS

The panel believes that a research agenda for child maltreatment studies should include attention to fundamental ethical and legal issues that pervade this field of inquiry. In particular, the panel recommends the following topics as research priorities:

Recommendation 9-1: The disclosure of unreported incidents of abuse by research subjects requires greater analysis to clarify the circumstances that foster such disclosures, the methods by which researchers respond to subject disclosures, and the outcomes for research subjects who disclose incidents of maltreatment.

Public awareness of the traumatic consequences of child abuse and neglect may begin to affect research participation. Children and adult survivors who disclose unreported incidents of maltreatment to researchers will require professional guidance and support in dealing with the consequences of their maltreatment. Furthermore, the ethical and legal role of researchers in responding to such disclosures requires methodological considerations in formulating appropriate guidance for the research community.

Recommendation 9-2: Methodological research is needed to develop design procedures and resources that can resolve ethical problems associated with recruitment, informed consent, privacy and confidentiality, and assignment of experimental and control groups.

In particular, the use of masked data strategies may acquire additional importance in the development of large data sets that will be used in secondary analyses by researchers who were not associated with the primary collection of the data. These issues would benefit from clarification of the nature of conflicting interests in the course of research, development of clinical advice and experience that can resolve such conflicts, and identification of methods by which such guidance could be communicated to researchers, institutional research boards, research administrators, research subjects, and others.

Ethical issues likely to arise in longitudinal prospective studies need to be identified, to clarify principles of responsible conduct regarding the treatment of risk factors, suspected abuse scenarios, and the rights of research subjects to privacy and confidentiality. Issues related to the sharing of research data, particularly in studies that were not designed as child maltreatment research projects, will need to be addressed in research that focuses on antecedents and consequences of various forms of abuse and neglect. The selection of appropriate models for long-term studies also requires consideration.

Recommendation 9-3: Research is needed to determine the impact of debriefings both on subjects' post-project perceptions as well as on research results. This research will have ethical implications for the inclusion or omission of such interviews in research designs.

Recommendation 9-4: Research on the institutional research board process should be done to improve the quality of the process by which studies of child abuse and neglect are initiated and approved.

The research community could benefit from studies that determine factors that influence approval and disapproval decisions by institutional research boards, the use of waivers and certificates of confidentiality, and other aspects of ethical decision making connected with research on child maltreatment.

NOTES

1. The term *research subject* has sometimes been replaced by the term *research participant* to convey more respect for those who participate in research studies. As noted by Sieber (1992b:13), however, the term subject "continually reminds the reader that the person being studied typically has less power than the researcher and must be accorded the protections that render this inequality morally acceptable." In the case of research on children, it is highly likely that they will more often be "subjects" than "participants."

2. Informed consent involves several basic components, including a description of the purpose of the research project, an explanation of the procedures in which the subject will participate, and a discussion of potential risks of the project. Following this presentation, the research subject is asked to sign a written form indicating that he or she understands the purpose of the study and agrees to participate. When children are involved as research subjects in the study, the parent or guardian is requested to sign an "assent" form as a proxy for the child. The documentation for informed consent may be waived in some instances.

3. Adapted from a statement developed by David H. Ruja, discussed in E. Gil, *The California Child Abuse Reporting Law: Issues and Answers for Professionals*. Publication 132(10/86). Sacramento, CA: California Department of Social Services, Office of Child Abuse Prevention.

REFERENCES

Adair, J.G., T.W. Dushenko, and R.C. Lindsay
     1985   Ethical regulations and their impact on research practice. *American Psychologist* 40:59-72.
American Psychological Association
     1987   *Casebook on Ethical Principles of Psychologists*. Washington, DC: American Psychological Association.
Bauer, W.D., and C.T. Twentyman
     1985   Abusing, neglectful and comparison mother's responses to child-related and non-child-related stressors. *Journal of Consulting Clinical Psychology* 53:335-343.
Bradley, E.J., and R.C. Lindsay
     1987   Methodological and ethical issues in child abuse research. *Journal of Family Violence* 2(3):239-255.
Conte, J.
     1987   Ethical issues in evaluation of prevention programs. *Child Abuse and Neglect*. 11(2):171-172.
Cook, T., and D. Campbell
     1979   *Quasi-Experimental Design and Analysis Issues for Field Settings*. Chicago: Rand McNally.

Duncan, G.T., T.B. Jabine, and V.A. deWolf, eds.
1993   *Private Lives and Public Policies: Confidentiality and Accessibility of Govern-ment Statistics.* Washington, DC: National Academy Press.
Finkelhor, D., and N. Strapko
1992   Sexual abuse and prevention education: A review of evaluation studies. Chapter 7 in D.J. Willis, E.W. Holden, and M. Rosenberg, eds., *Prevention of Child Mal-treatment.* New York: John Wiley and Sons.
Frodi, A.M., and M.E. Lamb
1980   Child abusers' responses to infant smiles and cries. *Child Development* 51:238-241.
Furstenberg, F.F., J. Brooks-Gunn, and L. Chase-Landsdale
1989   Adolescent fertility and public policy. *American Psychologist* 44(2):313-320.
Gil, E.
1982   The California child abuse reporting law: Issues and answers for professionals. Publication 132 (10/86). This booklet is printed and distributed by the State of California Department for Social Services, Office of Child Abuse Prevention, 744 P Street, M.S. 9-100, Sacramento, CA, 95815.
Holmes, D.S.
1976a   Debriefing after psychological experiment: I. Effectiveness of postdeception dehoaxing. *American Psychologist* 31:858-867.
1976b   Debriefing after psychological experiment: II. Effectiveness of experimental de-sensitizing. *American Psychologist* 31:868-875.
Kaufman, J., and E. Zigler
1992   The prevention of child maltreatment: Programming, research, and policy. Chap-ter 12 in D.J. Willis, E.W. Holden, and M. Rosenberg, eds., *Prevention of Child Maltreatment.* New York: John Wiley and Sons.
Keith-Spiegel, P., and G.P. Koocher
1985   *Ethics in Psychology Professional Standards and Cases.* New York: Random House.
Koocher, G.P., and P. Keith-Spiegel
1990   *Children, Ethics, and the Law: Professional Issues and Cases.* Lincoln: Univer-sity of Nebraska Press.
Levine, R.J.
1986   *Ethics and Regulation of Clinical Research.* Second edition. New Haven: Yale University Press.
1991   Respect for children as research subjects. Chapter 117 in M. Lewis, ed., *Child and Adolescent Psychiatry; A Comprehensive Textbook.* Baltimore: Williams and Wilkins.
Melton, G.
1982   Children's rights: Where are the children? *American Journal of Orthopsychiatry* 52(3):530-538.
1983   *Child Advocacy: Psychological Issues and Interventions.* New York: Plenum Press.
1990   Certificates of confidentiality under the Public Health Service Act: Strong protec-tion but not enough. *Violence and Victims* 12:369-386.
Myers, J.E.B.
1992   *Legal Issues in Child Abuse and Neglect.* Newbury Park, CA: Sage Publications.
National Institutes of Health
1991   NIH Guide to Grants and Contracts. 20(32):1-3. August 23.
Pruitt, D.L., and M.T. Erickson
1985   The Child Abuse Potential Inventory: A study of concurrent validity. *Journal of Clinical Psychology* 41:104-111.

Seitz, V.
    1987   Outcome evaluation of family support programs: Research design alternatives to true experiments. In S.L. Kagan, D. Powell, B. Weissbound, and E. Zigler, eds., *America's Family Support Programs: Perspectives and Prospects.* New Haven: Yale University Press.
Sieber, J.
    1992a   Issues Presented by Mandatory Reporting Requirements. Background paper prepared for the National Research Council's Panel on Research on Child Abuse and Neglect.
    1992b   *Planning Ethically Responsible Research.* Newbury Park, CA: Sage Publications.
Stanley, B., and J.E. Sieber, eds.
    1992   *Social Research on Children and Adolescents: Ethical Issues.* Newbury Park, CA: Sage Publications.
Thompson, R.A.
    1992   Developmental changes in research risk and benefit: A changing calculus of concerns. Chapter in B. Stanley and J.E. Sieber, eds., *Social Research on Children and Adolescents: Ethical Issues.* Newbury Park, CA: Sage Publications.
Weis, J.G.
    1989   Family violence research methodology and design. In L. Ohlin and M. Tonry, eds., *Family Violence.* Chicago: University of Chicago Press.
Widom, C.
    1988   Sampling biases and implications for child abuse research. *American Orthopsychiatric Association* 58(2):260-270.
Wolfe, D.A., J.A. Fairbank, J.A. Kelly, and A.S. Bradlyn
    1983   Child abusive parents' physiological responses to stressful and non-stressful behavior in children. *Behavior Assessment* 5:363-371.
Wyatt, G.E.
    1991   Examining ethnicity versus race in AIDS related research. *Social Science and Medicine* 33(1):37-45.
Wyatt, G.E., M. Newcombe, M. Riederlee, and C. Notgrass
    in press *The Effects of Child Sexual Abuse on Women's Sexual and Psychological Functioning.* Newbury Park, CA: Sage Publications.

10

Priorities for Child Maltreatment Research

Despite the magnitude and significance of the problem of child maltreatment, research in this area is still in an early stage of development. Understanding the complex nature of child maltreatment is a challenging task, one that requires a variety of methods and approaches to clarify the multiple dimensions of this phenomena. Although much insight has been gained over the past three decades, the field has not yet developed an integrated, organized base of knowledge or ongoing data collection efforts that can inform practice, guide the development of programs and policies relevant to child maltreatment, and shape the formation and testing of major hypotheses in this field. As a result, research programs are needed in diverse areas to explore promising directions. At the same time, research on child maltreatment requires guidance, coordination, and leadership to organize the research base and cultivate future generations of researchers who are well trained and informed about the evolution of research questions in this field. Federal agencies in the past have demonstrated leadership in helping to organize and foster research and training in other fields of family systems and child development studies (for example, the National Institute of Child Health and Human Development has played an important role in shaping the development of research on adolescent sexuality, pregnancy, and parenting) that provide examples of the type of institutional support that needs to be provided in developing research on child maltreatment.

The panel concludes that an agenda for child maltreatment research should address four separate objectives. We need knowledge that can:

(1) Clarify the nature and scope of child maltreatment, guided by well-developed research definitions and instrumentation;

(2) Provide an understanding of the origins and consequences of child maltreatment to establish a foundation for improving the quality of future policy and program efforts to address this problem;

(3) Provide empirical information about the strengths and limitations of existing interventions in preventing and treating child maltreatment to guide the development of new and more effective interventions; and

(4) Develop a science policy for child maltreatment research that recognizes the importance of national leadership, human resources, instrumentation, financial resources, and appropriate institutional arrangements for child maltreatment research.

A balance needs to be established within and among these four categories, requiring a systematic and coordinated effort among research sponsors both to meet existing needs and to develop a strong foundation for future research. In this chapter, the panel organizes its research priorities within these four headings as a plan for action to implement the research directions outlined in this report. Details regarding each priority area that is highlighted in this chapter appear in the preceding chapters, and reference guides are provided to facilitate cross-referencing.

Under each general heading below, the panel has organized the research priorities in order of their importance, with the most important recommendation listed first within each section.

THE NATURE AND SCOPE
OF CHILD MALTREATMENT

Our nation's ability to diagnose, treat, and prevent child maltreatment depends greatly on the quality of the tools that are available to address the problem. Good science requires good measurements and consistent characterizations of the phenomena under study, so that reported results can be replicated, extended, and subjected to critical comparative analysis. However, research definitions of child maltreatment are currently inconsistent, and the breadth and quality of instrumentation for child maltreatment studies are seriously incomplete. The variation in existing definitions and inadequate instrumentation impede high-quality research, inhibit the comparison of studies of related phenomena, and restrain the development of good evaluations of intervention efforts. Improved definitions and instrumentation will facilitate the development of small- and large-scale epidemiologic investigations that can clarify important dimensions as well as etiologic agents that are keys to understanding the nature and scope of child abuse and neglect.

Research Priority 1. A consensus on research definitions needs to be established for each form of child abuse and neglect.

The lack of a consensus on research definitions of child maltreatment is one of the major impediments to the development of a strong research base on all aspects of child maltreatment. The development of consensus requires a major federal and professional commitment to a dynamic, evolutionary process, guided by a series of expert multidisciplinary panels and developed in conjunction with agencies that support research in this area, that could review existing work on research definitions. The research definitions should be coordinated with case-report and legal definitions, be developmentally appropriate and culturally competent, provide clear inclusion and exclusion criteria, and provide clear guidance on issues of severity, duration, and frequency of acts of maltreatment (See Recommendations 2-1 and 2-3 in Chapter 2).

Research Priority 2: Reliable and valid clinical-diagnostic and research instruments for the measurement of child maltreatment are needed to operationalize the definitions discussed under Research Priority 1.

The absence of appropriate instrumentation and methodology is a second serious barrier to the development of good child maltreatment research. The use of appropriate measures in many different areas of child maltreatment is uneven. For example, although certain outcomes in terms of family functioning and individual development can be measured effectively, measures to classify different or multiple forms of child abuse and neglect are poorly developed. The behaviors, characteristics, and experiences of the child and the caretaker and the quality of the caretaking environment need to be assessed by research instruments rather than relying solely on administrative reports. The reliability and validity of these instruments must be established by sound testing for relevance and usefulness with economically and culturally diverse populations.

Since effective questioning strategies for children have not been established, programs are also necessary to foster diagnostic research in this field. Instrumentation studies, beginning with pilot studies in a variety of public and private settings, such as medical and educational systems, are necessary to determine the nature, incidence, and prevalence of abuse and neglect experiences among children and adolescents.

Research is also needed to train clinicians in the appropriate use of assessment instruments and techniques for obtaining maltreatment histories. Pilot instrumentation studies must incorporate age and culturally sensitive measures to protect families from the possible consequences of misdiagnosis and labeling. Recognizing that improved instruments may lead to detection of previously unreported cases of abuse, ways must be devised to enable clinicians and other service providers to refer potentially abusive parents and endangered children for direct assistance without requiring clear evidence of maltreatment prior to the delivery of services (See Recommendations 2-2 and 2-4 in Chapter 2).

Research Priority 3: Epidemiologic studies on the incidence and prevalence of child abuse and neglect should be encouraged, as well as the inclusion of research questions about child maltreatment in other national surveys.

After considerable work on instrumentation, including investigations into effective questioning strategies, the panel recommends the funding of a series of population-based epidemiologic studies of different size and scope, including children of different ages and different ethnic or cultural backgrounds, to address different child maltreatment research questions. Scientific information about the incidence and prevalence of child maltreatment has significant implications for advancing knowledge in the field. Improved measures of the scope of the problem will strengthen work on etiology, consequences, prevention, and treatment. Knowing more about the nature and scope of child maltreatment in the general population will also provide insights into the extent to which health professionals, social services staff, educators, law enforcement personnel, and others should be trained in this area. Better knowledge about the scope of child maltreatment will also inform the selection of appropriate sites for prevention and intervention, including the use of schools, hospitals, health clinics, juvenile detention facilities, homeless shelters, and community centers.

The panel believes that questions on child abuse and neglect should be included on future national surveys (the National Health Interview Survey, the National Survey of Children, and the National Longitudinal Survey of Youth) as part of an expanded data collection effort. Although the inclusion of questions on child maltreatment may raise issues of cost and administrative burdens, past surveys and secondary analyses of existing data sets represent important research opportunities that could provide further insights into the nature and frequency of child abuse and neglect. The data and information collected by child death fatality review teams in various localities may also serve as an important source of information for future research (See Recommendations 3-1 through 3-5 in Chapter 3).

UNDERSTANDING THE ORIGINS AND CONSEQUENCES OF CHILD MALTREATMENT

Research Priority 4: Research that examines the processes by which individual, family, community, and social factors interact will improve understanding of the causes of child maltreatment and should be supported.

Theoretical models that integrate a variety of risk and protective factors are a promising development in research on the origins of child maltreatment, and they deserve further research attention. Rather than endorsing a single approach, the panel recommends that diverse models be developed, incorporating multiple systems that use a variety of research strategies. Such models will allow researchers to learn more about mechanisms that activate or protect against individual child maltreatment and to distinguish between immediate precipitating factors and long-term chronic factors associated with maltreatment.

Multidimensional interactive models that capitalize on current knowledge should be strongly encouraged to facilitate examination of combinations of possible etiological factors. For example, rather than studying the role of poverty alone, future research should examine the interactive effects of poverty or unemployment, individual parental characteristics, and neighborhood conditions. Similarly, research on the intergenerational transmission of abusive parenting should focus on factors in the parent's social environment, such as social networks, that may distinguish individuals who do or do not repeat a pattern of abusive parenting. Continued reliance on simplistic univariate models or isolated risk factors in future research may not be productive (See Recommendation 4-1 in Chapter 4).

Research Priority 5: Research that clarifies the common and divergent pathways in the etiologies of different forms of child maltreatment for diverse populations is essential to improve the quality of future prevention and intervention efforts.

It is particularly important at this time to uncover key pathways for child victimization that may be amenable to prevention or other forms of intervention. Studies that compare the etiologies of different types of maltreatment, including the diverse patterns of risk and protective factors among populations that vary by ethnicity, culture, and economic status, should be supported. For example, being a victim of physical abuse or emotional maltreatment may increase the risk for a child to be victimized by sexual abuse (or vice versa), but the relationships among multiple forms of maltreatment are as yet unexamined.

We do not yet know if there are links between different forms of child maltreatment. We also do not know if the etiology for mild, moderate, and severe forms of abuse is the same within the general population and in specific cultural or ethnic groups. In a similar manner, it is not yet known if there is a continuum involving physical punishment, emotional maltreatment, and other forms of child abuse and neglect or whether these are distinctive behaviors with separate etiologies (See Recommendations 4-2 and 4-3 in Chapter 4).

Research Priority 6: Research that assesses the outcomes of specific and combined types of maltreatment should be supported.

We currently lack a clear understanding of the outcomes of specific and combined forms of child maltreatment in a variety of cultural contexts. Research is needed that assesses direct and indirect consequences of child maltreatment across different domains of life, such as health, cognitive and intellectual skills, and social behavior.

Tightly defined samples that use appropriate comparison groups can reveal significant information about the outcomes of specific forms of child maltreatment. Studies that examine multiple forms of abuse can help compare and contrast child maltreatment outcomes with the consequences of other childhood risk factors. The common practice of treating abused and neglected children together may reveal only a partial portrait of childhood victims' risk for later consequences. Furthermore, longitudinal studies of identified victims (i.e., those who have been reported to authorities) must keep in mind that reporting itself is an intervention in examining the outcomes of abused and neglected children.

In the short term, research efforts to describe, document, and evaluate relationships suggested by the clinical literature on the consequences of child maltreatment are necessary. However, in the long term, the field must build and test hypotheses in a longitudinal developmental framework that examines the timing, duration, severity, and nature of effects over the life course within a cultural context. This approach can reveal the real-world complexities of the outcomes of specific and general types of child maltreatment, including gender differences in vulnerability and manifestations of subsequent problem behaviors, the effects of the developmental stage, cultural environment, and belief system of the individual, and the role of protective factors and interventions in the lives of abused and neglected children that appear to lead to more positive outcomes.

Well-designed longitudinal research should begin as soon as possible. However, since longitudinal research is by nature a long-term analysis, cross-sectional retrospective designs may be the most effective interim means of identifying the prevalence and effects of maltreatment in adults. Cross-sectional studies conducted with techniques to minimize memory performance error (using anchoring and boundary techniques), can provide retrospective information that can be verified in prospective longitudinal studies (See Recommendations 6-1 through 6-4 in Chapter 6).

Research Priority 7: Research is needed to clarify the effects of multiple forms of child victimization that often occur in the social context of child maltreatment. The consequences of child maltreatment may be significantly influenced by a combination of risk factors that have not been well described or understood.

Child maltreatment often occurs against a background of chronic adversity. The assessment of consequences for abused and neglected children is complicated by the co-occurrence of other problems, such as poverty, unemployment, stress, alcohol and drug problems, racism, parental mental illness, and violence. These problems may constitute stressors that affect the psychological well-being of children, families, and communities. The presence or absence of certain characteristics and events in the child's environment may influence a child's response to maltreatment experiences; in some cases the combined effects of two stressors (such as family environment and poor caretaking) may be greater than the sum of the two considered separately. The social context is particularly important, since the effects of abuse or neglect often cannot be separated when families are experiencing a variety of problems.

Research in the area of childhood victimization has generally not examined interrelationships among problem behaviors and symptoms of dysfunction. It is not yet known, for example, whether some common underlying factors result in a syndrome of problem behaviors or combined risks or whether discrete behaviors have different etiologies. Researchers who emphasize syndromes believe that identifying and modifying common factors will reduce problem behaviors in a variety of areas. However, if specific problem behaviors represent specific etiologies, then a general intervention strategy might fail to reduce the problems of most individuals (See Recommendation 6-5 in Chapter 6).

Research Priority 8: Studies of similarities and differences in the etiologies and consequences of various forms of maltreatment across various cultural and ethnic groups are necessary.

The effects of risk potentiating and protective factors in diverse cultural and ethnic groups have not been adequately explored in examining both the origins and consequences of child maltreatment. Researchers have often relied primarily on clinical populations or subjects who have already been identified as offenders as representatives of entire cultural groups. Samples that are more representative of the diversity of American society are necessary to improve research quality. More needs to be known about the effects of what are considered to be normal or acceptable forms of physical discipline, sexual behavior, and parenting styles within various cultural, ethnic, and residential subgroups because cultural norms can have an impact on child maltreatment. Research must address both commonalities and diversity among populations in studying the interactions of variables that promote or prevent various forms of maltreatment and in studying the combinations of factors that foster or inhibit harmful consequences across various dimensions (See Recommendations 6-6 and 6-7 in Chapter 6).

IMPROVING TREATMENT AND PREVENTIVE INTERVENTIONS

The quality of existing treatment and preventive interventions is affected by many factors, including the social and legal context in which programs and policies are developed, the allocation of human and financial resources, and the strength of the research base that informs and guides intervention programs and services. At present, we have limited knowledge about the range or nature of treatment and preventive services for child maltreatment or the context in which these services are available to children and their families. Research evaluations in this area therefore must seek to broaden understanding of what currently exists as well as documenting what services appear to work for which individuals or groups, and under what circumstances. Research on service interventions must also seek to identify factors and mechanisms that facilitate, or impede, the exchange of knowledge between researchers who study the origins, nature, scope, and outcomes of child maltreatment and those who develop and implement policies and programs for child and family services in the public sector.

Research Priority 9: High-quality evaluation studies of existing program and service interventions are needed to develop criteria and instrumentation that can help identify promising developments in the delivery of treatment and prevention services.

Independent scientific evaluations are needed to clarify the outcomes to be assessed for service delivery programs in the area of child maltreatment. Such evaluations should identify the outcomes to be assessed, clarify the instrumentation and measures that can provide effective indicators of child and family well-being or dysfunction, develop the criteria that should be considered in evaluating the effectiveness of a specific program or service, and use appropriate control groups. Evaluation studies currently rely heavily on reported incidents of child maltreatment as a measure of program effectiveness. Given the uncertainties associated with official detection of child maltreatment, such outcomes may have limited value in measuring the achievements or limitations of a selected program intervention.

Rigorous evaluation studies should be an essential part of all major demonstration projects in the area of child maltreatment, and funds should also be available for investigator-initiated evaluation studies of smaller program efforts. Smaller programs should be encouraged to use similar assessment instruments, so that results can be compared across studies. Scientific program evaluations, published in the professional literature, are an important means of transferring the knowledge and experience gained in the service sector into the research community. Such information exchange can improve the quality of studies on the origins, consequences, and other aspects of child maltreatment, ultimately leading to improved services and programs.

Evaluation research is particularly important in the following areas:

• Evaluation studies are needed of specific program interventions, such as foster care, family preservation services, and self-help programs that examine the conditions and circumstances under which selected programs are beneficial or detrimental to the child. Special consideration should be given to factors that might be related to outcomes, such as characteristics of the process by which the service was provided, the circumstances under which the child was removed from the original home, characteristics of the child's original home environment and foster family, and characteristics of the child (including age at time of services provided) (See Recommendations 7-3 and 7-6 in Chapter 7).

• Empirical research is also needed to determine the degrees to which criminal sanctions deter child abuse and the degree to which removal of offenders or children from the home protects the child from abuse. For example, abuse rates and recidivism rates in jurisdictions making heavy use of criminal sanctions and child removal might be compared with matched jurisdictions that rarely use these approaches. Since the relative effectiveness of punitive compared with helping approaches could be different for physical abuse, sexual abuse, and neglect, each of these types of abuse needs to be distinguished.

• Rigorous scientific evaluations of home visiting programs, focused on the prenatal, postnatal, and toddler periods, are necessary prior to the development of nationwide home visiting programs. Such evaluations should include rigorous scientific measurements, appropriate measures of child abuse and neglect, and clarification of the theoretical assumptions that shaped the home visitation efforts.

Home visiting programs have great potential for enhancing family functioning and parenting skills and reducing the prevalence of child maltreatment. However, given the state of knowledge about what programs work, for whom they work, and whether they influence child abuse and neglect directly (via a reduction in child abuse and neglect) or indirectly (via changes in parenting skills and parental characteristics such as depression, problem solving, fertility, and employment), the panel recommends that no major home visiting programs be funded that do not include an evaluation component that incorporates appropriate social and behavioral science design, measures of child abuse and neglect, or both. Subgroup analyses are strongly recommended, requiring samples that are large enough to identify groups for whom the intervention was effective (See Recommendation 5-1 in Chapter 5).

• Evaluations of treatments for specific forms of child maltreatment are needed to identify criteria that promote recovery and to identify treatment modalities that are appropriate for children and offenders depending on their sex, age, social class, spoken language or culture, and type of abuse. Treatment evaluations need to incorporate a developmental perspective, including recognition of the impact of child maltreatment on children of different ages and in different contexts. Treatment strategies need to incorporate what we have learned about consequences of child abuse and neglect. The criteria selected for treatment outcome studies are also particularly important because they shape the emphasis of the intervention. The treatment of children with developmental disabilities, past histories of abuse, and factors associated with maintenance of treatment effects (e.g., concomitant therapy for parents), all require special attention because they can all influence treatment outcomes (See Recommendations 7-2 and 7-5 in Chapter 7).

• Research evaluations of sexual abuse prevention programs are necessary, particularly to determine the outcomes of personal reports of sexual abuse that are often disclosed as a result of such programs. Research needs to address the development of measures for sexual abuse prevention research, natural histories of post-prevention training experiences, factors that support or impede disclosure of abuse in the natural setting, and the roles of parents and other adults in the prevention of sexual abuse.

Evaluations of child sexual abuse prevention should incorporate knowledge about appropriate risk factors as well as the relationship between cognitive and behavioral skills, particularly in situations involving known or trusted adults. Sexual abuse prevention research also needs to integrate knowledge of factors that support or impede disclosure of abuse in the natural setting, including factors that influence adult recognition of sexual abuse and situations at risk for child abuse (See Recommendation 5-2 in Chapter 5).

• Research is needed on the extent to which community-based prevention and intervention programs (such as school-based violence and domestic violence prevention programs, and Head Start) focused on families at risk of multiple problems may affect the likelihood of child maltreatment. Research is also needed on these programs to identify methodological elements (such as designs that successfully engage the participation of at-risk communities) that could be incorporated into child maltreatment prevention programs.

If exposure to a greater number of risk factors increases the risk for violence and child abuse, then community-based prevention and intervention programs need to target multiple childhood risk factors in both the family and the school domains, as well as within the broader social context of the child (e.g., peers, neighborhood).

In addition to recommending comprehensive and intensive programs that address multiple risk factors associated with violence and abuse, we recommend research evaluations on the long-term effectiveness of home-school collaborations, supplemented by booster sessions at developmentally appropriate points in time. School and community-based programs need to be sensitive to the specific social, cultural, gender, and other characteristics and experiences of their participants. Furthermore, major prevention programs need to include a long-term follow-up as part of their evaluation, including information on long-term outcomes, such as arrests for violent behavior and child abuse (See Recommendation 5-3 in Chapter 5).

Research Priority 10: Research on the operation of the existing child protection and child welfare systems is urgently needed. Factors that influence different aspects of case handling decisions and the delivery and use of individual and family services require attention. The strengths and limitations of alternatives to existing institutional arrangements need to be described and evaluated.

We have very poor information about the methods and mechanisms used to identify and confirm cases of child maltreatment, to evaluate the severity of child and family dysfunction, to assess personal and social resources, family strengths, and extrafamilial influences, and to match clients to appropriate treatments based on these formulations. An analysis is needed of interactions among different agencies involved in intervention and treatment and the degree to which decisions made by one agency affect outcomes in others. A research framework that provides standardized classifications and descriptions of child maltreatment investigations, adjudications, and treatment services should be developed. Comparative studies are needed to describe the agencies involved in the system, the types of interventions available for selected forms of maltreatment, the costs of investigating and responding to reports of child maltreatment, and the outcomes of case reports. Such studies should also consider the development of alternatives to existing institutional arrangements to improve the quality of service delivery systems.

Research should be conducted on the detection processes that lead to the definition of cases identified in child protective services records and other social agencies that handle child maltreatment. Research is needed to evaluate the stages by which children receive services following reports of maltreatment as well as to identify methods by which developmental, social, and cultural variations in abuse symptomatology are integrated into treatment goals and assessment instruments. We lack data about accessibility and affordability of treatment services for abused and neglected children and their families. Information is needed on critical individual, social, cultural, and contextual factors that can determine the success or failure of child maltreatment interventions (See Recommendation 7-1 in Chapter 7).

Research Priority 11: Service system research on existing state data systems should be conducted to improve the quality of child maltreatment research information as well as to foster improved service interventions.

Variations in state definitions of child abuse and neglect as well as differences in verification procedures result in significant unevenness in the quality of research data on child maltreatment reports. Effort is needed on a national level to:

• mandate state compliance with data acquisition and reporting efforts, as in other federal efforts like Medicaid and Medicare;
• develop uniform case definitions with measurable criteria;
• identify the criteria used by social service agencies in making assessment, investigation, substantiation, and referral decisions;
• identify potential sources of bias in current procedures for reporting and investigation of reported cases;
• redesign state data-processing systems so that uniform individual-level data are available and unduplicated counts of children affected by abuse and neglect are easily obtainable;
• establish an expert panel to periodically review the data system, establish quality indicators, and identify key areas for services systems investigation;
• make available state-level data as public use data tapes;
• conduct ethnographic studies to identify the systems-level features that affect reporting and case verification; and
• provide sufficient incentive for state child welfare agencies to become equal partners in the research process while acknowledging the problems (e.g., understaffing, management emphasis) of state-level research (See Recommendation 3-1 in Chapter 3).

Research Priority 12: The role of the media in reinforcing or questioning social norms relevant to child maltreatment needs further study.

Important lessons can be learned from the role of the media in fostering healthy or unhealthy behaviors in areas such as the use of alcohol, smoking, drug use, and condom use. Research is needed that can identify the significant pathways by which key factors and behaviors affect child maltreatment, such as parenting styles, the use of corporal punishment, the use of violence and time-out periods in stress management and conflict resolution, and young children's relationships with strangers and abusive caretakers. Rather than simply highlighting sensational aspects of abusive cases, the media can play an important role in disseminating research results and encouraging behaviors that have relevance for fostering positive family relationships and the protection of children (See Recommendation 5-4 in Chapter 5).

A SCIENCE POLICY FOR RESEARCH ON CHILD MALTREATMENT

The complexity of the problem of child maltreatment requires a sustained commitment to high-quality research, national leadership, human resources, and adequate funds. Scientific knowledge can contribute to our understanding of the nature, scope, origins, and consequences of child maltreatment, but such knowledge cannot be developed in a haphazard manner. Thus the panel has formulated priorities for science policy and the research infrastructure that supports child maltreatment research in order to highlight key strengths and existing deficiencies that need attention.

Research Priority 13: Federal agencies concerned with child maltreatment research need to formulate a national research plan and provide leadership for child maltreatment research.

Existing fragmentation in the federal research effort focused on child maltreatment requires immediate attention. National leadership is necessary to develop a long-term plan that would implement the child maltreatment research priorities identified by the panel. Such a plan would help coordinate the field and focus it on key research questions.

Effective governmental research leadership requires:

• A commitment to high-quality research on child maltreatment, including the support of relevant theoretical work, instrumentation, and data collection efforts;
• Staff members who have experience in and understanding of the research process;
• Procedures that provide opportunities for researchers to receive feedback from their peers on the quality of their proposals and to incorporate that feedback in revised and improved research proposals;
• An administrative process that ensures that research proposals will be evaluated on the basis of the quality of the work proposed rather than the political or programmatic relationships of the research investigators;
• A broad-based relationship with service providers that effectively disseminates research findings and encourages their use in clinical services, treatment efforts, preventive interventions, and child maltreatment programs and policies.

At present, the lead federal research agency for child maltreatment studies (the National Center on Child Abuse and Neglect) does not meet all these criteria. As a result, the panel examined alternative methods of organizing federal research leadership in this field. Three possible approaches deserve further consideration:

(1) The research mission of the National Center on Child Abuse and Neglect could be strengthened with the necessary staff, budgetary, and program resources so that it can provide leadership in this area;

(2) The lead agency responsibility for research on child maltreatment could be transferred to an agency with a distinguished research record (such as the National Institute of Mental Health, the National Institute of Child Health and Human Development, or the Maternal and Child Health Bureau) that has established procedures and experience in supporting high-quality research;

(3) The research mission of the National Center on Child Abuse and Neglect could be consolidated with the research functions of other bureaus and centers within the Administration of Children, Youth, and Families (such as Head Start, the Children's Bureau, and others) so that a research institute within ACYF could develop scientific studies directly relevant to existing and proposed ACYF programs.

Each of these approaches has advantages and disadvantages. Strengthening the existing research effort of the National Center on Child Abuse and Neglect has the advantage of continuing the core research activity developed within that agency and ensuring an explicit focus on child maltreatment research. However, the center has not demonstrated that it has the resources or research expertise necessary to support long-term research studies, postgraduate training programs, and interdisciplinary centers. Its responsibilities in providing federal funds for state child maltreatment programs also create a political climate in which the expansion of the research program may be seen as a weakening of a commitment to child maltreatment services, if additional funds are not available for the full range of program activity.

Deficiencies in the existing research program could be addressed by designating a research agency, such as the the National Institute of Mental Health, the National Institute of Child Health and Human Development, or Maternal and Child Health, as the lead agency for child maltreatment research. This proposal has the advantage of placing child maltreatment research within an agency that has a record of scientific achievement and experienced research staff. However, it is not certain that another research agency would have the authority and the necessary commitment to child maltreatment research that are necessary to sustain an effective program focused explicitly on this topic. Other agencies may lack extensive ties with service providers and policy makers that would foster greater utilization and dissemination of research in this field.

The proposed creation of a research institute within ACYF appears to have substantial merit and attracted the interest of the panel. However, such a proposal requires clarification of the research programs of other ACYF components and the consideration of the sustainability of its research mission separated from programmatic activities. The panel was not able to develop this material in the limited time available for this study.

The panel believes that Congress, federal agency directors, and the research community should weigh the strengths and limitations of each approach discussed above in considering how federal leadership might best be provided in implementing a national research plan for child maltreatment. Once a course of action has been formulated, current and proposed agency research activities need to be examined so that areas of strength, duplication of effort, and gaps in current efforts can be identified (See Recommendation 8-2 and 8-6 in Chapter 8).

Research Priority 14: Governmental leadership is needed to sustain and improve the capabilities of the available pool of researchers who can contribute to studies of child maltreatment. National leadership is also required to foster the integration of research from related fields that offer significant insights into the causes, consequences, treatment, and prevention of child maltreatment.

The following steps need to be taken to foster career development and to expand the human resources that provide the foundation for studies of child maltreatment:

• The interdisciplinary nature of child maltreatment research requires the development of specialized disciplinary expertise as well as opportunities for collaborative research studies. Researchers in child maltreatment projects increasingly need to cross disciplinary boundaries, in terms of theories, instrumentation, and constructs, and to integrate relevant literature from multiple disciplines. For example, signs of behavioral distress patterns may be similar in physical and sexual abuse, although they may be labeled differently. Similarly, research on child abuse, stress, and trauma needs to integrate findings from the psychological literature with more recent physiological findings, such as those that examine the relationship between sexual abuse, stress, and early puberty. Governmental agencies and foundations that sponsor research in child maltreatment need to recognize the importance of strengthening research resources in the disciplines as well as fostering interdisciplinary collaboration that will contribute to understanding of child abuse and neglect.

• Federal and state agencies should develop mechanisms for interdisciplinary graduate and postgraduate training programs focused on the examination of child maltreatment issues. Postdoctoral training programs designed to deepen a young scientist's interests in research on child abuse and neglect should be given preference at this time over graduate student dissertation support, although both training efforts are desirable in the long term. External fellowship training for health professionals interested in child maltreatment research is particularly important, given the broad range of roles that health professionals are expected to play in detecting, identifying, confirming, treating, and preventing child abuse and neglect. Postdoctoral training programs should include an emphasis on working with diverse ethnic and cultural groups.

• The creation of a corps of research-practitioners familiar with studies of child maltreatment should be an explicit goal of federal, state, and private agencies that operate programs in areas of child welfare, child protection, maternal and child health, spousal violence, and child maltreatment. The proposed corps of research-practitioners will encourage the development of studies on selected child maltreatment issues as well as facilitate the integration of relevant research findings into agency services and programs.

• A directory of active research investigators, identifying key fields of research interests, should be developed in collaboration between professional societies and child advocacy organizations whose members have research experience on child abuse and neglect. A consortium of university research programs should also be developed to provide expanded opportunities for information exchange and dissemination among multiple institutions and research disciplines.

• The cultural and ethnic diversity of the corps of research investigators concerned with child maltreatment studies is not broad enough to explore the importance of culture and ethnicity in theories, instrumentation, and other aspects of research on child abuse and neglect. Special efforts are needed at this time to train child maltreatment researchers in the importance of ethnic and cultural factors in this field. Efforts are also needed to provide educational and research support for researchers from ethnic and cultural minority groups to strengthen the diversity of human resources dedicated to this topic.

• When a sufficient research budget is available to support an expanded corps of research investigators from multiple disciplines, multidisciplinary research centers should be established to foster collaboration in research on child maltreatment. The purpose of these centers should be to assemble a corps of faculty and practitioners focused on selected aspects of child abuse and neglect, including medical, psychological, social, legal, and cultural aspects of child abuse and neglect. The proposed centers could provide a critical mass in developing long-term research studies and evaluating major demonstration projects to build on and expand the existing base of empirical knowledge. The proposed centers should have a regional distribution, be associated with major academic centers, have the capacity to educate professionals of various disciplines, and launch major research efforts. Examples of the cancer and diabetes research centers funded by the National Institutes of Health could serve as models, as could the Prevention Intervention Research Centers sponsored by the National Institute of Mental Health (See Recommendations 8-1, 8-3, 8-4, 8-5, and 8-7 in Chapter 8).

Research Priority 15: Recognizing that fiscal pressures and budgetary deficits diminish prospects for significant increases in research budgets generally, special efforts are required to find new funds for research on child abuse and neglect and to encourage research collaboration and data collection in related fields.

The federal government spent about $15 million in fiscal year 1992 on research directly related to child maltreatment. As a first step, the panel recommends that the relevant budgets for child maltreatment research of the National Center on Child Abuse and Neglect, the National Institute of Mental Health, the National Institute of Child Health and Human Development, the Centers for Disease Control and Prevention, and the Department of Justice be doubled over the next three years. Second, the panel recommends that the National Center on Child Abuse and Neglect convene a consortium of government agencies, private foundations, and research scientists to identify ways in which research on programs relevant to child maltreatment (such as substance abuse, spousal violence, child homicides, juvenile delinquency, and so forth) can be more systematically integrated into the research infrastructure for child abuse and neglect.

Congress needs to recognize the centrality of the issue of child maltreatment in contributing to a wide range of social problems and family pathologies. Our country spends little on building the knowledge and resource base we need to treat and prevent incidents of child abuse and neglect, particularly in light of the enormous human, economic, and social costs associated with violence toward children. Furthermore, Congress should recognize that the level of financial support currently available for research on child maltreatment is not well understood or easily obtainable. Congress should request that the General Accounting Office conduct a thorough review of all ongoing federally supported research on child abuse and neglect, identifying and categorizing research programs that are relevant to this area, even if their primary goal is in support of a different objective, such as the reduction of spousal violence, childhood injuries, and infant mortality.

Since child maltreatment is known to be a significant factor in the

development of many social pathologies, research on child abuse and neglect should be an integral part of the programmatic activity for each of
these areas. The proposed task force should develop a formula whereby
each agency sponsoring research on social problems should be encouraged
to allocate 10 percent of its funds to studies on basic and applied research
studies on child maltreatment, administered through a consortium effort that
would encourage the transfer of knowledge among these separate programs
(See Recommendations 8-9, 8-10, and 8-12 in Chapter 8).

**Research Priority 16: Research is needed to identify organizational
innovations that can improve the process by which child maltreatment
research findings are disseminated to practitioners and policy makers.
The role of state agencies in supporting, disseminating, and utilizing
empirical research deserves particular attention.**

We currently know very little about the ways in which empirical research findings are disseminated to such individuals as social agency officials, educators, judges, law enforcement officers, and many others who are
responsible for the social welfare and protection of children. Research on
the information dissemination process can strengthen the ways in which
science is used to inform and advise legislative and judicial decision makers. Such research can also contribute to effective partnerships among
scientists, practitioners, clinicians, and governmental officials to encourage
the use of sound research results in formulating policies, programs, and
services that affect the lives of thousands of children and their families.

State agencies have an important role in fostering and disseminating
knowledge about factors that affect the identification, treatment, and prevention of child maltreatment. The National Center on Child Abuse and
Neglect should encourage the development of a collaborative state consortium to serve as a documentation and research support center. One potential model of a state collaborative research consortium is the Strategic High-
way Research Program administered by the Transportation Research Board
in the National Research Council.

The empirical base of knowledge that guides state programs and practices in the area of child maltreatment needs national attention and sustained organization. The states need a consortium device through which
regional and national research seminars can be organized, collaborative research studies can be developed, and relevant research findings can be disseminated to a wide pool of personnel. A national child abuse and neglect
research information service, similar to the "Research in Brief" program
operated through the Department of Justice, would be a significant asset to
the state agency personnel and service providers (See Recommendation 8-
11 in Chapter 9).

Research Priority 17: Researchers should design methods, procedures, and resources that can resolve ethical problems associated with recruitment of research subjects; informed consent; privacy, confidentiality, and autonomy; assignment of experimental and control research participants; and debriefings.

Research is needed to clarify the nature of individual and group interests in the course of research, to develop clinical advice and experience that can resolve such conflicts among such interests, and to identify methods by which such guidance could be communicated to researchers, institutional research boards, research administrators, research subjects, and others. Such advice should include consideration of spoken language, language comprehension, literacy, and reading orientation (left to right or vice versa).

Issues of data sharing, privacy, confidentiality, and autonomy in the field of child maltreatment research need further development, especially in prospective studies of maltreating and nonmaltreating families. Ethical issues likely to arise in longitudinal prospective studies need to be identified, to clarify principles of responsible conduct regarding the treatment of risk factors, researcher responses to suspected abuse scenarios, and the rights of research subjects to privacy, confidentiality, and autonomy. The ethical and legal role of researchers in responding to suspected or unreported disclosures of maltreatment requires methodological considerations in formulating appropriate guidance for the research community.

Finally, empirical analyses of research protocols and institutional research board reviews of proposed research projects on child maltreatment should be conducted to determine factors that influence approval and disapproval decisions, the use of waivers and certificates of confidentiality, and other factors that affect the manner in which research investigators address ethical and legal issues in the course of their research (See Recommendations 9-1 through 9-4 in Chapter 9).

APPENDIXES

A

Panel Activities

The panel wishes to thank the individuals who provided assistance and information during the course of this study, including:

Jean Adnopoz, Yale University
Pam Alexander, University of Maryland
Bernard Auchter, National Institute of Justice
Diana Baumrind, University of California—Berkeley
Judith Becker, University of Arizona
Jay Belsky, The Pennsylvania State University
Marilyn Benoit, Children's Hospital National Medical Center,
    Washington, DC
Lucy Berliner, Harborview Treatment Center
Jeanne Bertolli, University of California—Los Angeles
Thomas Birch, National Child Abuse Coalition
Rosemary Bolig, Ohio State University
Barbara L. Bonner, University of Oklahoma Health Sciences Center
Jim Breiling, National Institute of Mental Health
John Briere, University of Southern California
Ann Burgess, University of Pennsylvania
Mary Campbell, American Psychological Association
Dante Cicchetti, University of Rochester
Joann Corbin, Yale University School of Medicine
Patrick Curtis, Child Welfare League of America
Howard Davidson, American Bar Association
Esther Deblinger, University of Medicine and Dentistry of New Jersey

Anne Cohn Donnelly, National Committee for the Prevention of Child
  Abuse
Edward Donnerstein, University of California—Santa Barbara
Dennis Drotar, Metropolitan Hospital, Cleveland
Howard Dubowitz, University of Maryland at Baltimore
Richard Famularo, Boston Juvenile Court
Martin Finkel, University of Medicine and Dentistry of New Jersey
Robert Flores, U.S. Department of Justice
Brad Garrett, Federal Bureau of Investigation
James Gaudin, University of Georgia
Jeanne Giovannoni, University of California—Los Angeles
Gail Goodman, State University of New York—Buffalo
Robert Gossart, Yale University
Martin H. Gerry, U.S. Department of Health and Human Services
Stuart Hart, Indiana University
Hope Hill, Howard University
Wade F. Horn, Administration for Children, Youth, and Families
Carole Jenny, Children's Hospital, Denver, Colorado
Coryl Jones, National Institute of Drug Abuse
Joan Kaufman, Western Psychiatric Insititute and Clinic
James Kavanagh, National Institute of Child Health and Human
  Development
Lorraine Klerman, Yale University
Dean Knudsen, Purdue University
David Kolko, Western Psychiatric Institute and Clinic
Richard D. Krugman, University of Colorado
Kenneth Lanning, Federal Bureau of Investigation
Alan Leshner, National Institute of Mental Health
John Leventhal, Yale University
Carolyn Levitt, Midwest Children's Resource Center
Dan Linz, University of California—Santa Barbara
Julie Lipovsky, Medical University of South Carolina
Marsha Liss, National Center on Child Abuse and Neglect
David Lloyd, National Center on Child Abuse and Neglect
Neil Malamuth, University of Michigan
Harold Morgenstern, University of California—Los Angeles
Patricia Mrazek, Institute of Medicine
Steven Nagler, Yale University
Kim Oates, Children's Hospital, Camperdown, Australia
David Olds, University of Rochester
Carol Petrie, National Institute of Justice
Patricia A. Place, National Research Council
Norman Polansky, Athens, Georgia

N. Dickon Reppucci, University of Virginia
Desmond Runyan, University of North Carolina
Joan Sieber, California State University—Hayward
Ray Smith, U.S. Postal Service
Joyce Thomas, Center for Child Protection and Family Support
Penelope Trickett, University of Southern California
Deborah Daro Tuggle, National Committee for Prevention of Child Abuse
Kathryn M. Turman, U.S. Department of Justice
Michael S. Wald, Stanford Law School
Roger Weissberg, Yale University
Debra Whitcomb, Educational Development Center
Diane Willis, University of Oklahoma
Charles Wilson, Child Welfare Services, Tennessee
David Wolfe, Western Ontario University
Ying-Ying Yuan, McDonald and Associates
Edward Zigler, Yale University

SURVEY RESPONDENTS

During spring and fall 1992, the panel conducted a mail survey to gather perspectives on current and future priorities in the field of child maltreatment research from officials of organizations with active interests in policy, advocacy, and education related to the prevention and treatment of abuse and neglect of children. The following organizations proposed research priorities for consideration by the panel in formulating this report:

Alaska Children and Youth, AK
American Academy of Child and Adolescent Psychiatry, DC
American Academy of Pediatrics, Committee on Child Abuse and
    Neglect, IL
American Association of Psychiatric Services for Children, NY
American Association of Sex Educators, Counselors and Therapists, IL
American Bar Association, Center on Children and the Law, DC
American Civil Liberties Union, Children's Rights Project, NY
American Humane Association, CO
American Indian Health Care Association, MN
American Indian Institute, Continuing Education and Public Service, OK
American Medical Association, IL
American Public Welfare Association, DC
Arkansas Committee for Prevention of Child Abuse, AR
Boulder County Safehouse, CO
California Consortium for the Prevention of Child Abuse, CA
Center for Family Resources, NY

Center for the Improvement of Child Caring, CA
Child Abuse Prevention Council, KS
Child Welfare League of America, DC
Children and Youth Advisory Committee, KS
Children's Services Division, OR
Children's Trust Fund, CO
Children's Trust Fund, Department of Children and Youth Services, CT
Children's Trust Fund, Department of Individual and Family Studies, DE
Children's Trust Fund Commission, GA
Children's Trust Fund, LA
Children's Trust Fund, MI
Children's Trust Fund, MN
Children's Trust Fund, MO
Children's Trust Fund, MS
Children's Trust Fund, NJ
Children's Trust Fund and Institutional Protective Services, ND
Children's Trust Fund, NC
Children's Trust Fund, Vermont State Agency of Human Services, VT
Coalition on Abuse and Disabilities, NY
Committee for Children, WA
Community and Family Support Services, Healthy Start Department, State
    Department of Health, Maternal and Child Health Branch, HI
Council on Child Abuse, KY
Crime Victims Research and Treatment Center, SC
D.C. Hotline, Inc., DC
Department of Children, Youth and Family Services, SD
Department of Human Resource Services - Children, Youth, and
    Families, FL
Department of Public Welfare, Office of Children, Youth, and
    Families, PA
Department of Social Services, NE
Disability, Abuse and Personal Rights Project, CA
Division of Child and Family Services, NV
Division of Family Services, UT
Effective Parenting Information for Children, NY
Effectiveness Training, Inc., CA
Exchange Club Center for Prevention of Child Abuse, SC
Family and Children Services, Division of Health and Welfare, ID
Family and Children's Trust Fund of Virginia, VA
Family and Social Services Administration, Division of Family and
    Children, IN
Family Nurturing Center, UT
Father Flanagan's Boy's Home, NE

First Steps, Georgia Council on Child Abuse, GA
Friends for Prevention of Child Abuse, Inc., WV
George Warren Brown School of Social Work, MO
Governor's Office for Children and Youth, MD
Harborview Sexual Assault Center, WA
Implementation Committee on Social Work Research, DC
Manilaq Association, AK
Massachusetts Committee for Children and Youth, MA
Meld, MN
Molesters/Batterers Anonymous, CA
Montana Council for Families, MT
National Adolescent Perpetrator Network, CO
National Association of Children's Hospitals and Related Institutions, VA
National Association of Social Workers, DC
National Center for Youth Law, CA
National Coalition Against Domestic Violence, CO
National Coalition on Child Abuse and Disabilities, NY
National Coalition to Abolish Corporal Punishment in Schools, OH
National Committee for the Prevention of Child Abuse (NCPCA), Alamo
     Chapter, Child Abuse Resources and Educational Services, TX
NCPCA, Delawareans United to Prevent Child Abuse, Delaware
     Chapter, DE
NCPCA, East Texas Chapter, TX
NCPCA, Florida Chapter, FL
NCPCA, Franklin County Chapter, ME
NCPCA, Greater Chicago Council, IL
NCPCA, Greater Philadelphia Chapter, PA
NCPCA, Illinois Chapter, IL
NCPCA, Indiana Chapter, IN
NCPCA, Iowa Chapter, IA
NCPCA, Lancaster County Chapter, PA
NCPCA, Michigan Chapter, MI
NCPCA, Missouri Chapter, MO
NCPCA, North Alabama Chapter, AL
NCPCA, North Carolina Chapter, NC
NCPCA, Quad Cities Affiliate, IL
NCPCA, Rhode Island Chapter, RI
NCPCA, South Plains Chapter TX
NCPCA, Southern Nevada Chapter, NV
NCPCA, Utah Chapter, UT
NCPCA, Western Pennsylvania Chapter, PA
NCPCA, Wisconsin Chapter, WI
National Court Appointed Special Advocates, WA

National Directory of Children, Youth and Family Services, CO
National Exchange Club Foundation, OH
National Network of Runaway and Youth Services Inc., DC
National Resource Center for Youth Services, OK
National Resource Center on Family-Based Services, IA
National Resource Center on Child Sexual Abuse, AL
New Hampshire Department of Education, NH
New Hampshire Task Force on Child Abuse and Neglect, NH
New Mexico Human Services Department, NM
Office for the Development of Ministry Personnel, CT
Office for Family Policy and Support, VA
Office of Child Abuse Prevention, OK
Ohio Department of Human Services, OH
Ohio League Against Child Abuse, OH
Ohio Research Institute on Child Abuse Prevention, OH
PACER Center, MN
Pediatrician, NE
People Against Child Abuse, Inc., MD
Primary Children's Medical Center Child Protection Team, UT
Tennessee Department of Human Services, TN
Texas Coalition for the Prevention of Child Abuse, TX
Texas Department of Human Services, TX
U.S. Navy Family Advocacy Program, DC
Union of Pan Asian Communities, CA
University of South Carolina, College of Social Work SC
University of Wisconsin, Department of Social Work WI
Vermont Center for Prevention of Child Abuse, VT
Washington Council for Prevention of Child Abuse, WA
Western South Dakota Child Protection Council, SD
York County Child Abuse and Neglect Council, Inc., ME

B

Supplementary Views

Panel members Dorothy O. Lewis, Murray A. Straus, and Gail E. Wyatt
concur with the recommendations in Chapter 10 and the Summary of this
report and wish to propose the following additional recommendation:

The United States has significantly more violent crime than either Western Europe or Canada. Its homicide rate alone is many times those of Great Britain and Canada. Homicide is the second leading cause of death among teens in the United States and the leading cause of death among black male teenagers in the United States. This raises questions about the relationship between societal violence and child maltreatment. Does a violent environment encourage maltreatment? To what extent does having been a victim of maltreatment contribute to societal violence? Are societal violence and maltreatment correlates or consequences of other factors? Thus, research on the possible relationship of societal violence and child maltreatment should be encouraged and supported.

Dorothy O. Lewis and Murray A. Straus wish to propose a second
additional recommendation:

There is evidence that harsh parenting practices, specifically corporal punishment, are associated with aggressive styles of adaptation. Research is needed to learn more about the relationship of different forms of corporal punishment to the development of aggressive, abusive practices. Research is also needed on the relationship of escalating corporal punishment to actual child abuse.

March 23, 1993

C

Biographical Sketches

ANNE C. PETERSEN (panel chair) is vice president for research and dean of the Graduate School as well as professor of adolescent development and pediatrics at the University of Minnesota. Previously she served as dean of the College of Health and Human Development and professor in the department of human development and women's studies at Pennsylvania State University. She is a former president of the Society for Research on Adolescence and a member of the advisory council of the National Institute of Child Health and Human Development. Dr. Petersen studies biopsychosocial development in adolescence, developmental psychopathology, gender differences in development, and methods for development and change. She has a Ph.D. in measurement, evaluation, and statistical analysis from the University of Chicago.

J. LAWRENCE ABER is associate professor in the Department of Psychology at Barnard College and director of the Barnard Center for Toddler Development at Columbia University. He has served as a consultant to the National Center on Children in Poverty since its inception. He teaches and has directed numerous research studies concerning the social, emotional, motivational, and behavioral development of high-risk infants, children, and youth. His developmental research has included the design of conceptual models and recommendations for program and policy changes that recognize the relationships between individual development and community, neighborhood, and family environments. He has a Ph.D. in clinical and developmental psychology from Yale University.

ANDREW BILLINGSLEY is professor and chair of the Department of Family and Community Development at the University of Maryland. He has held this position since 1987. Previously he served as president of Morgan State University and vice president for academic affairs at Howard University. He is author of 4 books and more than 200 technical and professional articles, primarily on the social and economic status of African American families in the United States. He is currently completing a book on the role of black churches as an American social institution. He has a Ph.D. in social policy and social research from Brandeis University.

JEANNE BROOKS-GUNN is Virginia and Leonard Marx professor in child and parent development and education and director of the Center for the Development and Education of Young Children and Their Parents at Columbia University. She was previously senior research scientist in the Division of Education Policy Research for the Educational Testing Service. She has coedited or authored about a dozen books and numerous research articles on youth and adolescence, focusing on teen parenting, adolescent transitions, and parent-child relationships. She has a Ph.D. in human learning and development from the University of Pennsylvania.

ROSEMARY CHALK (study director) is a science policy analyst in the Commission on Behavioral and Social Sciences and Education in the National Research Council/National Academy of Sciences. She has previously directed four studies for the Institute of Medicine and the National Academy of Sciences, including the study that produced the two-volume report *Responsible Science* (1993), a study on integrity and misconduct in science. Before joining the Academy staff in 1987, Ms. Chalk was program head for the Office of Scientific Freedom and Responsibility of the American Association for the Advancement of Science. She has consulted and written extensively on a range of science policy issues, including human rights and the civil liberties of scientists, social responsibility in the development and use of science and technology, and whistle-blowing in science. She has a B.A. in political science from the University of Cincinnati.

DONALD J. COHEN is Irving B. Harris professor of child psychiatry, pediatrics and psychology and director of the Child Study Center at the Yale University School of Medicine. A child psychiatrist and psychoanalyst, he joined the faculty of the School of Medicine in 1972 and has been the director of the Child Study Center since 1983. His clinical and research activities have focused on the serious neuropsychiatric disorders of childhood, including pervasive developmental disorders (such as autism) and stereotypic and tick disorders (such as Tourette's syndrome). He has published hundreds of articles and monographs. He is codirector of the Yale

Mental Health Clinical Research Center and vice-president (for North America) of the International Association of Child and Adolescent Psychiatry and Allied Professions. He is a member of the Institute of Medicine and the National Commission on Children. He has an M.D. from the Yale School of Medicine.

MICHAEL I. COHEN has been chairman of the Department of Pediatrics at Albert Einstein College of Medicine/Montefiore Medical Center since 1980 and has been a member of the faculty of the same institution since 1972. He is also an attending pediatrician at the Bronx Municipal Hospital and former president and chief executive officer of the Montefiore Medical Center in New York. Dr. Cohen is a member of the Institute of Medicine and a member of the Council on Adolescent Development of the Carnegie Corporation of New York. He has an M.D. from Columbia University.

JON ROBERT CONTE is associate professor in the School of Social Work at the University of Washington and editor of *The Journal of Interpersonal Violence* and *Violence Update*. His research interests include preventing the sexual victimization of young children, the effects of sexual abuse on children, and studies of the effects of intervention in child sexual abuse. He is a former president of the American Professional Society on the Abuse of Children and a former member of the criminal and violence research review committee of the National Institute of Mental Health. He has a Ph.D. in social work from the University of Washington.

BYRON EGELAND is the Irving B. Harris professor of child psychology for the Institute of Child Development at the University of Minnesota, where he has been a member of the faculty since 1972. Dr. Egeland has directed a comprehensive prospective study on high-risk mothers and the antecedents of child abuse. His research interests include patterns of adaptation to stressful events in childhood, profiles of women at risk for child abuse, and prevention interventions for high-risk parents. He is a member of the board of directors of the National Committee for the Prevention of Child Abuse, a member of the board of directors of the National Archives for Research in Child Abuse and Neglect at Cornell University, and a member of the Board of Directors of Project MELD in Minneapolis. Dr. Egeland has a Ph.D. in educational psychology from the University of Iowa.

E. MAVIS HETHERINGTON is the James Page professor of psychology at the University of Virginia. She has been a member of the faculty at the University of Virginia since 1970 and is a former chair of the psychology department. Dr. Hetherington has edited 10 books and numerous research articles on the role of family structure and the effects of parental characteristics on child development. Her research interests include the effects of divorce, single parenting, and stepparenting on children; the role of family systems in child development; and environmental influences on adolescence. She is a former president of the Society for Research in Child Development, former president of the Society for Research in Adolescence, and a member of the Board of Directors of the Foundation for Child Development. She has a Ph.D. in psychology from the University of California, Berkeley.

SARAH McCUE HORWITZ is associate professor of public health in the Department of Public Health and Epidemiology at the Yale University School of Medicine, where she has been a member of the faculty since 1986. Her research interests include the health and treatment of children born to teenage mothers and methodological issues in research on children. She has a Ph.D. in epidemiology and health services from Yale University and was a postdoctoral fellow in the Yale Institution for Social and Policy Studies.

JILL E. KORBIN is associate professor and acting chair in the Department of Anthropology at Case Western Reserve University. She received the 1986 Margaret Mead Award from the American Anthropological Association, served as a Society for Research in Child Development congressional science fellow in 1985-1986, and was a scholar-in-residence at the Kempe National Center in 1977-1978. Dr. Korbin has published numerous articles on culture and child maltreatment, including her edited book, *Child Abuse and Neglect: Cross-Cultural Perspectives*. She has conducted research on women incarcerated for fatal child maltreatment, on child and elder abuse in Ohio, and currently on the impact of neighborhood factors on child maltreatment in Cleveland. She earned a Ph.D. in anthropology from the University of California at Los Angeles.

DOROTHY OTNOW LEWIS is professor of psychiatry at the New York University School of Medicine and clinical professor of psychiatry at the Yale University Child Study Center. She is the recipient of the 1992 Norbert Rieger Award of the American Academy of Child and Adolescent Psychiatry for her research paper on the physical consequences of child maltreatment. Her research interests include studies of juvenile violence, delinquency and psychopathology, and the psychophysiological consequences of child maltreatment. She has edited three books and numerous research articles and is a frequent consultant and speaker on the problems of youthful offenders. She has an M.D. from the Yale School of Medicine.

RODERICK J.A. LITTLE is professor and chair of the Department of Biostatistics at the University of Michigan. He was formerly professor and vice-chair of the department of biomathematics in the School of Medicine at the University of California, Los Angeles. His research interests include the improvement of survey accuracy and the improvement of methodology and software for mental health research. He has a Ph.D. in statistics from London University, England.

MURRAY STRAUS is a professor of sociology and founder and codirector of the Family Research Laboratory at the University of New Hampshire. He has also taught at the universities of Minnesota, Cornell, Wisconsin, Washington State, York (England), Bombay (India), and the University of Ceylon (now Sri Lanka). He has been elected to a number of offices in scientific societies, including president of the Society for the Study of Social Problems, president of the Eastern Sociological Society, president of the National Council on Family Relations, and member of the Council of the American Association for the Advancement of Science. He received the Ernest W. Burgess Award of the National Council of Family Relations for outstanding research on the family and an American Sociological Association award for contributions to undergraduate teaching. Dr. Straus is author or coauthor of over 150 articles on the family, research methods, and South Asia; and 15 books on physical violence in American families, violence and crime in intimate relationships, and social stress in the United States. He is currently writing a book on the use of corporal punishment in American families. He has a Ph.D. in sociology from the University of Wisconsin.

CATHY SPATZ WIDOM is professor of criminal justice and psychology and director of the Hindelang Criminal Justice Research Center at the State University of New York at Albany. She is a former faculty member in psychology and social relations at Harvard University and in criminal justice and psychology at Indiana University. She received the 1989 American Association for the Advancement of Science Behavioral Science Research Prize and was elected a fellow of the American Psychological Association in 1993. She has published extensively on topics that include child abuse and neglect, juvenile delinquency, female criminality, and violence. Her recent research interests focus on the intergenerational transmission of violence and the long-term consequences of early childhood abuse and neglect. She has a Ph.D. in psychology from Brandeis University.

GAIL E. WYATT is a licensed clinical psychologist and professor in the Department of Psychiatry and Biobehavioral Sciences at the University of California, Los Angeles, where she has been a member of the faculty since 1974. She has been a National Institute of Mental Health research scientist since 1982, examining a range of women's consensual and nonconsensual sexual experiences and the effects on psychological functioning and sexual decision making. Dr. Wyatt is an internationally recognized sex educator, certified sex therapist, and lecturer. She is also a diplomate and founding clinical fellow of the American Academy of Clinical Sexologists and a fellow of the American Psychological Association. She is the principal investigator of research projects examining AIDS-related sexual decision making in Jamaica among men and women and African American, Latina, and white women in Los Angeles County. Dr. Wyatt's numerous scientific publications and books involve ethnic and cultural considerations and methodological issues in research and the effects of sexual victimization on women. Her current research interests include cultural factors that influence understanding of human sexuality and decision making. She has a Ph.D. in developmental studies in education from the University of California, Los Angeles.

Index

A

Abandonment, 60, 63
Academic performance, 2, 17, 39, 41, 138, 174–175, 198n, 212
Accidents, 68, 73n
Addiction, *see* Substance abuse
Administration on Children, Youth, and Families (ACYF), 304, 306–308, 356–357
Administrative records, 59, 61–62, 69–70, 73n, 79–83, 87, 90–91, 345, 350
Adolescents, 58, 124–125, 217–223
as sexual abuse offenders, 18–19, 84, 139, 260
see also Juvenile delinquency; Teenage pregnancy
Adult survivors, 18, 87, 224–226, 228, 229, 258–259, 335
recall bias, 6, 8, 44, 45, 90, 224–225
Advisory organizations, 27, 313
Advocacy organizations, 24, 165, 315
African Americans, 67, 88, 98n, 130–131, 136, 175, 185, 371
Age, 15, 58, 66, 113, 124–125
parental, 7, 122–123, 133, 220
see also Adolescents; Developmental stages; Infants

Aggression, 51, 61, 119–121, 128, 212, 215–216, 371
Aid to Families with Dependent Children (AFDC), 19, 266, 303
Alcoholism, 2, 16, 39, 220–221, 223
parental, 7–8, 17, 118–119, 141, 221
of sexual abusers, 114
American Bar Association, 61
American Humane Association (AHA), 79–80, 98n
American Medical Association, 72n, 86
American Professional Society on the Abuse of Children, 294
Amphetamines, 114
Anatomical dolls, 280n
Anger, 8, 109, 215–216
Animal models and studies, 119–122, 144n
Antipoverty programs, 12, 19–20, 182–183, 266
Antisocial behavior, 215–216, 226
parental, 7, 111–112, 117, 128
personality disorder, 7, 16, 113, 119, 223
Anxiety, 61, 111–112, 124, 128, 213, 224
Archives and databases, 23, 25, 97, 298, 299–300